DrMaster
Publications Inc.
www.DrMasterbooks.com

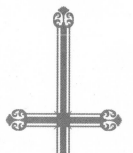

Author:	Gokurakuin Sakurako
Translators:	Daniel Sullivan and Asako Otomo
Production Artist:	Bryce Gunkel
US Cover Design:	Bryce Gunkel
English Adaptation:	Ken Li
Editor:	Ailen Lujo
Supervising Editor:	Matthew A. Scrivner
Marketing:	Shawn Sander
V.P of Operations:	Yuki Chung
President:	Jennifer Chen

Category Freaks

Publisher
DrMaster Publications, Inc.
4044 Clipper Ct.
Fremont, CA 94538
www.DrMasterbooks.com

Second Edition: August 2006
ISBN 1-59796-095-0

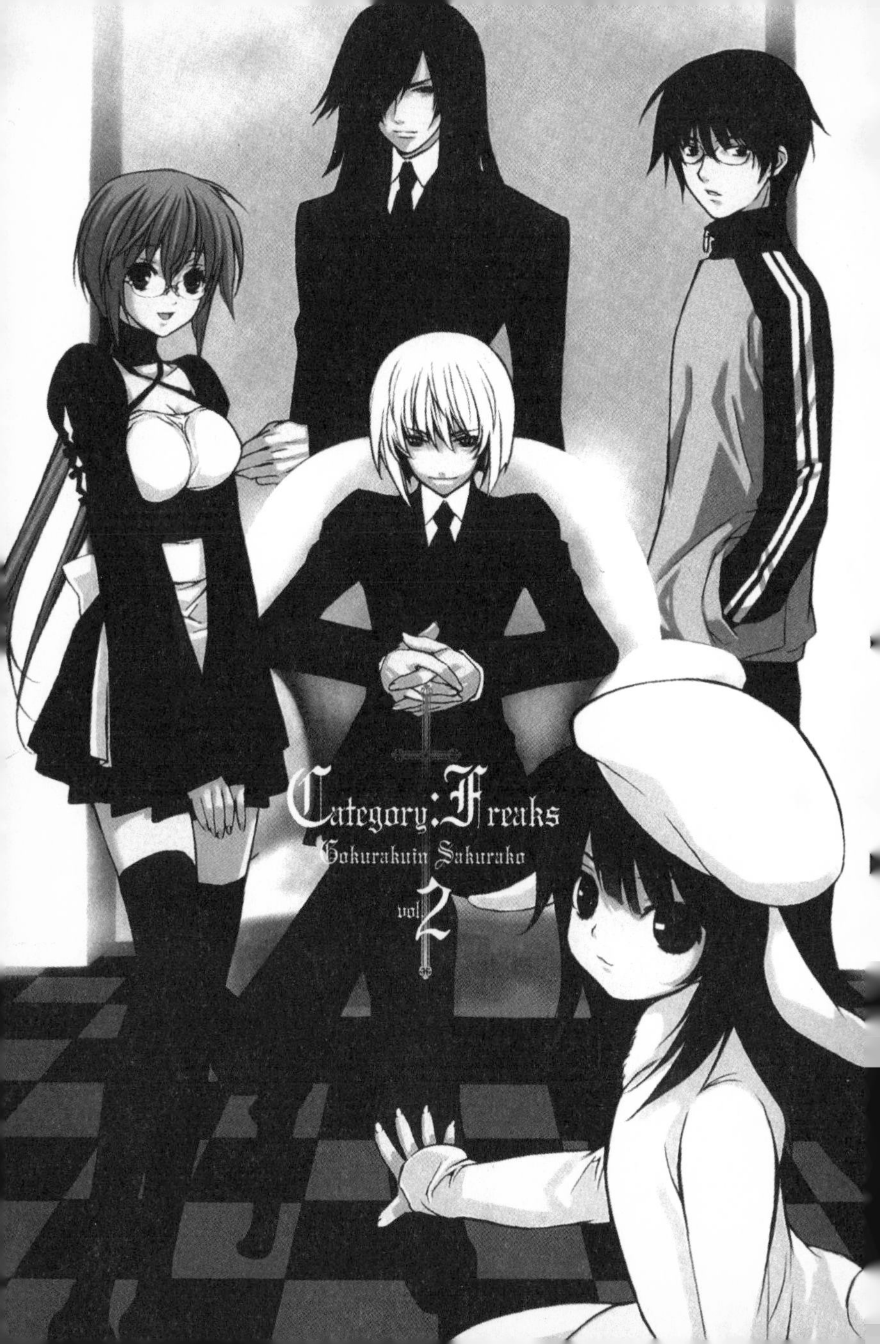
Category: Freaks
Gokurakuin Sakurako
vol. 2

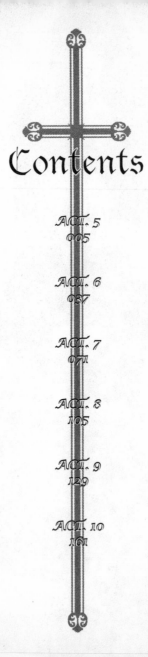

Contents

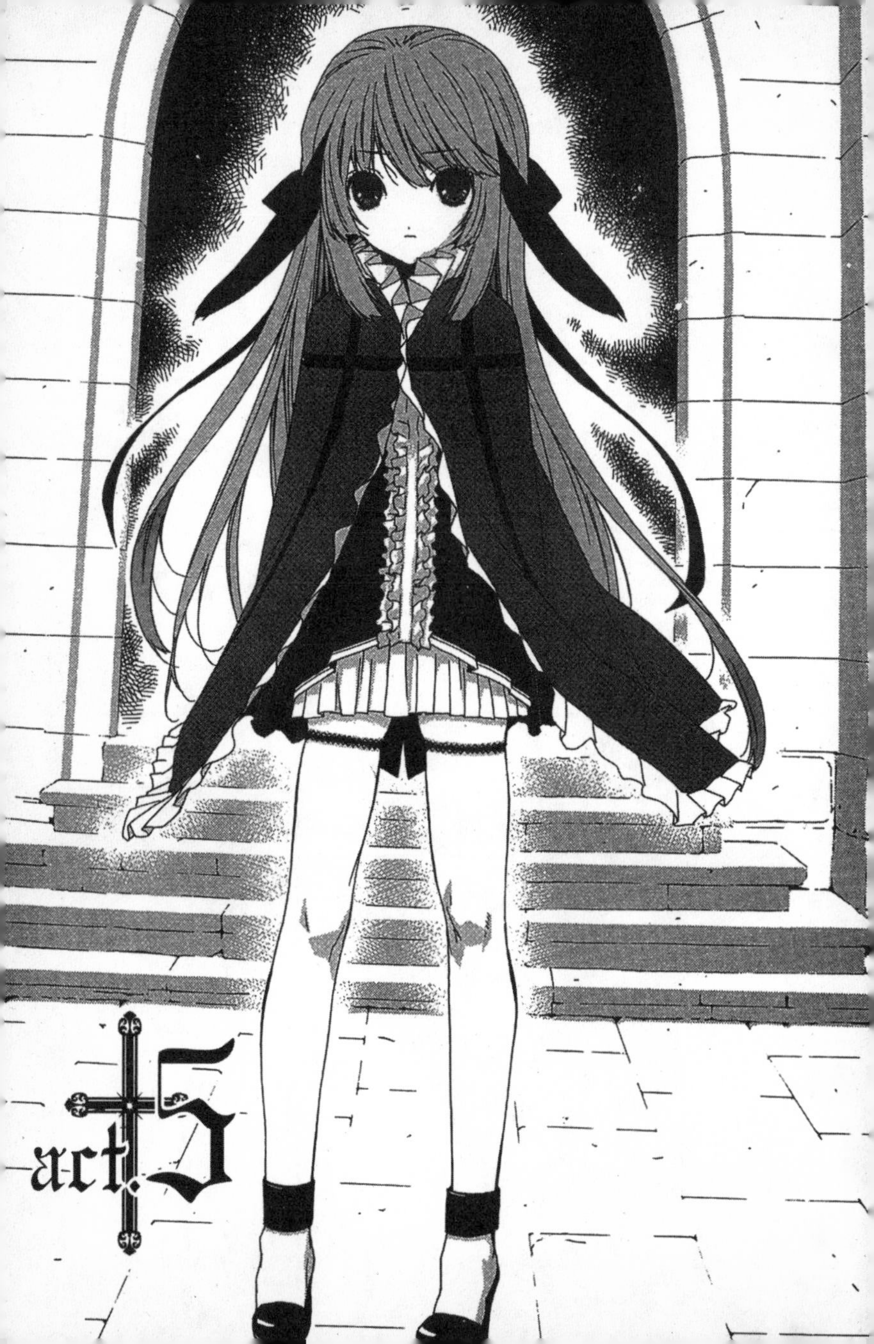
act 5

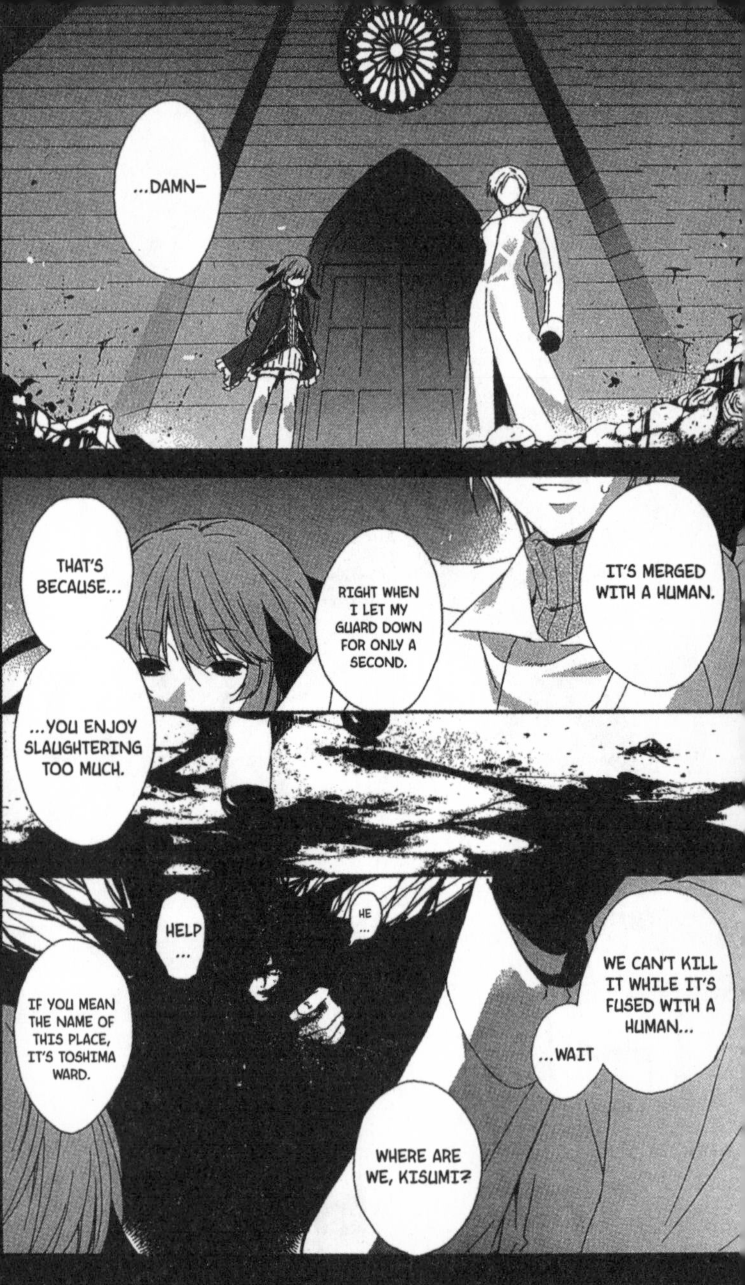
...DAMN—
IT'S MERGED WITH A HUMAN.
RIGHT WHEN I LET MY GUARD DOWN FOR ONLY A SECOND.
THAT'S BECAUSE...
...YOU ENJOY SLAUGHTERING TOO MUCH.
WE CAN'T KILL IT WHILE IT'S FUSED WITH A HUMAN...
...WAIT
HE ...
HELP ...
WHERE ARE WE, KISUMI?
IF YOU MEAN THE NAME OF THIS PLACE, IT'S TOSHIMA WARD.

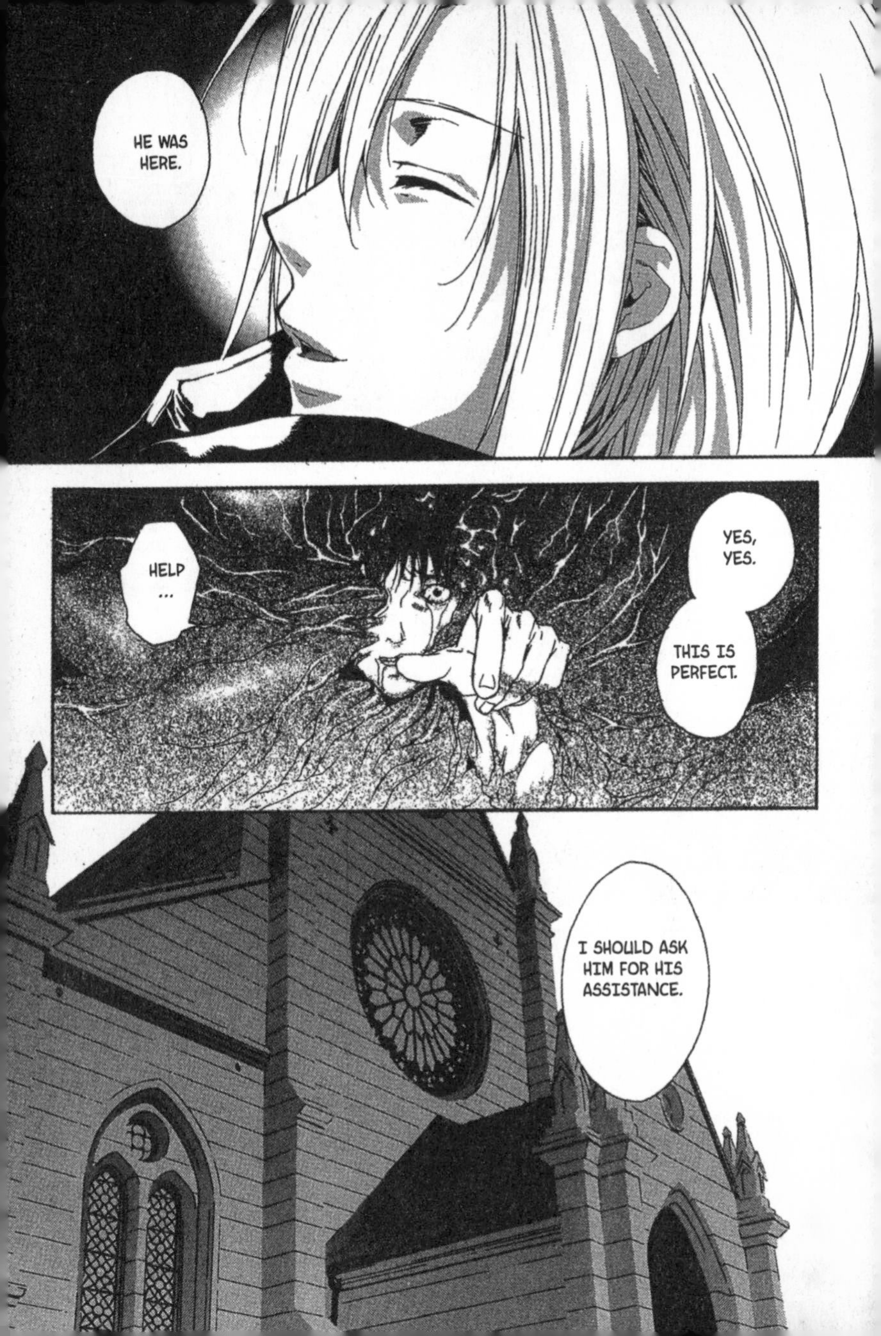
HE WAS HERE.
YES, YES.
THIS IS PERFECT.
HELP ...
I SHOULD ASK HIM FOR HIS ASSISTANCE.

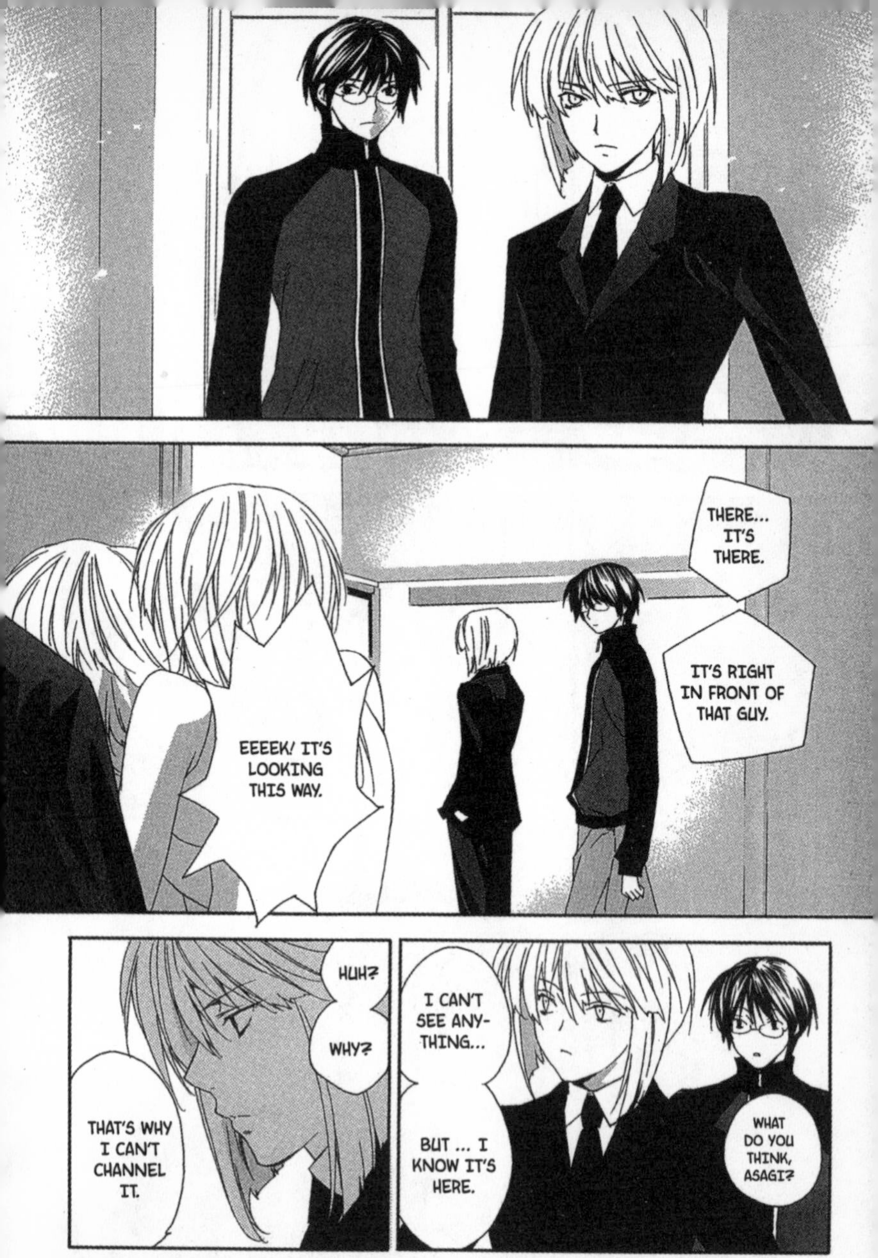
THERE... IT'S THERE.
IT'S RIGHT IN FRONT OF THAT GUY.
EEEEK! IT'S LOOKING THIS WAY.
WHAT DO YOU THINK, ASAGI?
I CAN'T SEE ANY-THING...
BUT ... I KNOW IT'S HERE.
HUH?
WHY?
THAT'S WHY I CAN'T CHANNEL IT.

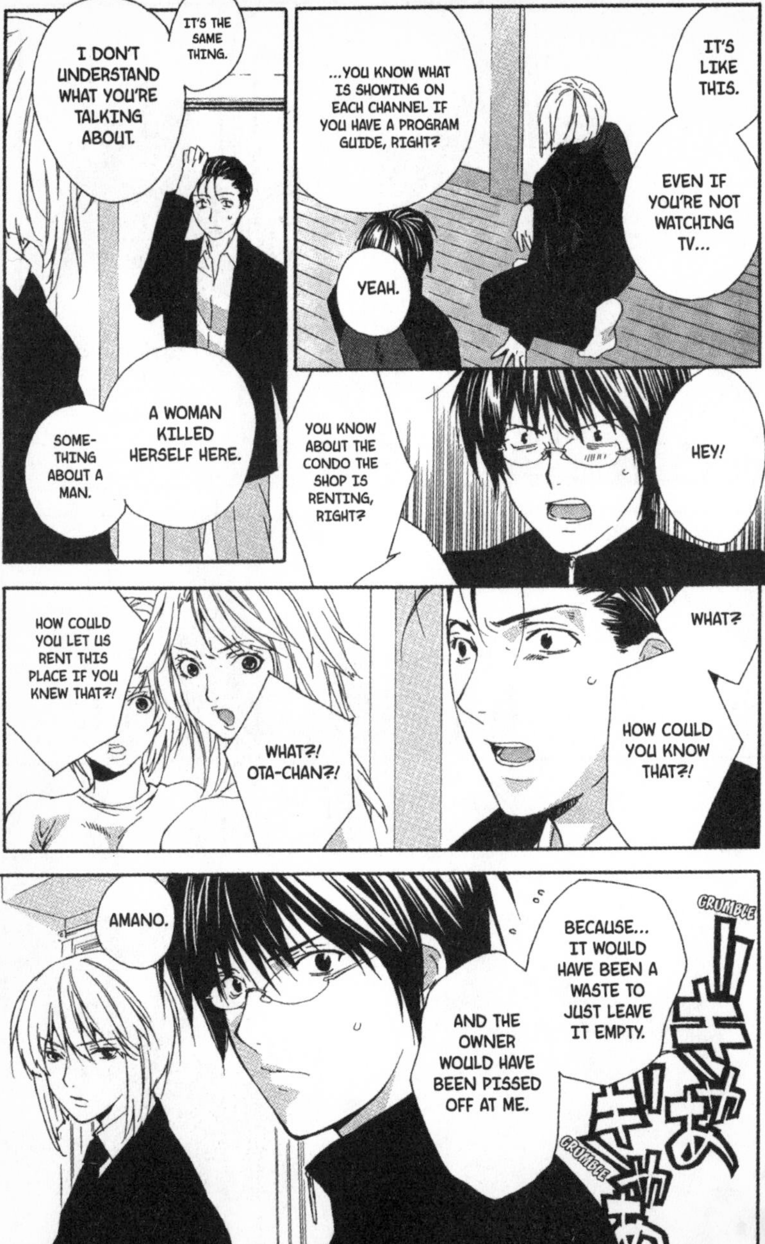
IT'S LIKE THIS.
EVEN IF YOU'RE NOT WATCHING TV...
...YOU KNOW WHAT IS SHOWING ON EACH CHANNEL IF YOU HAVE A PROGRAM GUIDE, RIGHT?
YEAH.
HEY!
YOU KNOW ABOUT THE CONDO THE SHOP IS RENTING, RIGHT?
IT'S THE SAME THING.
I DON'T UNDERSTAND WHAT YOU'RE TALKING ABOUT.
A WOMAN KILLED HERSELF HERE.
SOME-THING ABOUT A MAN.
WHAT?
HOW COULD YOU KNOW THAT?!
WHAT?! OTA-CHAN?!
HOW COULD YOU LET US RENT THIS PLACE IF YOU KNEW THAT?!
GRUMBLE
BECAUSE... IT WOULD HAVE BEEN A WASTE TO JUST LEAVE IT EMPTY.
AND THE OWNER WOULD HAVE BEEN PISSED OFF AT ME.
AMANO.
GRUMBLE

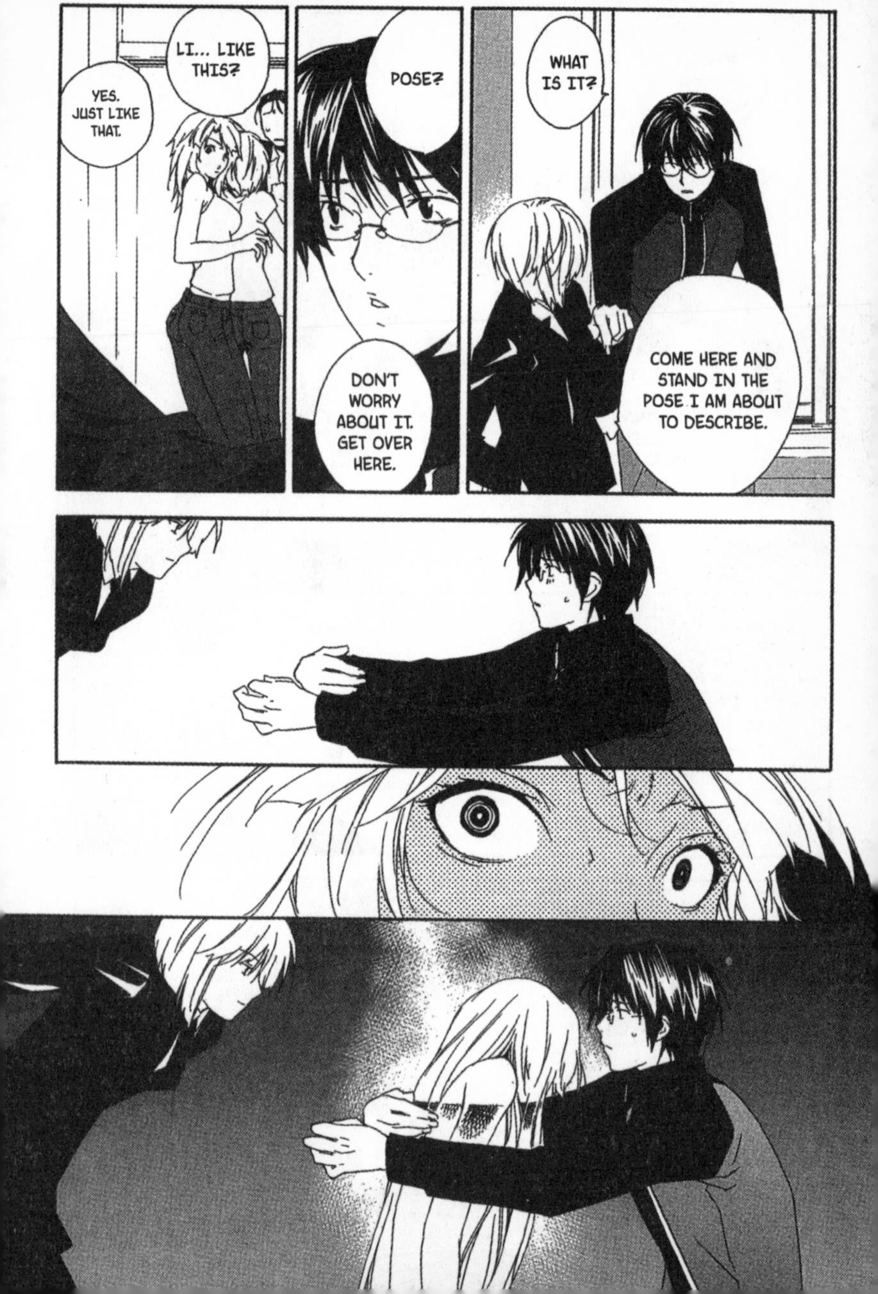
WHAT IS IT?
COME HERE AND STAND IN THE POSE I AM ABOUT TO DESCRIBE.
POSE?
DON'T WORRY ABOUT IT. GET OVER HERE.
LI... LIKE THIS?
YES. JUST LIKE THAT.

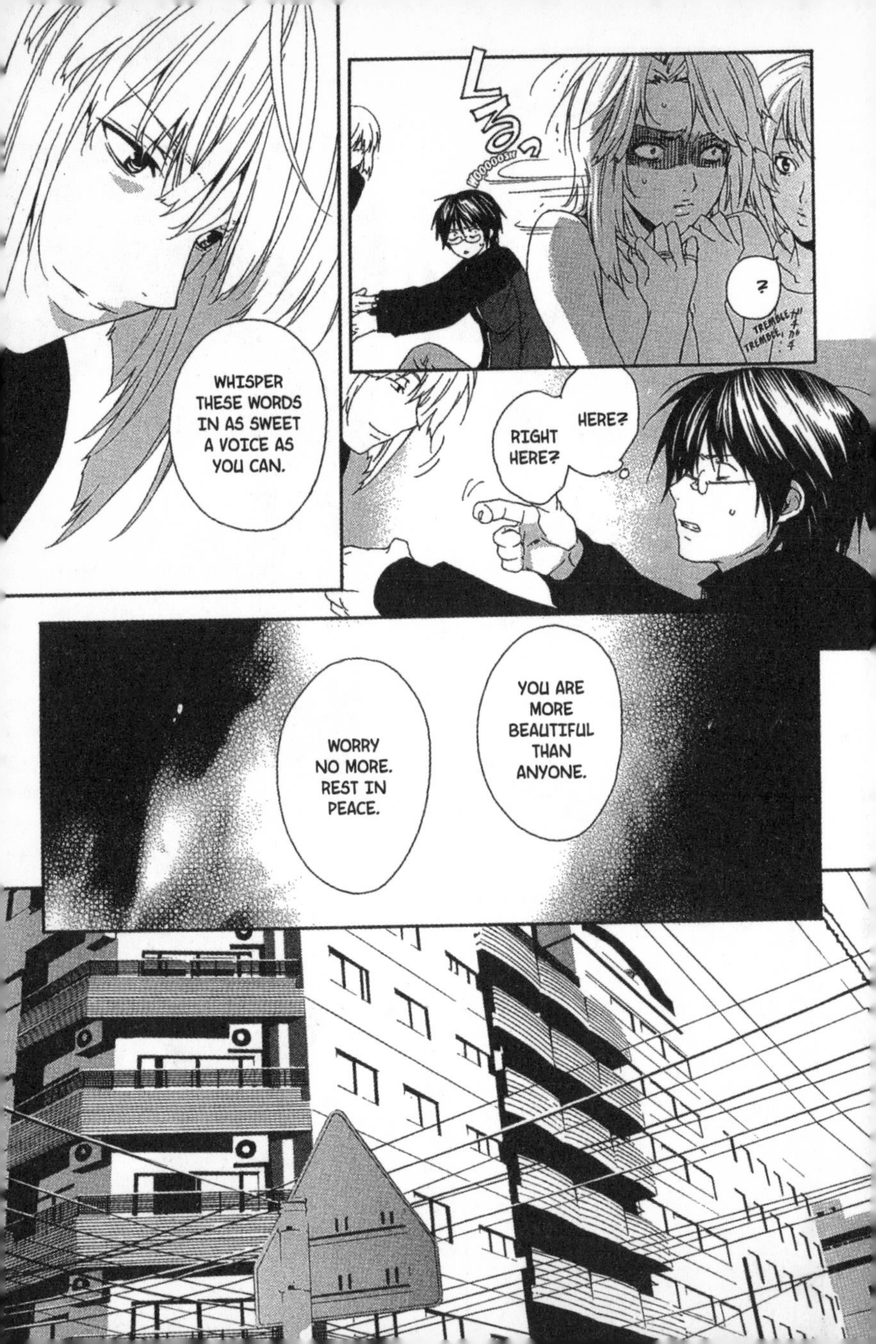
WOOOOOSH
?
TREMBLE TREMBLE
RIGHT HERE?
HERE?
WHISPER THESE WORDS IN AS SWEET A VOICE AS YOU CAN.
YOU ARE MORE BEAUTIFUL THAN ANYONE.
WORRY NO MORE. REST IN PEACE.

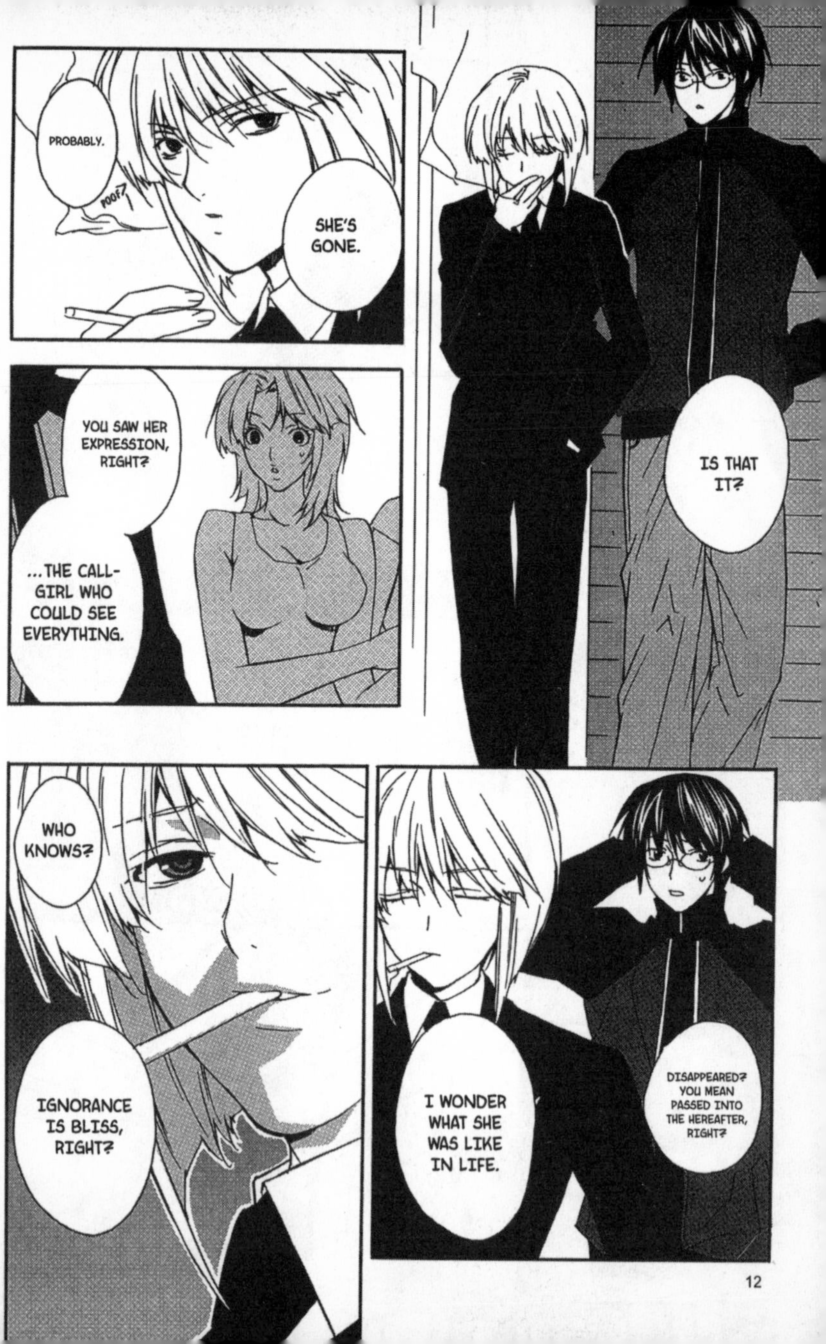
IS THAT IT?
PROBABLY.
POOF
SHE'S GONE.
YOU SAW HER EXPRESSION, RIGHT?
...THE CALL-GIRL WHO COULD SEE EVERYTHING.
DISAPPEARED? YOU MEAN PASSED INTO THE HEREAFTER, RIGHT?
I WONDER WHAT SHE WAS LIKE IN LIFE.
WHO KNOWS?
IGNORANCE IS BLISS, RIGHT?

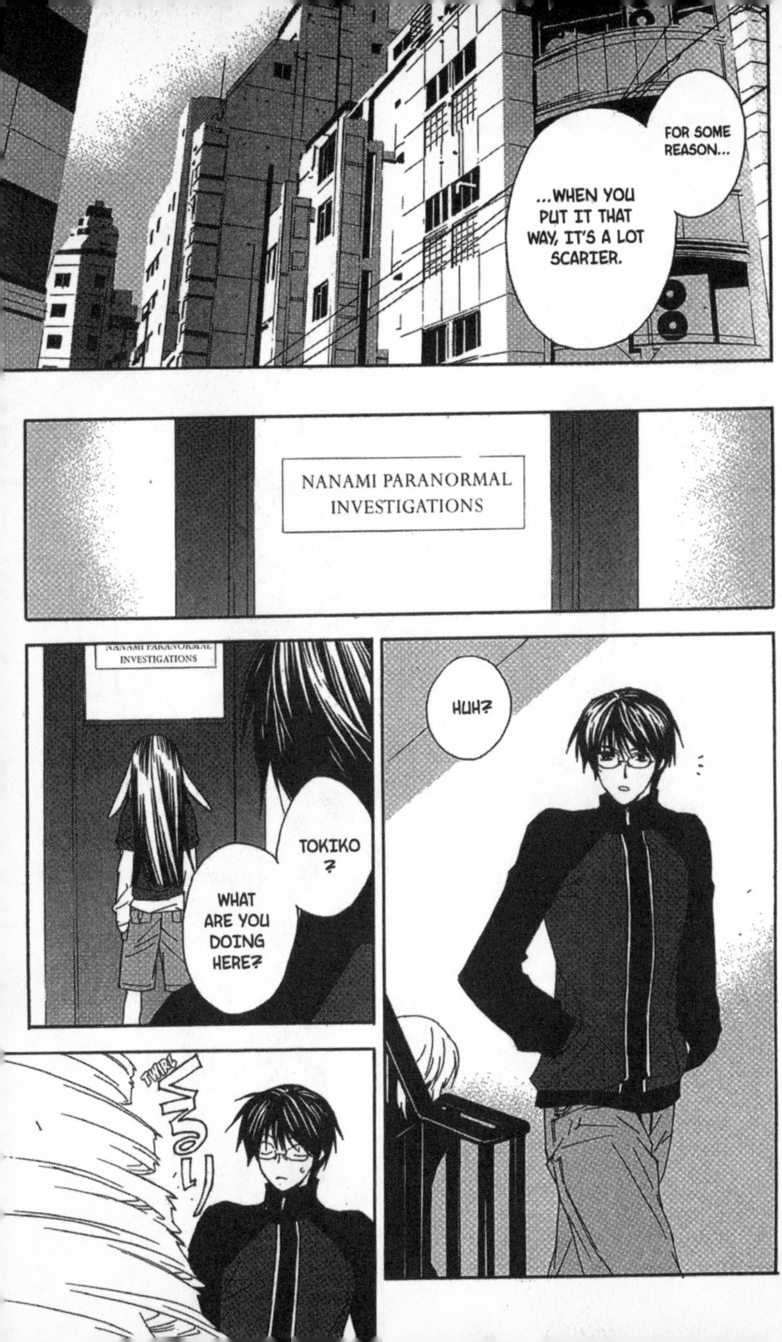
FOR SOME REASON...
...WHEN YOU PUT IT THAT WAY, IT'S A LOT SCARIER.
NANAMI PARANORMAL INVESTIGATIONS
HUH?
NANAMI PARANORMAL INVESTIGATIONS
TOKIKO?
WHAT ARE YOU DOING HERE?
TWIRL

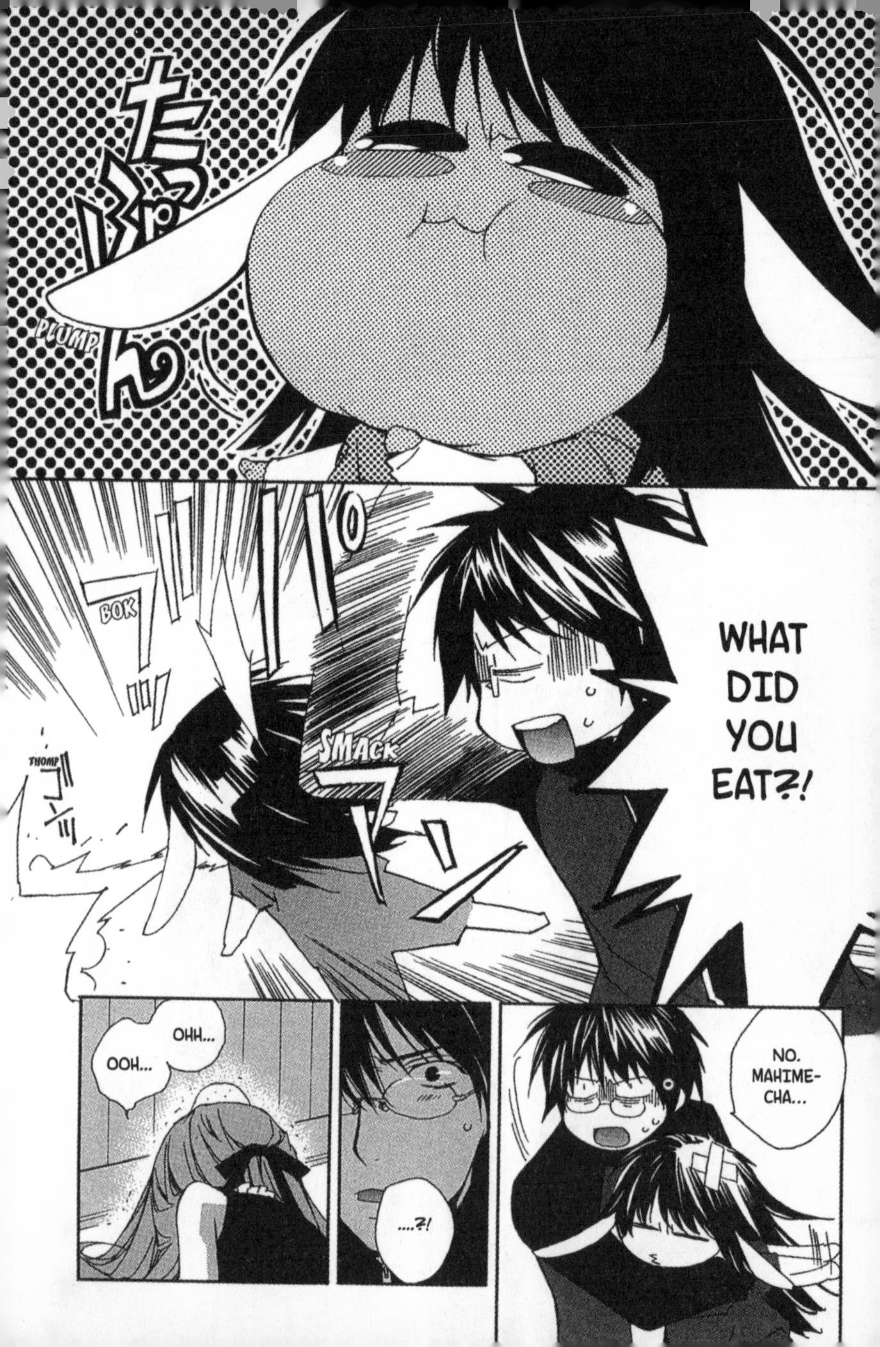
PLUMP
WHAT DID YOU EAT?!
SMACK
BOK
THOMP
NO. MAHIME-CHA...
....?!
OHH...
OOH...

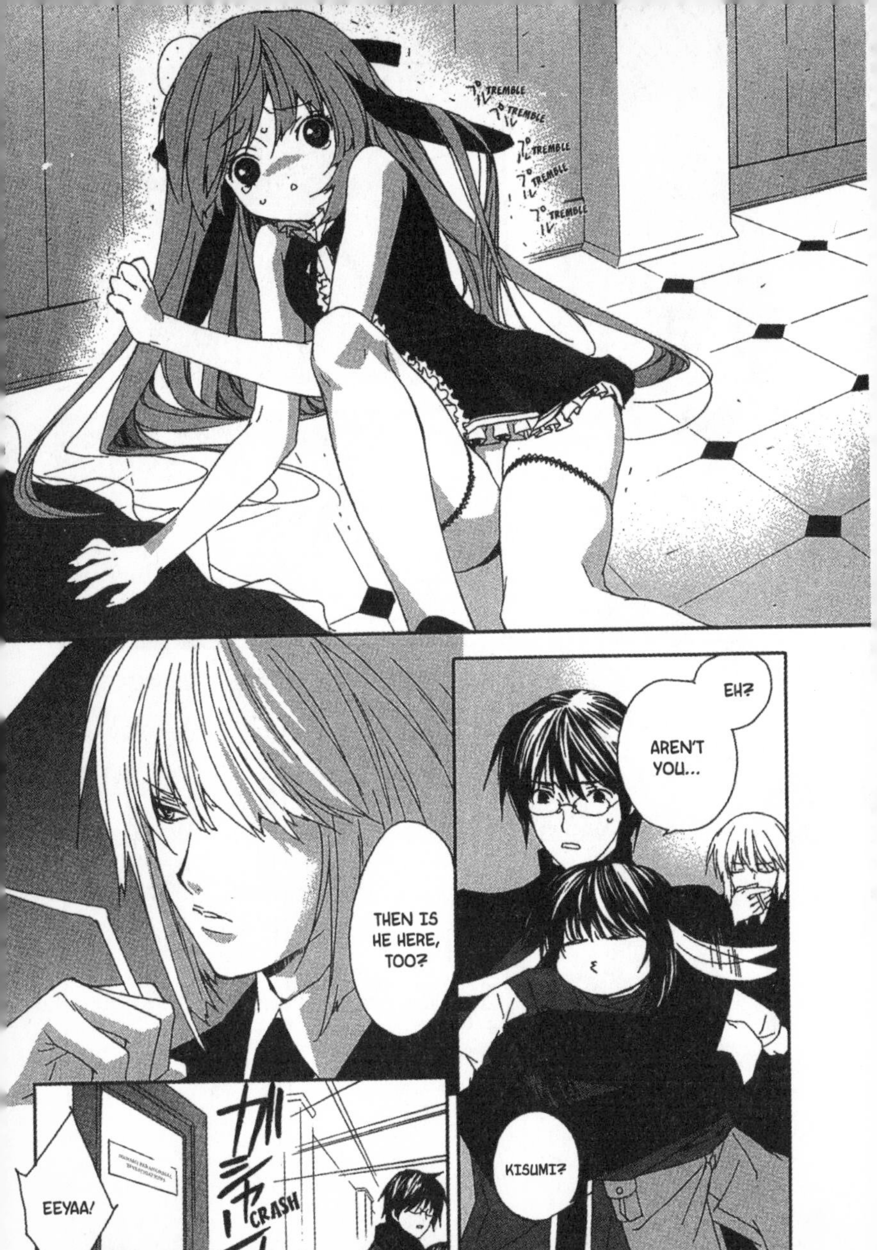
TREMBLE
TREMBLE
TREMBLE
TREMBLE
TREMBLE
EH?
AREN'T YOU...
KISUMI?
THEN IS HE HERE, TOO?
CRASH
EEYAA!

WAIT.

MAHIME-CHAN?

DO NOT ENTER UNTIL I GIVE YOU THE OK.

YOU STAY HERE.

STOP IT.

NO...

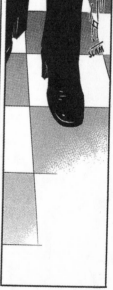

SLAM

16

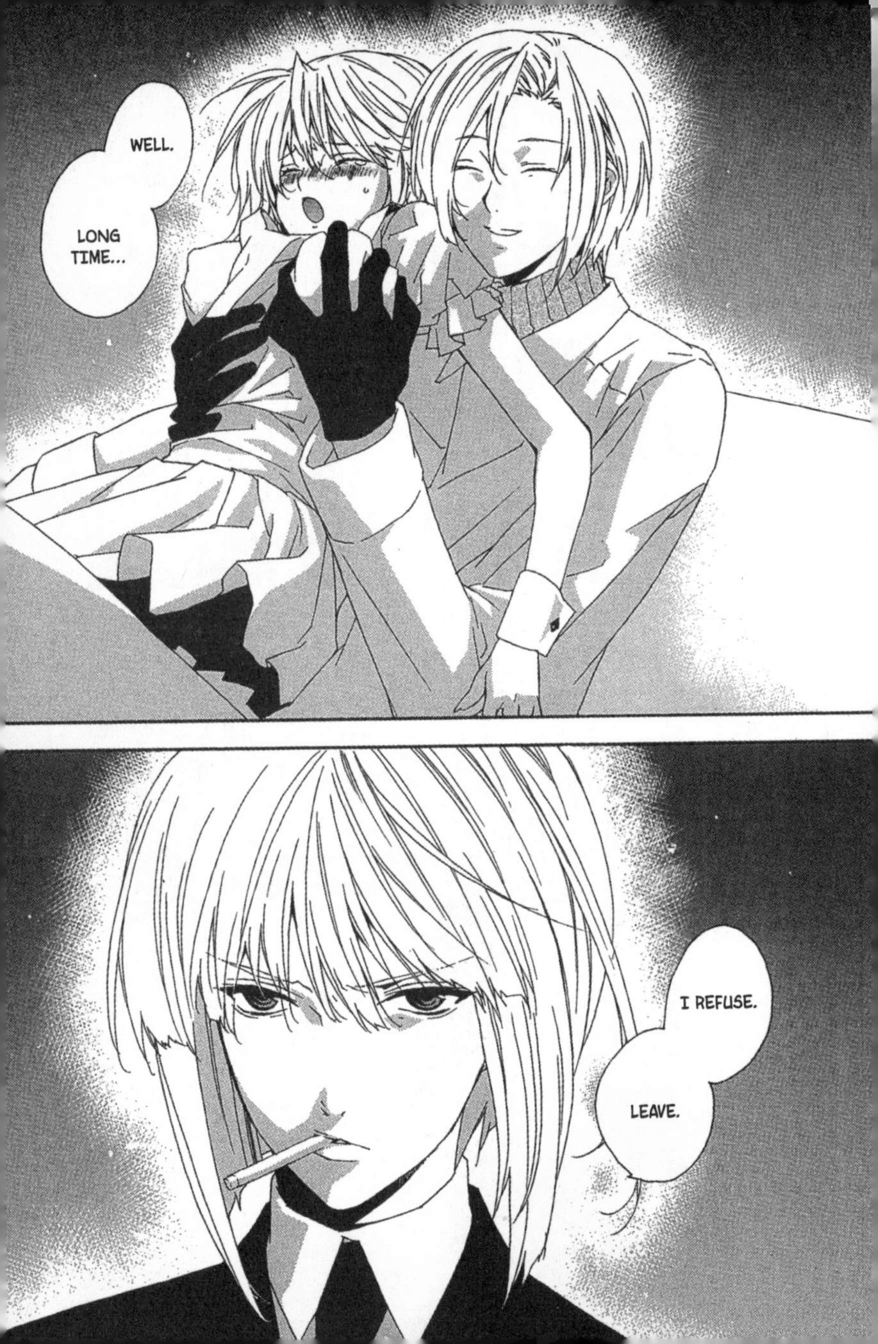
WELL.
LONG TIME...
I REFUSE.
LEAVE.

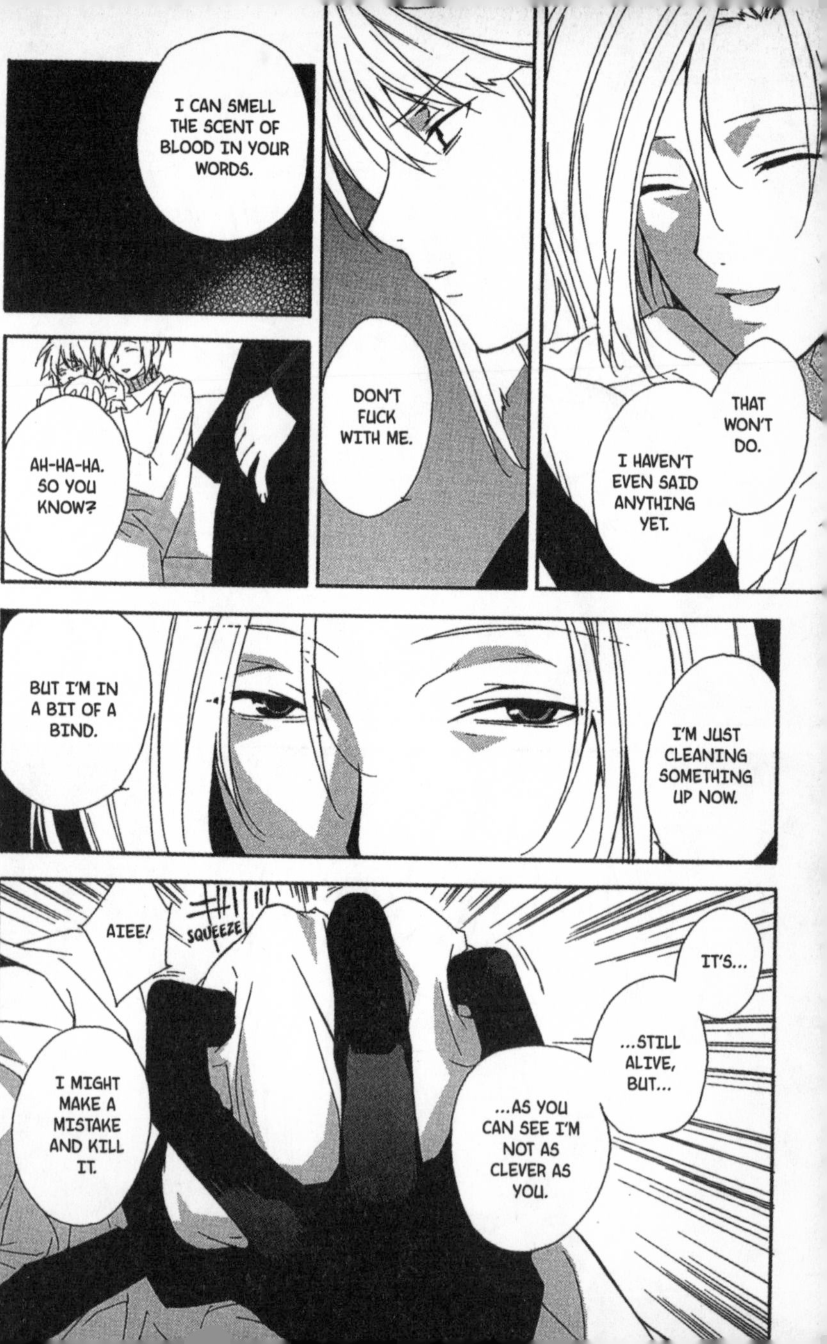
THAT WON'T DO.
I HAVEN'T EVEN SAID ANYTHING YET.
DON'T FUCK WITH ME.
I CAN SMELL THE SCENT OF BLOOD IN YOUR WORDS.
AH-HA-HA. SO YOU KNOW?
I'M JUST CLEANING SOMETHING UP NOW.
BUT I'M IN A BIT OF A BIND.
IT'S...
...STILL ALIVE, BUT...
...AS YOU CAN SEE I'M NOT AS CLEVER AS YOU.
SQUEEZE
AIEE!
I MIGHT MAKE A MISTAKE AND KILL IT.

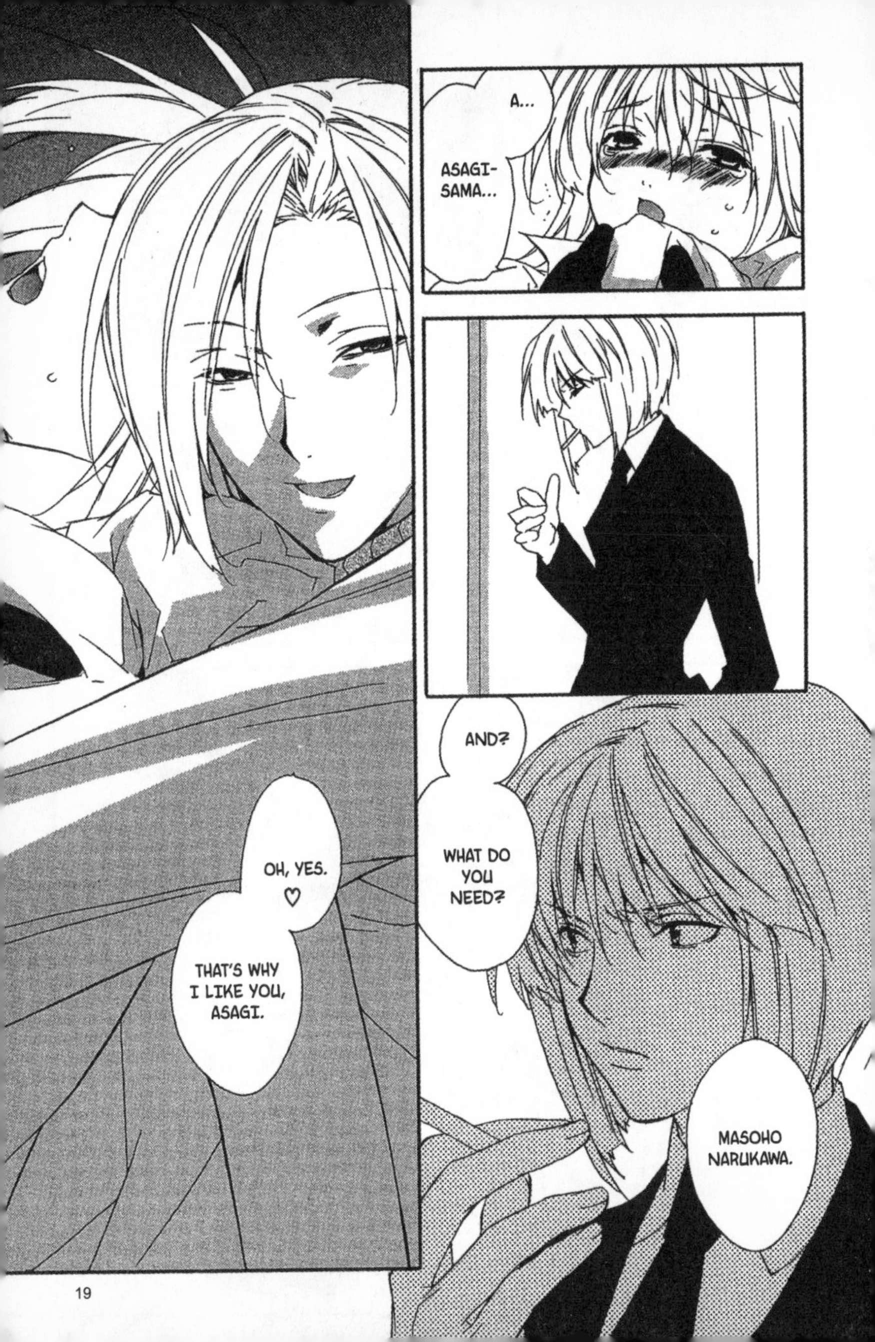
A...
ASAGI-SAMA...
AND?
WHAT DO YOU NEED?
MASOHO NARUKAWA.
OH, YES. ♡
THAT'S WHY I LIKE YOU, ASAGI.

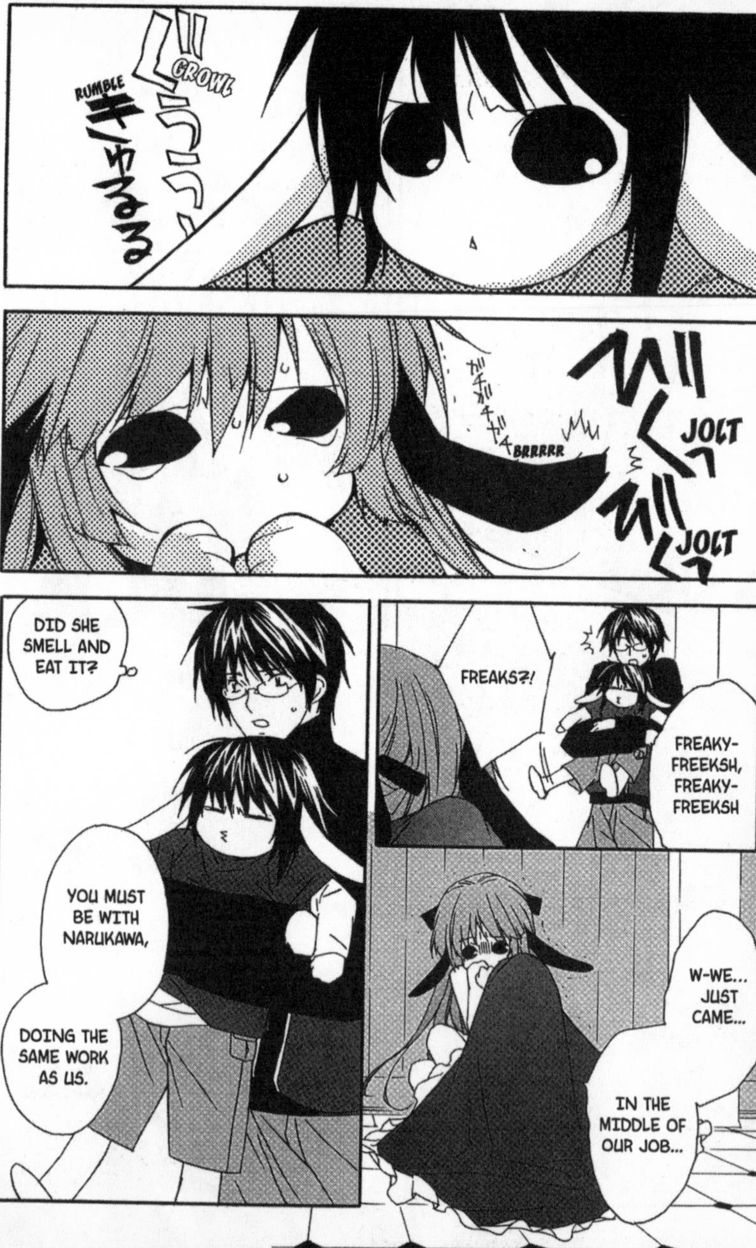
GROWL
RUMBLE
きゅるる
JOLT
JOLT
BRRRRR
FREAKY-FREEKSH, FREAKY-FREEKSH
FREAKS?!
W-WE... JUST CAME...
IN THE MIDDLE OF OUR JOB...
DID SHE SMELL AND EAT IT?
YOU MUST BE WITH NARUKAWA,
DOING THE SAME WORK AS US.

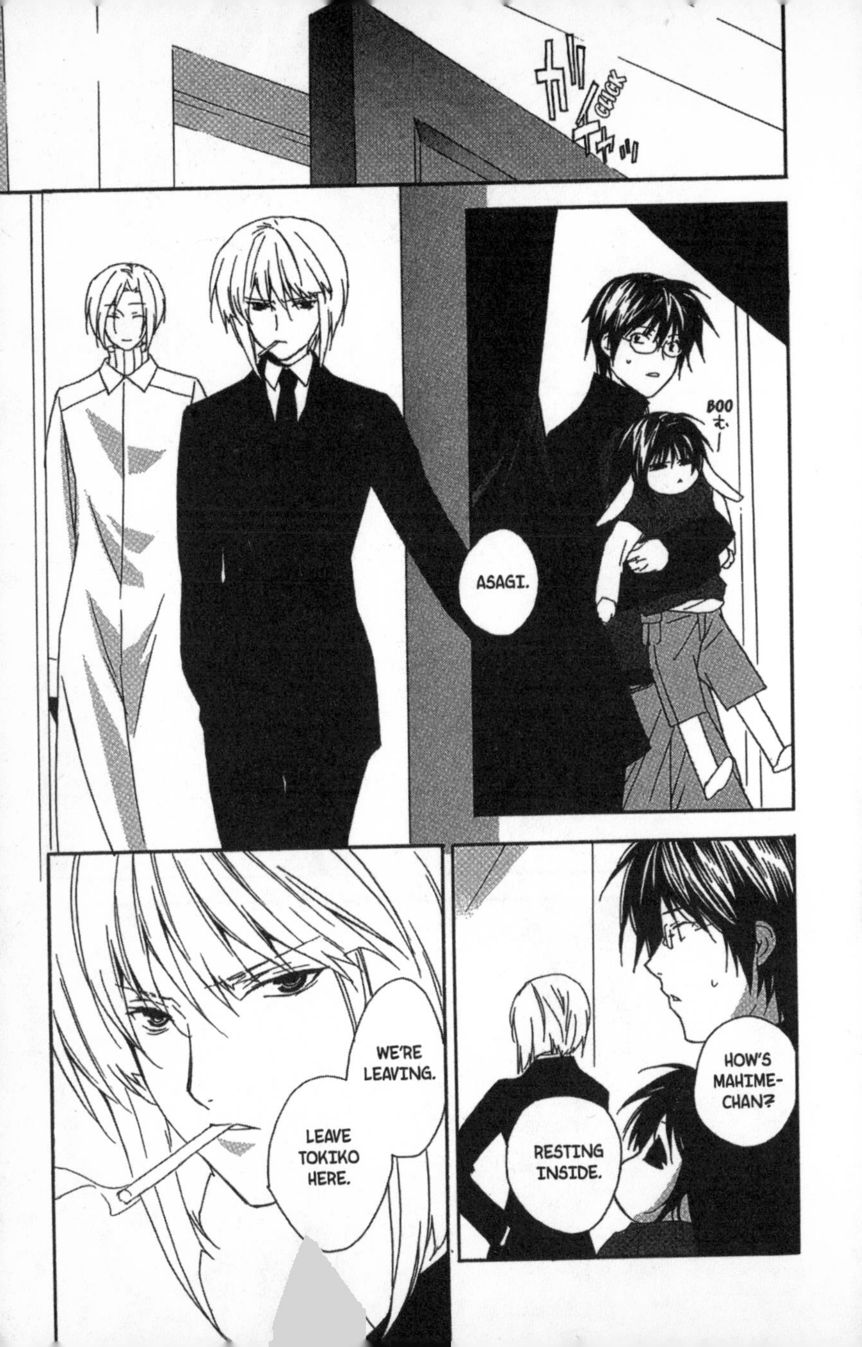
CLICK
BOO
ASAGI.
HOW'S MAHIME-CHAN?
RESTING INSIDE.
WE'RE LEAVING.
LEAVE TOKIKO HERE.

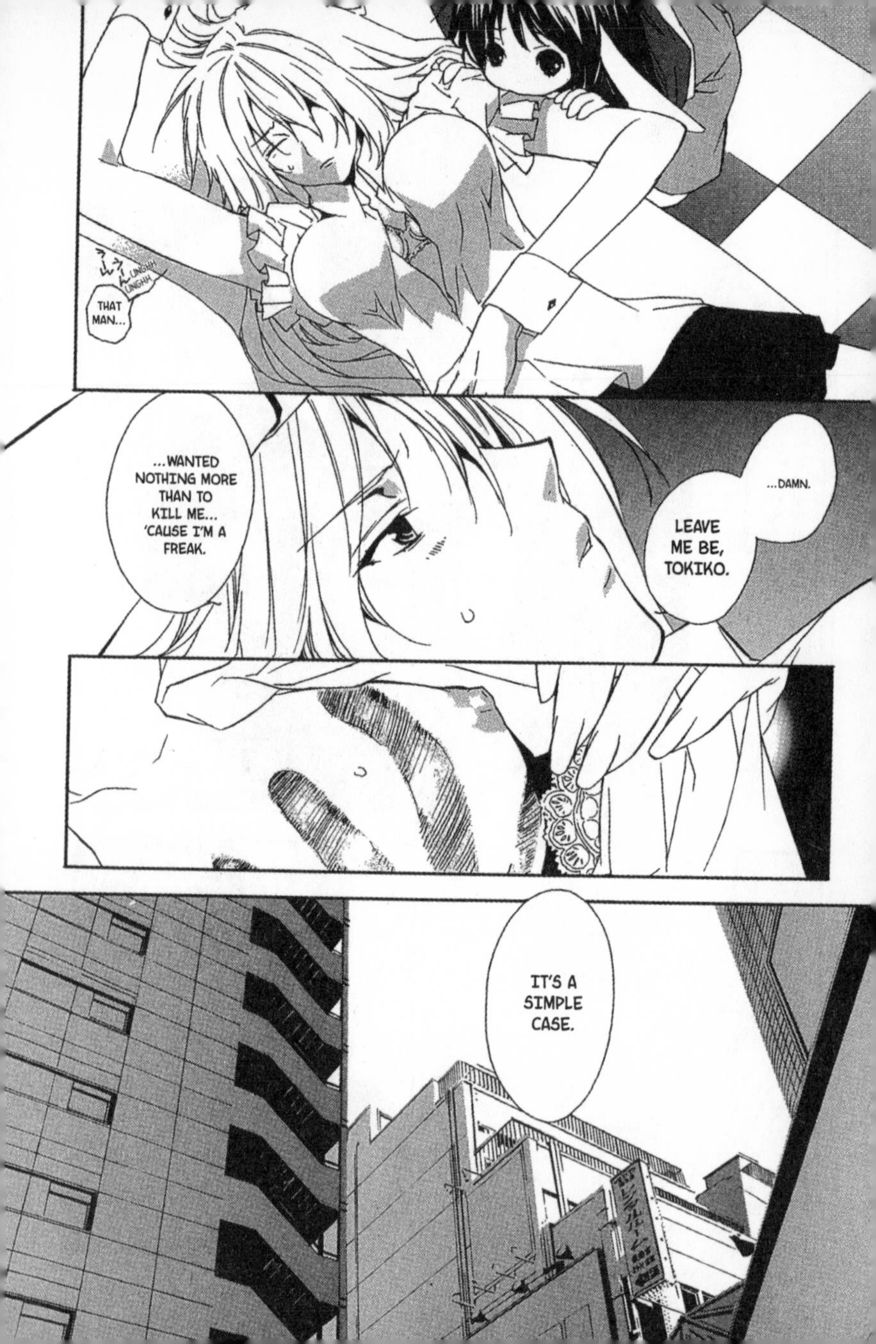
UNGHH
UNGHH
THAT MAN...
...DAMN.
LEAVE ME BE, TOKIKO.
...WANTED NOTHING MORE THAN TO KILL ME... 'CAUSE I'M A FREAK.
IT'S A SIMPLE CASE.

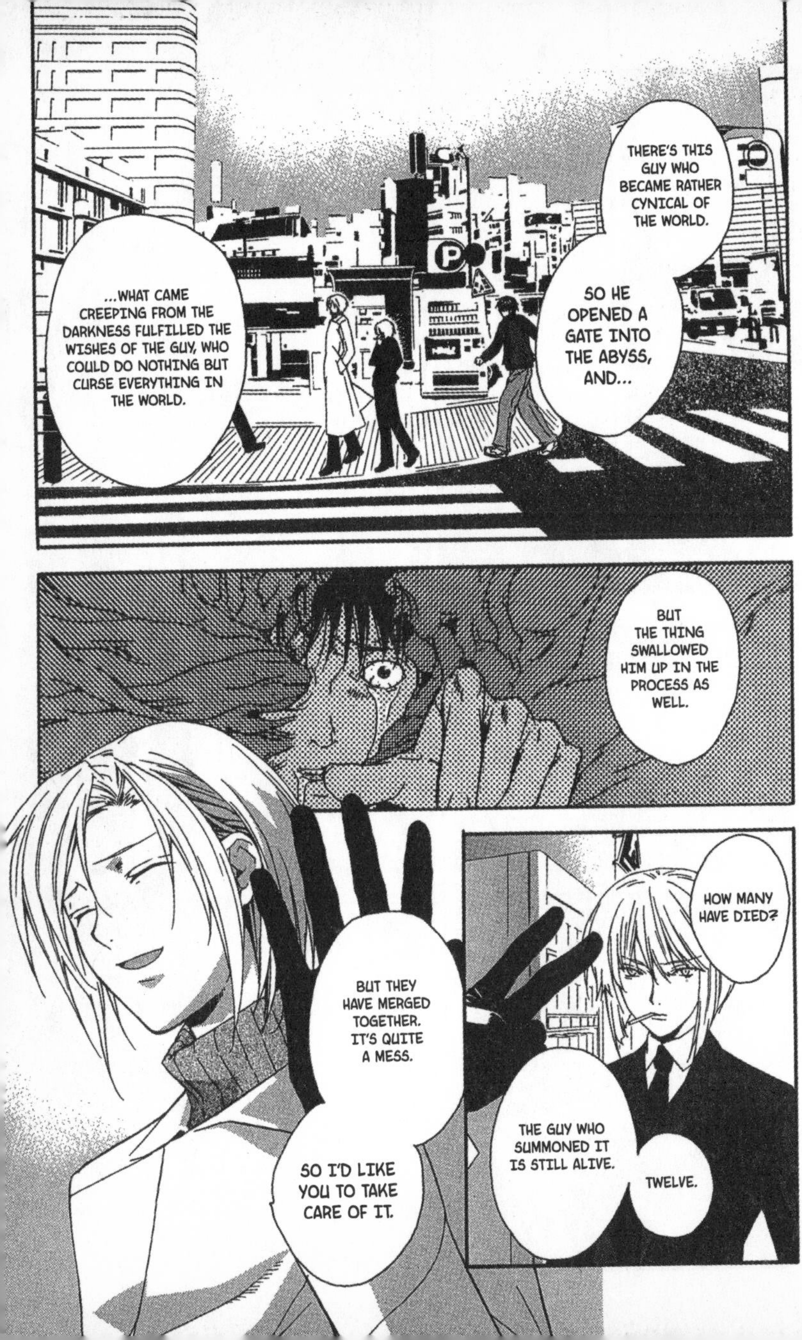
THERE'S THIS GUY WHO BECAME RATHER CYNICAL OF THE WORLD.
SO HE OPENED A GATE INTO THE ABYSS, AND...
...WHAT CAME CREEPING FROM THE DARKNESS FULFILLED THE WISHES OF THE GUY, WHO COULD DO NOTHING BUT CURSE EVERYTHING IN THE WORLD.
BUT THE THING SWALLOWED HIM UP IN THE PROCESS AS WELL.
HOW MANY HAVE DIED?
TWELVE.
THE GUY WHO SUMMONED IT IS STILL ALIVE.
BUT THEY HAVE MERGED TOGETHER. IT'S QUITE A MESS.
SO I'D LIKE YOU TO TAKE CARE OF IT.

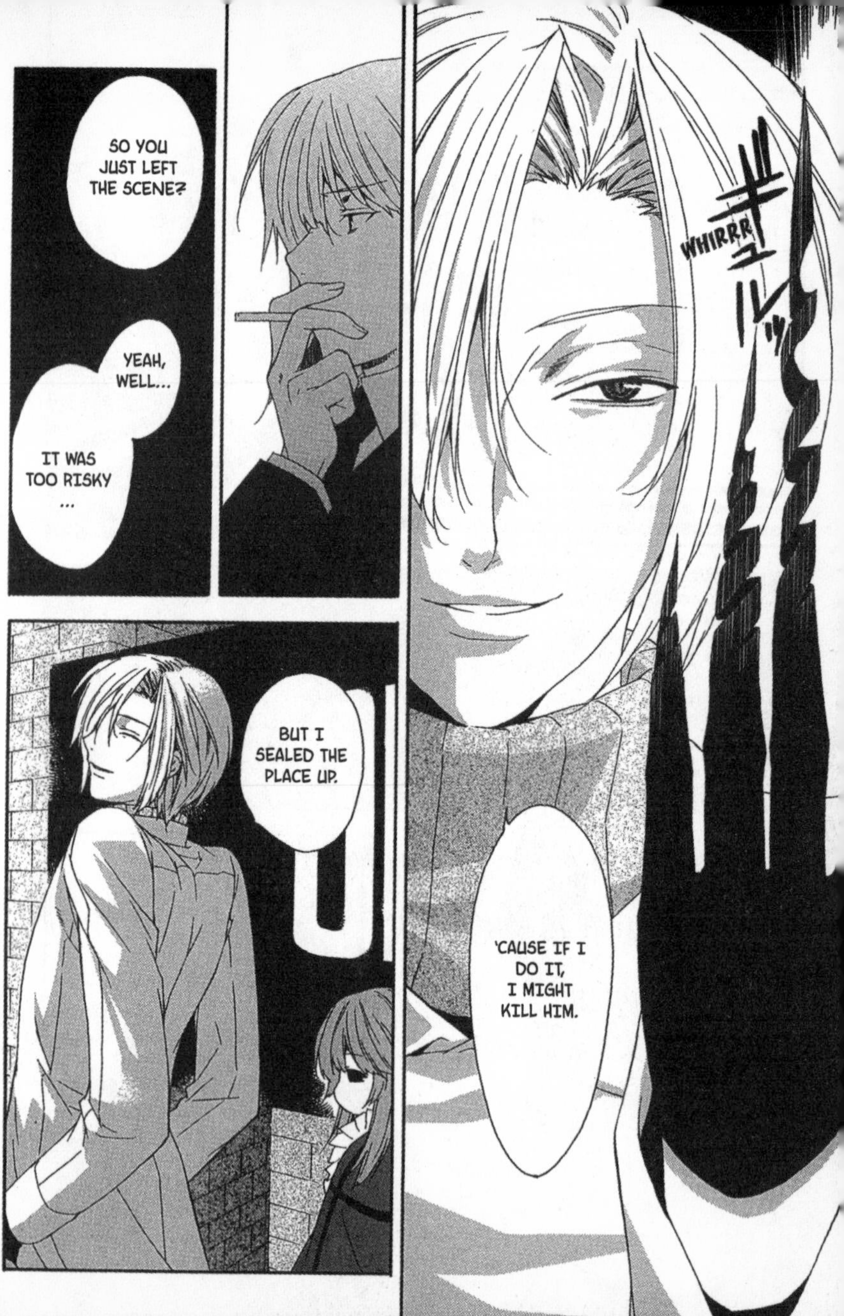
WHIRRR
'CAUSE IF I DO IT, I MIGHT KILL HIM.
SO YOU JUST LEFT THE SCENE?
YEAH, WELL...
IT WAS TOO RISKY ...
BUT I SEALED THE PLACE UP.

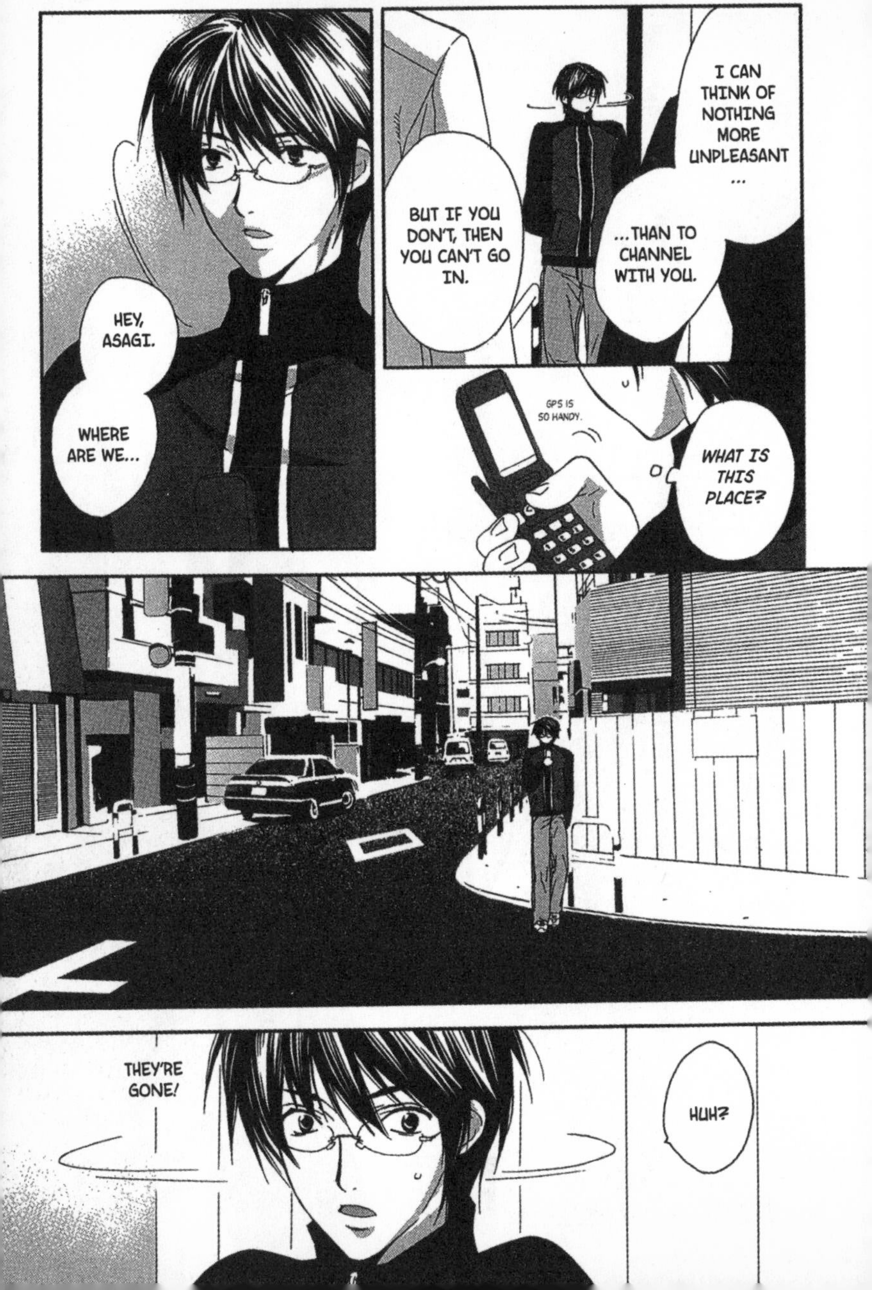
I CAN THINK OF NOTHING MORE UNPLEASANT...
...THAN TO CHANNEL WITH YOU.
BUT IF YOU DON'T, THEN YOU CAN'T GO IN.
WHAT IS THIS PLACE?
GPS IS SO HANDY.
HEY, ASAGI.
WHERE ARE WE...
HUH?
THEY'RE GONE!

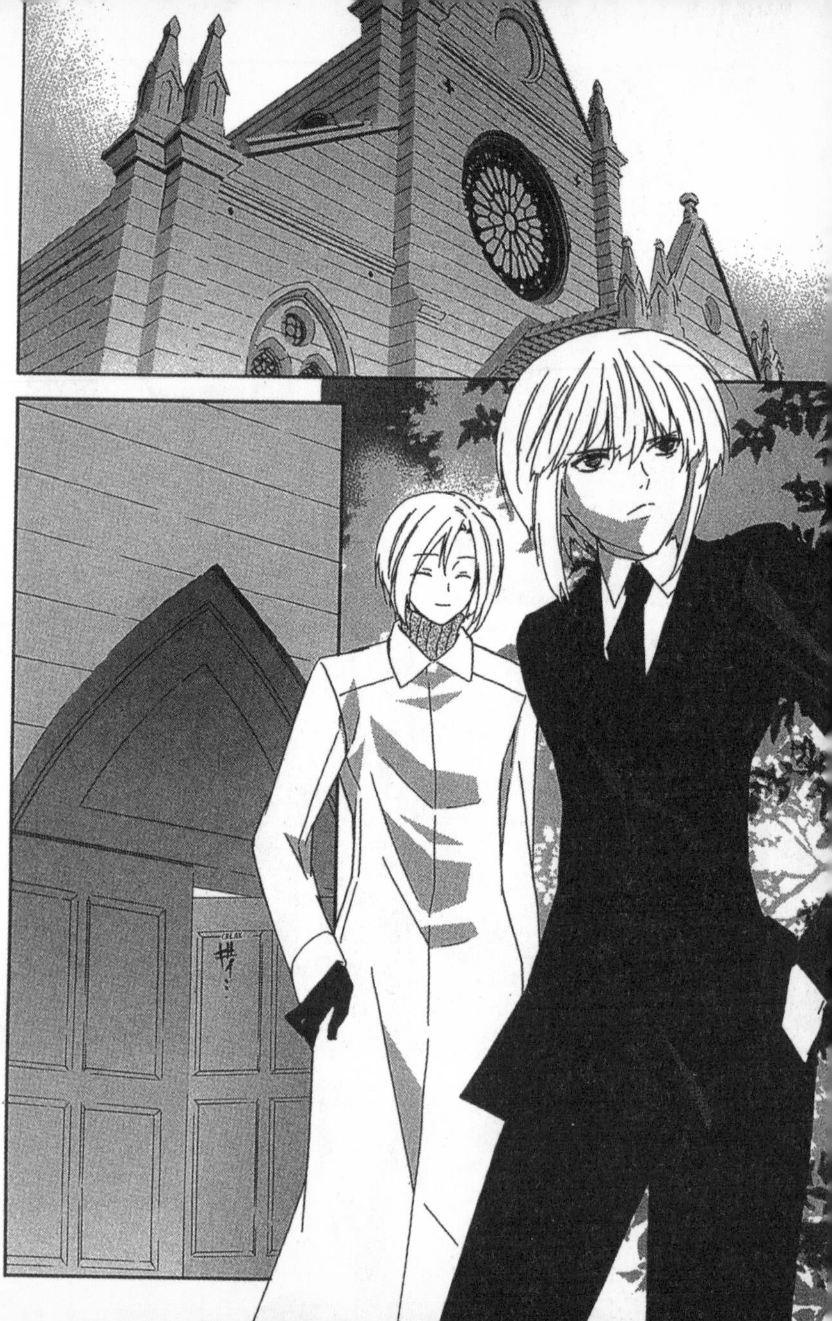
CREAK

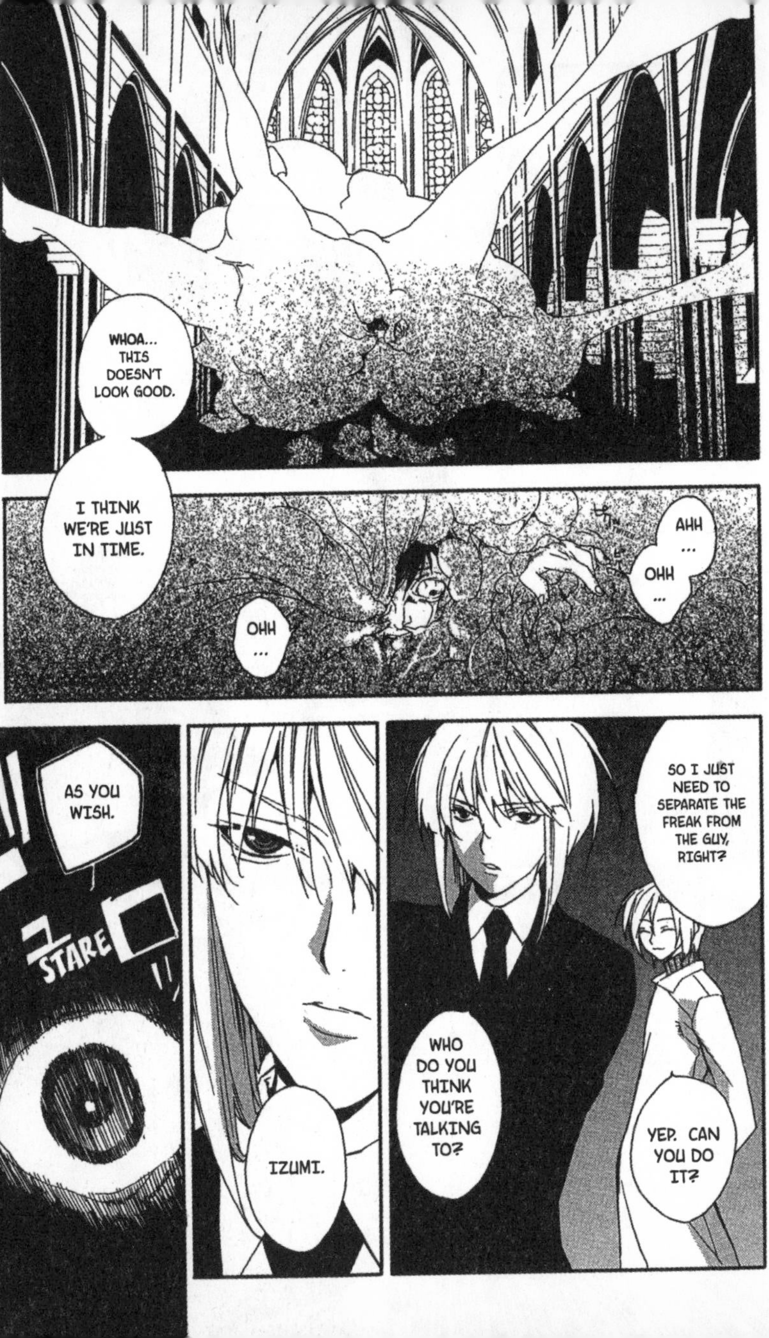
WHOA... THIS DOESN'T LOOK GOOD.
AHH ... OHH ...
I THINK WE'RE JUST IN TIME.
OHH ...
SO I JUST NEED TO SEPARATE THE FREAK FROM THE GUY, RIGHT?
YEP. CAN YOU DO IT?
WHO DO YOU THINK YOU'RE TALKING TO?
IZUMI.
AS YOU WISH.
STARE

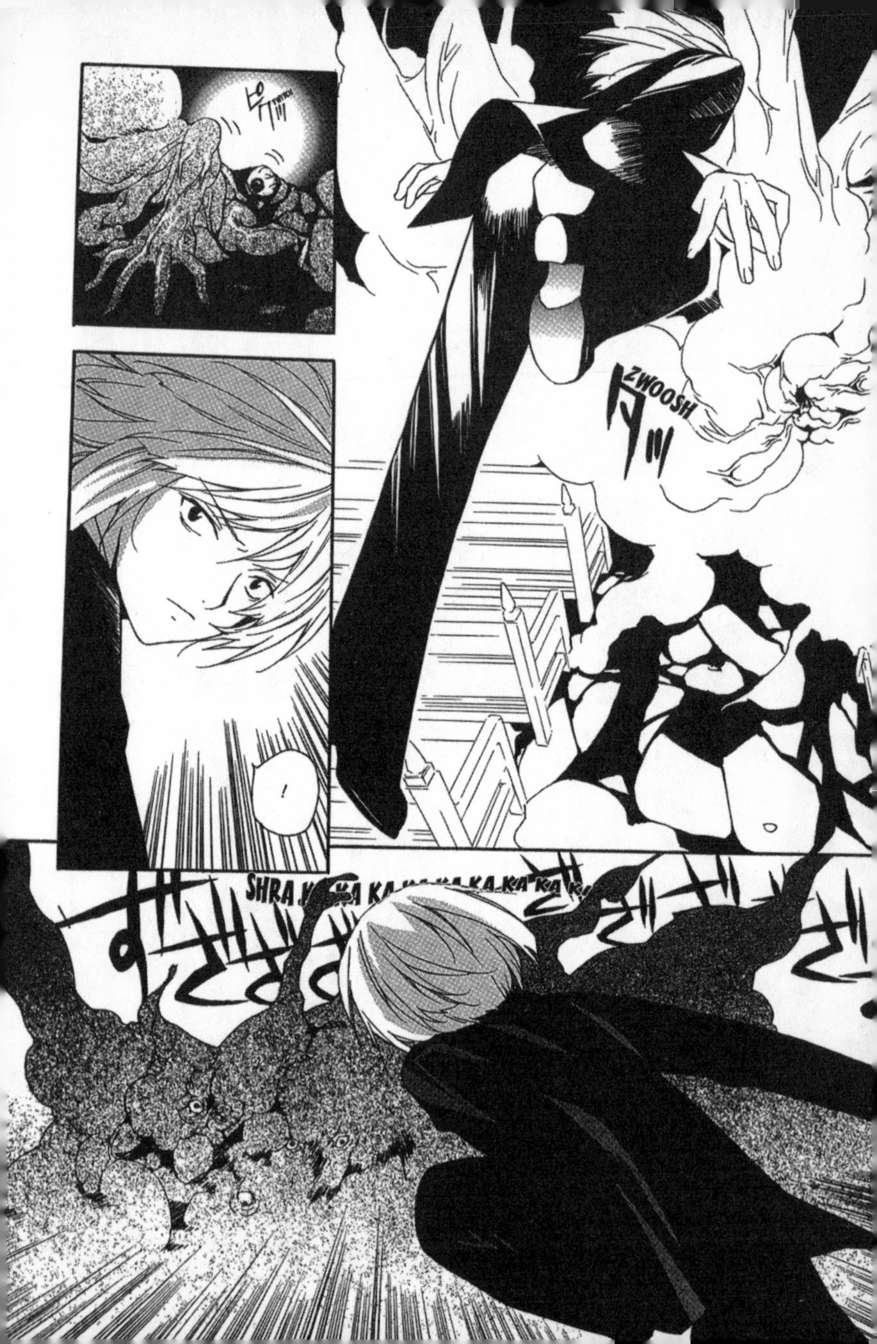
ZWOOSH
TWITCH
!
SHRA KA KA KA KA KA KA KA K

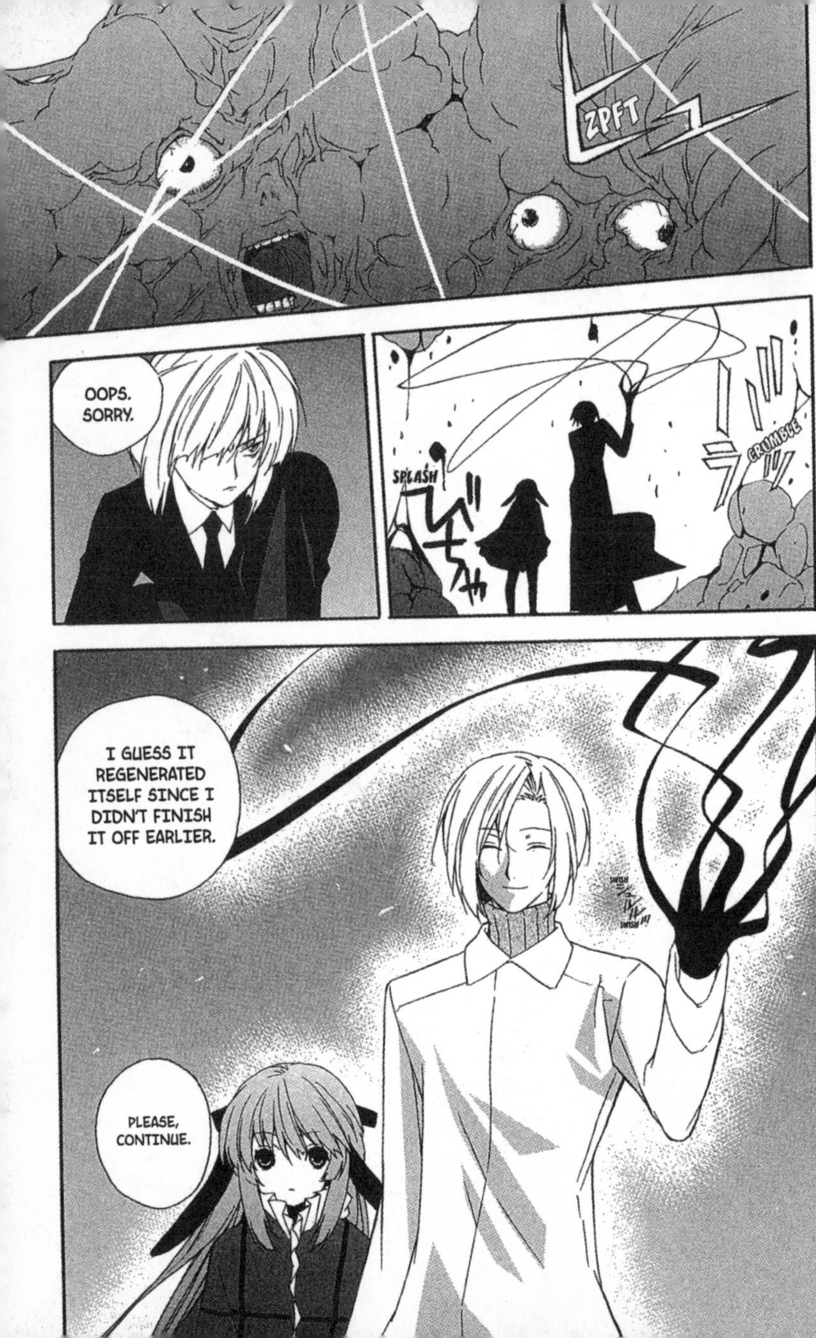
ZPFT
SPLASH
CRUMBLE
OOPS. SORRY.
I GUESS IT REGENERATED ITSELF SINCE I DIDN'T FINISH IT OFF EARLIER.
SWISH
SWISH!!
PLEASE, CONTINUE.

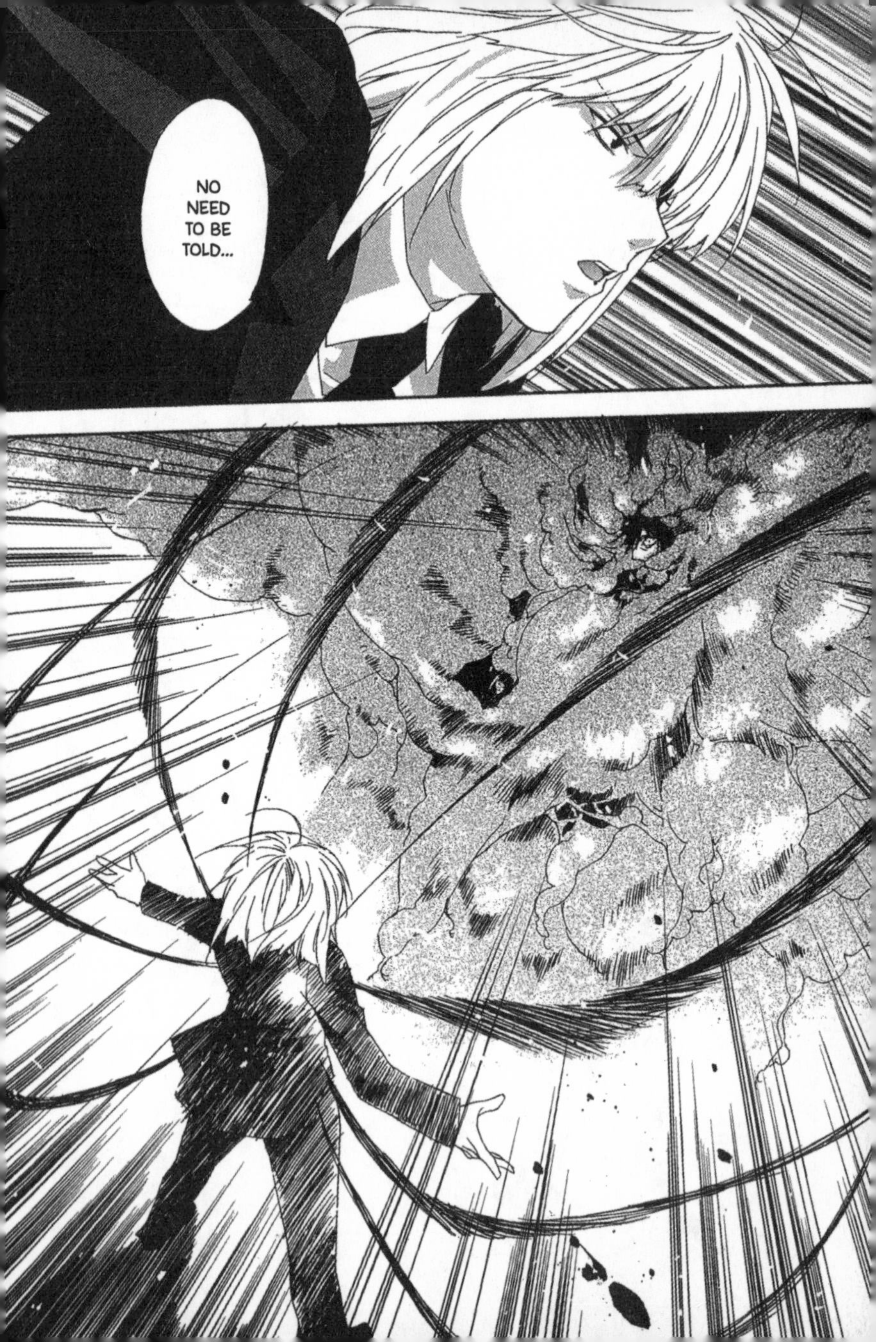
NO NEED TO BE TOLD...

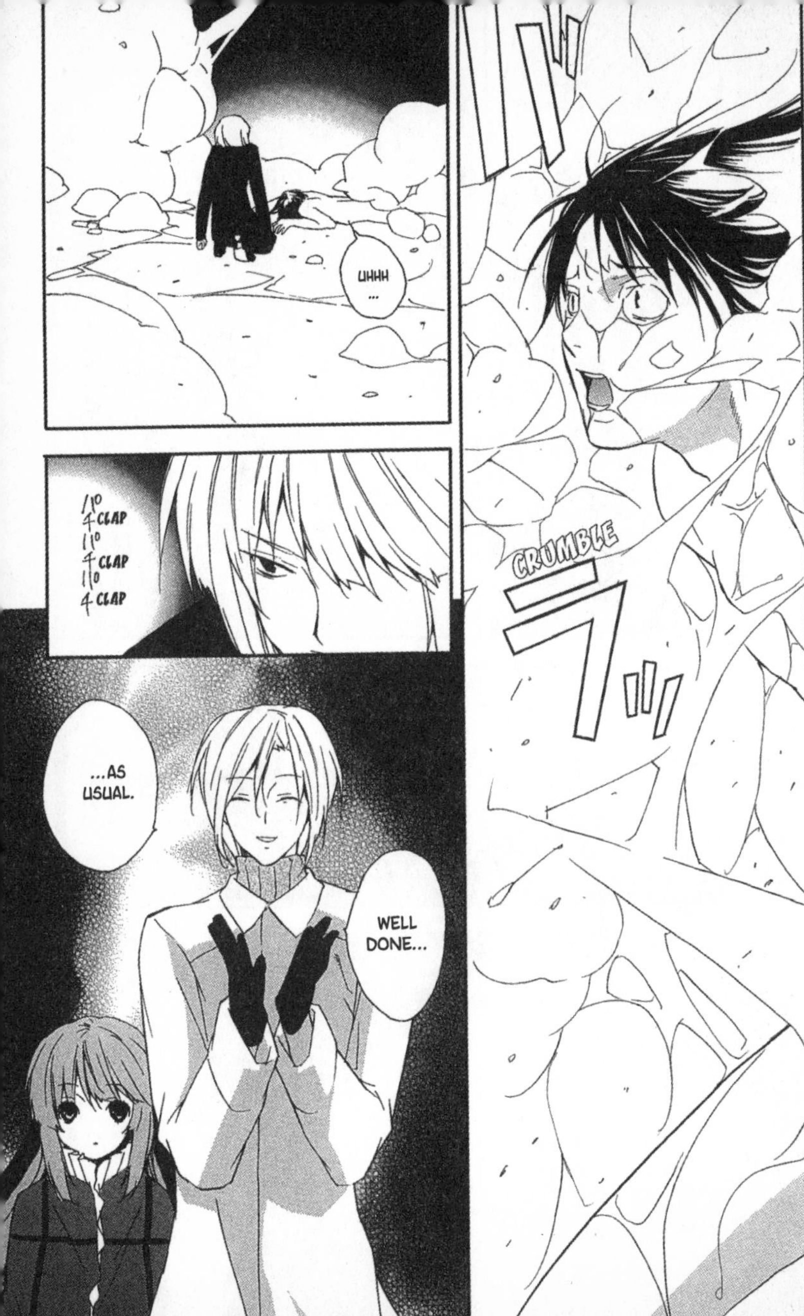
CRUMBLE
UHHH ...
CLAP
CLAP
CLAP
WELL DONE...
...AS USUAL.

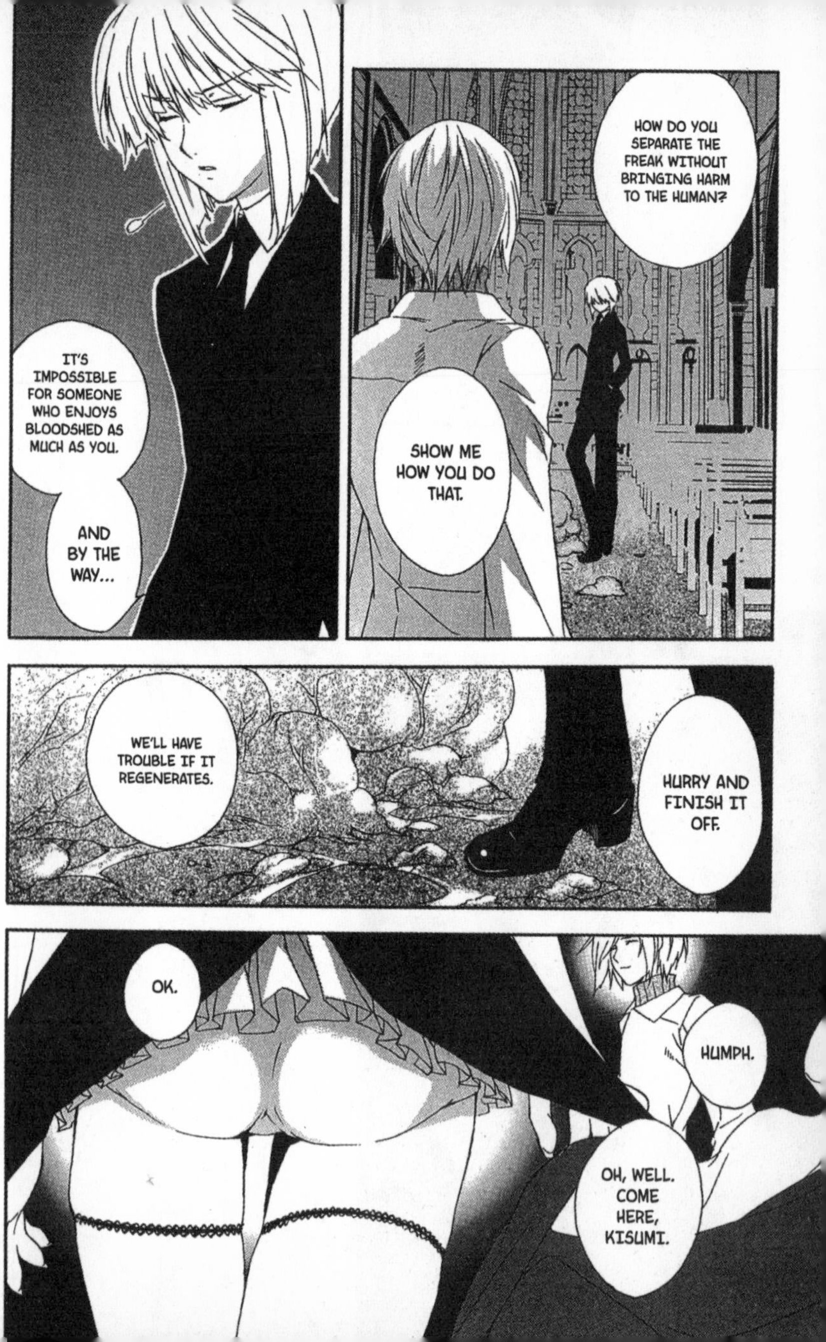
HOW DO YOU SEPARATE THE FREAK WITHOUT BRINGING HARM TO THE HUMAN?
SHOW ME HOW YOU DO THAT.
IT'S IMPOSSIBLE FOR SOMEONE WHO ENJOYS BLOODSHED AS MUCH AS YOU.
AND BY THE WAY...
HURRY AND FINISH IT OFF.
WE'LL HAVE TROUBLE IF IT REGENERATES.
HUMPH.
OK.
OH, WELL. COME HERE, KISUMI.

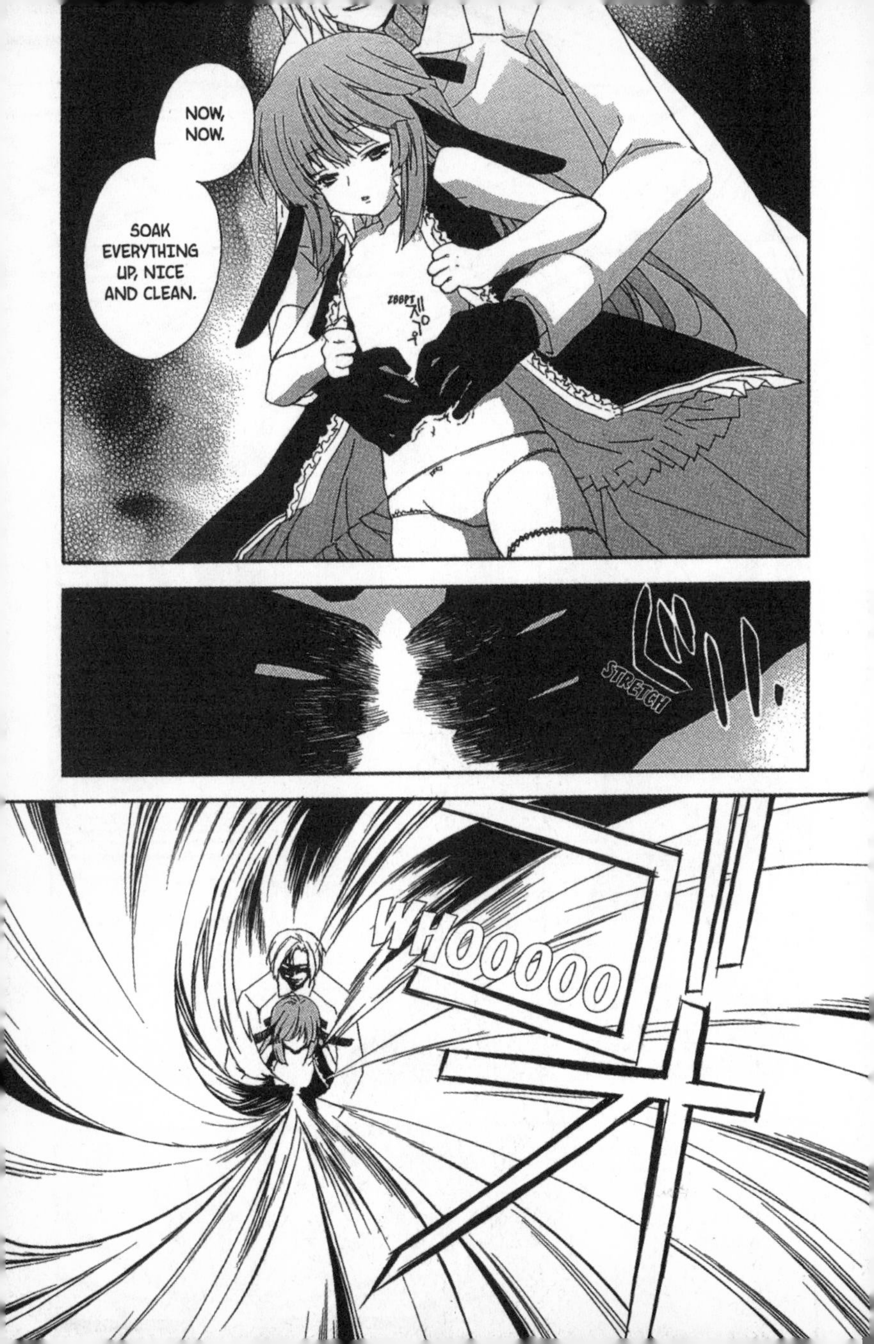
NOW, NOW.
SOAK EVERYTHING UP, NICE AND CLEAN.
ZBBPT
STRETCH
WHOOOOO

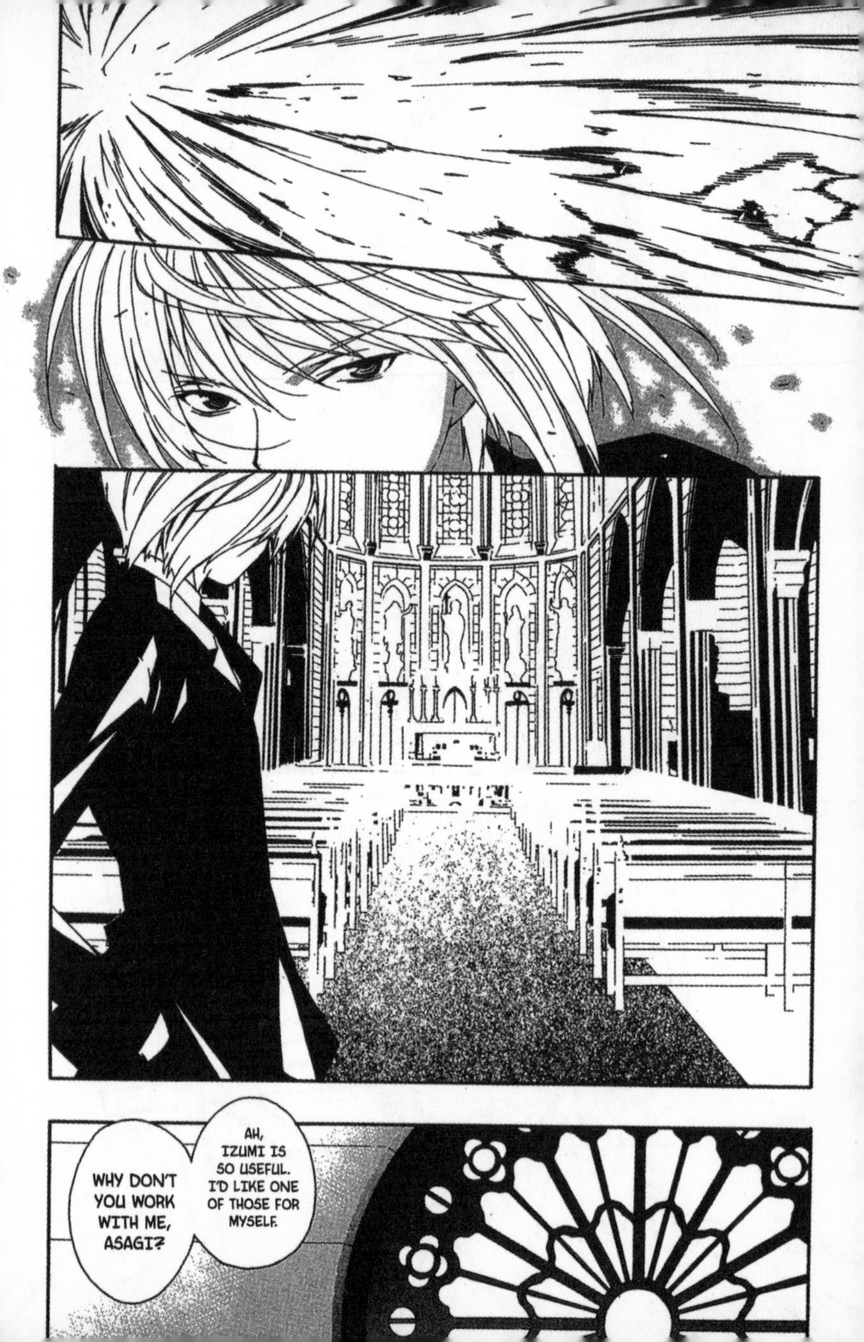
AH, IZUMI IS SO USEFUL. I'D LIKE ONE OF THOSE FOR MYSELF.
WHY DON'T YOU WORK WITH ME, ASAGI?

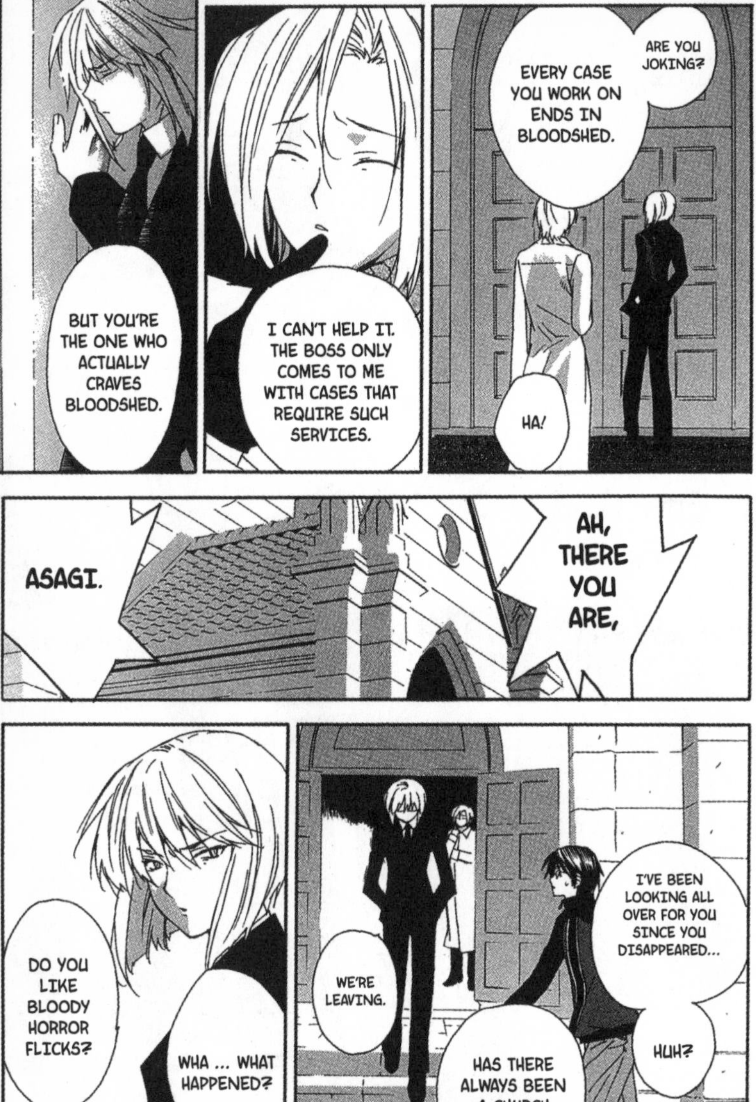
ARE YOU JOKING?
EVERY CASE YOU WORK ON ENDS IN BLOODSHED.
HA!
I CAN'T HELP IT. THE BOSS ONLY COMES TO ME WITH CASES THAT REQUIRE SUCH SERVICES.
BUT YOU'RE THE ONE WHO ACTUALLY CRAVES BLOODSHED.
AH, THERE YOU ARE,
ASAGI.
I'VE BEEN LOOKING ALL OVER FOR YOU SINCE YOU DISAPPEARED...
HUH?
HAS THERE ALWAYS BEEN A CHURCH HERE?
WE'RE LEAVING.
WHA ... WHAT HAPPENED?
DO YOU LIKE BLOODY HORROR FLICKS?

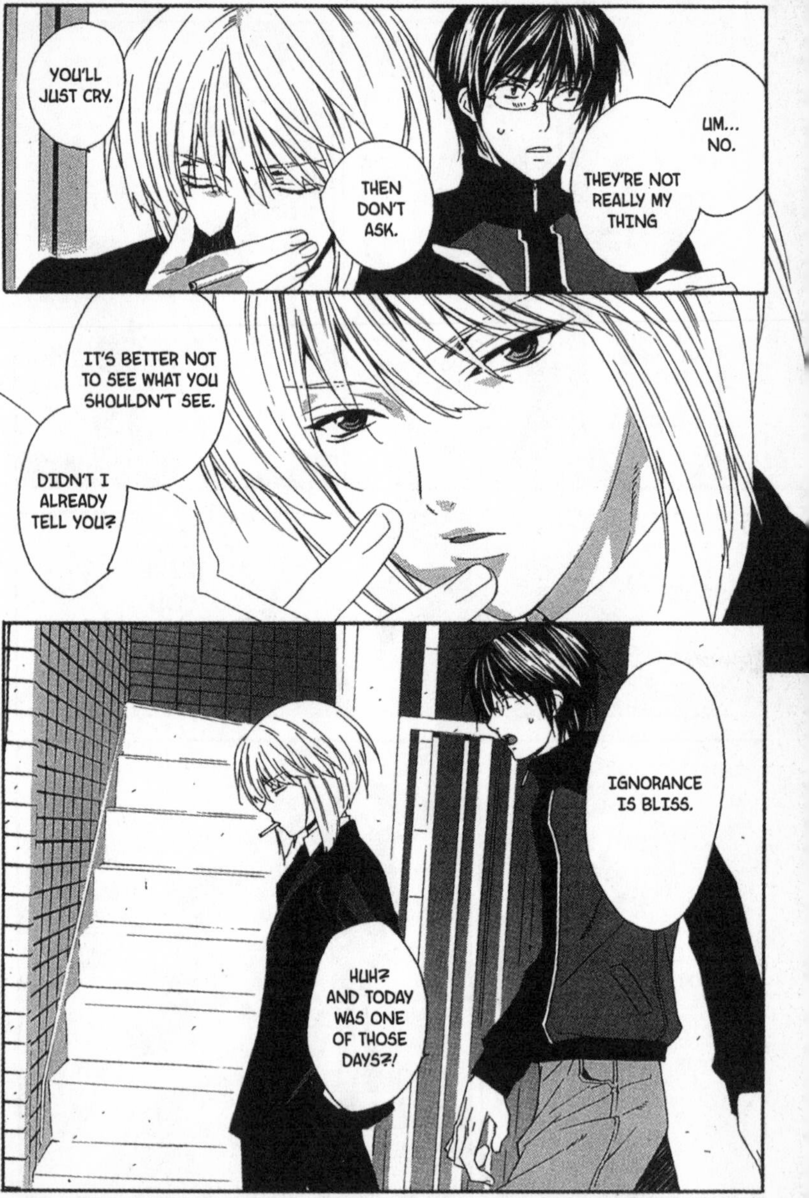
UM... NO.
THEY'RE NOT REALLY MY THING
THEN DON'T ASK.
YOU'LL JUST CRY.
IT'S BETTER NOT TO SEE WHAT YOU SHOULDN'T SEE.
DIDN'T I ALREADY TELL YOU?
IGNORANCE IS BLISS.
HUH? AND TODAY WAS ONE OF THOSE DAYS?!

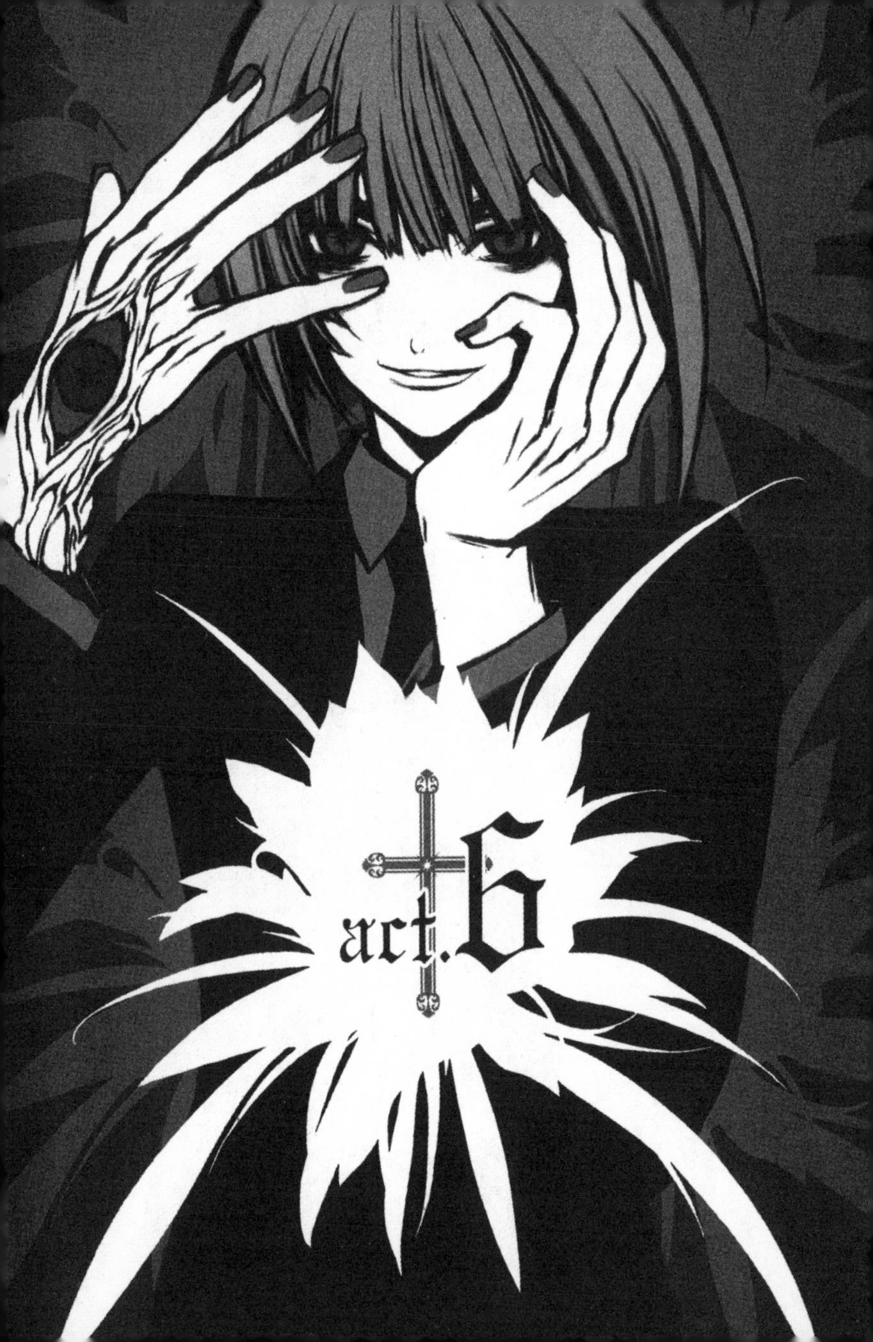
act. 6

NAPPING RABBIT
PRINCESSES

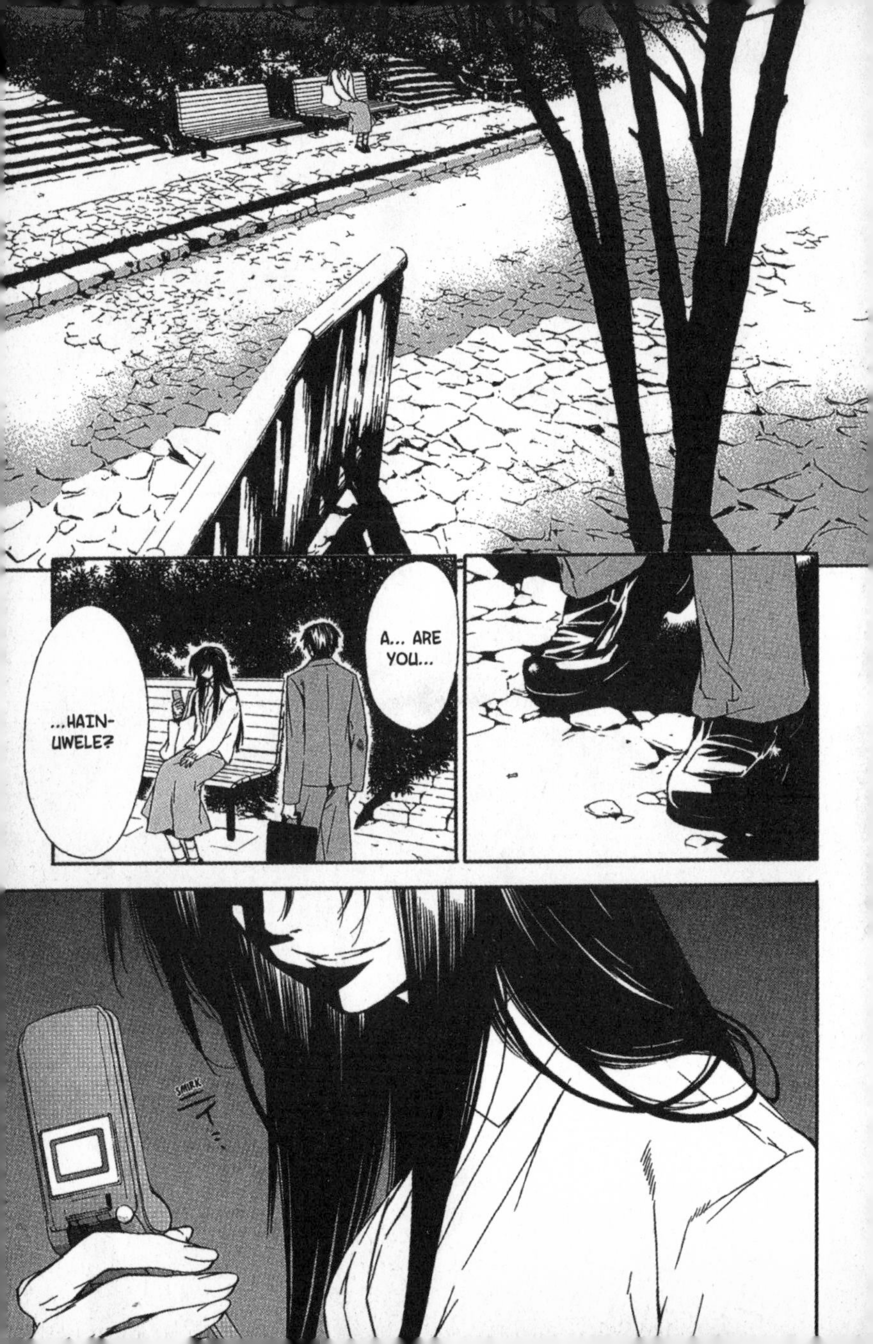
A... ARE YOU...
...HAIN-UWELE?
SMIRK

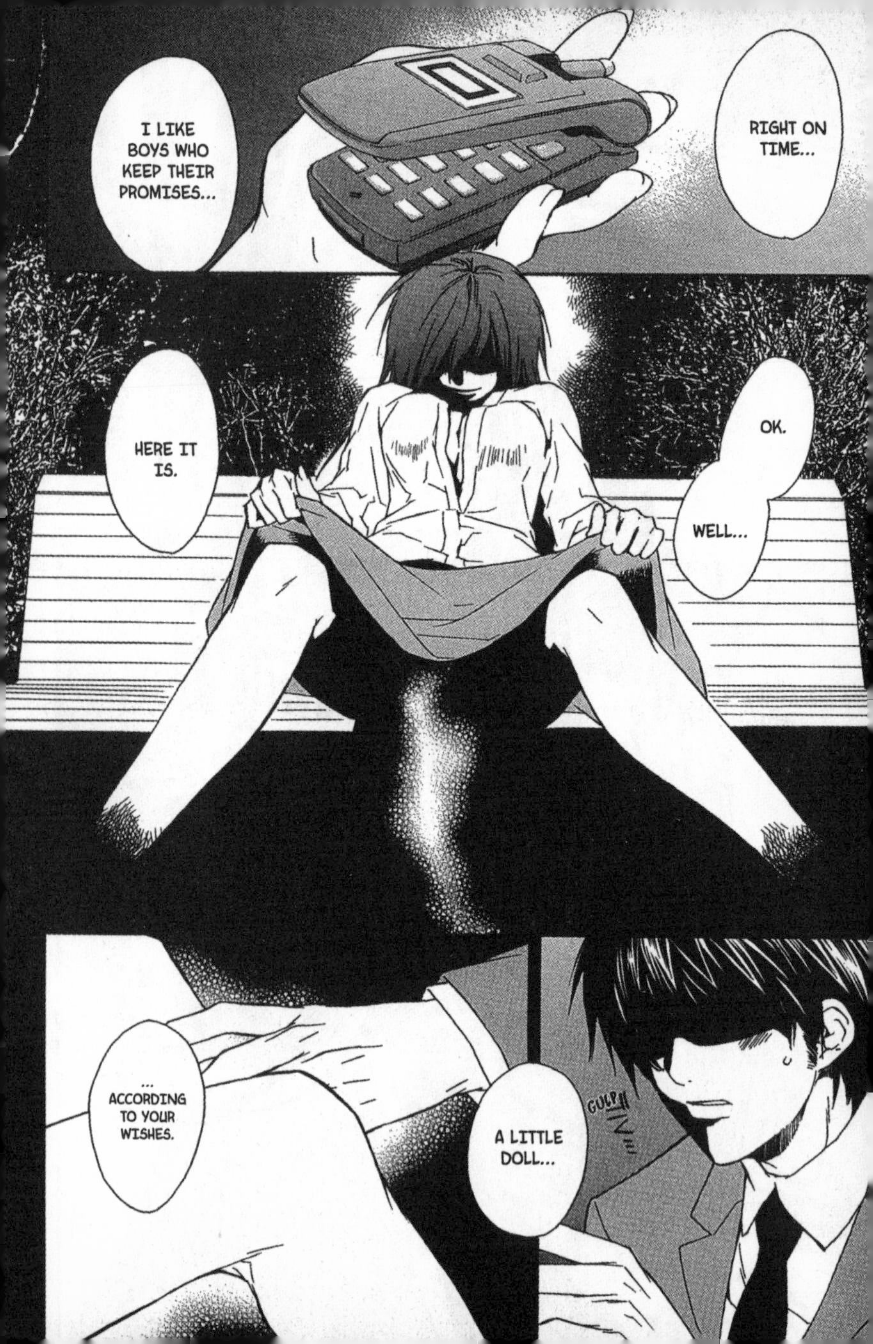
RIGHT ON TIME...
I LIKE BOYS WHO KEEP THEIR PROMISES...
OK.
WELL...
HERE IT IS.
GULP!!
A LITTLE DOLL...
... ACCORDING TO YOUR WISHES.

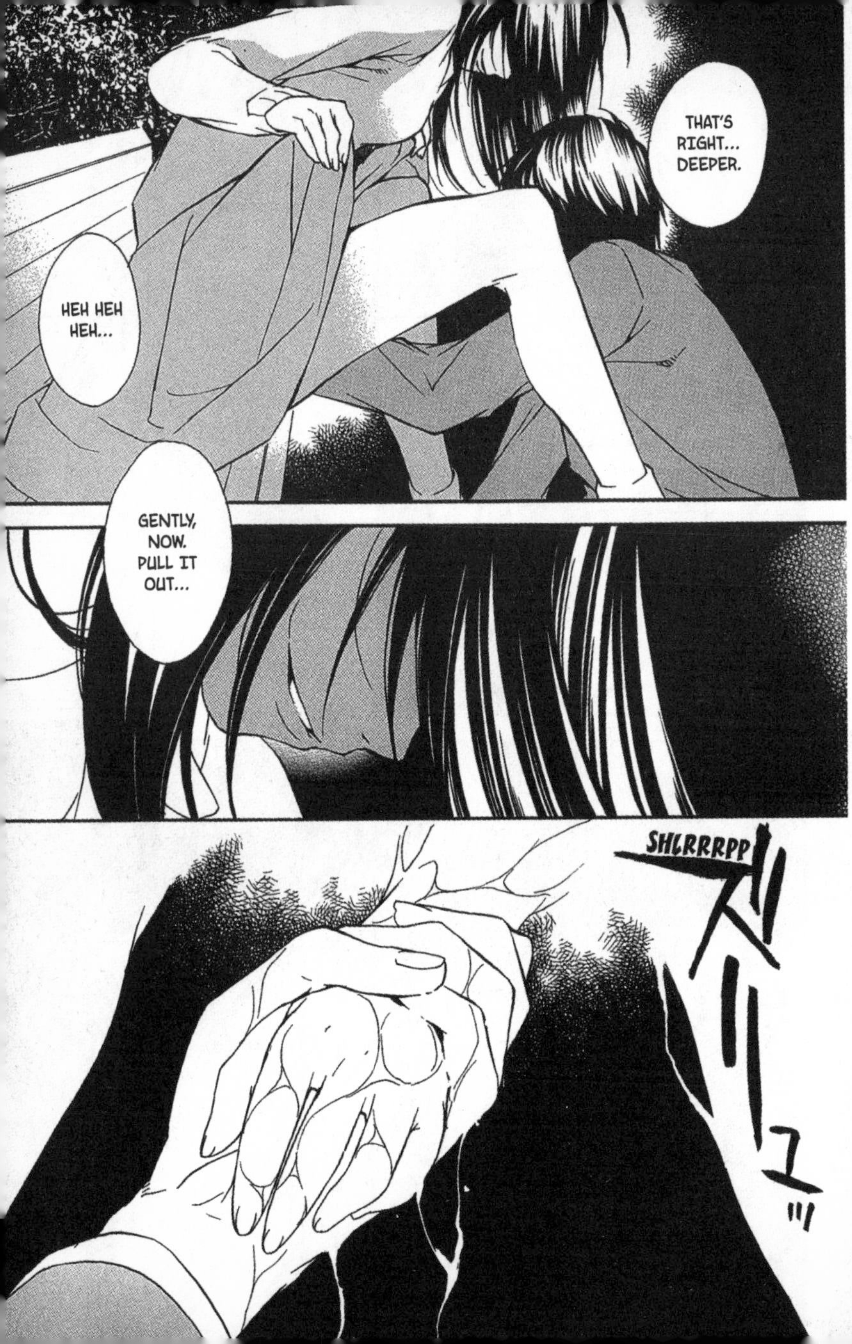
THAT'S RIGHT... DEEPER.
HEH HEH HEH...
GENTLY, NOW. PULL IT OUT...
SHLRRRPP

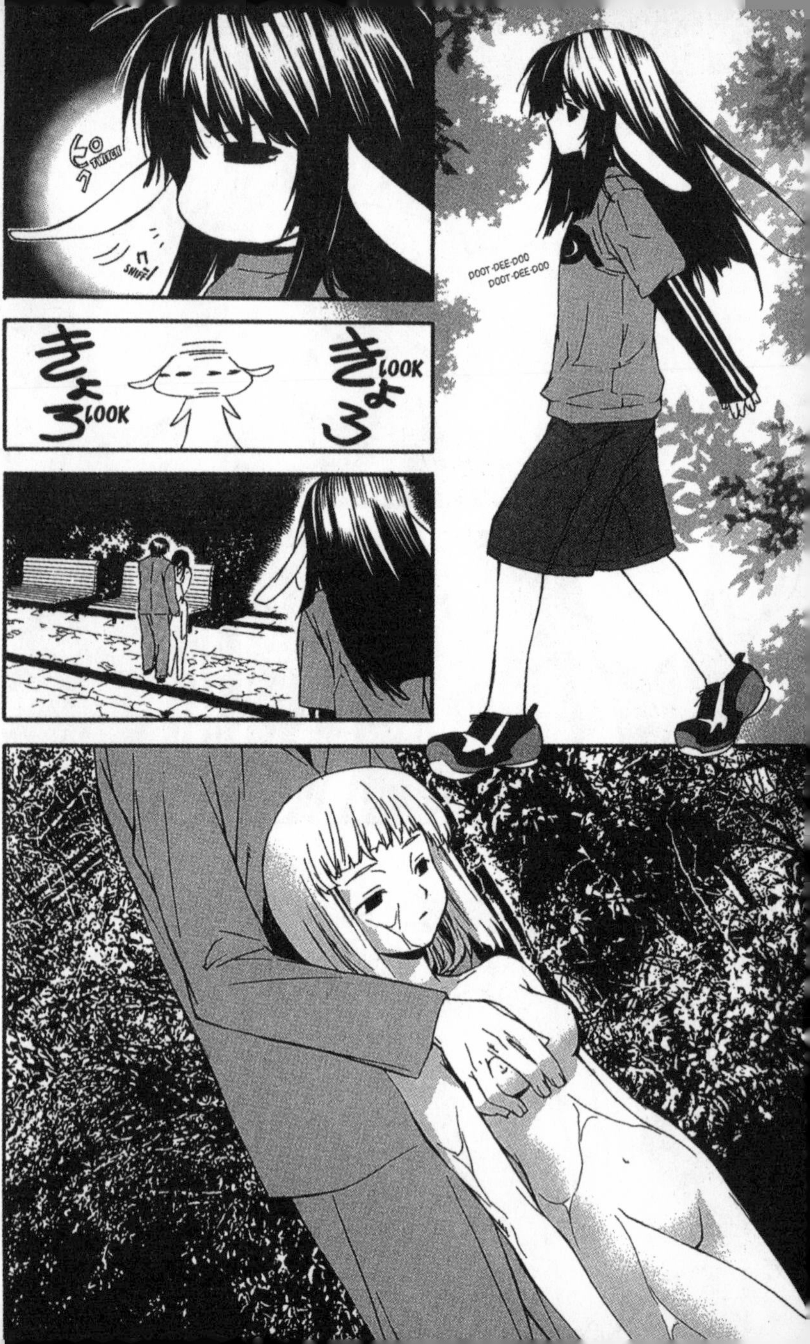
DOOT-DEE-DOO
DOOT-DEE-DOO
TWITCH
SNIFF!
きょろ LOOK
きょろ LOOK

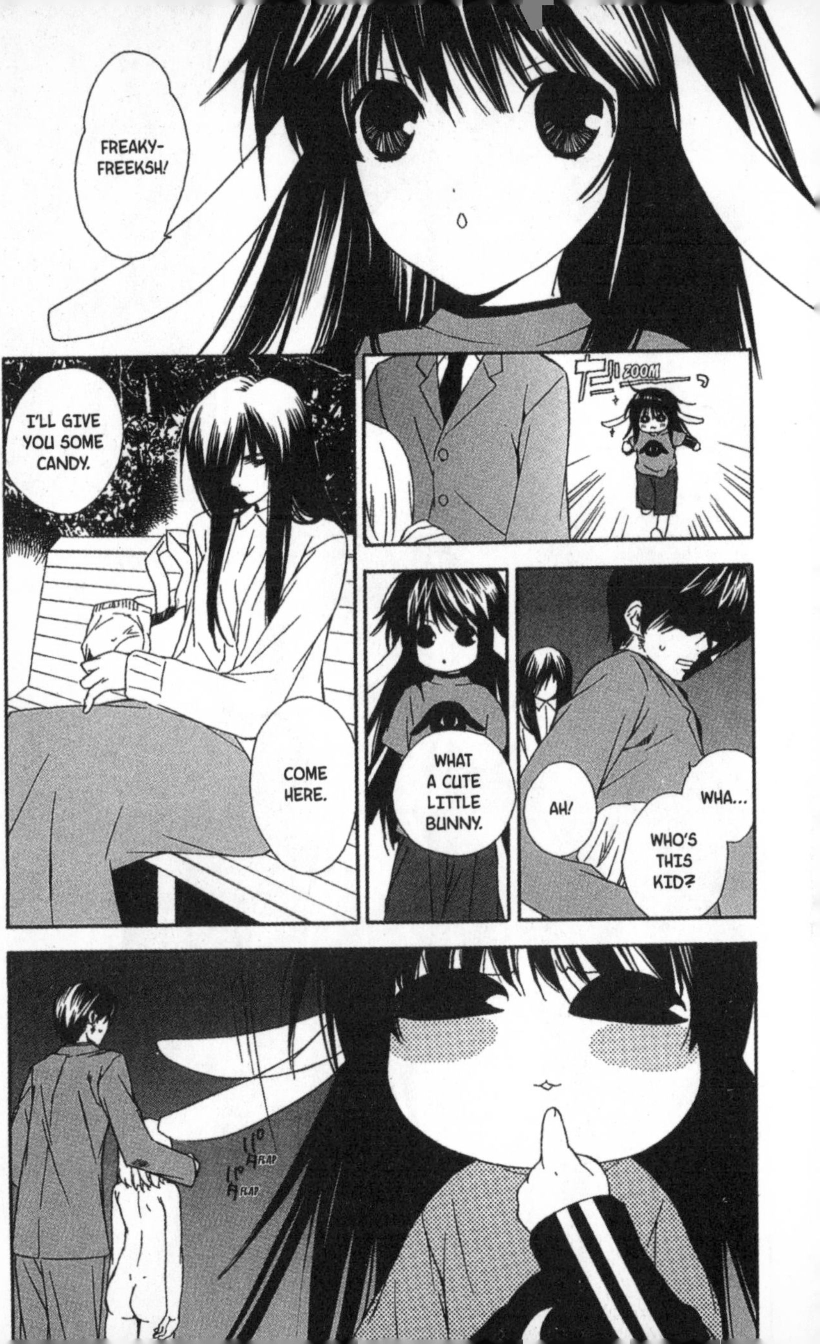
FREAKY-FREEKSH!
ZOOM
WHA...
WHO'S THIS KID?
AH!
WHAT A CUTE LITTLE BUNNY.
I'LL GIVE YOU SOME CANDY.
COME HERE.
FLAP
FLAP

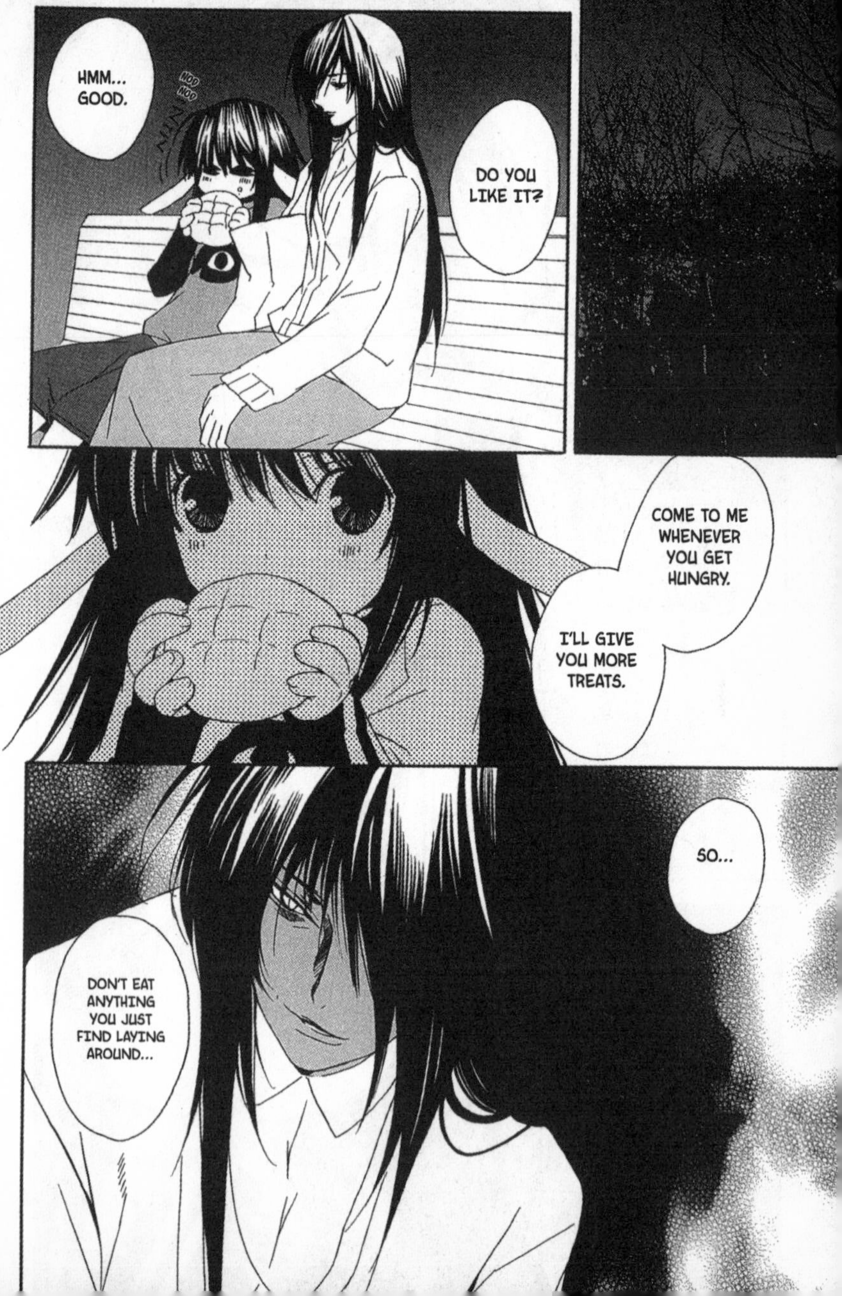
DO YOU LIKE IT?
NOD NOD
HMM... GOOD.
COME TO ME WHENEVER YOU GET HUNGRY.
I'LL GIVE YOU MORE TREATS.
SO...
DON'T EAT ANYTHING YOU JUST FIND LAYING AROUND...

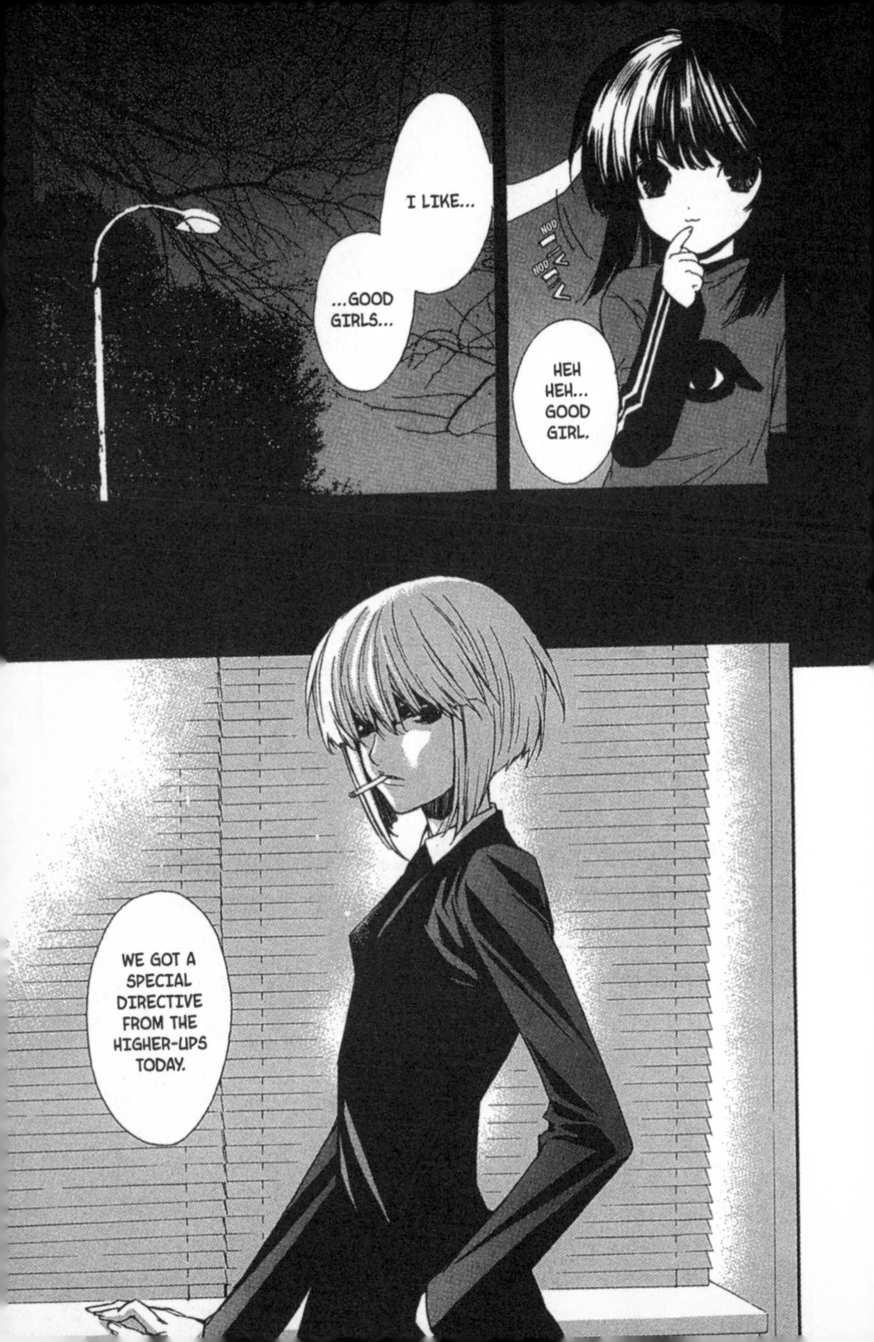
I LIKE...
...GOOD GIRLS...
NOD NOD
HEH HEH... GOOD GIRL.
WE GOT A SPECIAL DIRECTIVE FROM THE HIGHER-UPS TODAY.

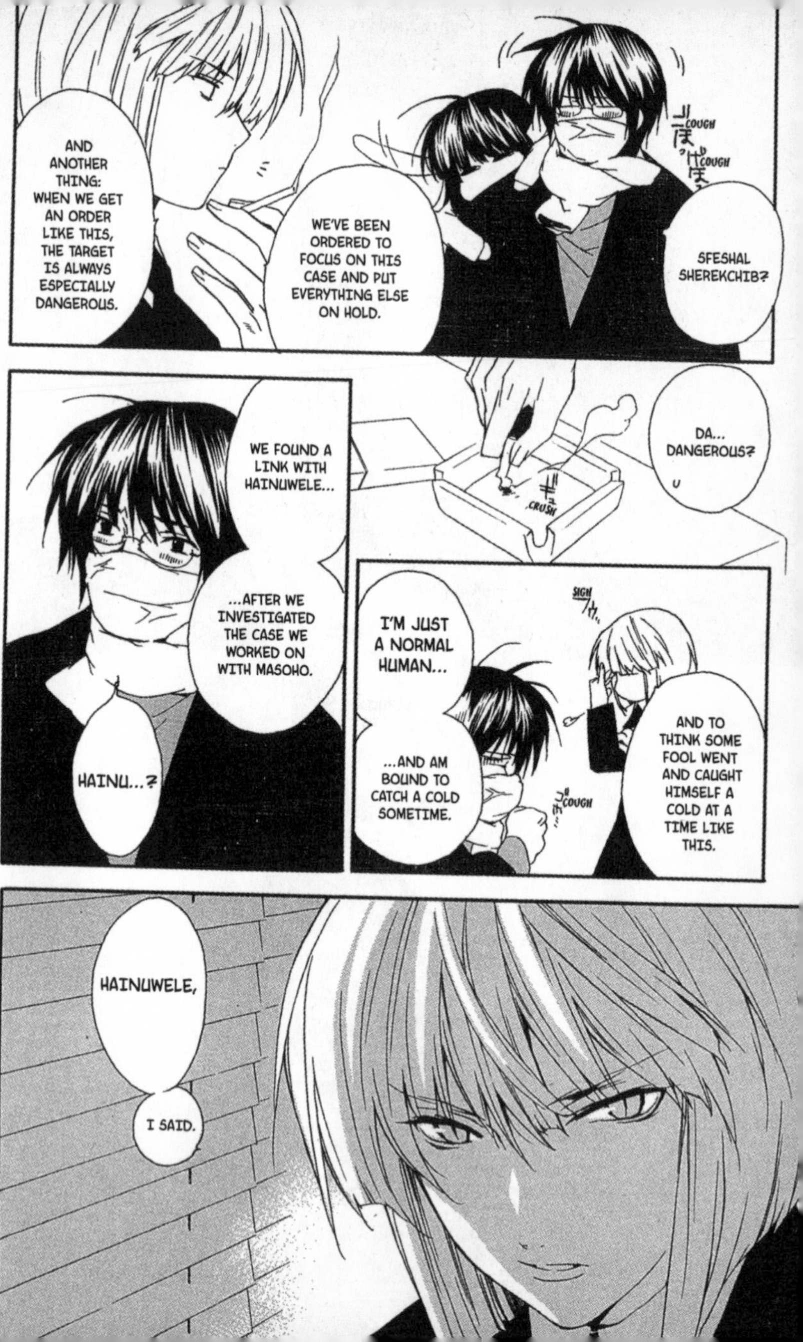
COUGH
COUGH
SFESHAL SHEREKCHIB?
WE'VE BEEN ORDERED TO FOCUS ON THIS CASE AND PUT EVERYTHING ELSE ON HOLD.
AND ANOTHER THING: WHEN WE GET AN ORDER LIKE THIS, THE TARGET IS ALWAYS ESPECIALLY DANGEROUS.
DA... DANGEROUS?
CRUSH
SIGH
AND TO THINK SOME FOOL WENT AND CAUGHT HIMSELF A COLD AT A TIME LIKE THIS.
COUGH
I'M JUST A NORMAL HUMAN...
...AND AM BOUND TO CATCH A COLD SOMETIME.
WE FOUND A LINK WITH HAINUWELE...
...AFTER WE INVESTIGATED THE CASE WE WORKED ON WITH MASOHO.
HAINU...?
HAINUWELE,
I SAID.

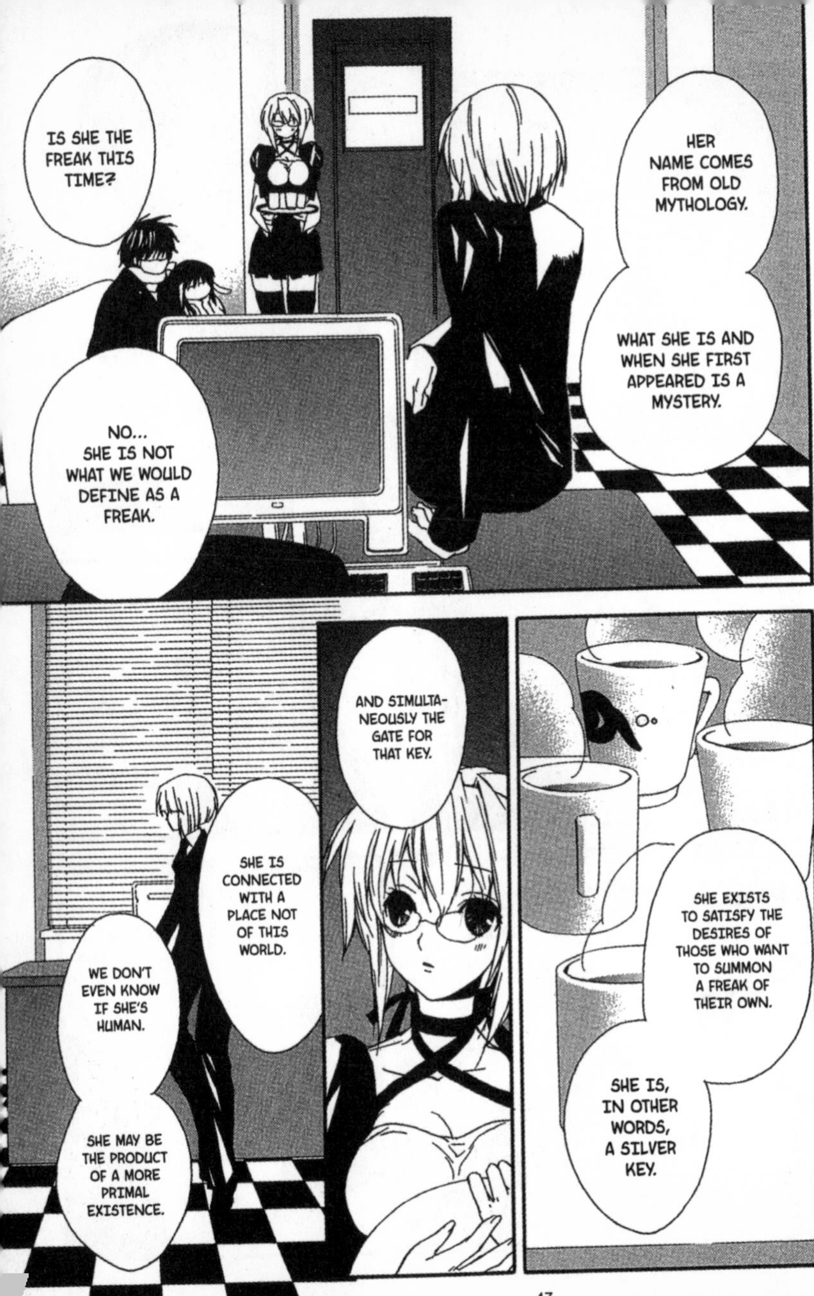
HER NAME COMES FROM OLD MYTHOLOGY.
WHAT SHE IS AND WHEN SHE FIRST APPEARED IS A MYSTERY.
IS SHE THE FREAK THIS TIME?
NO... SHE IS NOT WHAT WE WOULD DEFINE AS A FREAK.
SHE EXISTS TO SATISFY THE DESIRES OF THOSE WHO WANT TO SUMMON A FREAK OF THEIR OWN.
SHE IS, IN OTHER WORDS, A SILVER KEY.
AND SIMULTA-NEOUSLY THE GATE FOR THAT KEY.
SHE IS CONNECTED WITH A PLACE NOT OF THIS WORLD.
WE DON'T EVEN KNOW IF SHE'S HUMAN.
SHE MAY BE THE PRODUCT OF A MORE PRIMAL EXISTENCE.

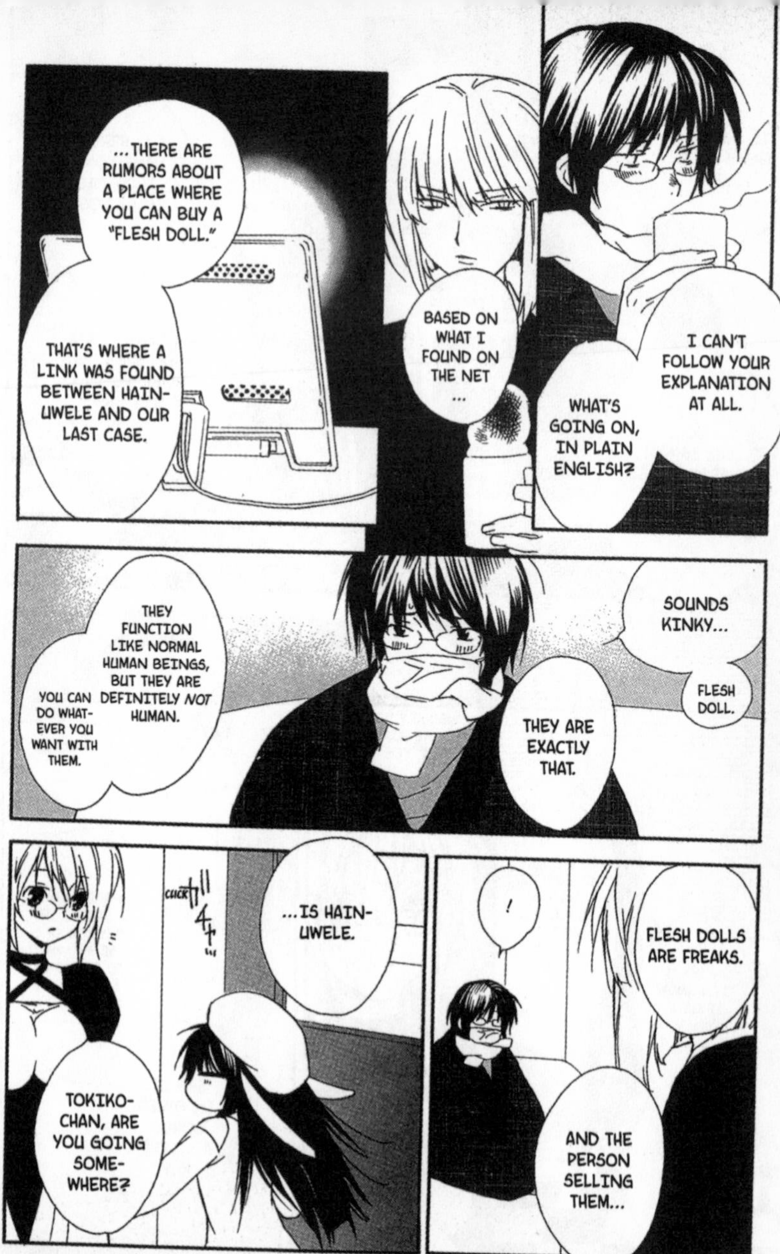

I CAN'T FOLLOW YOUR EXPLANATION AT ALL.
WHAT'S GOING ON, IN PLAIN ENGLISH?
BASED ON WHAT I FOUND ON THE NET ...
...THERE ARE RUMORS ABOUT A PLACE WHERE YOU CAN BUY A "FLESH DOLL."
THAT'S WHERE A LINK WAS FOUND BETWEEN HAIN-UWELE AND OUR LAST CASE.
SOUNDS KINKY...
FLESH DOLL.
THEY ARE EXACTLY THAT.
THEY FUNCTION LIKE NORMAL HUMAN BEINGS, BUT THEY ARE DEFINITELY *NOT* HUMAN.
YOU CAN DO WHAT-EVER YOU WANT WITH THEM.
FLESH DOLLS ARE FREAKS.
!
AND THE PERSON SELLING THEM...
...IS HAIN-UWELE.
CLICK
TOKIKO-CHAN, ARE YOU GOING SOME-WHERE?

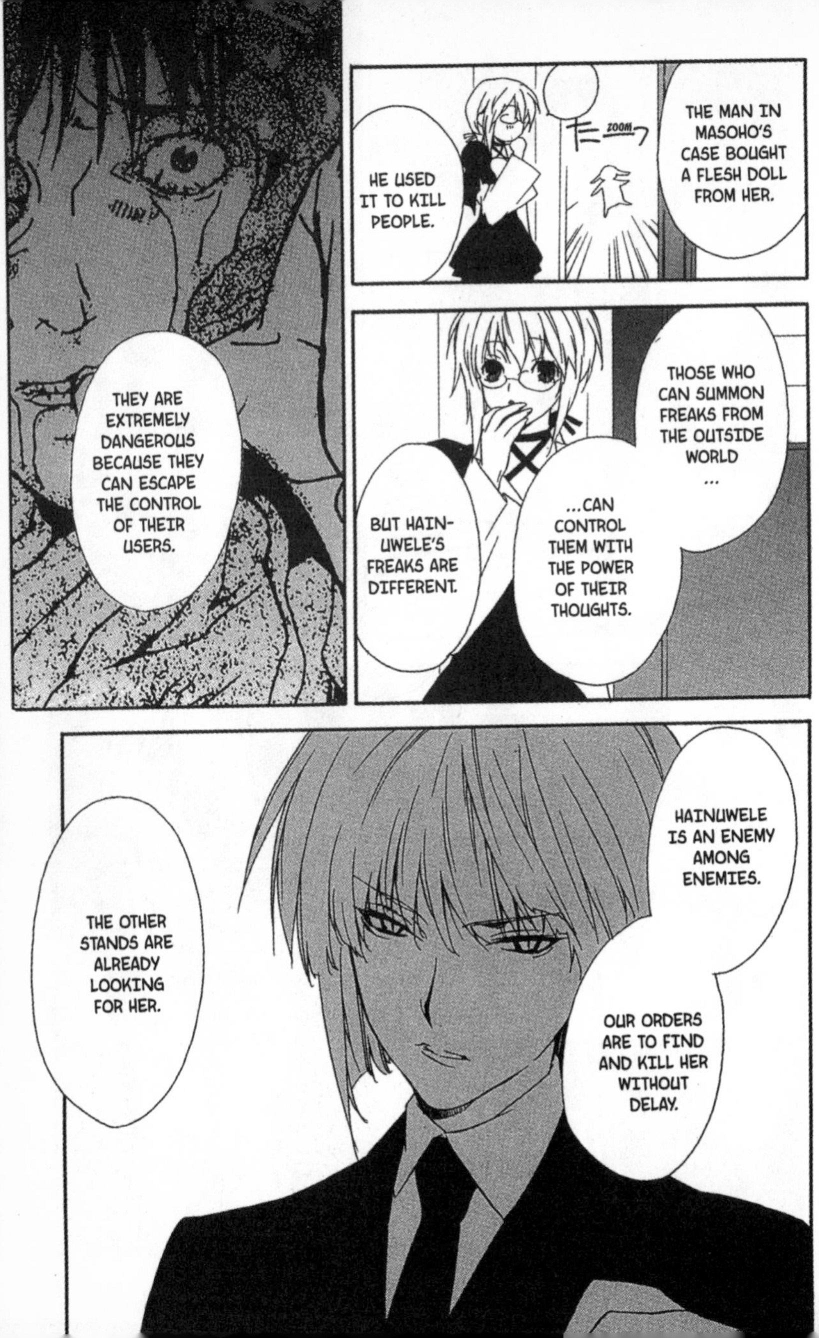
THE MAN IN MASOHO'S CASE BOUGHT A FLESH DOLL FROM HER.
ZOOM
HE USED IT TO KILL PEOPLE.
THOSE WHO CAN SUMMON FREAKS FROM THE OUTSIDE WORLD ...
...CAN CONTROL THEM WITH THE POWER OF THEIR THOUGHTS.
BUT HAIN-UWELE'S FREAKS ARE DIFFERENT.
THEY ARE EXTREMELY DANGEROUS BECAUSE THEY CAN ESCAPE THE CONTROL OF THEIR USERS.
HAINUWELE IS AN ENEMY AMONG ENEMIES.
OUR ORDERS ARE TO FIND AND KILL HER WITHOUT DELAY.
THE OTHER STANDS ARE ALREADY LOOKING FOR HER.

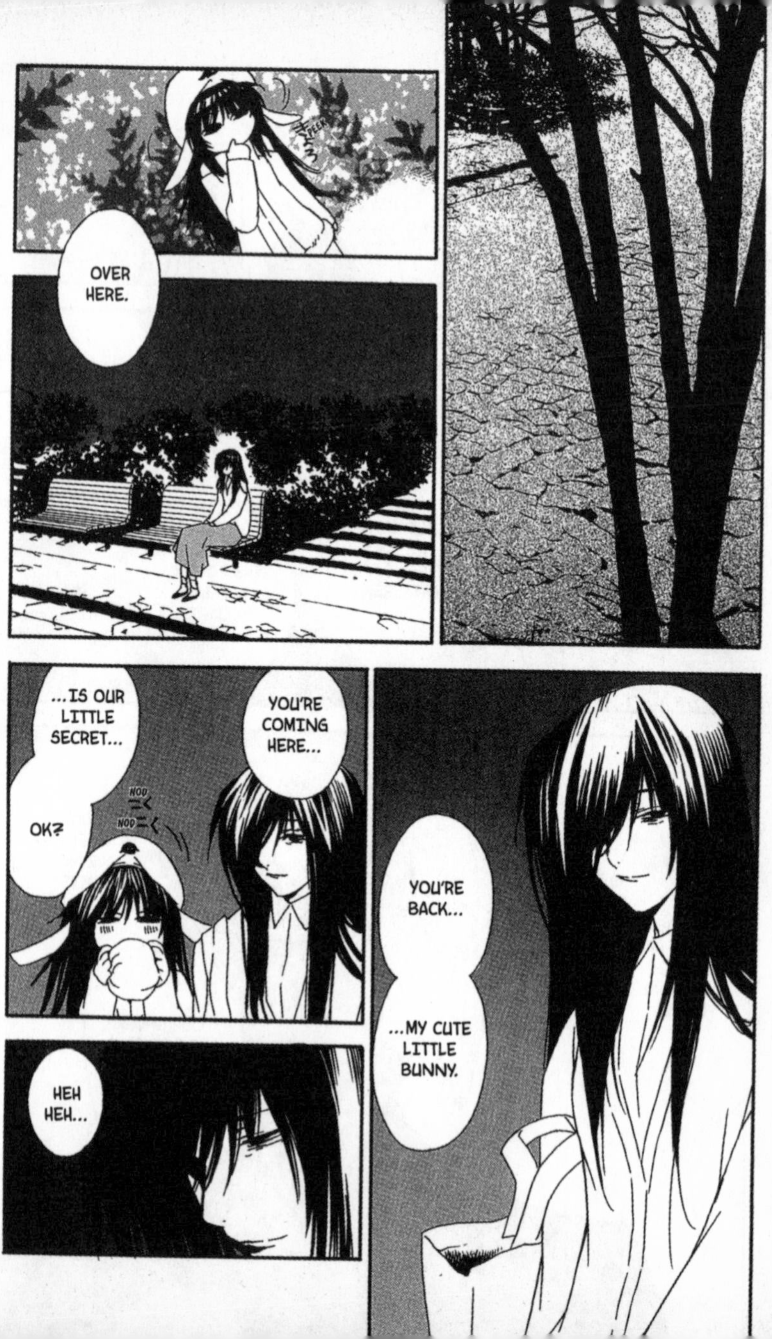
PEEK
OVER HERE.
YOU'RE BACK...
...MY CUTE LITTLE BUNNY.
YOU'RE COMING HERE...
...IS OUR LITTLE SECRET...
NOD
NOD
OK?
HEH HEH...

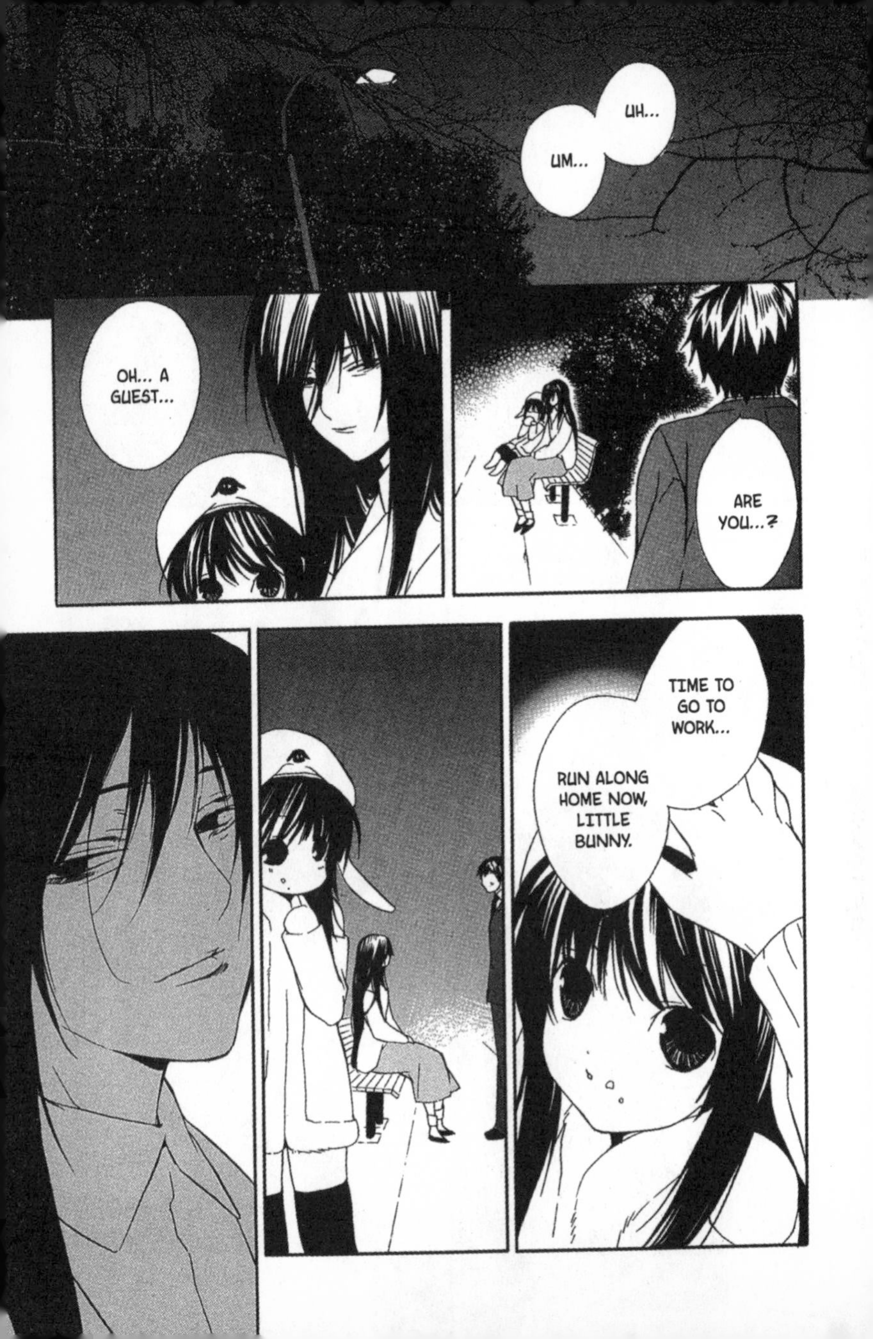
UH...
UM...
ARE YOU...?
OH... A GUEST...
TIME TO GO TO WORK...
RUN ALONG HOME NOW, LITTLE BUNNY.

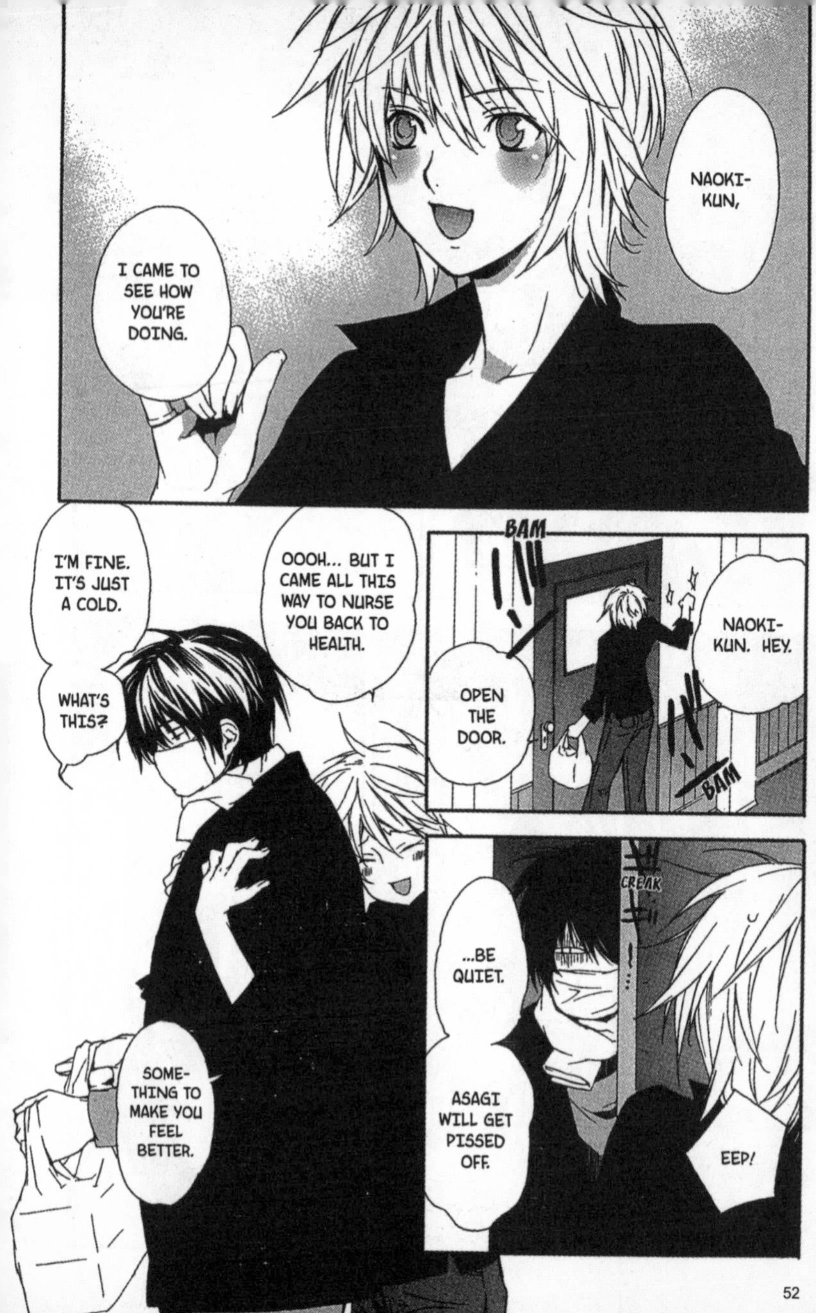
NAOKI-KUN,
I CAME TO SEE HOW YOU'RE DOING.
BAM
NAOKI-KUN. HEY.
OPEN THE DOOR.
BAM
CREAK
...BE QUIET.
ASAGI WILL GET PISSED OFF.
EEP!
OOOH... BUT I CAME ALL THIS WAY TO NURSE YOU BACK TO HEALTH.
I'M FINE. IT'S JUST A COLD.
WHAT'S THIS?
SOME-THING TO MAKE YOU FEEL BETTER.

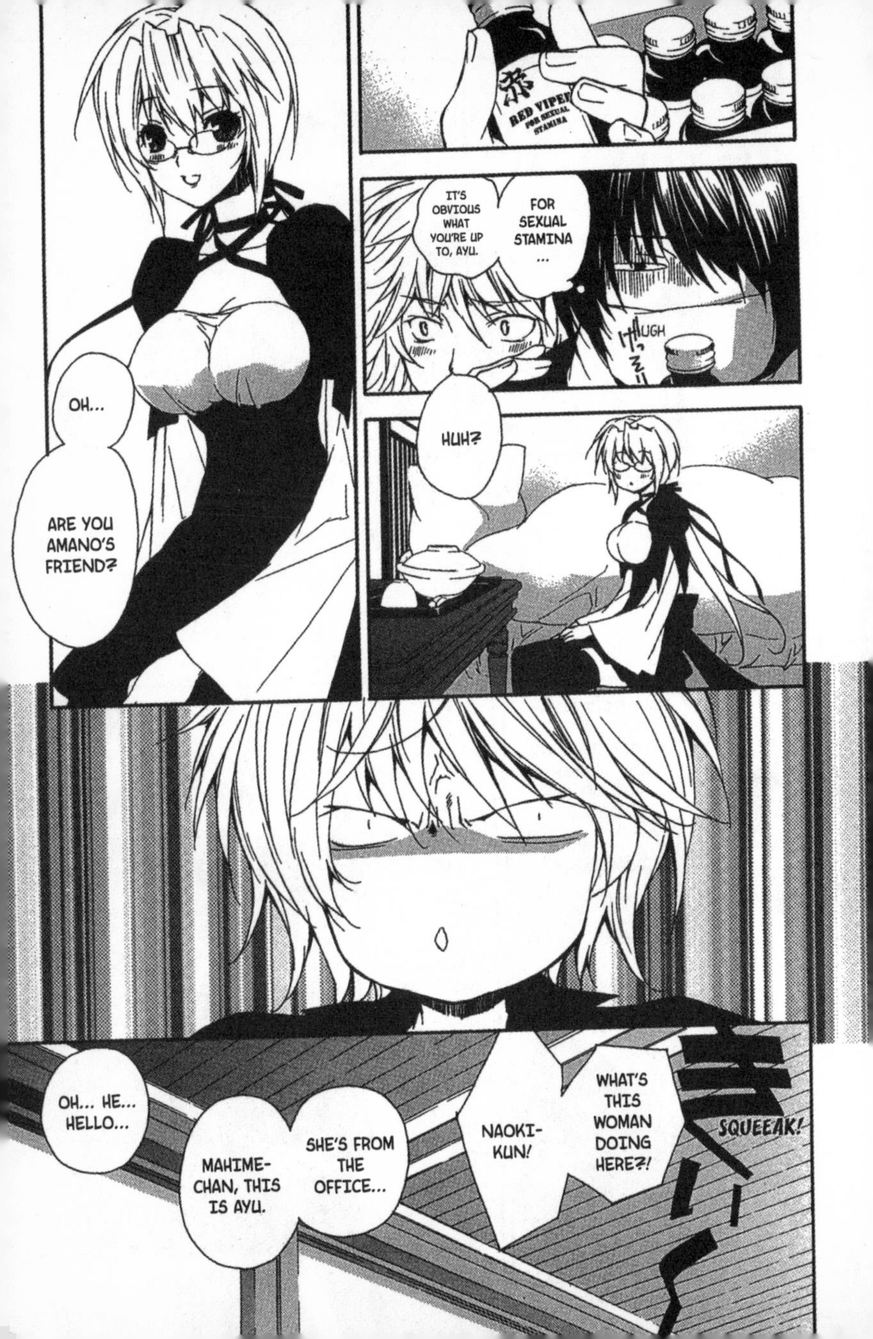
RED VIPER FOR SEXUAL STAMINA
FOR SEXUAL STAMINA ...
IT'S OBVIOUS WHAT YOU'RE UP TO, AYU.
UGH
HUH?
OH...
ARE YOU AMANO'S FRIEND?
SQUEEAK!
WHAT'S THIS WOMAN DOING HERE?!
NAOKI-KUN!
SHE'S FROM THE OFFICE...
MAHIME-CHAN, THIS IS AYU.
OH... HE... HELLO...

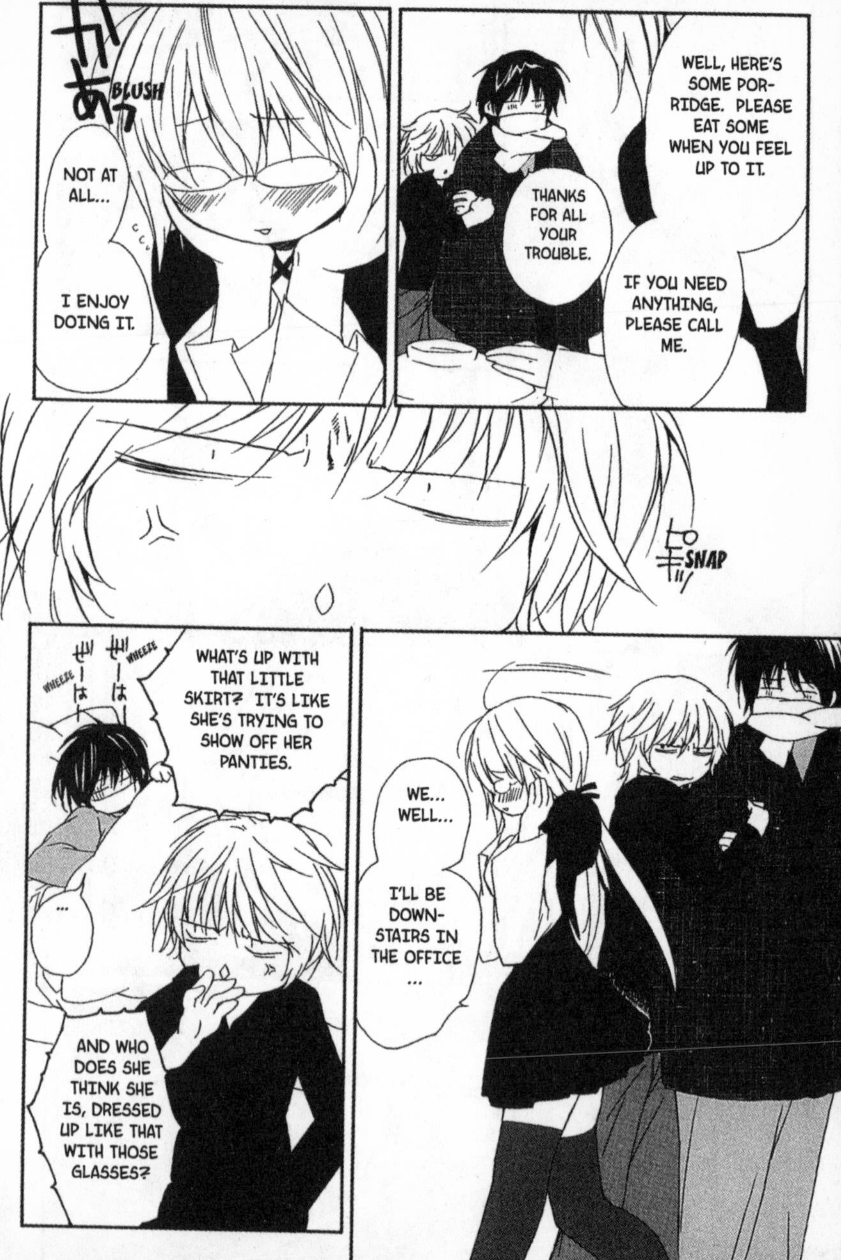

WELL, HERE'S SOME POR-RIDGE. PLEASE EAT SOME WHEN YOU FEEL UP TO IT.
IF YOU NEED ANYTHING, PLEASE CALL ME.
THANKS FOR ALL YOUR TROUBLE.
かあっ
BLUSH
NOT AT ALL...
I ENJOY DOING IT.
SNAP
WE... WELL...
I'LL BE DOWN-STAIRS IN THE OFFICE ...
ぜーはー
WHEEZE
ぜーはー
WHEEZE
WHAT'S UP WITH THAT LITTLE SKIRT? IT'S LIKE SHE'S TRYING TO SHOW OFF HER PANTIES.
...
AND WHO DOES SHE THINK SHE IS, DRESSED UP LIKE THAT WITH THOSE GLASSES?

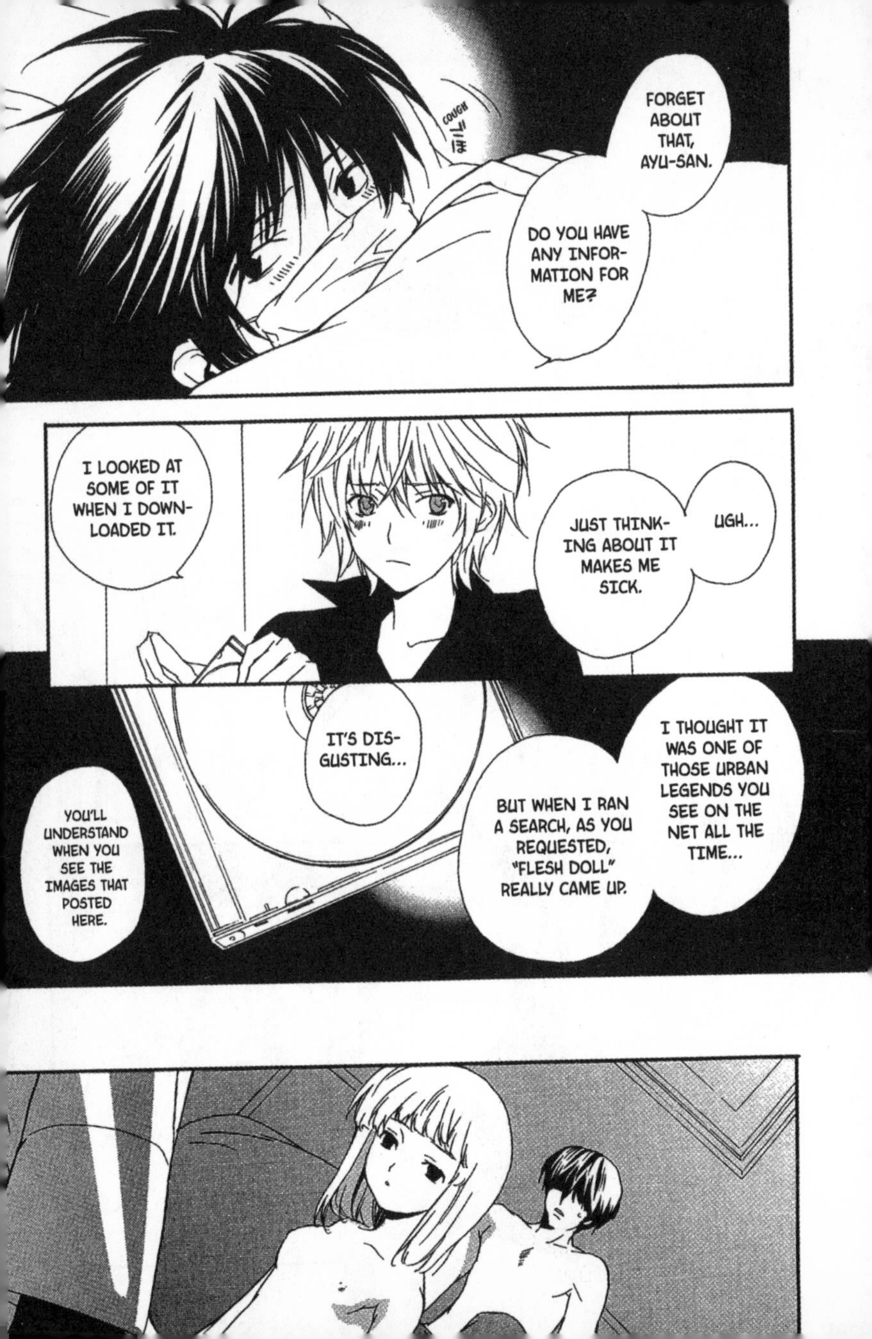
COUGH
FORGET ABOUT THAT, AYU-SAN.
DO YOU HAVE ANY INFORMATION FOR ME?
UGH...
JUST THINKING ABOUT IT MAKES ME SICK.
I LOOKED AT SOME OF IT WHEN I DOWNLOADED IT.
I THOUGHT IT WAS ONE OF THOSE URBAN LEGENDS YOU SEE ON THE NET ALL THE TIME...
BUT WHEN I RAN A SEARCH, AS YOU REQUESTED, "FLESH DOLL" REALLY CAME UP.
IT'S DISGUSTING...
YOU'LL UNDERSTAND WHEN YOU SEE THE IMAGES THAT POSTED HERE.

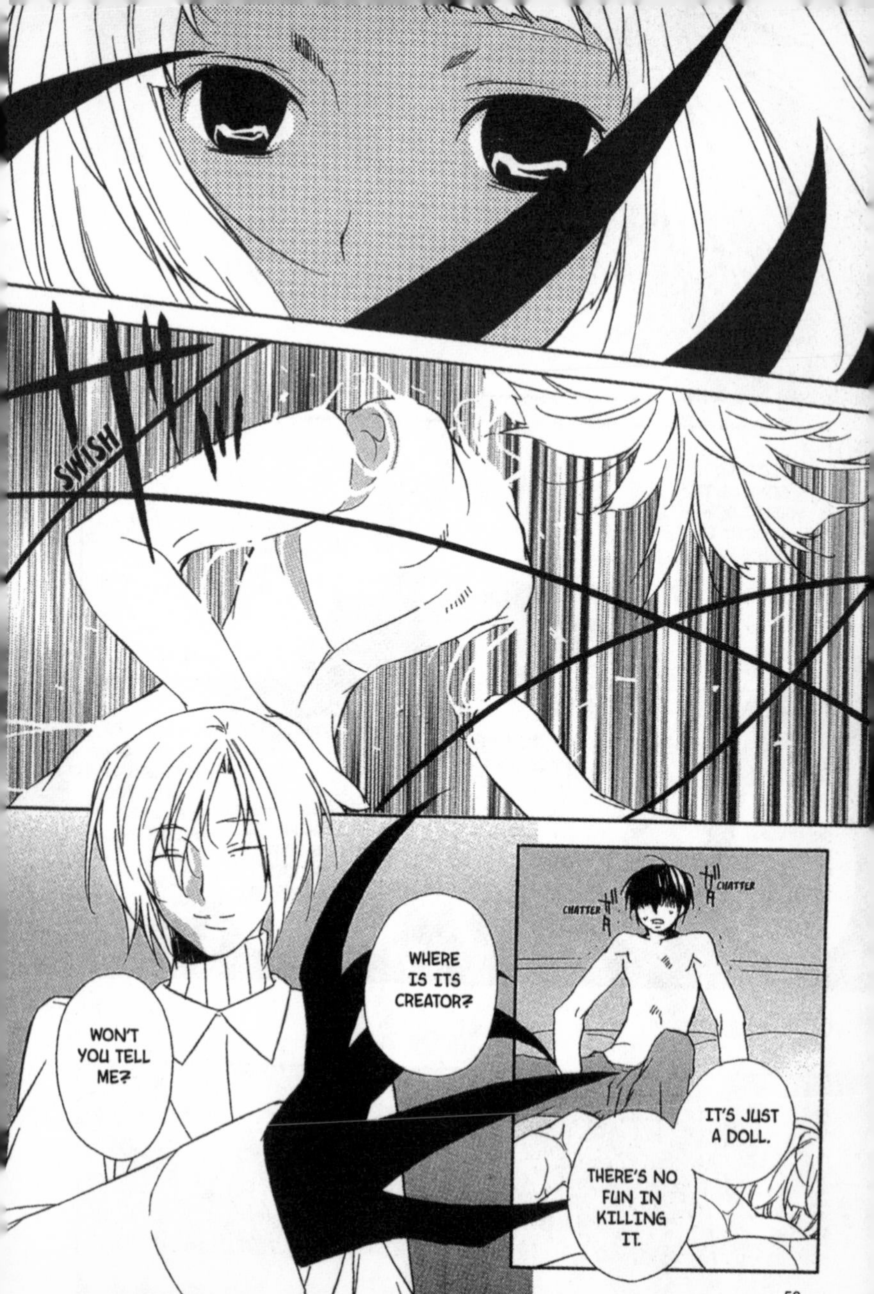
SWISH
CHATTER
CHATTER
IT'S JUST A DOLL.
THERE'S NO FUN IN KILLING IT.
WHERE IS ITS CREATOR?
WON'T YOU TELL ME?

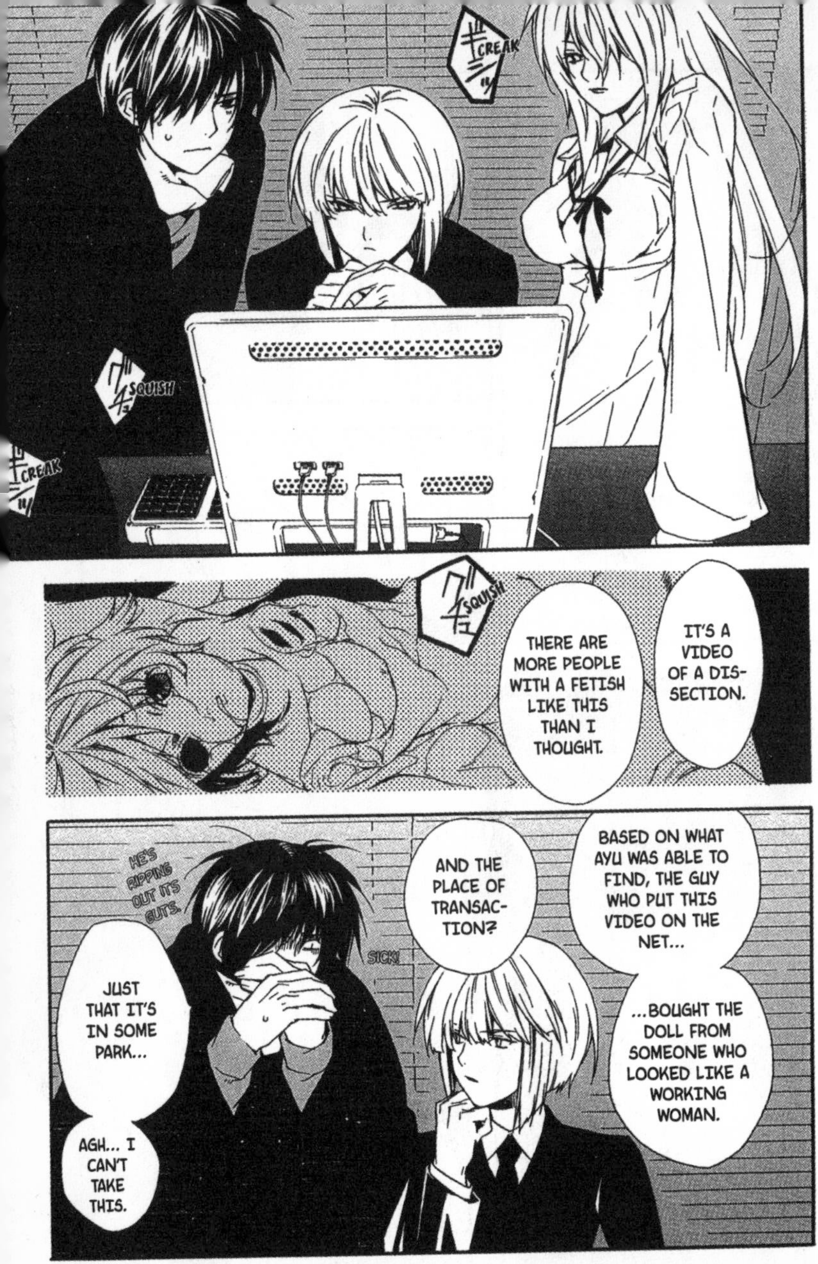
CREAK
SQUISH
CREAK
IT'S A VIDEO OF A DIS-SECTION.
THERE ARE MORE PEOPLE WITH A FETISH LIKE THIS THAN I THOUGHT.
SQUISH
BASED ON WHAT AYU WAS ABLE TO FIND, THE GUY WHO PUT THIS VIDEO ON THE NET...
...BOUGHT THE DOLL FROM SOMEONE WHO LOOKED LIKE A WORKING WOMAN.
AND THE PLACE OF TRANSAC-TION?
JUST THAT IT'S IN SOME PARK...
HE'S RIPPING OUT ITS GUTS.
SICK!
AGH... I CAN'T TAKE THIS.

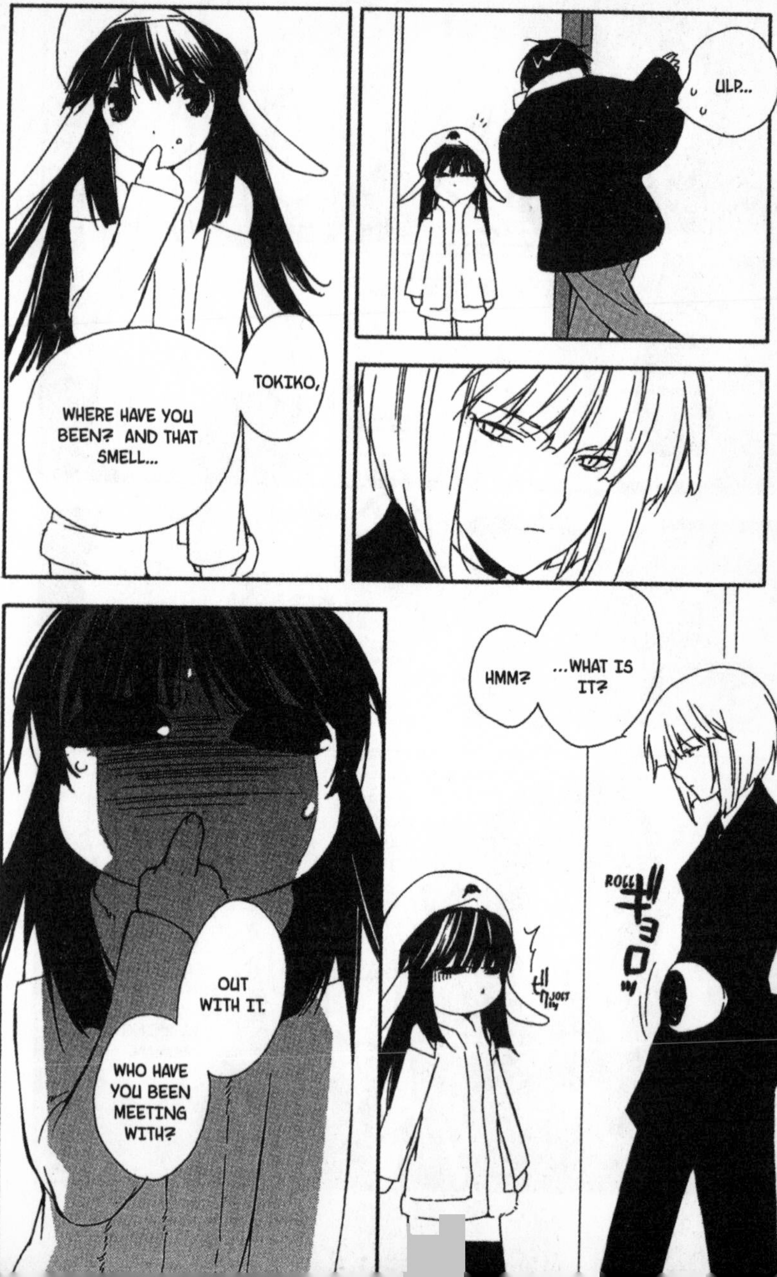
ULP...
TOKIKO,
WHERE HAVE YOU BEEN? AND THAT SMELL...
HMM? ...WHAT IS IT?
ROLL
JOLT
OUT WITH IT.
WHO HAVE YOU BEEN MEETING WITH?

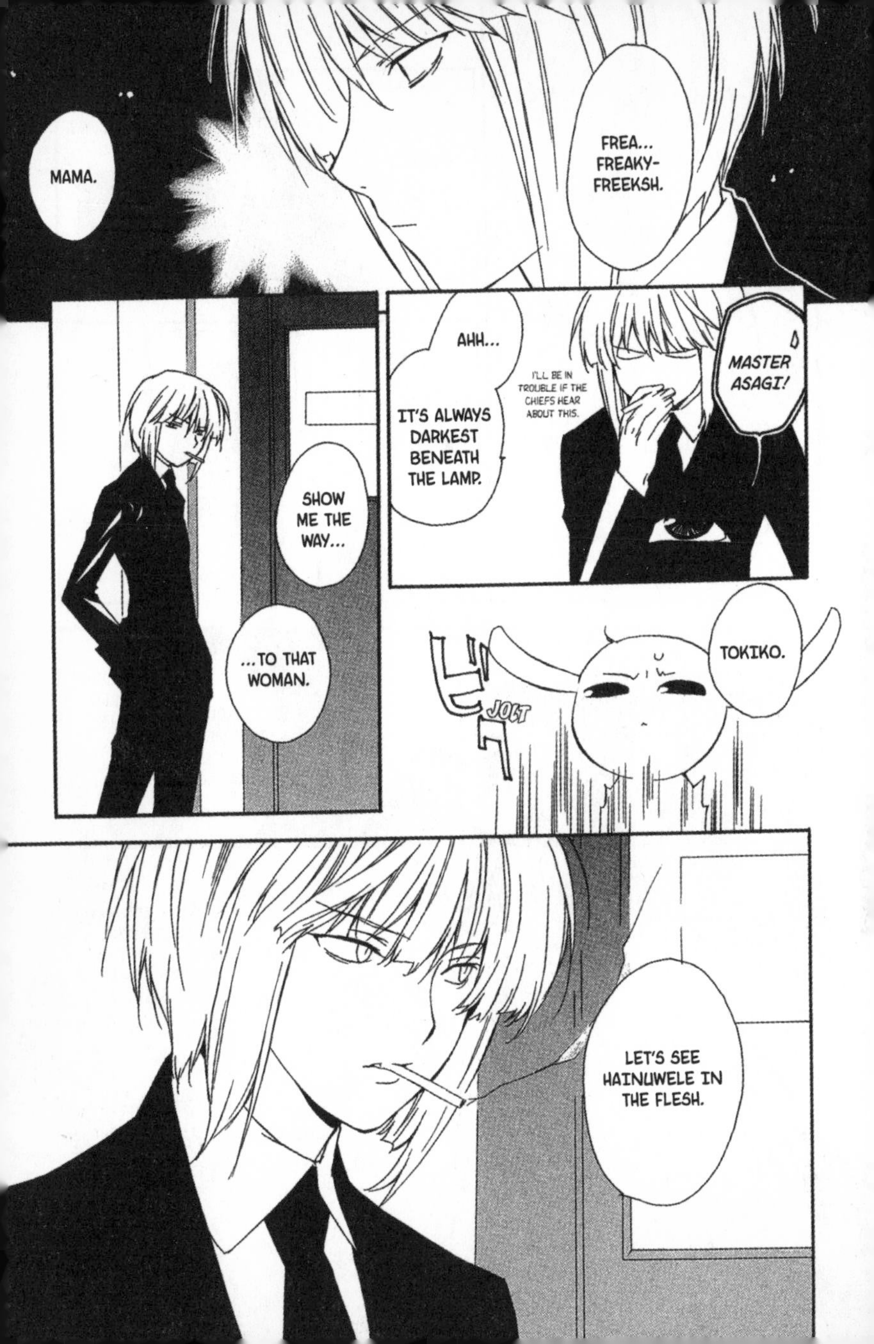
FREA... FREAKY-FREEKSH.
MAMA.
MASTER ASAGI!
I'LL BE IN TROUBLE IF THE CHIEFS HEAR ABOUT THIS.
AHH...
IT'S ALWAYS DARKEST BENEATH THE LAMP.
TOKIKO.
JOLT
SHOW ME THE WAY...
...TO THAT WOMAN.
LET'S SEE HAINUWELE IN THE FLESH.

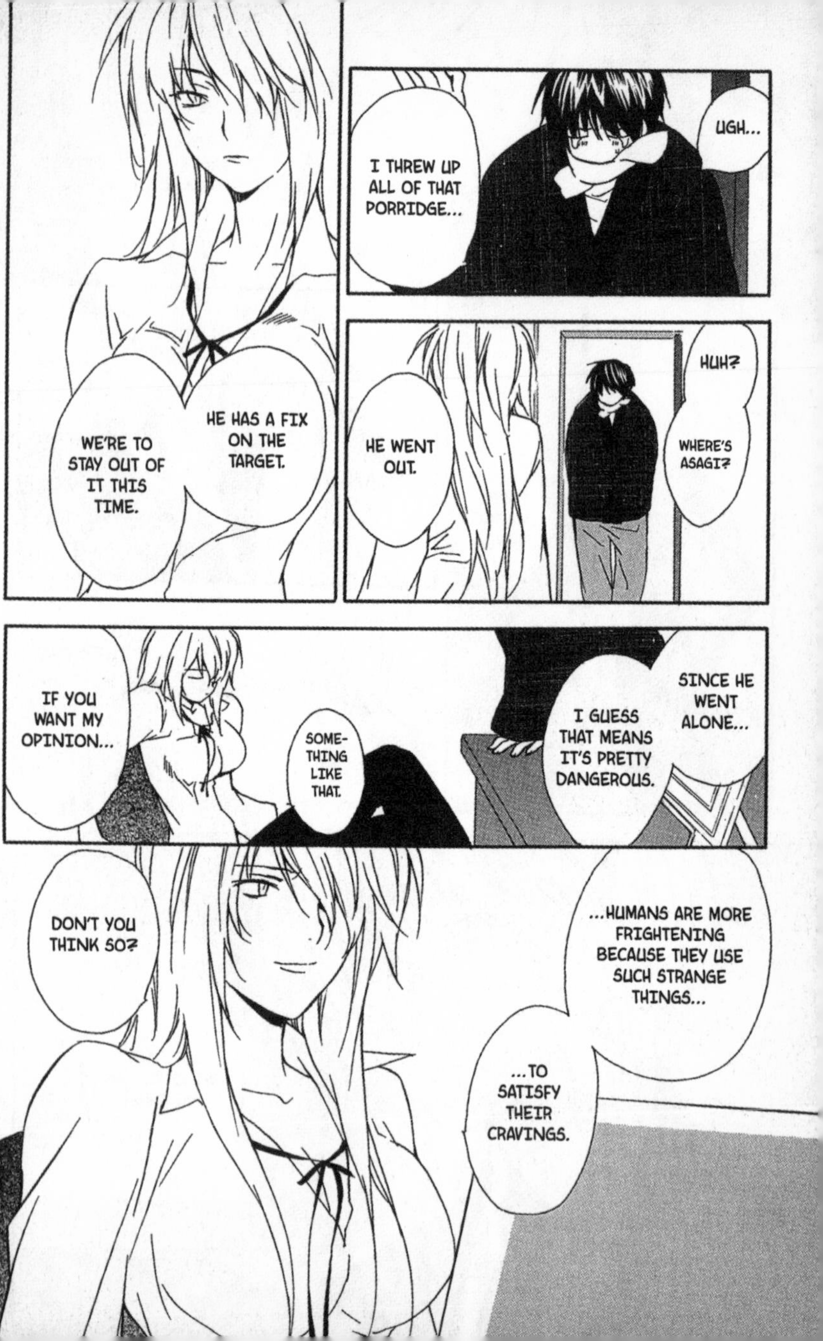
UGH...
I THREW UP ALL OF THAT PORRIDGE...
HUH?
WHERE'S ASAGI?
HE WENT OUT.
HE HAS A FIX ON THE TARGET.
WE'RE TO STAY OUT OF IT THIS TIME.
SINCE HE WENT ALONE...
I GUESS THAT MEANS IT'S PRETTY DANGEROUS.
SOME-THING LIKE THAT.
IF YOU WANT MY OPINION...
...HUMANS ARE MORE FRIGHTENING BECAUSE THEY USE SUCH STRANGE THINGS...
...TO SATISFY THEIR CRAVINGS.
DON'T YOU THINK SO?

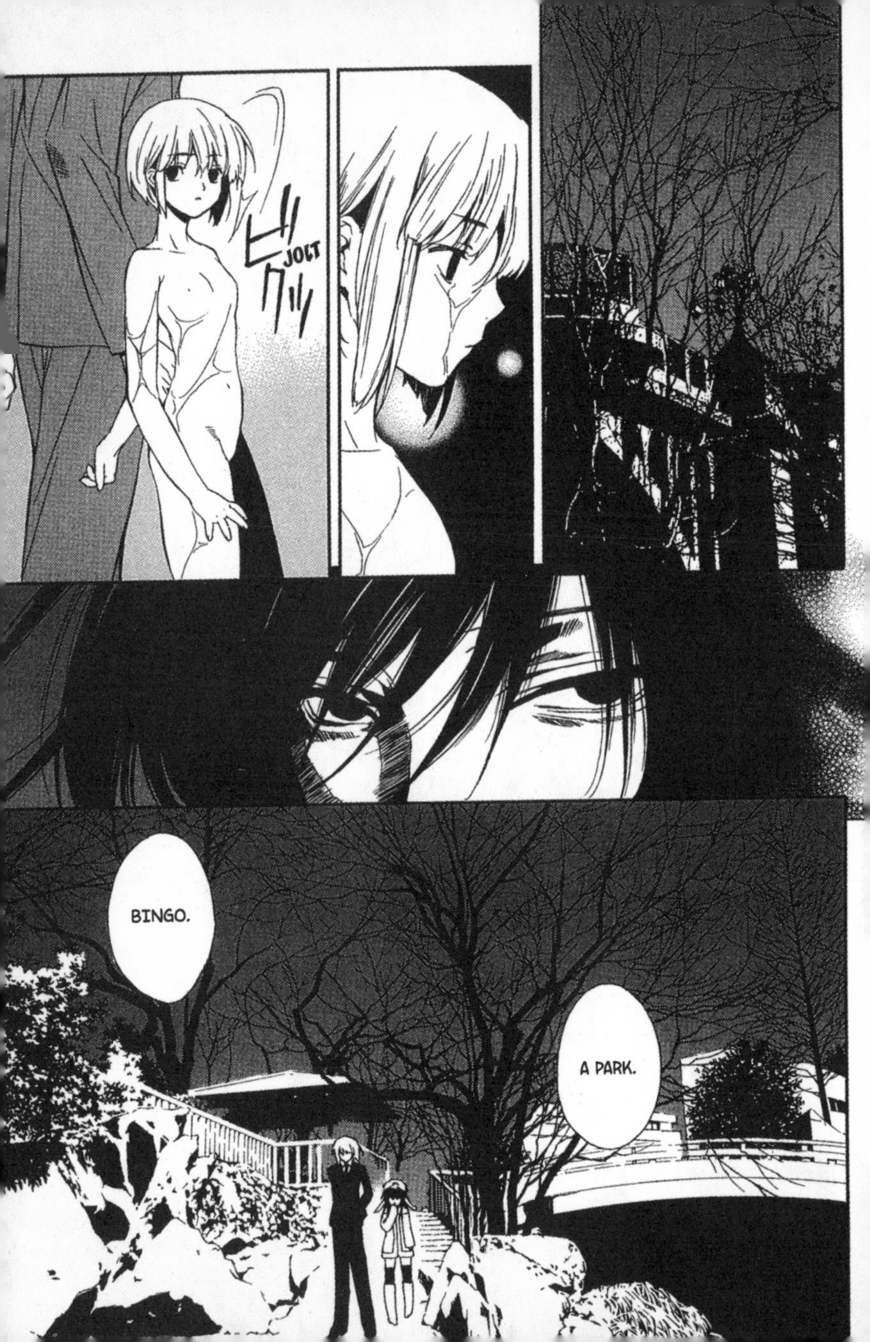
ビクッ
JOLT
BINGO.
A PARK.

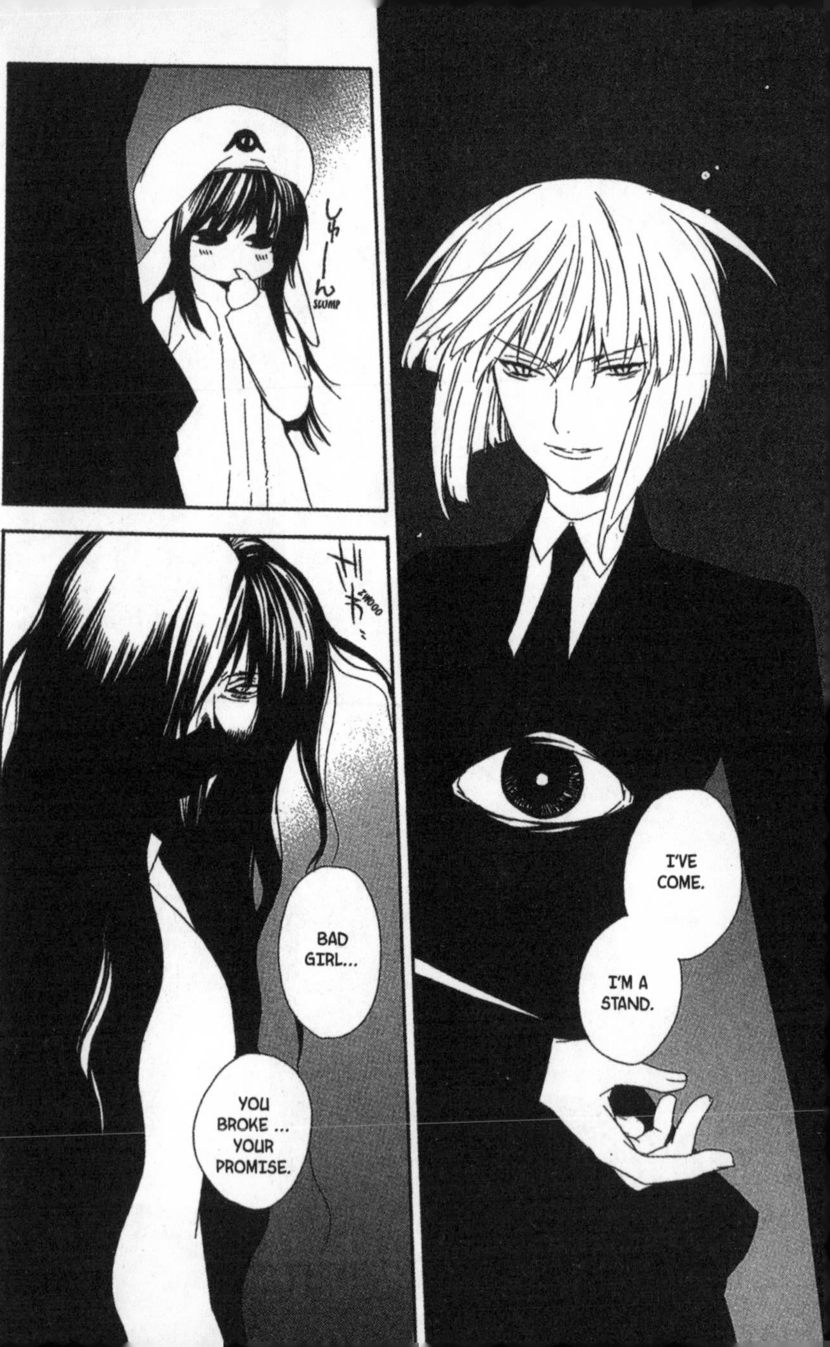
I'VE COME.
I'M A STAND.
しゅーん
SLUMP
ZWOOO
BAD GIRL...
YOU BROKE ... YOUR PROMISE.

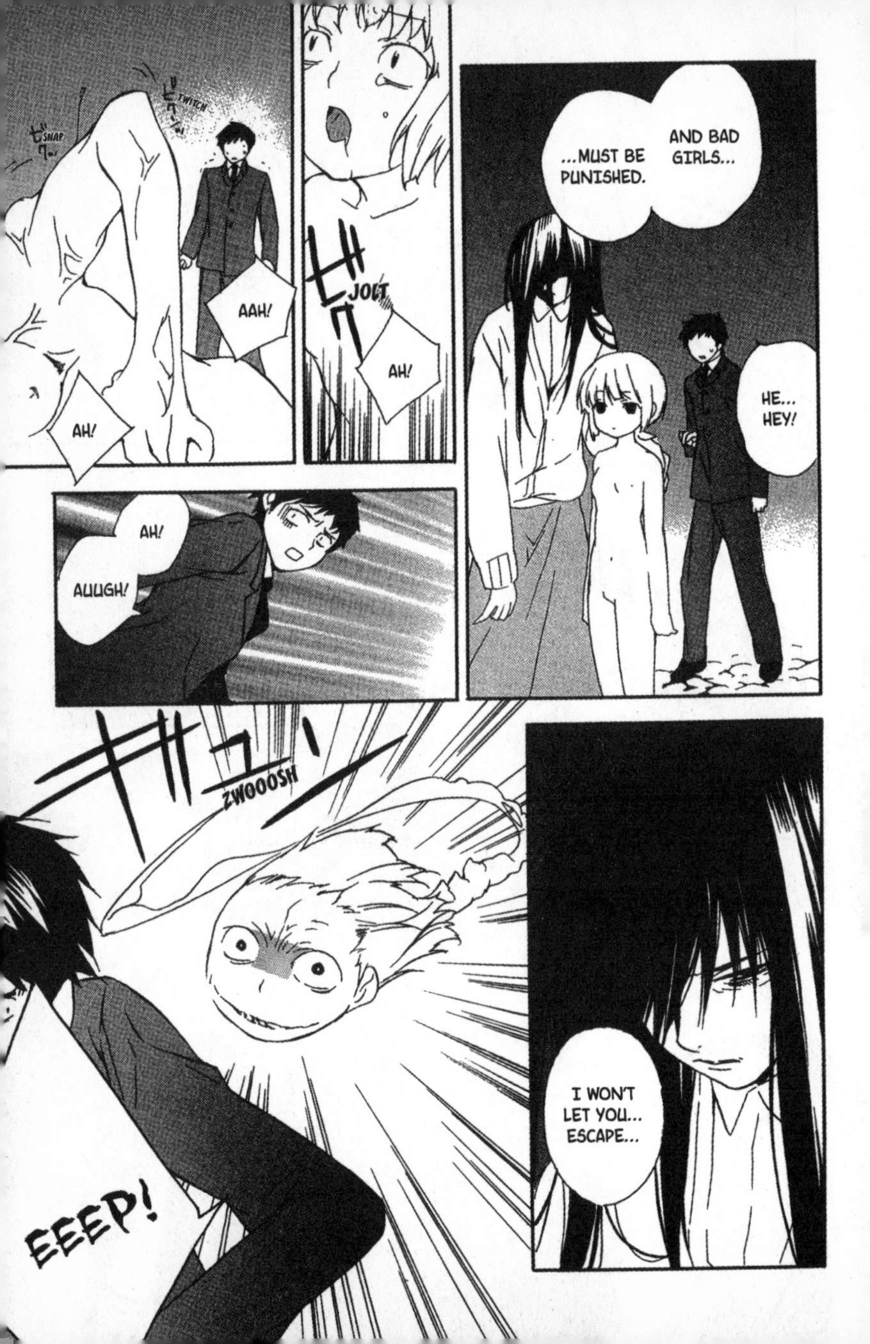
AND BAD GIRLS...
...MUST BE PUNISHED.
HE... HEY!
JOLT
AH!
TWITCH
SNAP
AAH!
AH!
AH!
AUUGH!
I WON'T LET YOU... ESCAPE...
ZWOOOSH
EEEP!

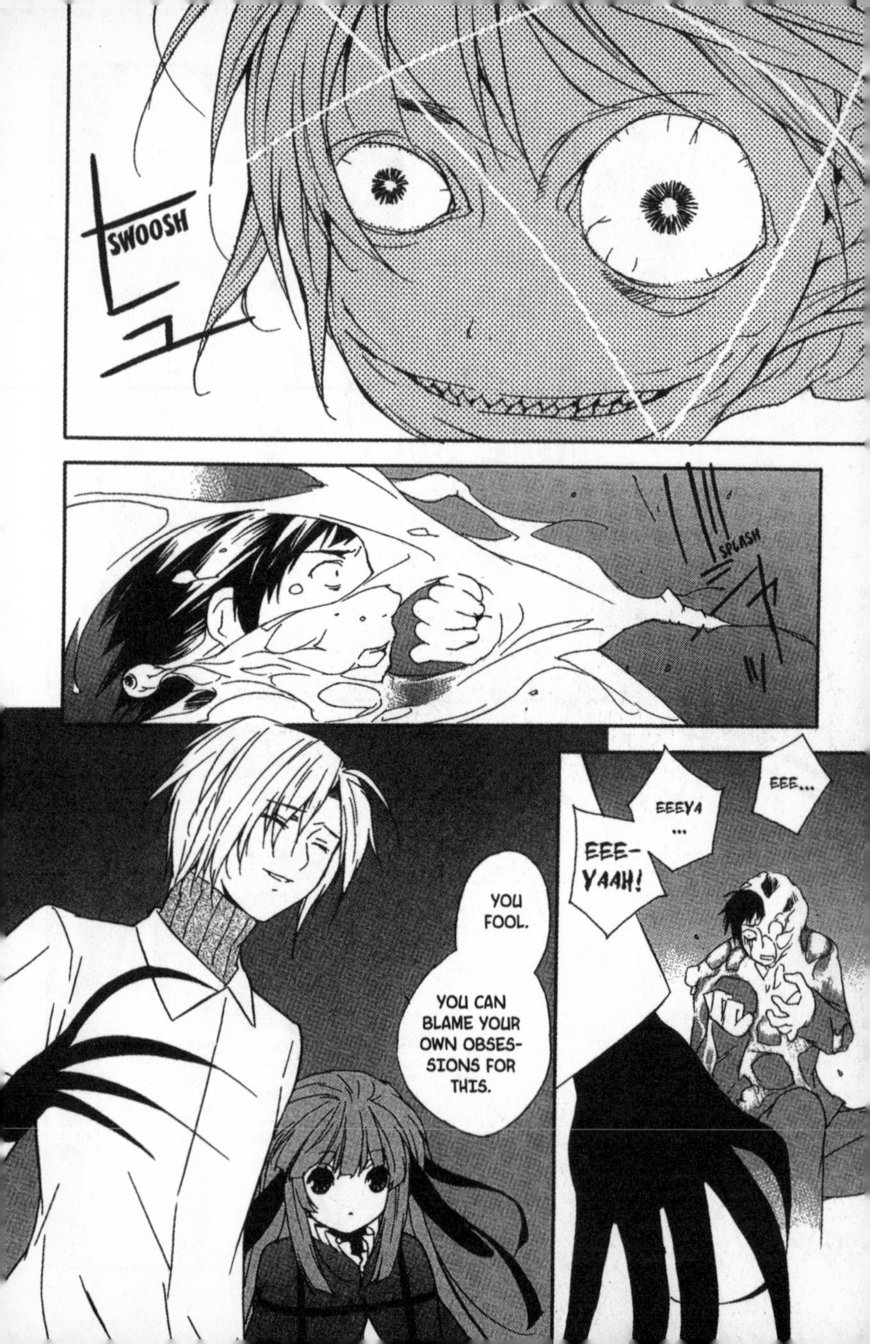
SWOOSH
SPLASH
EEE...
EEEYA ...
EEE-YAAH!
YOU FOOL.
YOU CAN BLAME YOUR OWN OBSES-SIONS FOR THIS.

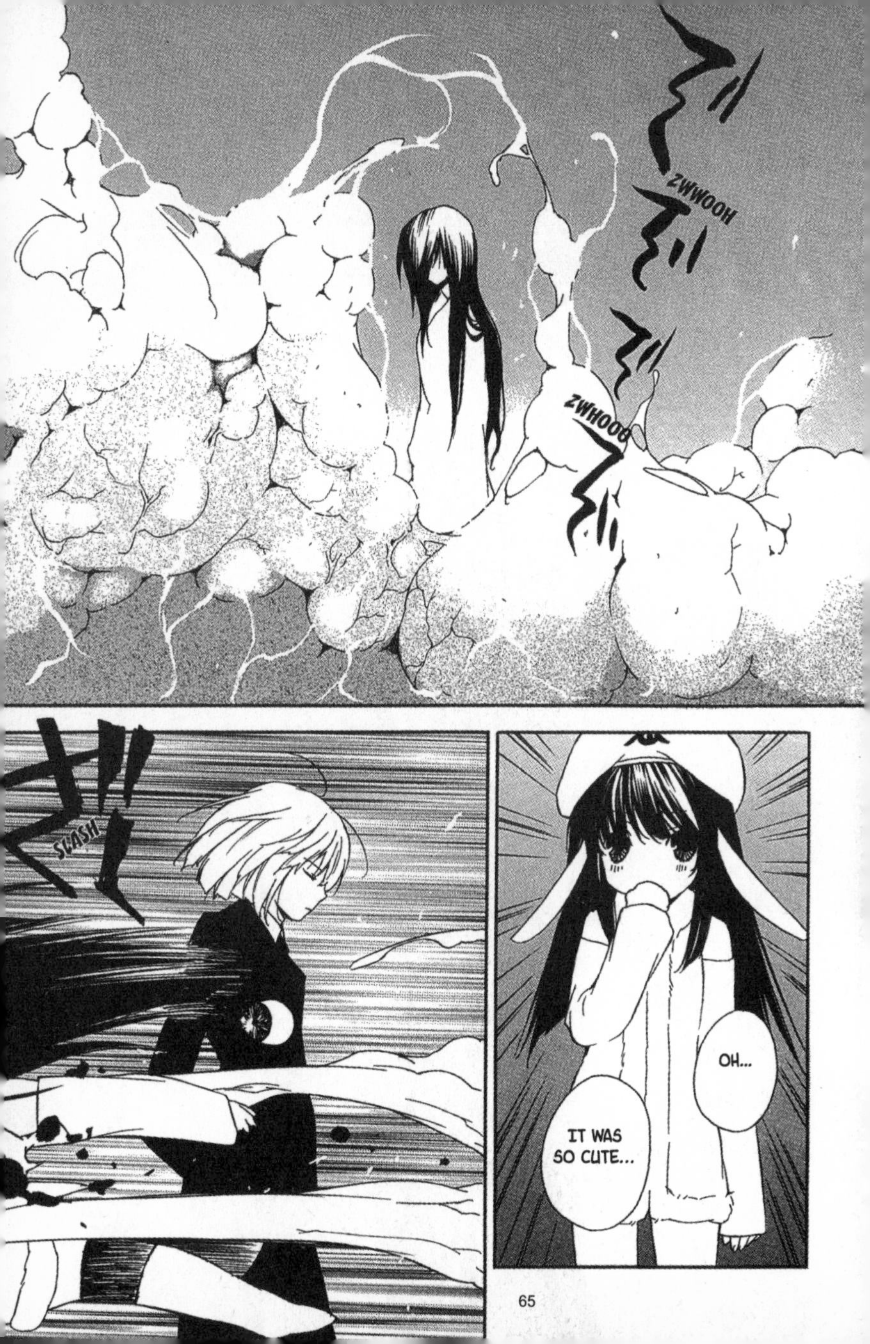
ZWWOOH
ZWHOOO
OH...
IT WAS SO CUTE...
SLASH

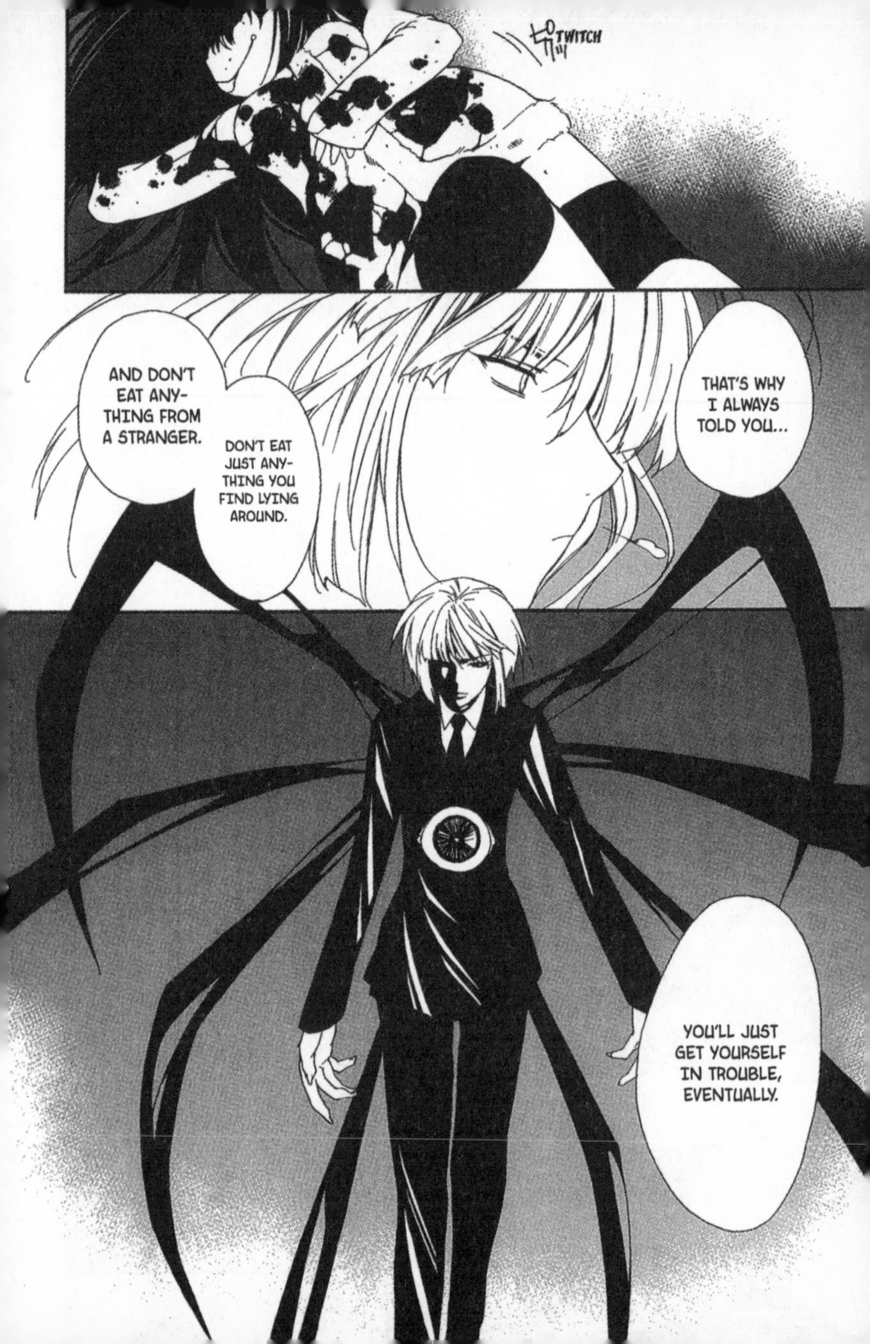
TWITCH
THAT'S WHY I ALWAYS TOLD YOU...
DON'T EAT JUST ANYTHING YOU FIND LYING AROUND.
AND DON'T EAT ANY-THING FROM A STRANGER.
YOU'LL JUST GET YOURSELF IN TROUBLE, EVENTUALLY.

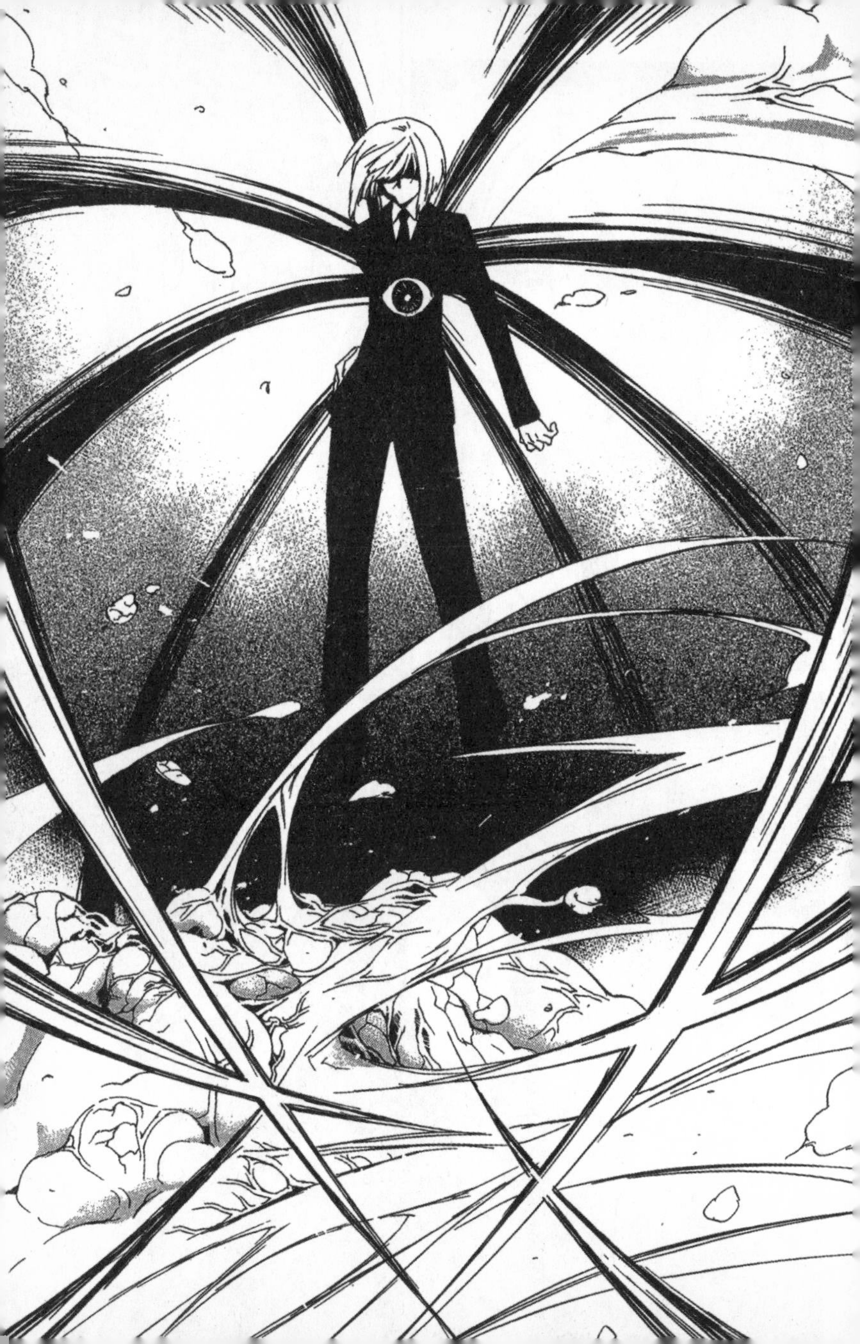

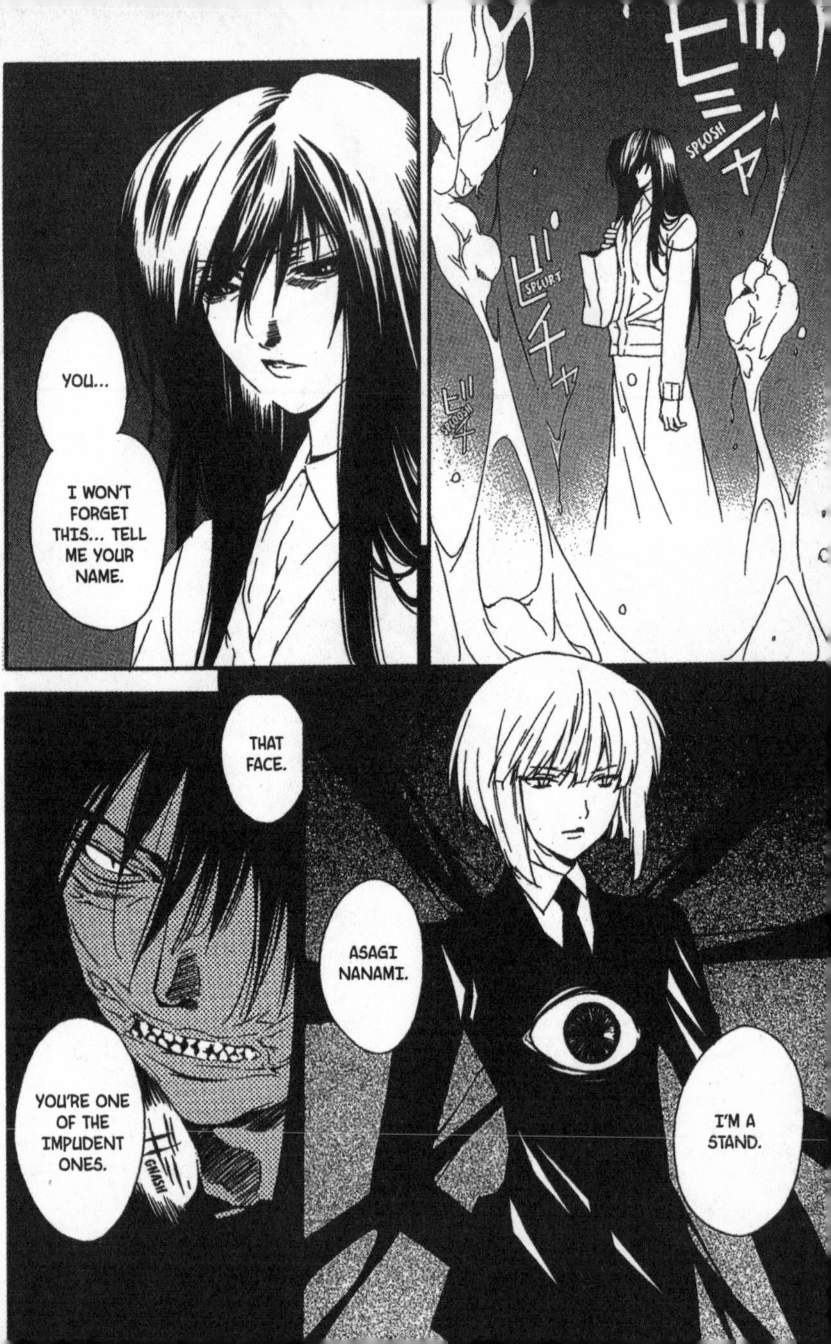

ビシャ
SPLOSH
ビチャ
SPLURT
SPLOOSH
YOU...
I WON'T FORGET THIS... TELL ME YOUR NAME.
ASAGI NANAMI.
I'M A STAND.
THAT FACE.
YOU'RE ONE OF THE IMPUDENT ONES.
GNASH

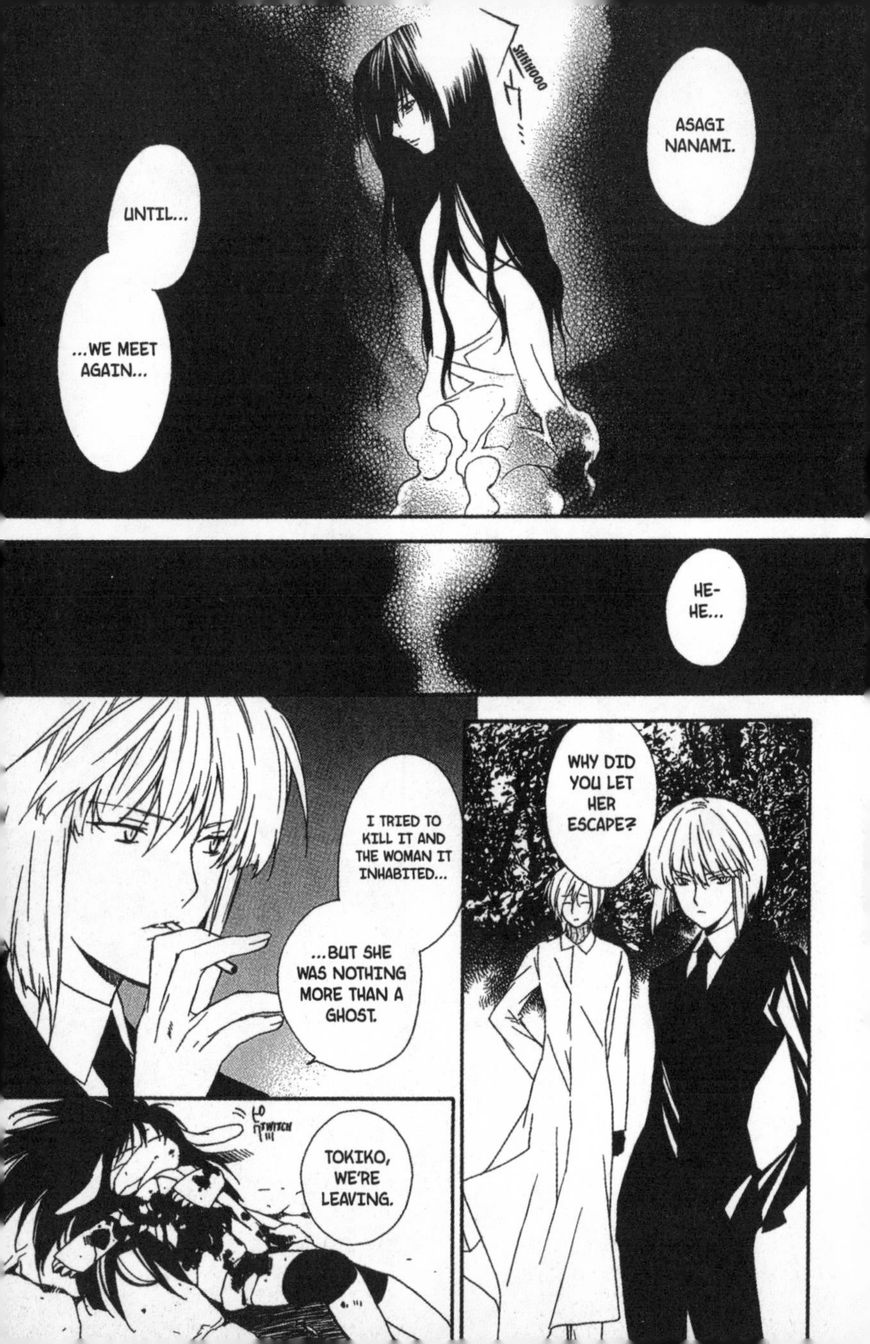
ASAGI NANAMI.
SHHHOOO
UNTIL...
...WE MEET AGAIN...
HE-HE...
WHY DID YOU LET HER ESCAPE?
I TRIED TO KILL IT AND THE WOMAN IT INHABITED...
...BUT SHE WAS NOTHING MORE THAN A GHOST.
TWITCH
TOKIKO, WE'RE LEAVING.

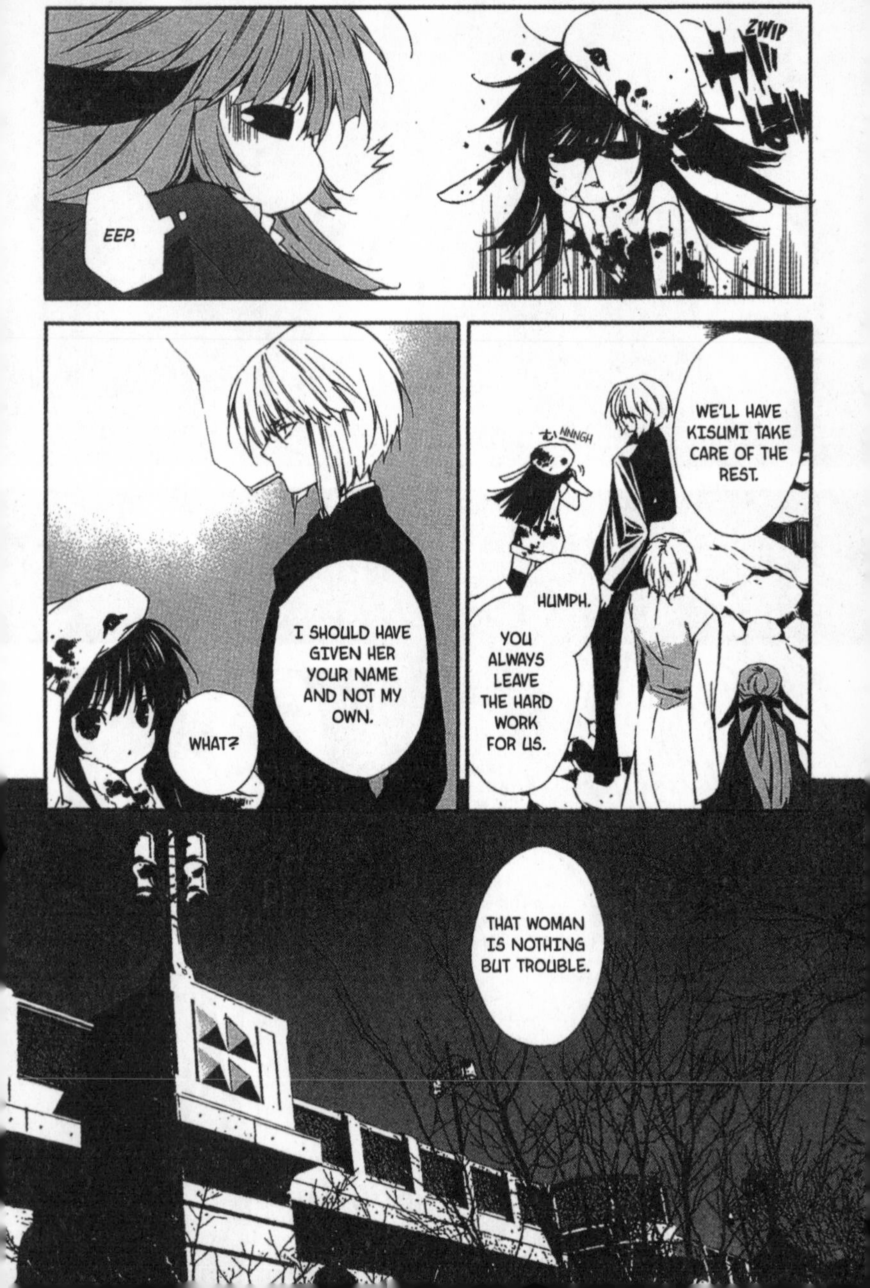
ZWIP
EEP.
WE'LL HAVE KISUMI TAKE CARE OF THE REST.
NNNGH
HUMPH.
YOU ALWAYS LEAVE THE HARD WORK FOR US.
I SHOULD HAVE GIVEN HER YOUR NAME AND NOT MY OWN.
WHAT?
THAT WOMAN IS NOTHING BUT TROUBLE.

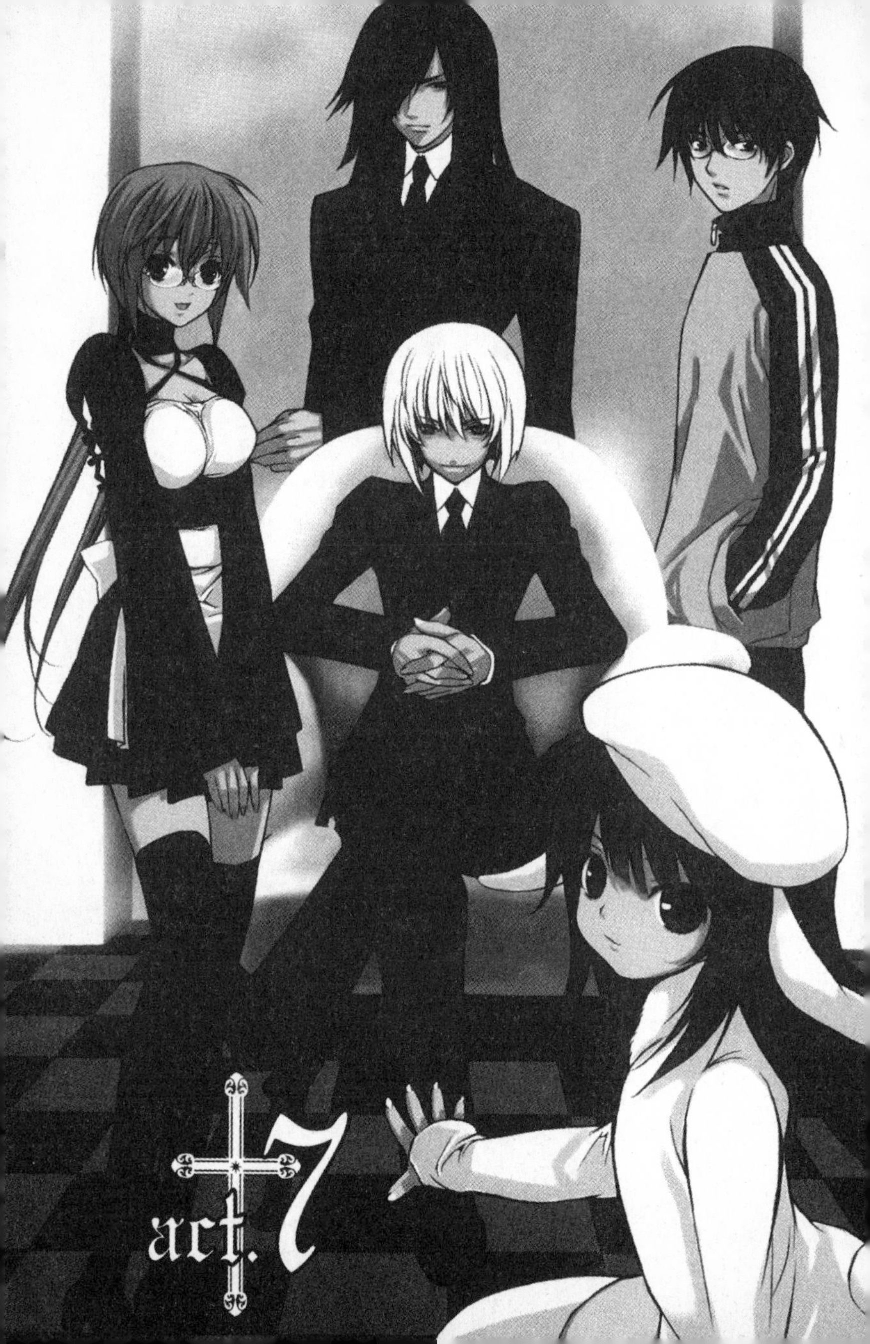
act. 7

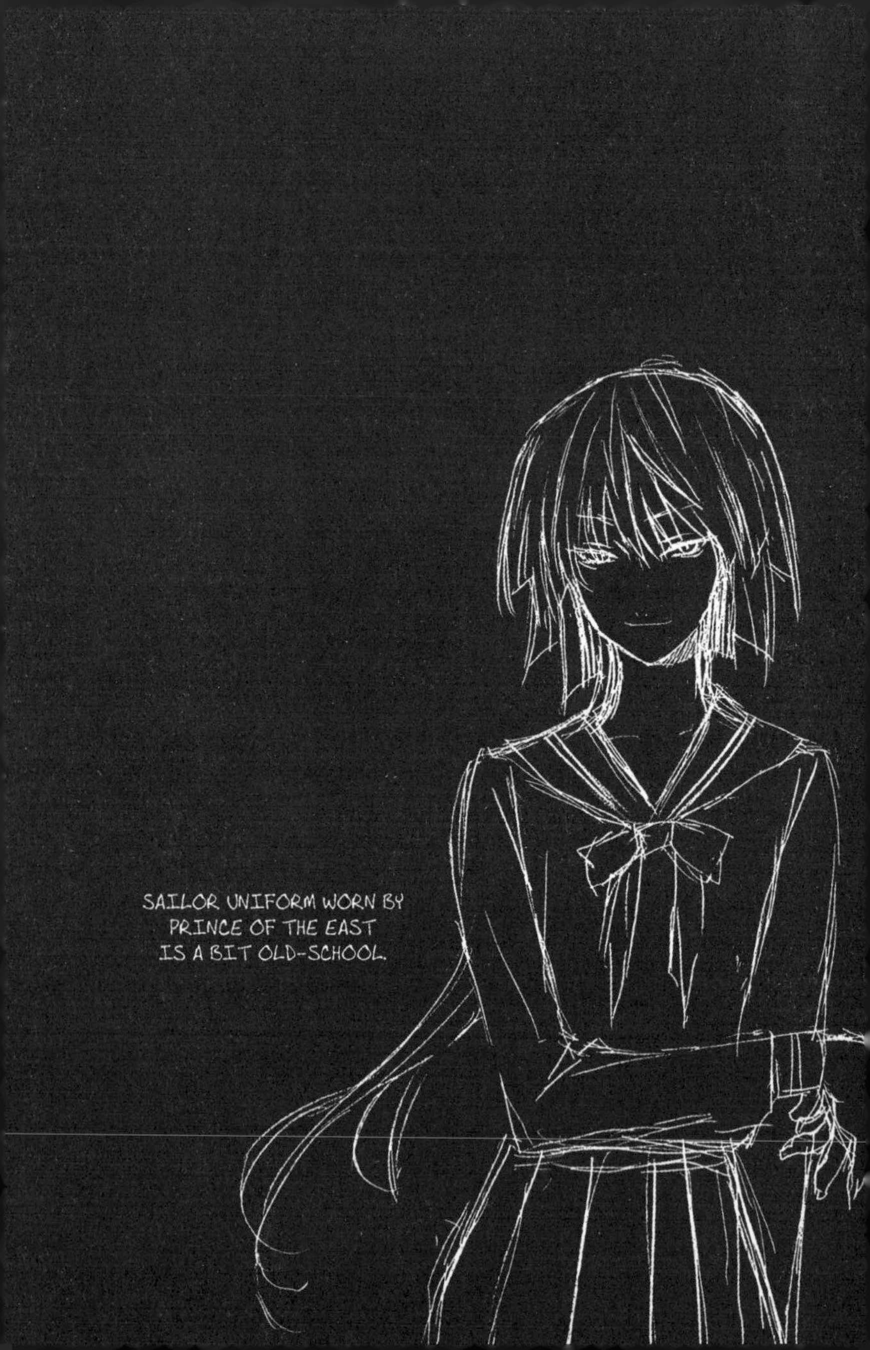
SAILOR UNIFORM WORN BY
PRINCE OF THE EAST
IS A BIT OLD-SCHOOL.

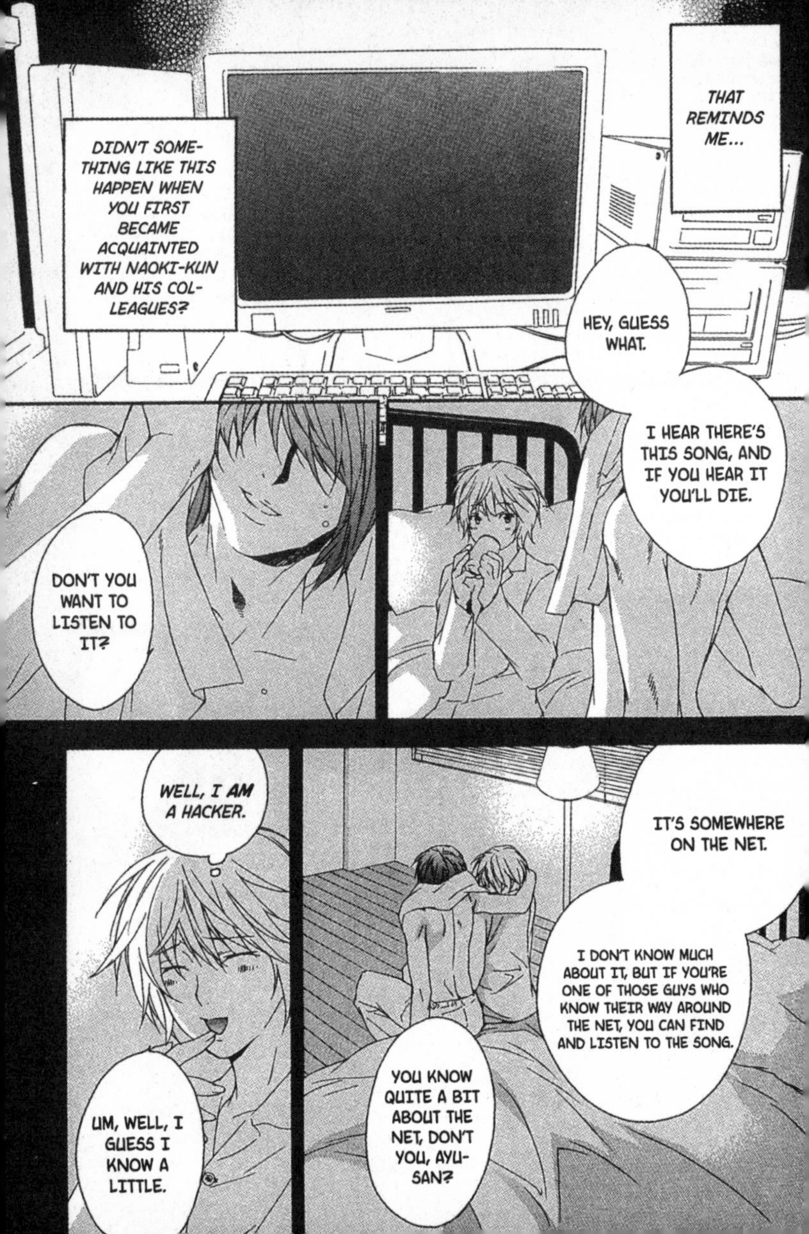
THAT REMINDS ME...
DIDN'T SOMETHING LIKE THIS HAPPEN WHEN YOU FIRST BECAME ACQUAINTED WITH NAOKI-KUN AND HIS COLLEAGUES?
HEY, GUESS WHAT.
I HEAR THERE'S THIS SONG, AND IF YOU HEAR IT YOU'LL DIE.
DON'T YOU WANT TO LISTEN TO IT?
IT'S SOMEWHERE ON THE NET.
I DON'T KNOW MUCH ABOUT IT, BUT IF YOU'RE ONE OF THOSE GUYS WHO KNOW THEIR WAY AROUND THE NET, YOU CAN FIND AND LISTEN TO THE SONG.
YOU KNOW QUITE A BIT ABOUT THE NET, DON'T YOU, AYU-SAN?
WELL, I AM A HACKER.
UM, WELL, I GUESS I KNOW A LITTLE.

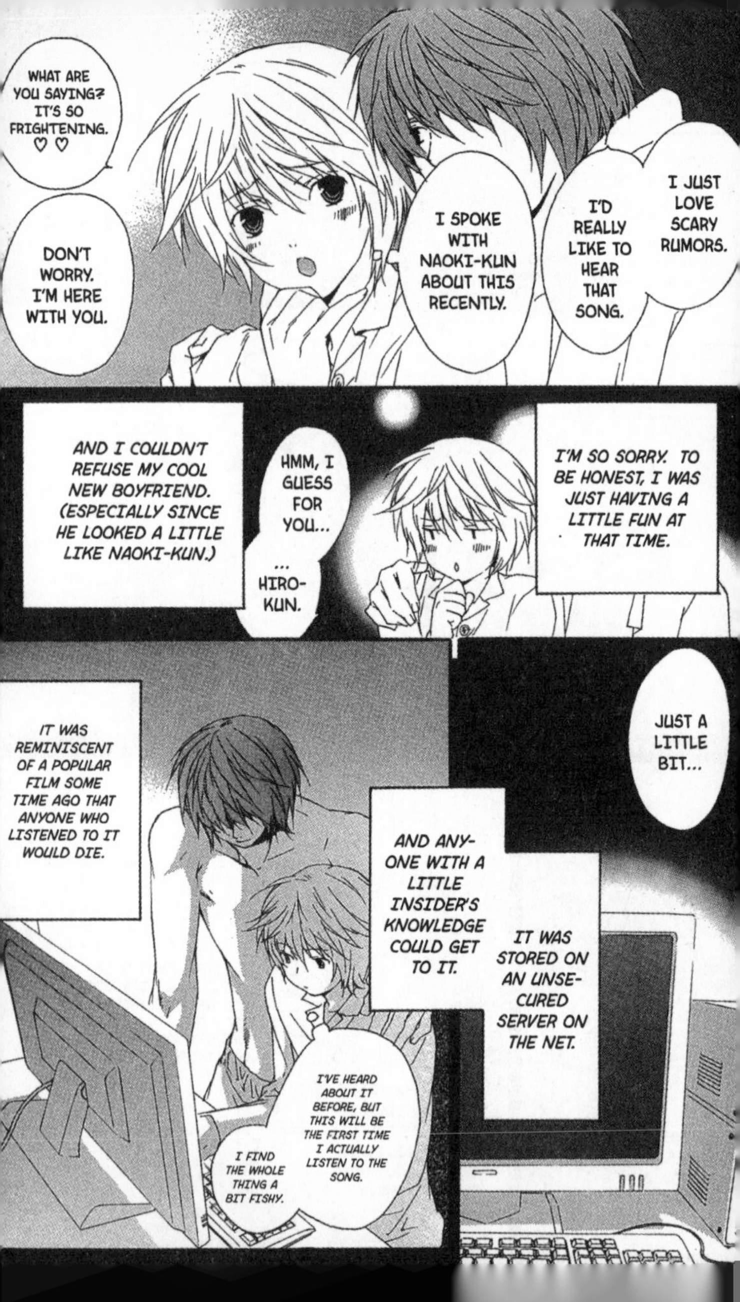

I JUST LOVE SCARY RUMORS.
I'D REALLY LIKE TO HEAR THAT SONG.
I SPOKE WITH NAOKI-KUN ABOUT THIS RECENTLY.
WHAT ARE YOU SAYING? IT'S SO FRIGHTENING. ♡ ♡
DON'T WORRY. I'M HERE WITH YOU.
I'M SO SORRY. TO BE HONEST, I WAS JUST HAVING A LITTLE FUN AT THAT TIME.
HMM, I GUESS FOR YOU...
...HIRO-KUN.
AND I COULDN'T REFUSE MY COOL NEW BOYFRIEND. (ESPECIALLY SINCE HE LOOKED A LITTLE LIKE NAOKI-KUN.)
JUST A LITTLE BIT...
IT WAS STORED ON AN UNSECURED SERVER ON THE NET.
AND ANYONE WITH A LITTLE INSIDER'S KNOWLEDGE COULD GET TO IT.
IT WAS REMINISCENT OF A POPULAR FILM SOME TIME AGO THAT ANYONE WHO LISTENED TO IT WOULD DIE.
I'VE HEARD ABOUT IT BEFORE, BUT THIS WILL BE THE FIRST TIME I ACTUALLY LISTEN TO THE SONG.
I FIND THE WHOLE THING A BIT FISHY.

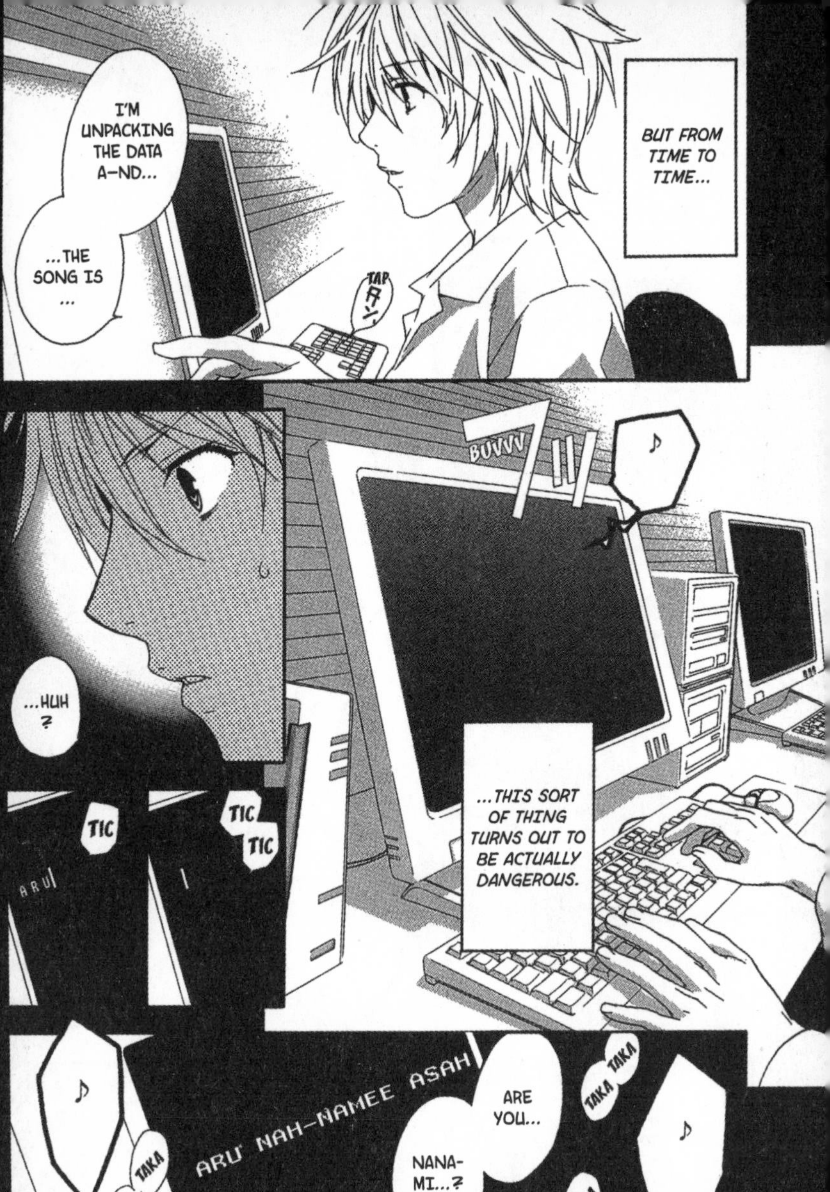
BUT FROM TIME TO TIME...
I'M UNPACKING THE DATA A-ND...
...THE SONG IS ...
TAP
BUVVV
♪
...THIS SORT OF THING TURNS OUT TO BE ACTUALLY DANGEROUS.
...HUH?
TIC TIC
TIC
ARU
♪
TAKA TAKA
ARE YOU...
NANA-MI...?
TAKA
ARU NAH-NAMEE ASAH
♪
TAKA TAKA

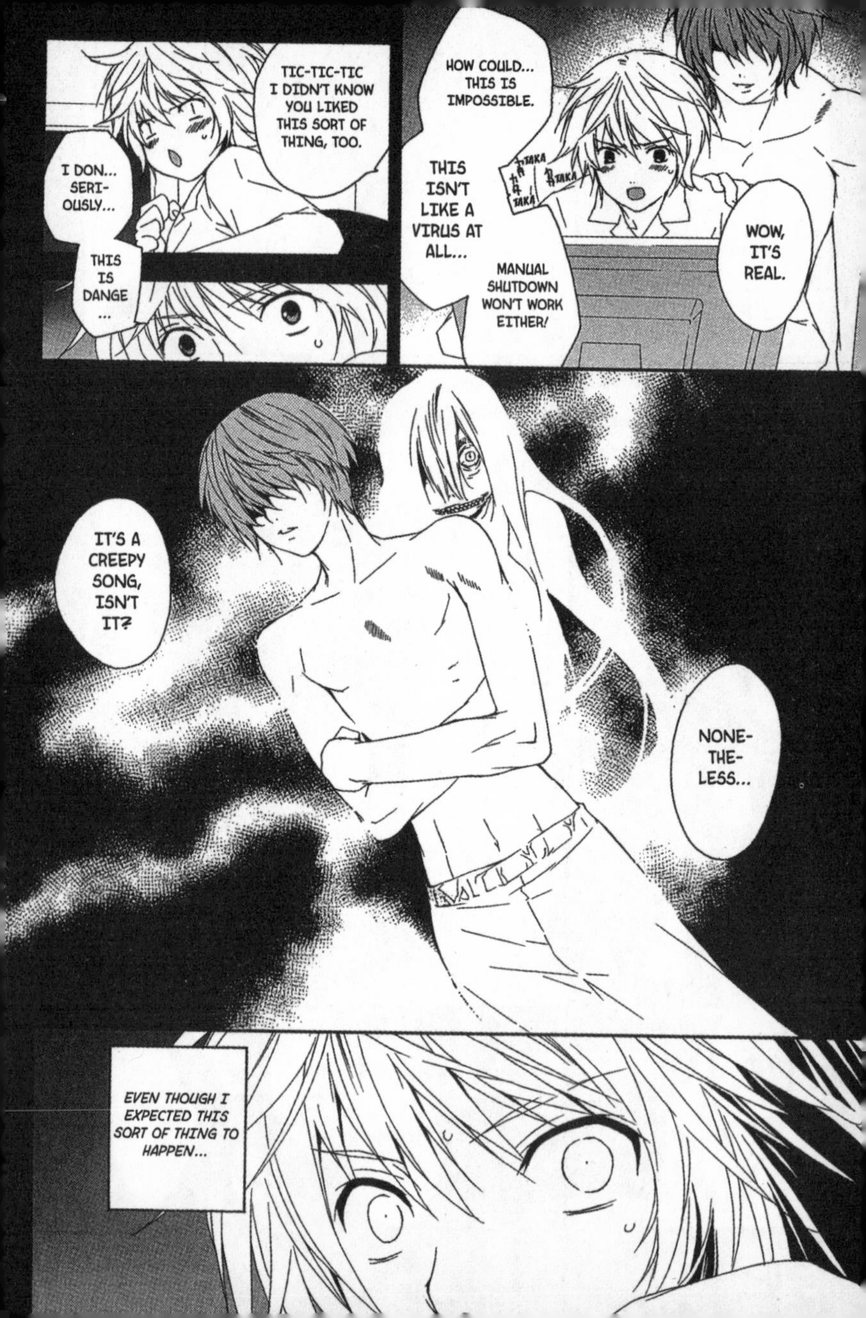
HOW COULD... THIS IS IMPOSSIBLE.
TAKA TAKA TAKA TAKA
THIS ISN'T LIKE A VIRUS AT ALL...
MANUAL SHUTDOWN WON'T WORK EITHER!
WOW, IT'S REAL.
TIC-TIC-TIC I DIDN'T KNOW YOU LIKED THIS SORT OF THING, TOO.
I DON... SERI-OUSLY...
THIS IS DANGE ...
IT'S A CREEPY SONG, ISN'T IT?
NONE-THE-LESS...
EVEN THOUGH I EXPECTED THIS SORT OF THING TO HAPPEN...

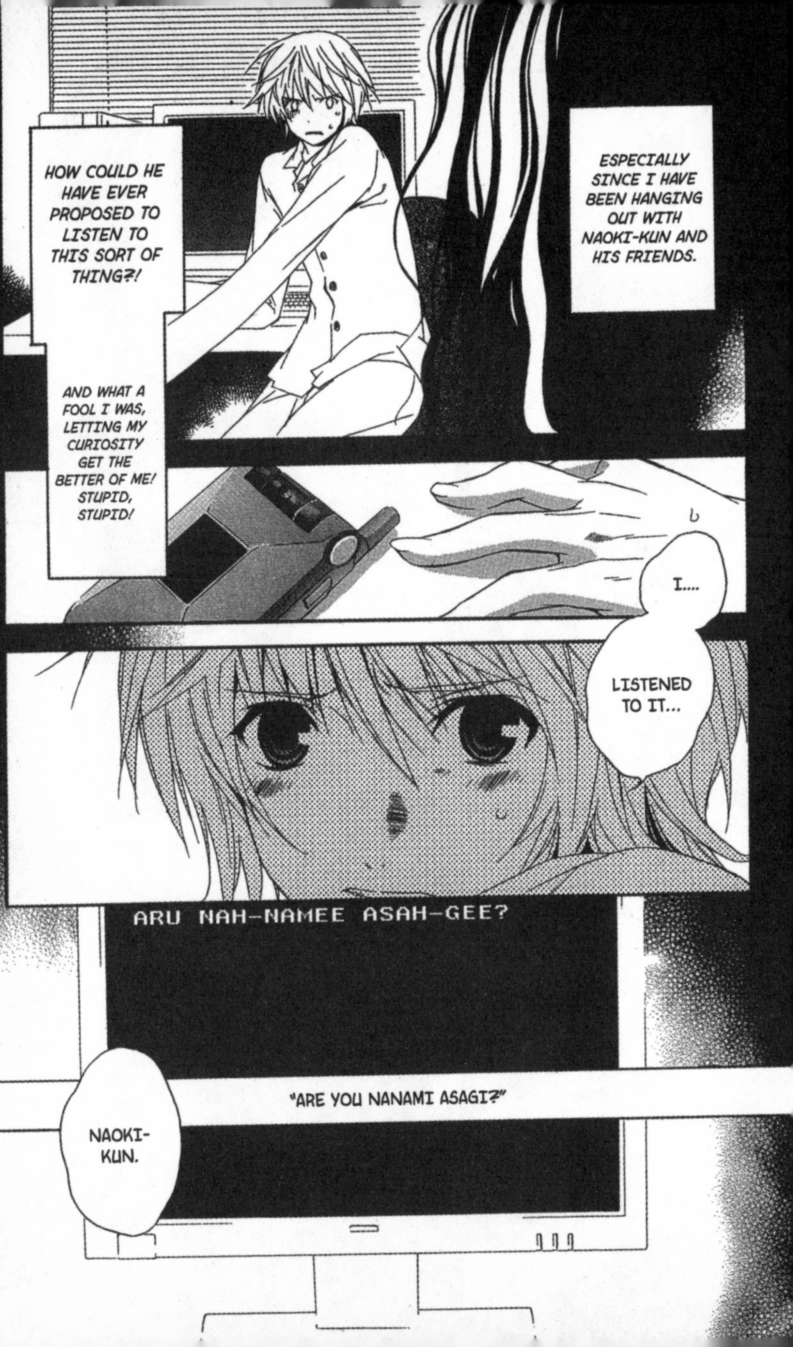
ESPECIALLY SINCE I HAVE BEEN HANGING OUT WITH NAOKI-KUN AND HIS FRIENDS.
HOW COULD HE HAVE EVER PROPOSED TO LISTEN TO THIS SORT OF THING?!
AND WHAT A FOOL I WAS, LETTING MY CURIOSITY GET THE BETTER OF ME! STUPID, STUPID!
I....
LISTENED TO IT...
ARU NAH-NAMEE ASAH-GEE?
"ARE YOU NANAMI ASAGI?"
NAOKI-KUN.

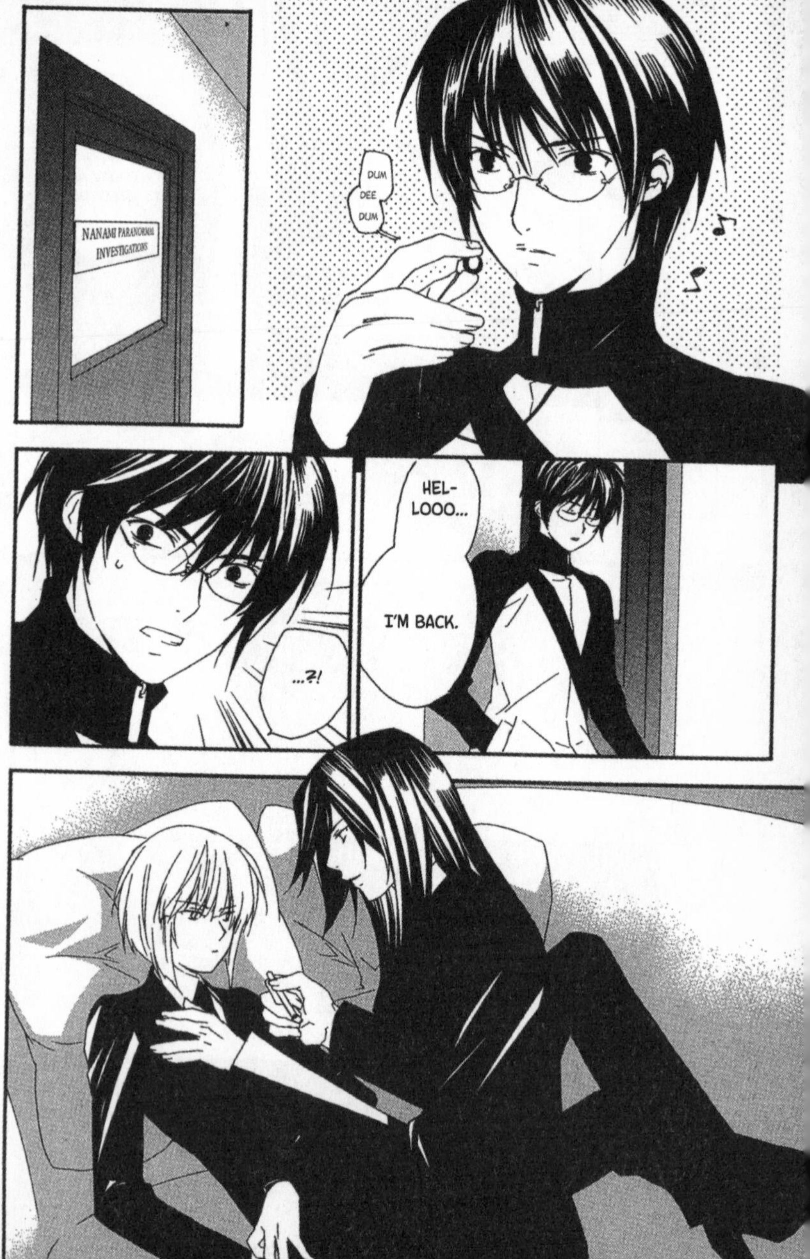
DUM DEE DUM
NANAMI PARANORMAL INVESTIGATIONS
HEL-LOOO...
I'M BACK.
...?!

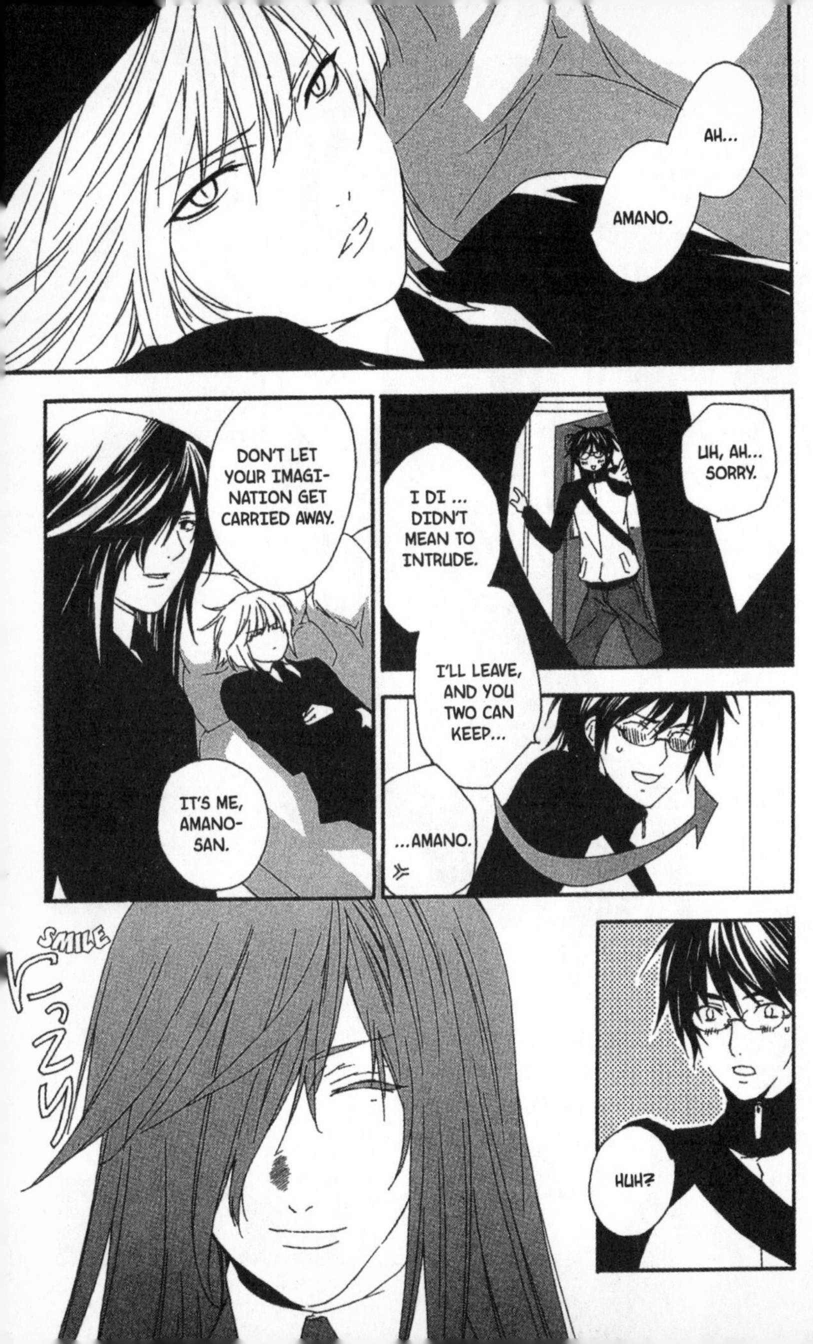
AH...
AMANO.
UH, AH... SORRY.
I DI ... DIDN'T MEAN TO INTRUDE.
I'LL LEAVE, AND YOU TWO CAN KEEP...
...AMANO.
DON'T LET YOUR IMAGINATION GET CARRIED AWAY.
IT'S ME, AMANO-SAN.
HUH?
SMILE

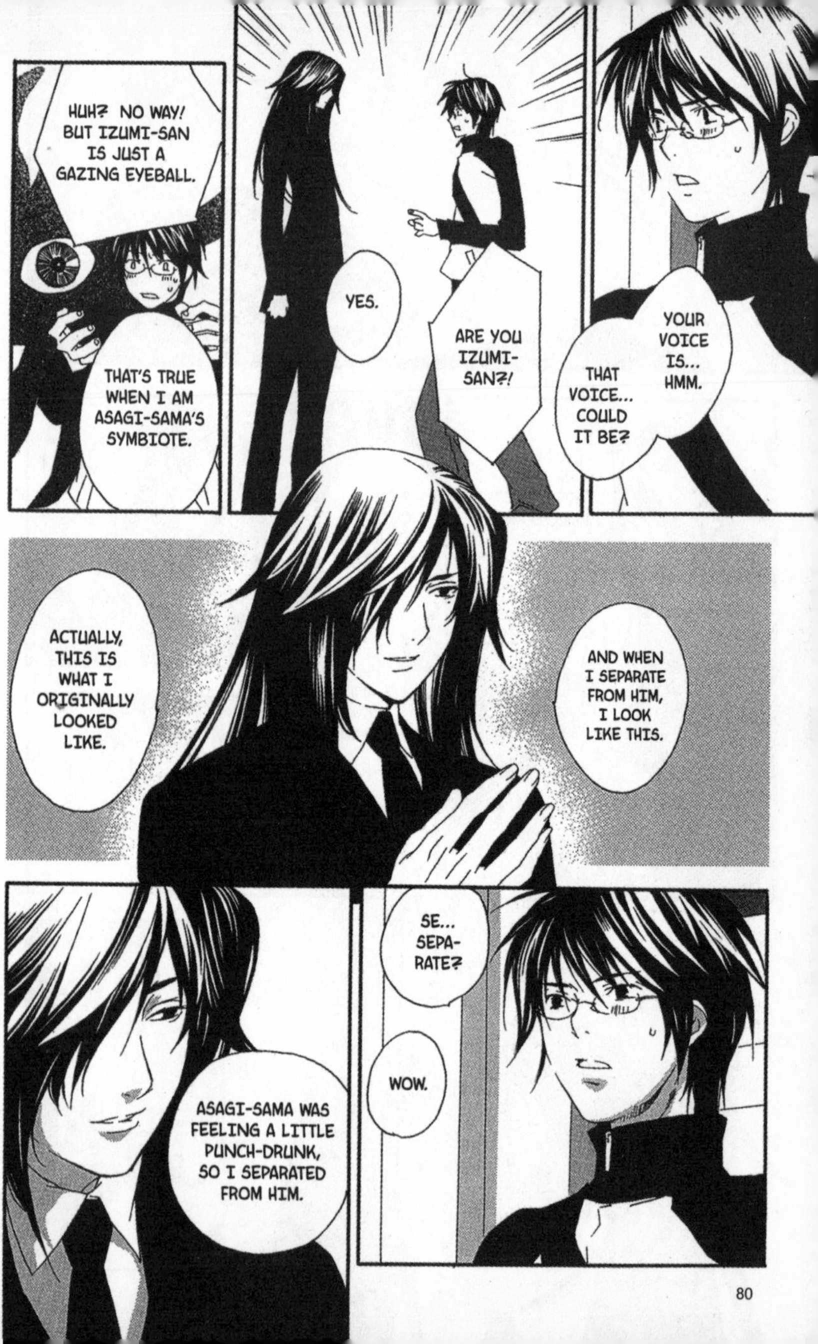
YOUR VOICE IS... HMM.
THAT VOICE... COULD IT BE?
ARE YOU IZUMI-SAN?!
YES.
HUH? NO WAY! BUT IZUMI-SAN IS JUST A GAZING EYEBALL.
THAT'S TRUE WHEN I AM ASAGI-SAMA'S SYMBIOTE.
AND WHEN I SEPARATE FROM HIM, I LOOK LIKE THIS.
ACTUALLY, THIS IS WHAT I ORIGINALLY LOOKED LIKE.
SE... SEPARATE?
WOW.
ASAGI-SAMA WAS FEELING A LITTLE PUNCH-DRUNK, SO I SEPARATED FROM HIM.

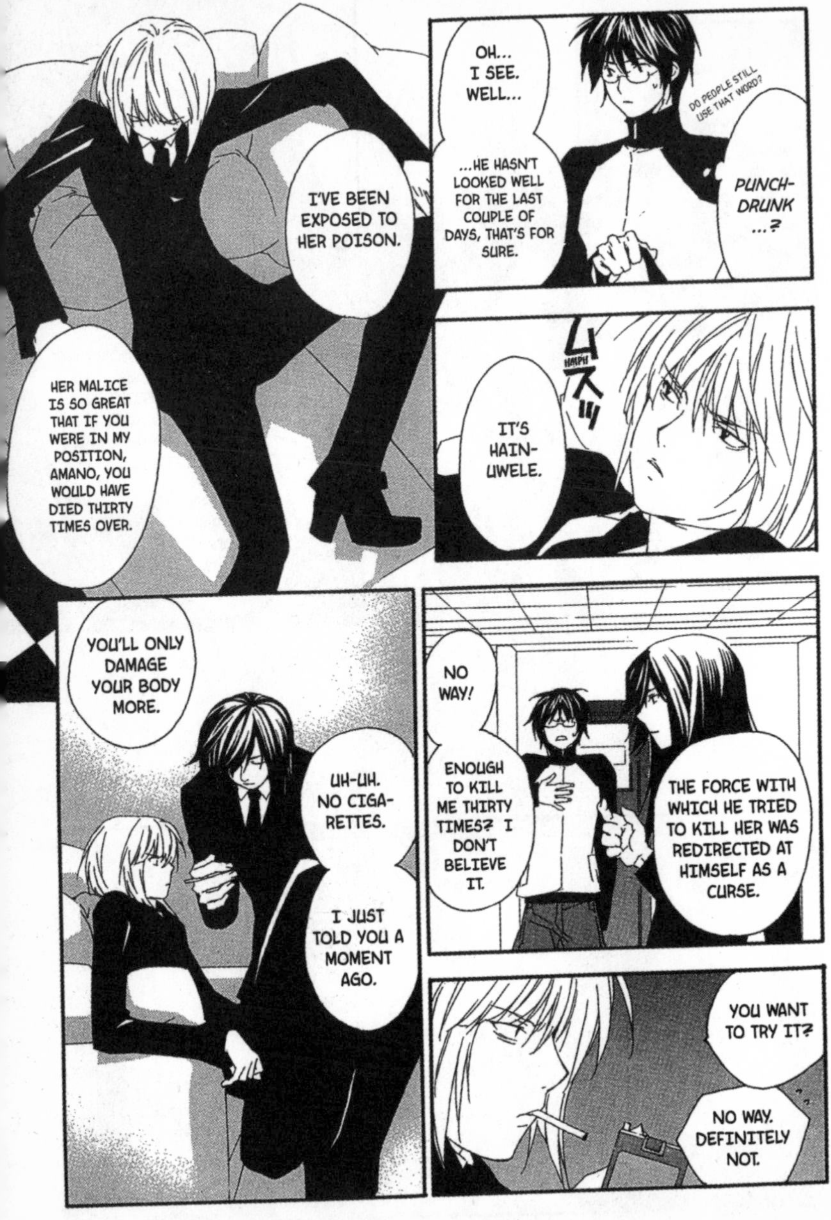
DO PEOPLE STILL USE THAT WORD?
PUNCH-DRUNK ...?
OH... I SEE. WELL...
...HE HASN'T LOOKED WELL FOR THE LAST COUPLE OF DAYS, THAT'S FOR SURE.
HMPH
IT'S HAIN-UWELE.
I'VE BEEN EXPOSED TO HER POISON.
HER MALICE IS SO GREAT THAT IF YOU WERE IN MY POSITION, AMANO, YOU WOULD HAVE DIED THIRTY TIMES OVER.
NO WAY!
ENOUGH TO KILL ME THIRTY TIMES? I DON'T BELIEVE IT.
THE FORCE WITH WHICH HE TRIED TO KILL HER WAS REDIRECTED AT HIMSELF AS A CURSE.
YOU WANT TO TRY IT?
NO WAY. DEFINITELY NOT.
YOU'LL ONLY DAMAGE YOUR BODY MORE.
UH-UH. NO CIGA-RETTES.
I JUST TOLD YOU A MOMENT AGO.

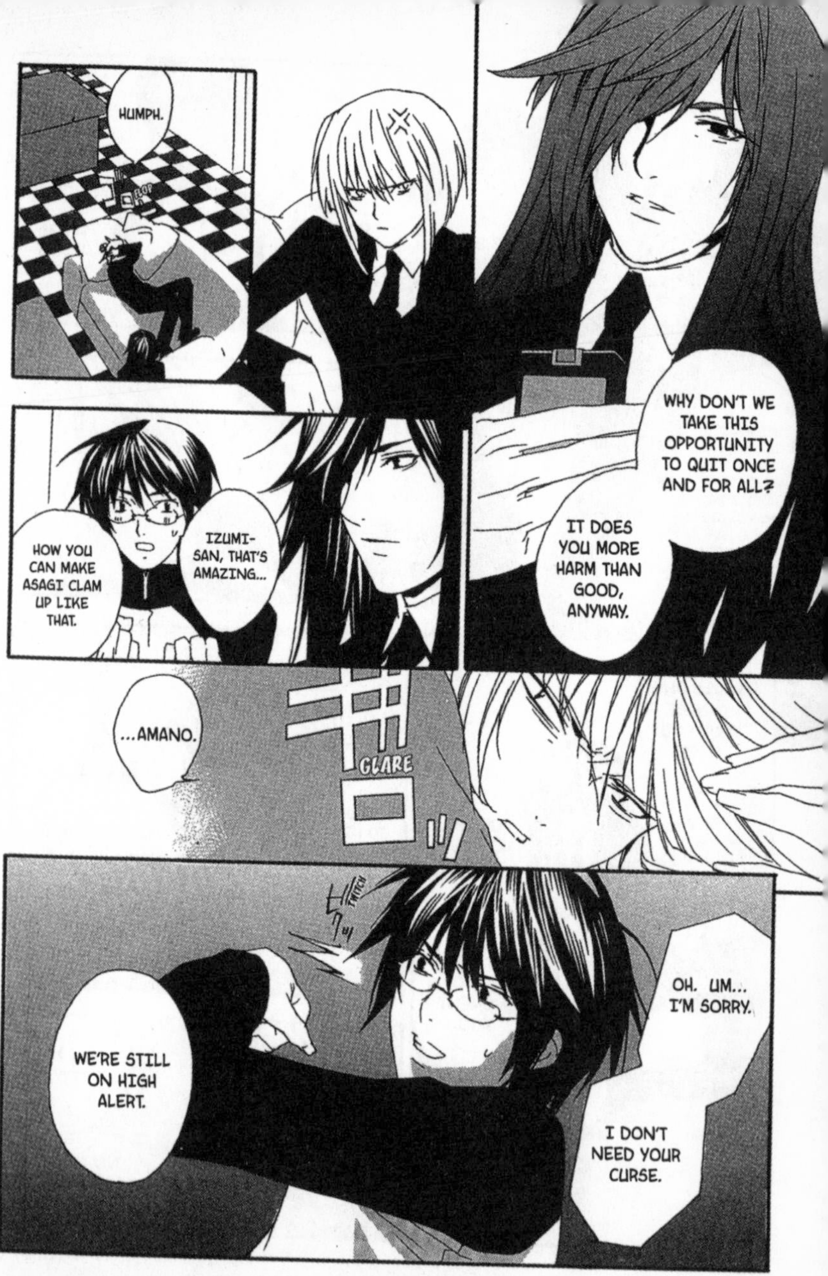

HUMPH.
FLOP
WHY DON'T WE TAKE THIS OPPORTUNITY TO QUIT ONCE AND FOR ALL?
IT DOES YOU MORE HARM THAN GOOD, ANYWAY.
IZUMI-SAN, THAT'S AMAZING...
HOW YOU CAN MAKE ASAGI CLAM UP LIKE THAT.
GLARE
...AMANO.
TWITCH
OH. UM... I'M SORRY.
WE'RE STILL ON HIGH ALERT.
I DON'T NEED YOUR CURSE.

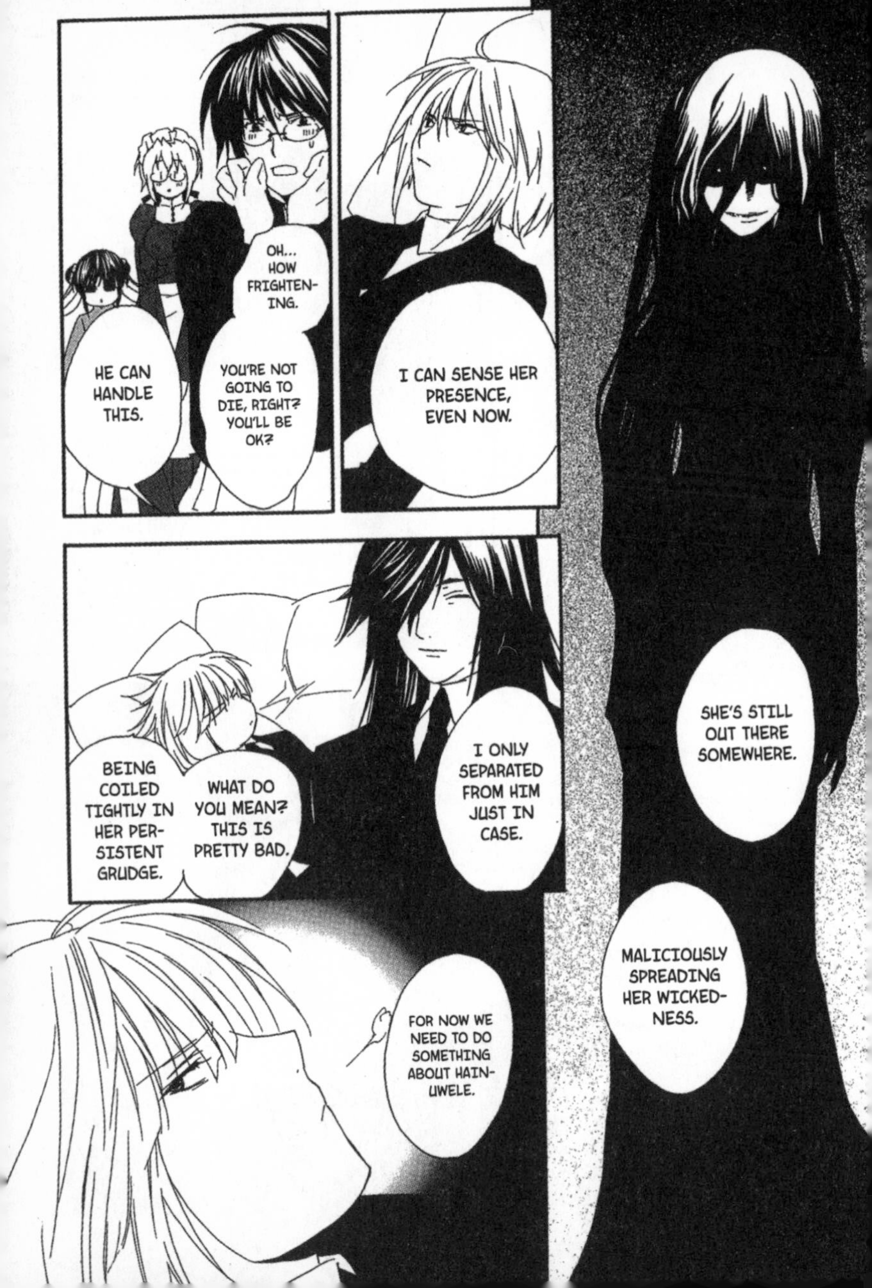
SHE'S STILL OUT THERE SOMEWHERE.
MALICIOUSLY SPREADING HER WICKEDNESS.
I CAN SENSE HER PRESENCE, EVEN NOW.
OH... HOW FRIGHTENING.
YOU'RE NOT GOING TO DIE, RIGHT? YOU'LL BE OK?
HE CAN HANDLE THIS.
I ONLY SEPARATED FROM HIM JUST IN CASE.
WHAT DO YOU MEAN? THIS IS PRETTY BAD.
BEING COILED TIGHTLY IN HER PERSISTENT GRUDGE.
FOR NOW WE NEED TO DO SOMETHING ABOUT HAINUWELE.

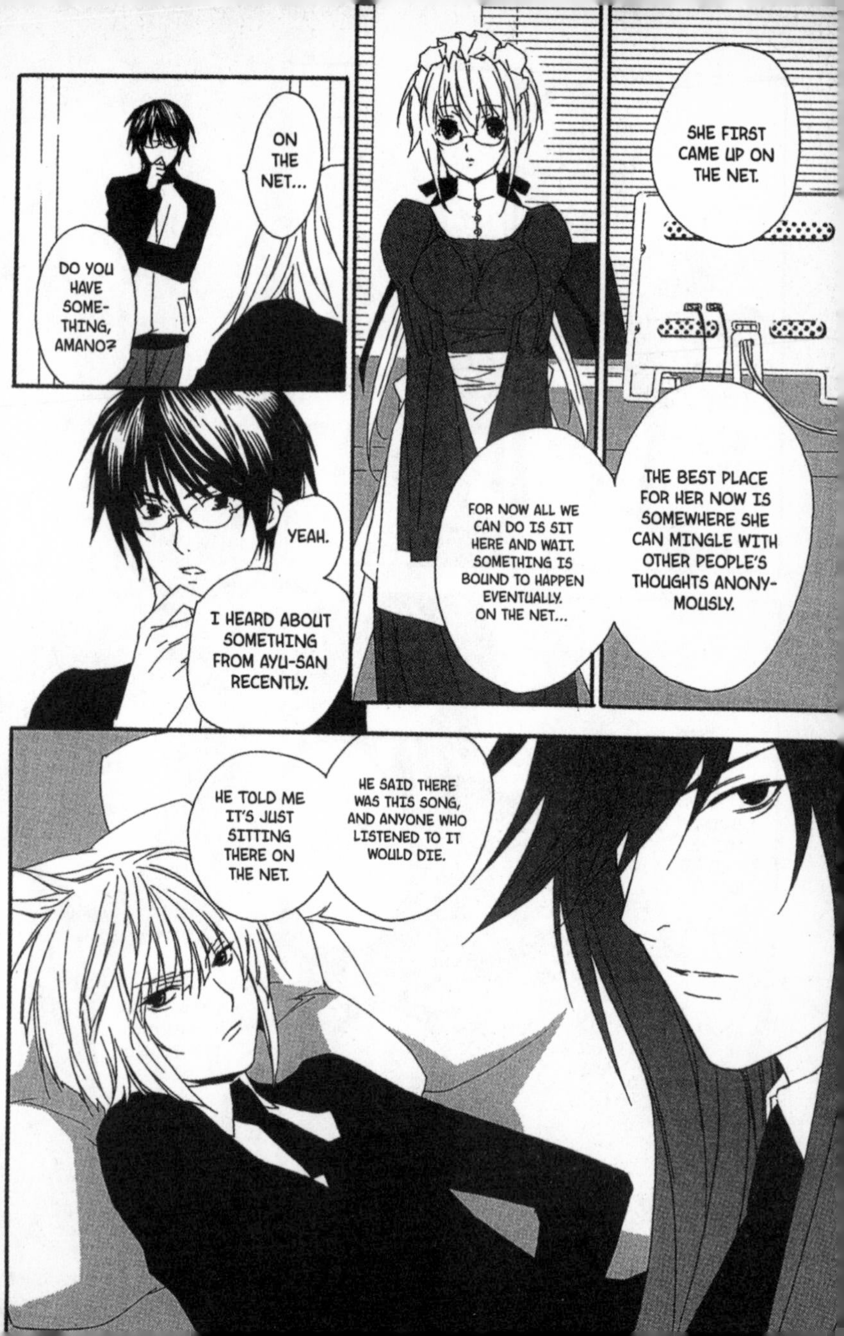
SHE FIRST CAME UP ON THE NET.
THE BEST PLACE FOR HER NOW IS SOMEWHERE SHE CAN MINGLE WITH OTHER PEOPLE'S THOUGHTS ANONYMOUSLY.
FOR NOW ALL WE CAN DO IS SIT HERE AND WAIT. SOMETHING IS BOUND TO HAPPEN EVENTUALLY. ON THE NET...
ON THE NET...
DO YOU HAVE SOMETHING, AMANO?
YEAH.
I HEARD ABOUT SOMETHING FROM AYU-SAN RECENTLY.
HE SAID THERE WAS THIS SONG, AND ANYONE WHO LISTENED TO IT WOULD DIE.
HE TOLD ME IT'S JUST SITTING THERE ON THE NET.

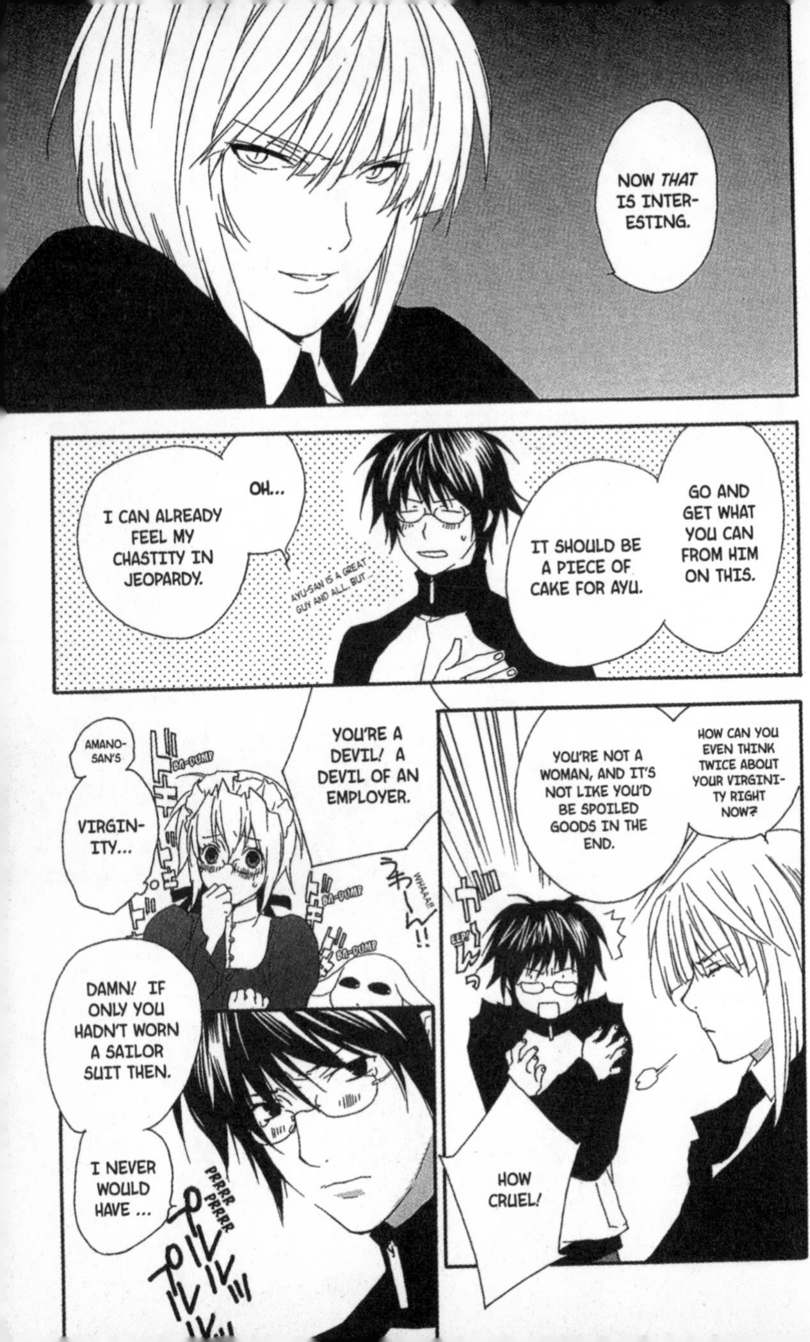
NOW *THAT* IS INTER-ESTING.
GO AND GET WHAT YOU CAN FROM HIM ON THIS.
IT SHOULD BE A PIECE OF CAKE FOR AYU.
AYU-SAN IS A GREAT GUY AND ALL, BUT...
OH...
I CAN ALREADY FEEL MY CHASTITY IN JEOPARDY.
HOW CAN YOU EVEN THINK TWICE ABOUT YOUR VIRGINI-TY RIGHT NOW?
YOU'RE NOT A WOMAN, AND IT'S NOT LIKE YOU'D BE SPOILED GOODS IN THE END.
EEP!
HOW CRUEL!
YOU'RE A DEVIL! A DEVIL OF AN EMPLOYER.
WHAAA!!
BA-DUMP
BA-DUMP
BA-DUMP
AMANO-SAN'S
VIRGIN-ITY...
DAMN! IF ONLY YOU HADN'T WORN A SAILOR SUIT THEN.
I NEVER WOULD HAVE ...
PRRRR PRRRR

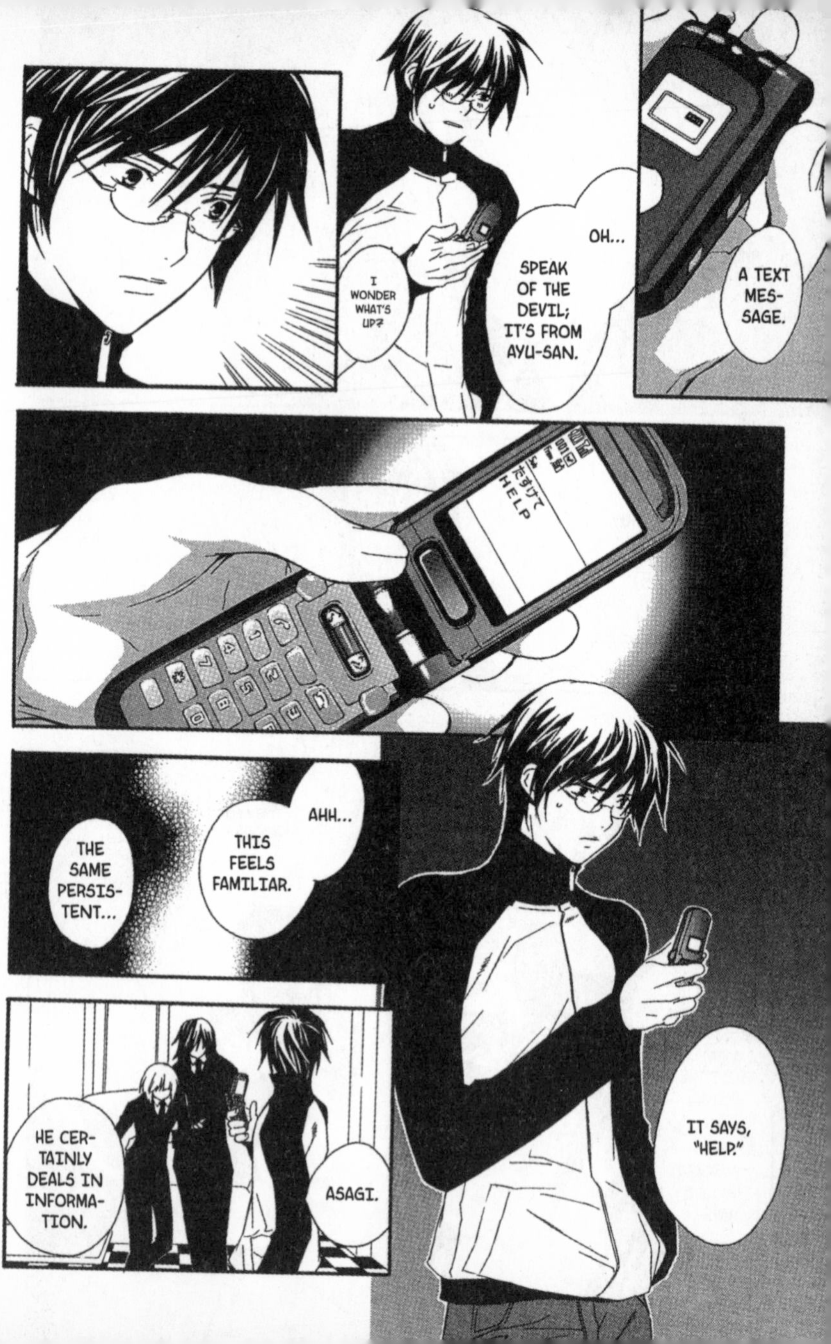
A TEXT MES-SAGE.
OH...
SPEAK OF THE DEVIL; IT'S FROM AYU-SAN.
I WONDER WHAT'S UP?
たすけて
HELP
IT SAYS, "HELP."
AHH...
THIS FEELS FAMILIAR.
THE SAME PERSIS-TENT...
ASAGI.
HE CER-TAINLY DEALS IN INFORMA-TION.

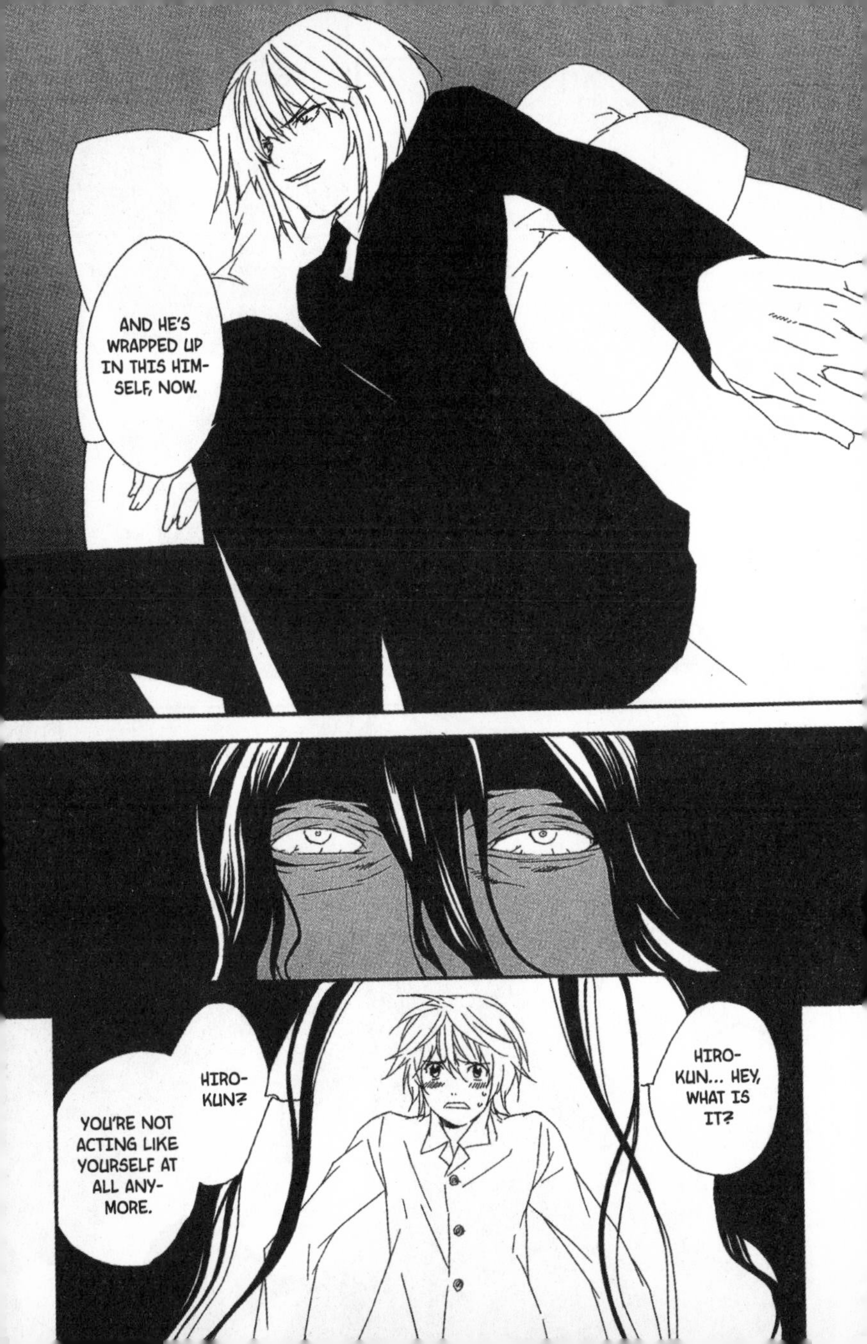
AND HE'S WRAPPED UP IN THIS HIMSELF, NOW.
HIRO-KUN... HEY, WHAT IS IT?
HIRO-KUN?
YOU'RE NOT ACTING LIKE YOURSELF AT ALL ANYMORE.

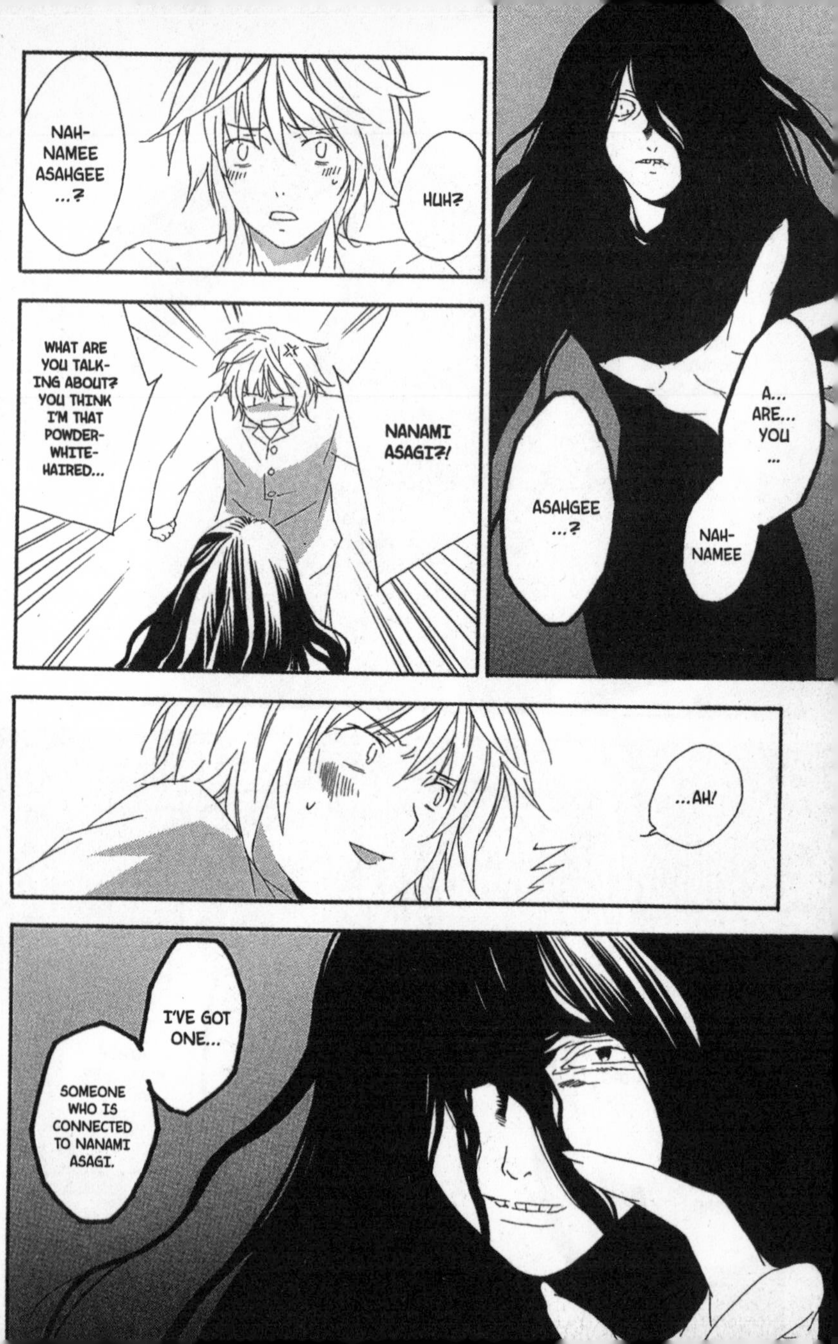
A... ARE... YOU ...
NAH-NAMEE
ASAHGEE ...?
HUH?
NAH-NAMEE ASAHGEE ...?
NANAMI ASAGI?!
WHAT ARE YOU TALKING ABOUT? YOU THINK I'M THAT POWDER-WHITE-HAIRED...
...AH!
I'VE GOT ONE...
SOMEONE WHO IS CONNECTED TO NANAMI ASAGI.

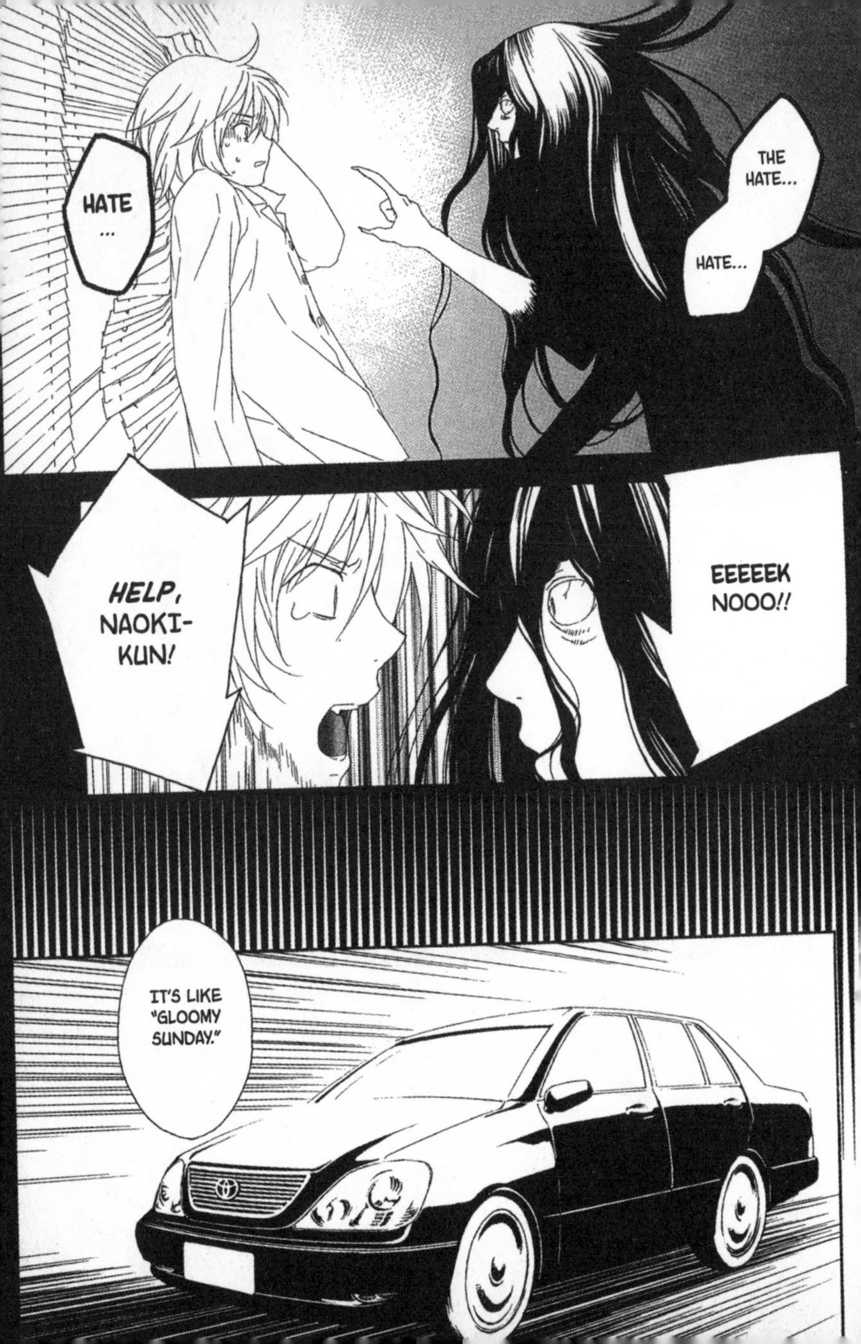
THE HATE...
HATE...
HATE ...
EEEEEK NOOO!!
HELP, NAOKI-KUN!
IT'S LIKE "GLOOMY SUNDAY."

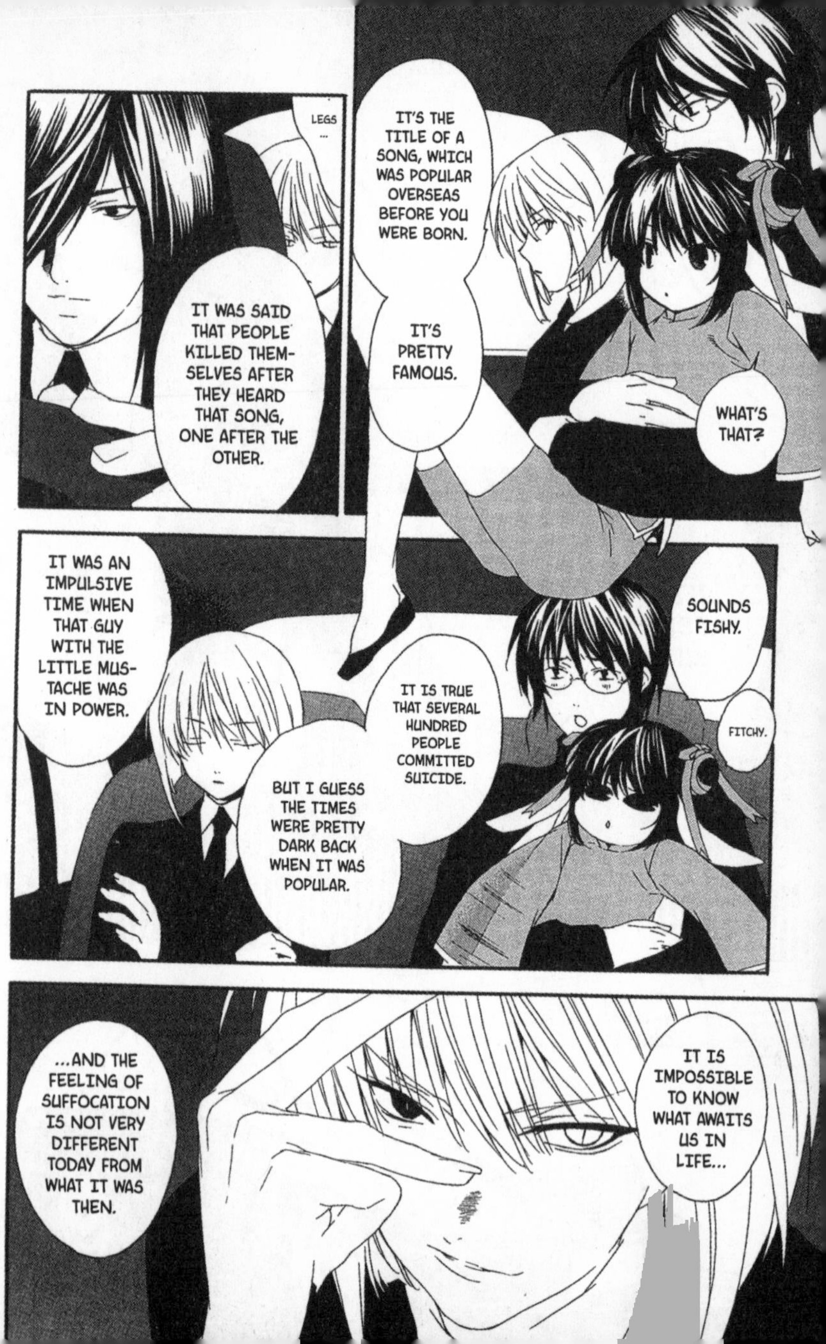
WHAT'S THAT?
IT'S THE TITLE OF A SONG, WHICH WAS POPULAR OVERSEAS BEFORE YOU WERE BORN.
IT'S PRETTY FAMOUS.
LEGS ...
IT WAS SAID THAT PEOPLE KILLED THEM-SELVES AFTER THEY HEARD THAT SONG, ONE AFTER THE OTHER.
SOUNDS FISHY.
FITCHY.
IT IS TRUE THAT SEVERAL HUNDRED PEOPLE COMMITTED SUICIDE.
BUT I GUESS THE TIMES WERE PRETTY DARK BACK WHEN IT WAS POPULAR.
IT WAS AN IMPULSIVE TIME WHEN THAT GUY WITH THE LITTLE MUS-TACHE WAS IN POWER.
IT IS IMPOSSIBLE TO KNOW WHAT AWAITS US IN LIFE...
...AND THE FEELING OF SUFFOCATION IS NOT VERY DIFFERENT TODAY FROM WHAT IT WAS THEN.

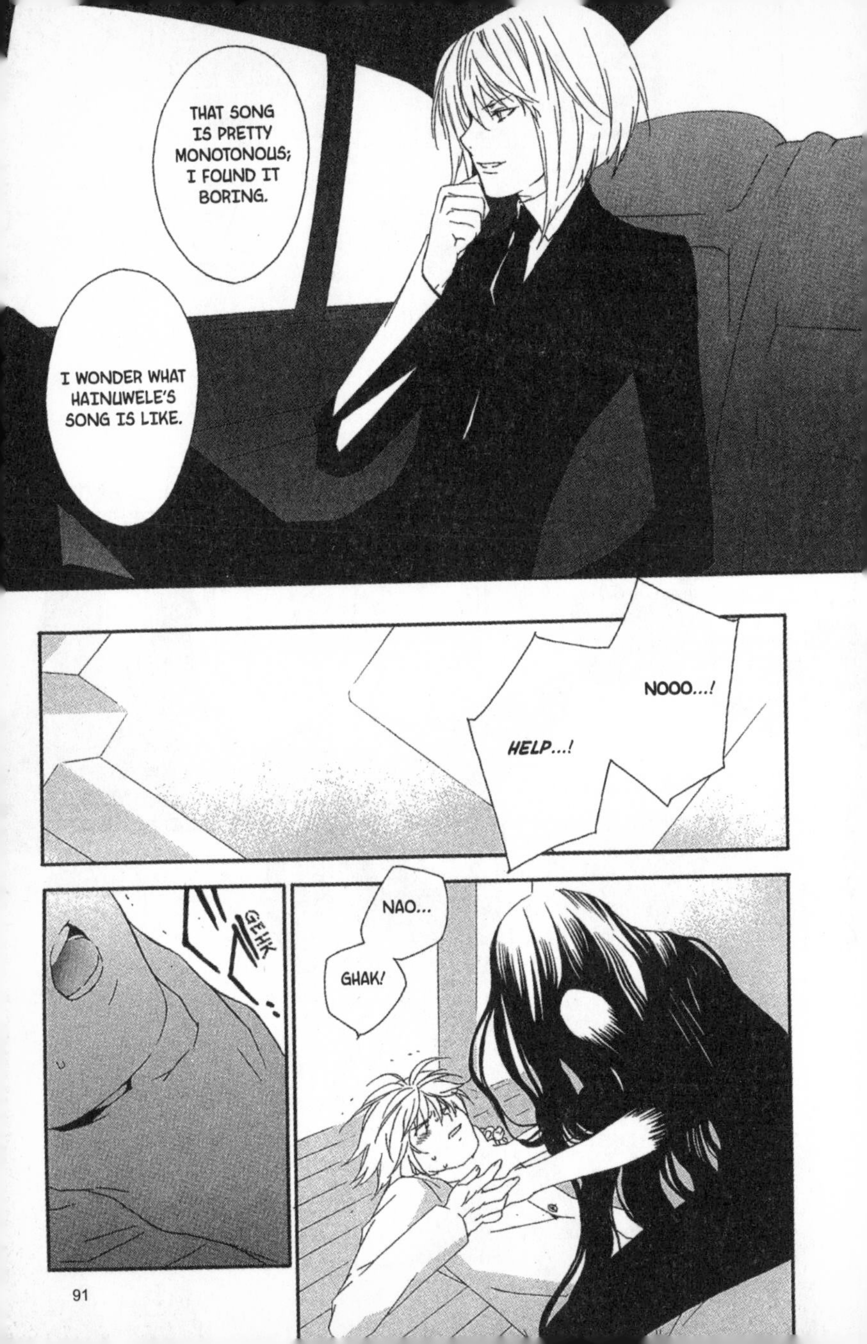
THAT SONG IS PRETTY MONOTONOUS; I FOUND IT BORING.
I WONDER WHAT HAINUWELE'S SONG IS LIKE.
NOOO...!
HELP...!
NAO...
GHAK!
GEHK

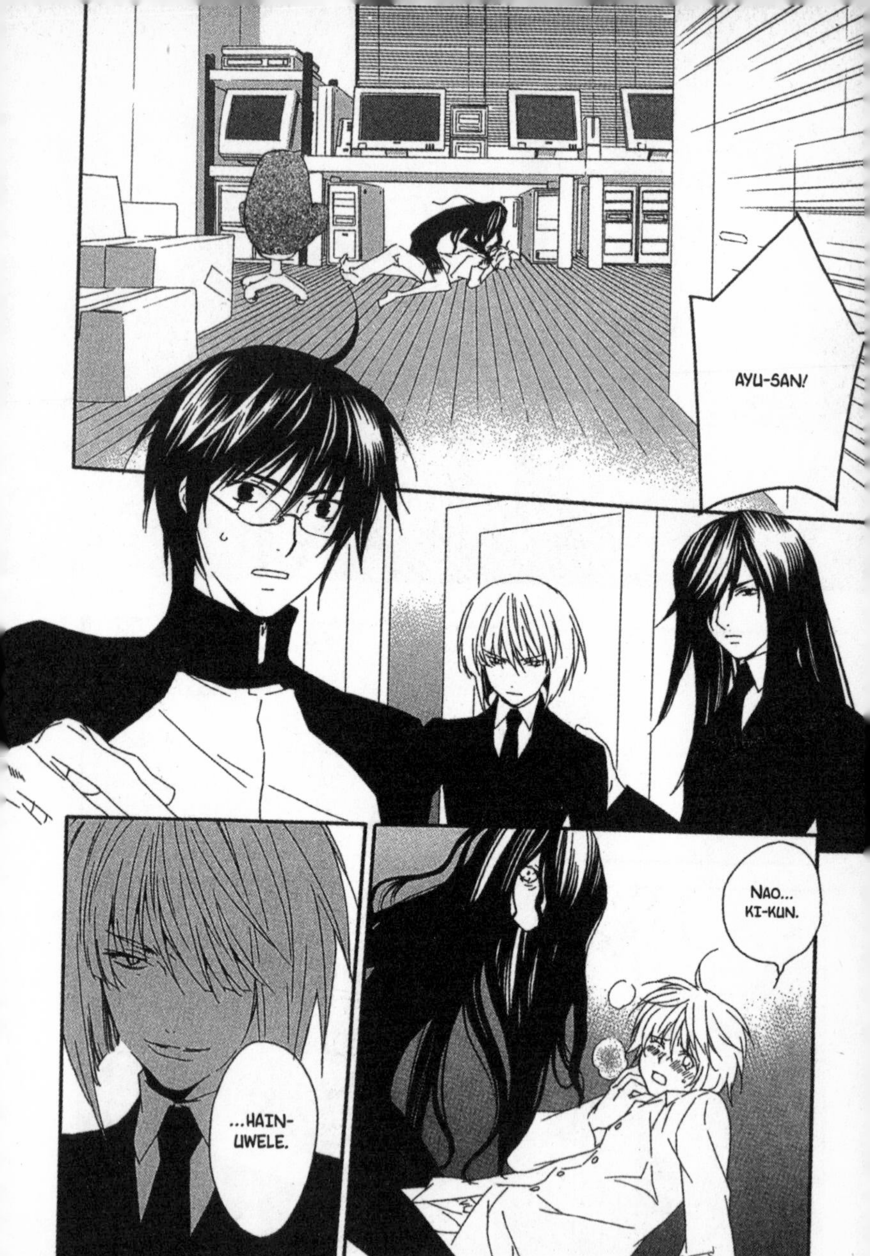
AYU-SAN!
NAO... KI-KUN.
...HAIN-UWELE.

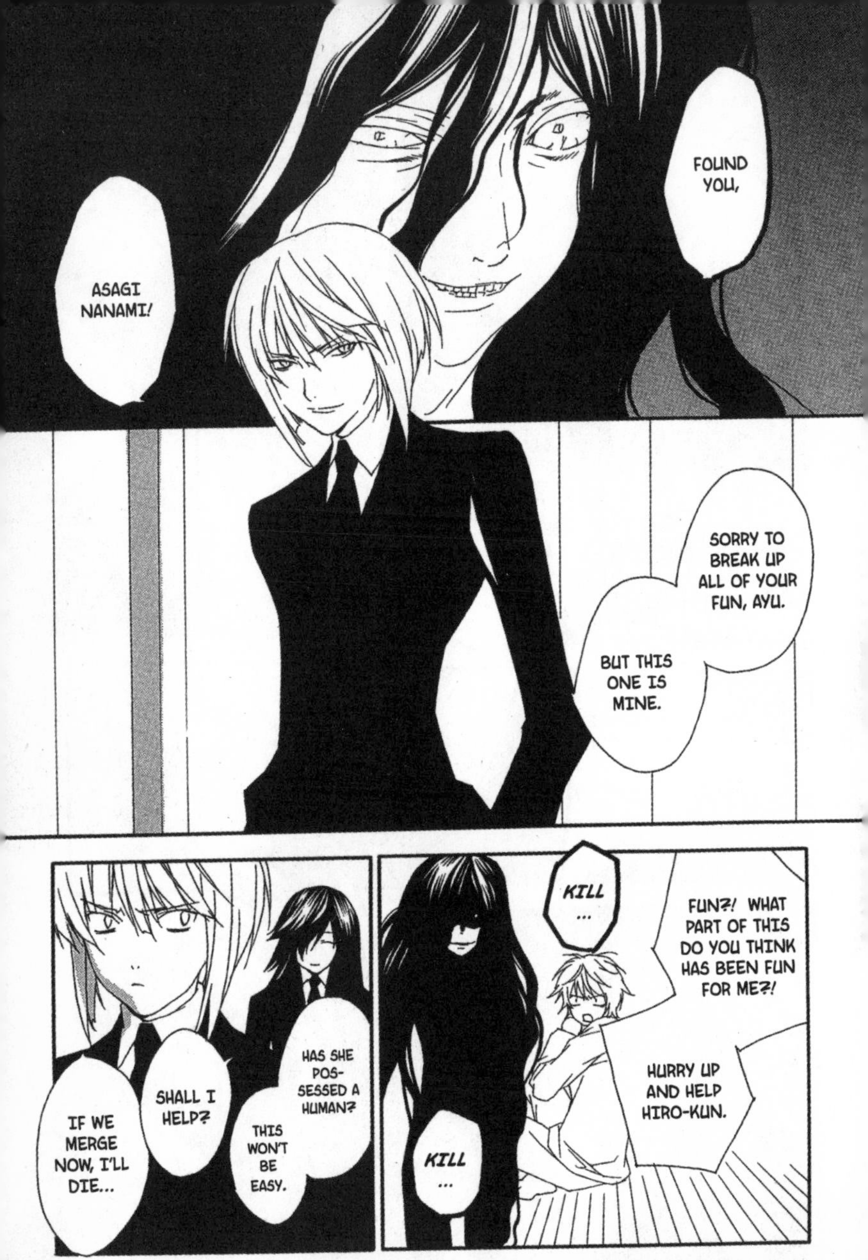
FOUND YOU,
ASAGI NANAMI!
SORRY TO BREAK UP ALL OF YOUR FUN, AYU.
BUT THIS ONE IS MINE.
KILL ...
FUN?! WHAT PART OF THIS DO YOU THINK HAS BEEN FUN FOR ME?!
HURRY UP AND HELP HIRO-KUN.
KILL ...
HAS SHE POS-SESSED A HUMAN?
THIS WON'T BE EASY.
SHALL I HELP?
IF WE MERGE NOW, I'LL DIE...

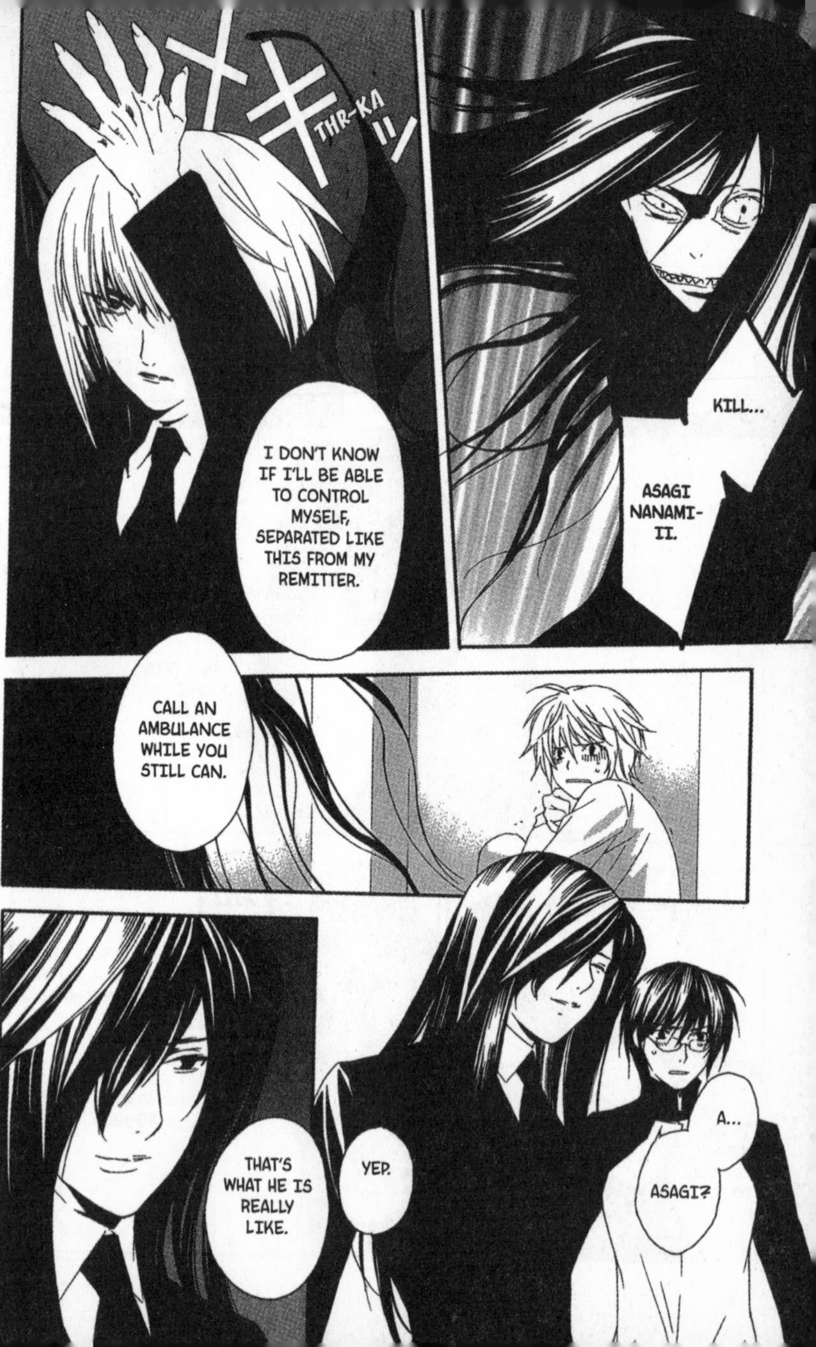
KILL...
ASAGI NANAMI-II.
THR-KA
I DON'T KNOW IF I'LL BE ABLE TO CONTROL MYSELF, SEPARATED LIKE THIS FROM MY REMITTER.
CALL AN AMBULANCE WHILE YOU STILL CAN.
A...
ASAGI?
YEP.
THAT'S WHAT HE IS REALLY LIKE.

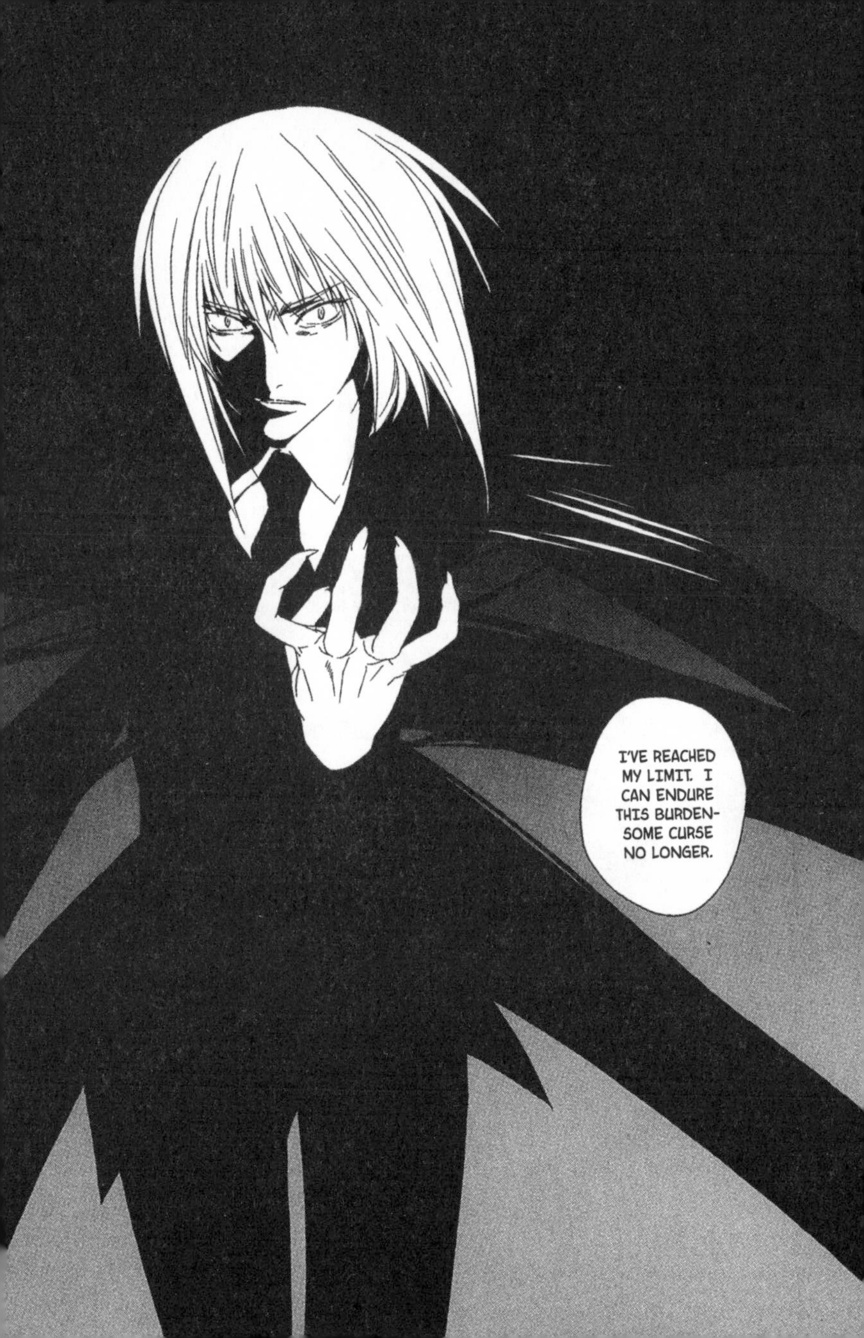
I'VE REACHED MY LIMIT. I CAN ENDURE THIS BURDEN-SOME CURSE NO LONGER.

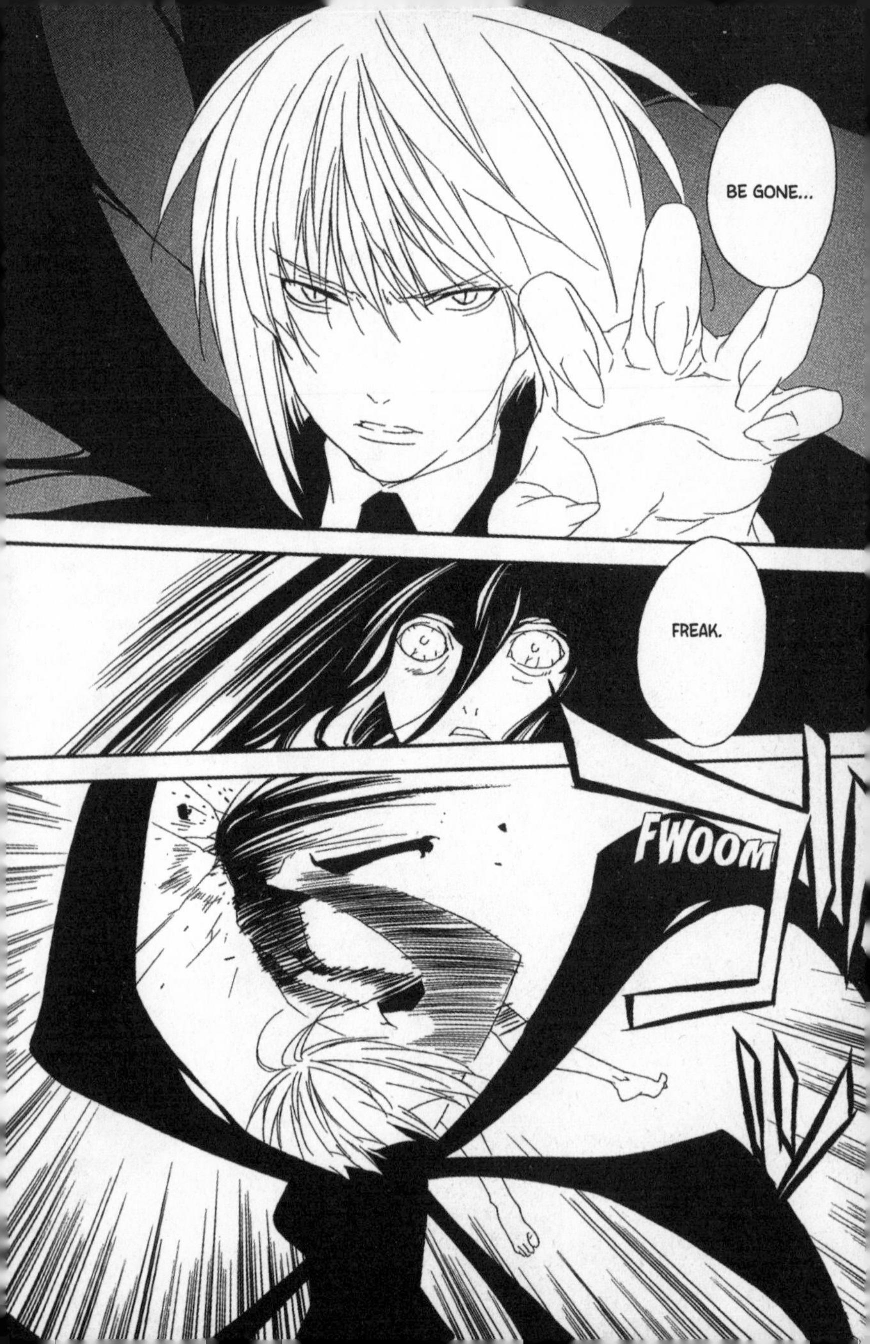
BE GONE...
FREAK.
FWOOM

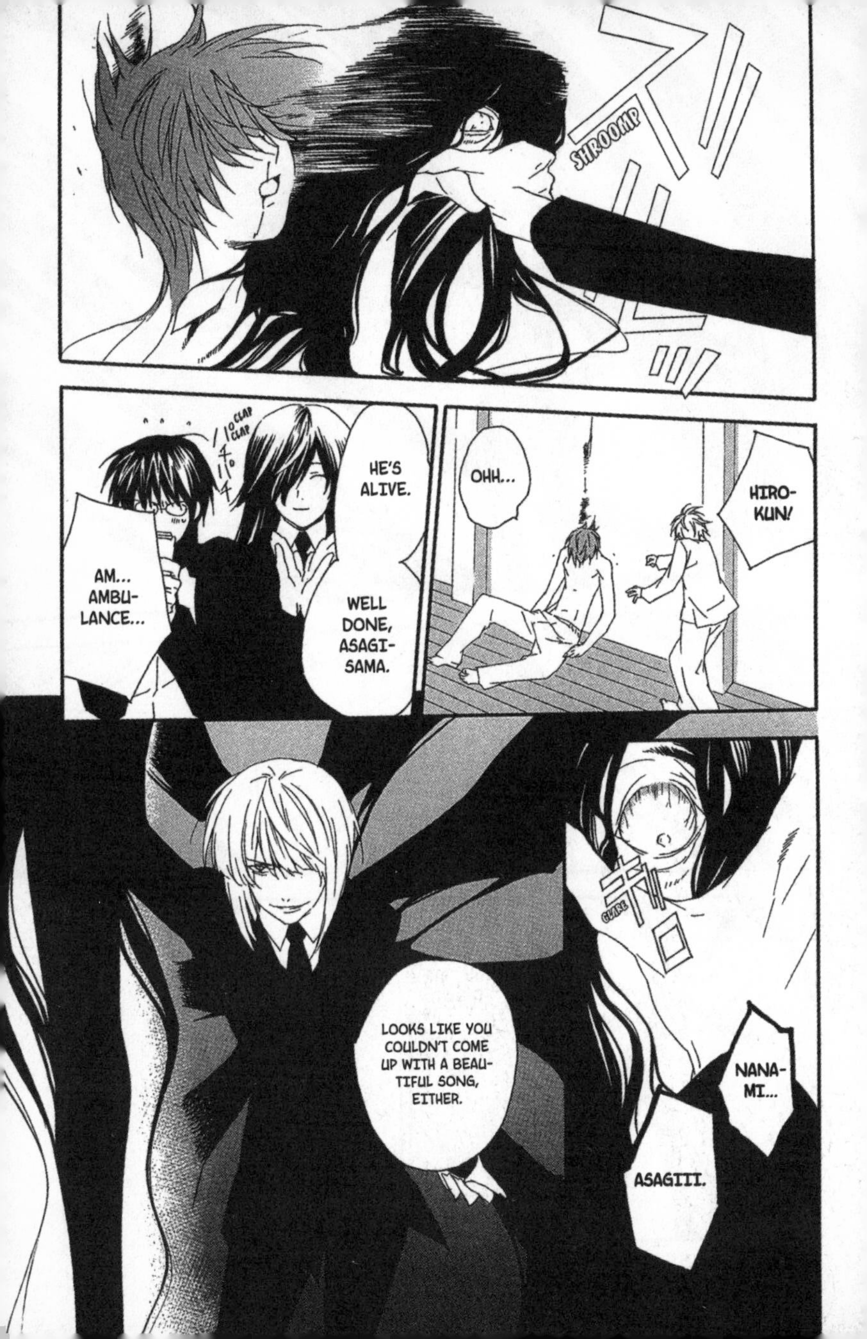

SHROOMP
HIRO-KUN!
OHH...
HE'S ALIVE.
CLAP CLAP
WELL DONE, ASAGI-SAMA.
AM... AMBULANCE...
GLARE
NANA-MI...
ASAGITI.
LOOKS LIKE YOU COULDN'T COME UP WITH A BEAUTIFUL SONG, EITHER.

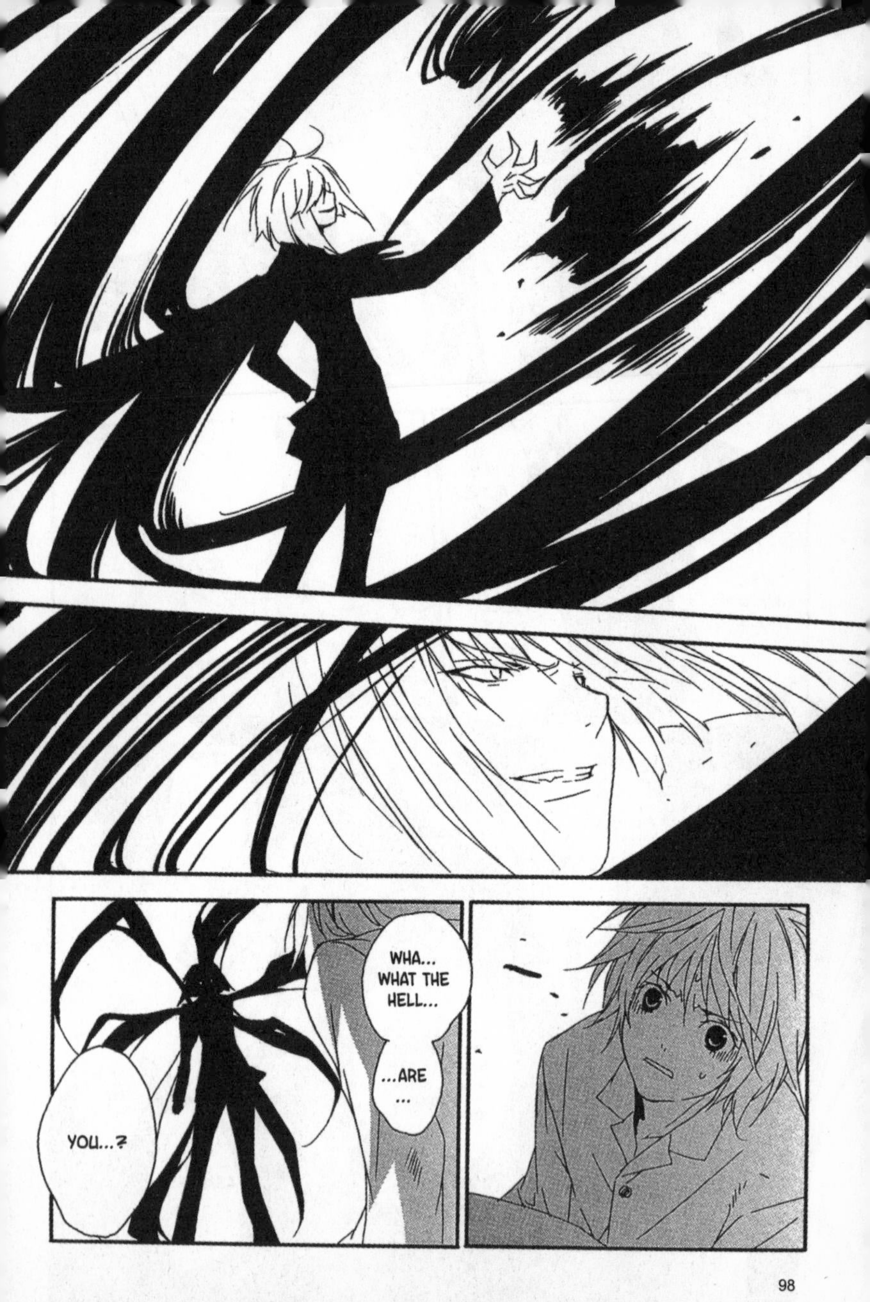
WHA... WHAT THE HELL...
...ARE ...
YOU...?

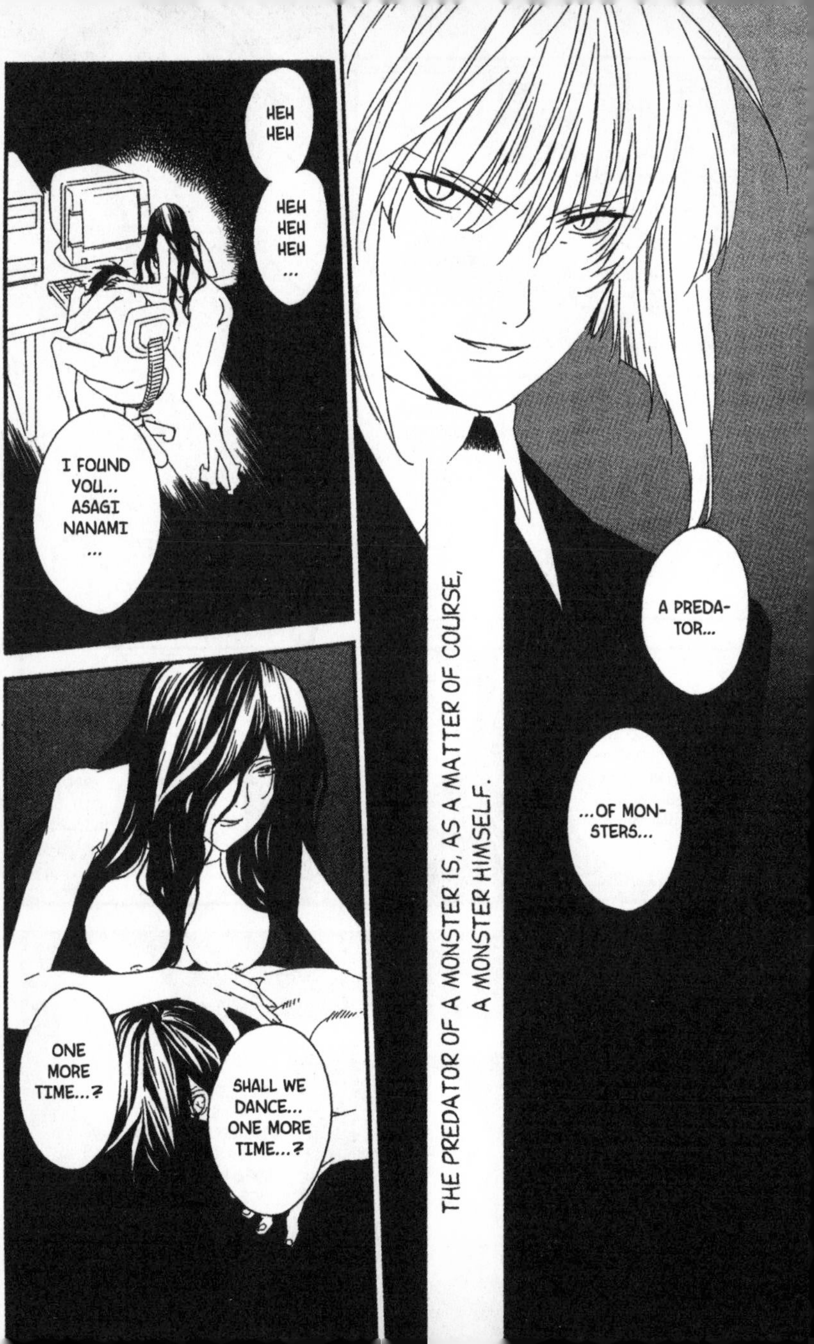
A PREDATOR...
...OF MONSTERS...
THE PREDATOR OF A MONSTER IS, AS A MATTER OF COURSE, A MONSTER HIMSELF.
HEH HEH
HEH HEH HEH ...
I FOUND YOU... ASAGI NANAMI ...
SHALL WE DANCE... ONE MORE TIME...?
ONE MORE TIME...?

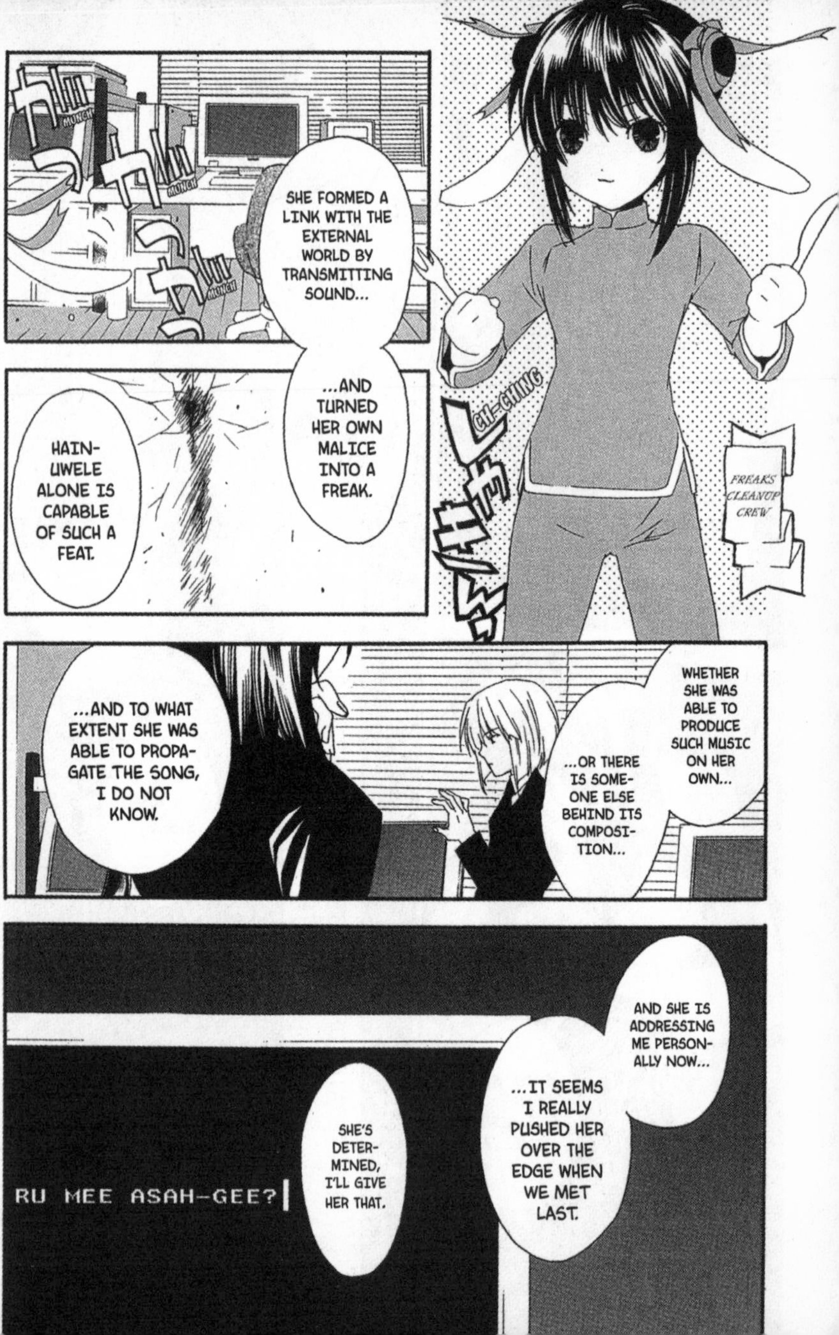
CH-CHING
FREAKS CLEANUP CREW
SHE FORMED A LINK WITH THE EXTERNAL WORLD BY TRANSMITTING SOUND...
...AND TURNED HER OWN MALICE INTO A FREAK.
MUNCH
MUNCH
MUNCH
HAIN-UWELE ALONE IS CAPABLE OF SUCH A FEAT.
WHETHER SHE WAS ABLE TO PRODUCE SUCH MUSIC ON HER OWN...
...OR THERE IS SOME-ONE ELSE BEHIND ITS COMPOSI-TION...
...AND TO WHAT EXTENT SHE WAS ABLE TO PROPA-GATE THE SONG, I DO NOT KNOW.
AND SHE IS ADDRESSING ME PERSON-ALLY NOW...
...IT SEEMS I REALLY PUSHED HER OVER THE EDGE WHEN WE MET LAST.
SHE'S DETER-MINED, I'LL GIVE HER THAT.
RU MEE ASAH-GEE?

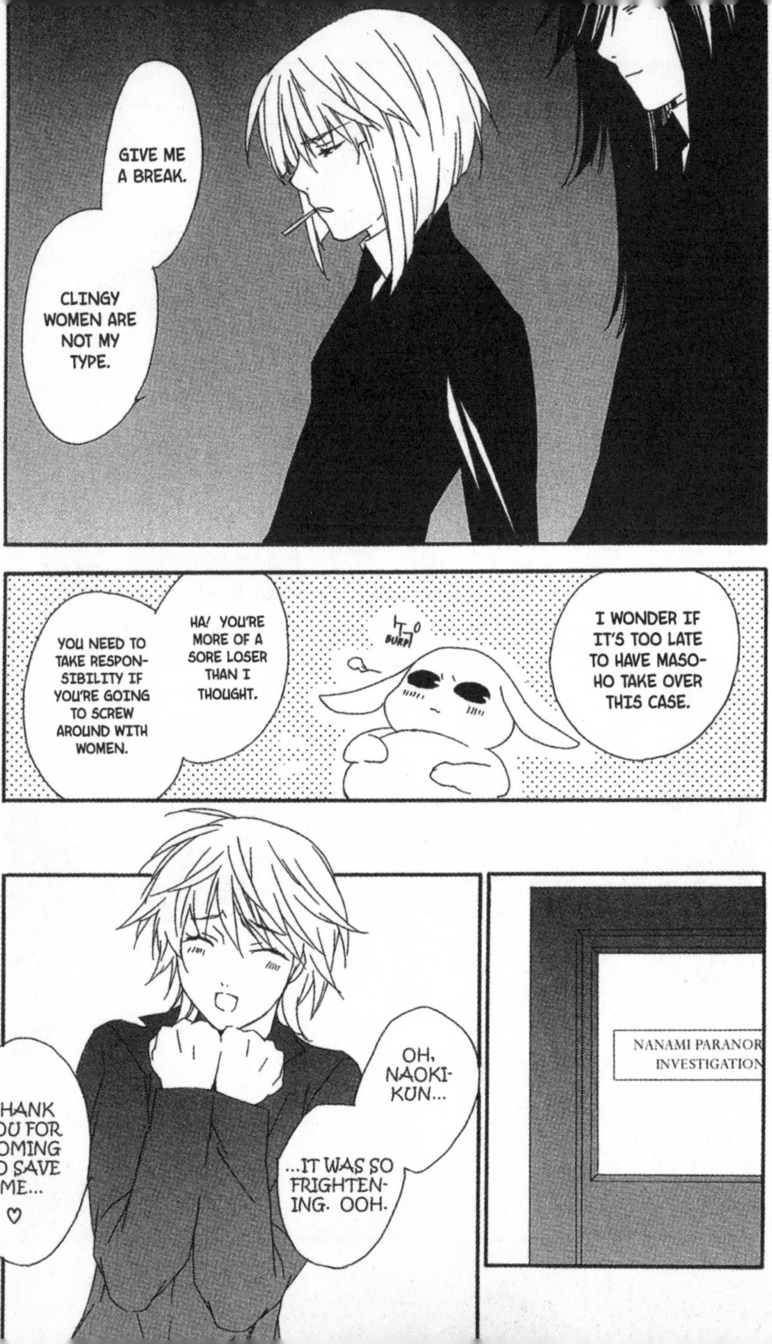
GIVE ME A BREAK.
CLINGY WOMEN ARE NOT MY TYPE.
I WONDER IF IT'S TOO LATE TO HAVE MASO-HO TAKE OVER THIS CASE.
BURP!
HA! YOU'RE MORE OF A SORE LOSER THAN I THOUGHT.
YOU NEED TO TAKE RESPON-SIBILITY IF YOU'RE GOING TO SCREW AROUND WITH WOMEN.
NANAMI PARANOR
INVESTIGATION
OH, NAOKI-KUN...
...IT WAS SO FRIGHTEN-ING. OOH.
THANK YOU FOR COMING TO SAVE ME... ♡

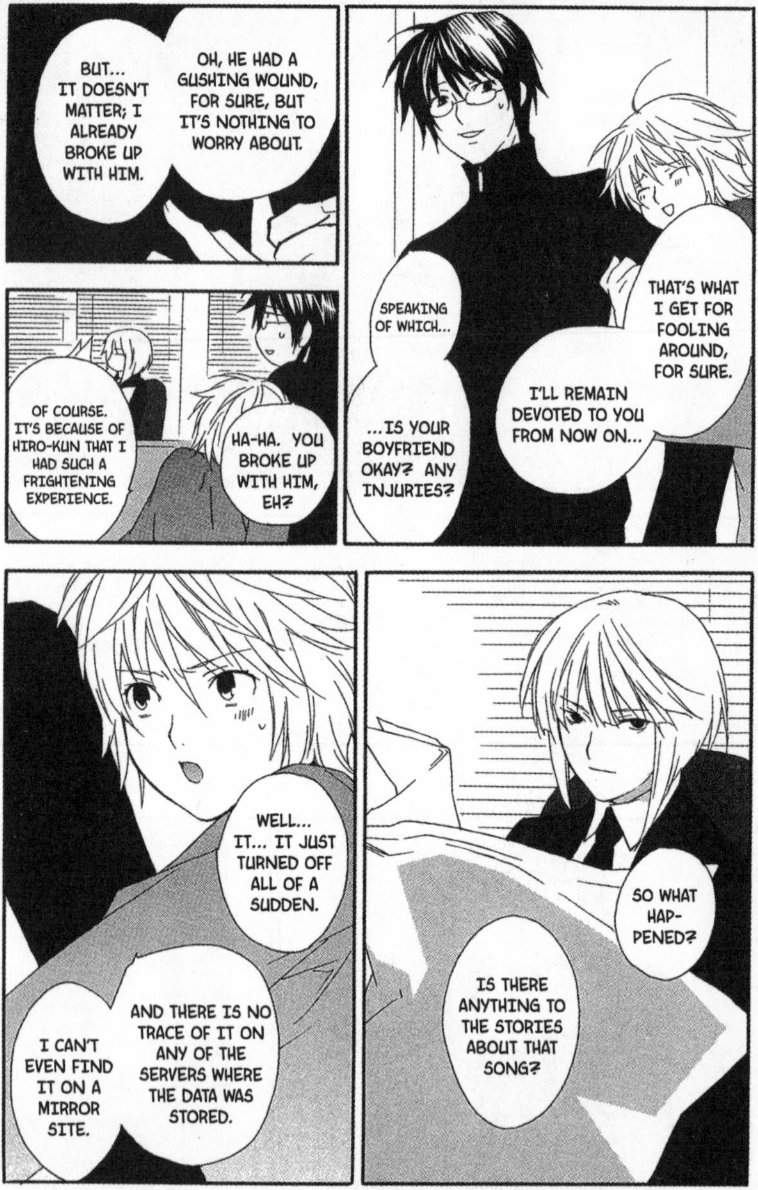
THAT'S WHAT I GET FOR FOOLING AROUND, FOR SURE.
I'LL REMAIN DEVOTED TO YOU FROM NOW ON...
SPEAKING OF WHICH...
...IS YOUR BOYFRIEND OKAY? ANY INJURIES?
OH, HE HAD A GUSHING WOUND, FOR SURE, BUT IT'S NOTHING TO WORRY ABOUT.
BUT... IT DOESN'T MATTER; I ALREADY BROKE UP WITH HIM.
HA-HA. YOU BROKE UP WITH HIM, EH?
OF COURSE. IT'S BECAUSE OF HIRO-KUN THAT I HAD SUCH A FRIGHTENING EXPERIENCE.
SO WHAT HAPPENED?
IS THERE ANYTHING TO THE STORIES ABOUT THAT SONG?
WELL... IT... IT JUST TURNED OFF ALL OF A SUDDEN.
AND THERE IS NO TRACE OF IT ON ANY OF THE SERVERS WHERE THE DATA WAS STORED.
I CAN'T EVEN FIND IT ON A MIRROR SITE.

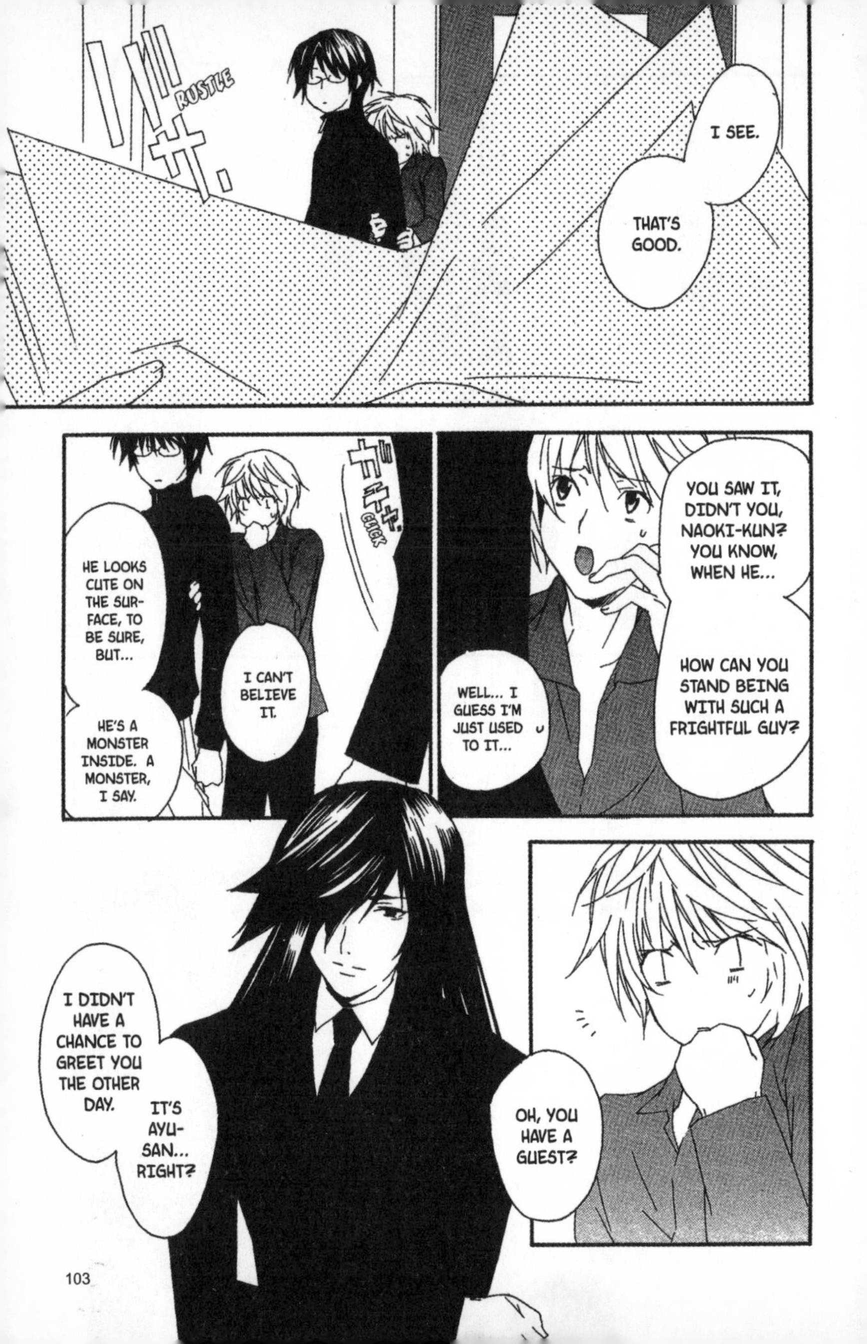

I SEE.
THAT'S GOOD.
RUSTLE
YOU SAW IT, DIDN'T YOU, NAOKI-KUN? YOU KNOW, WHEN HE...
HOW CAN YOU STAND BEING WITH SUCH A FRIGHTFUL GUY?
WELL... I GUESS I'M JUST USED TO IT...
CLICK
HE LOOKS CUTE ON THE SUR-FACE, TO BE SURE, BUT...
I CAN'T BELIEVE IT.
HE'S A MONSTER INSIDE. A MONSTER, I SAY.
OH, YOU HAVE A GUEST?
I DIDN'T HAVE A CHANCE TO GREET YOU THE OTHER DAY.
IT'S AYU-SAN... RIGHT?

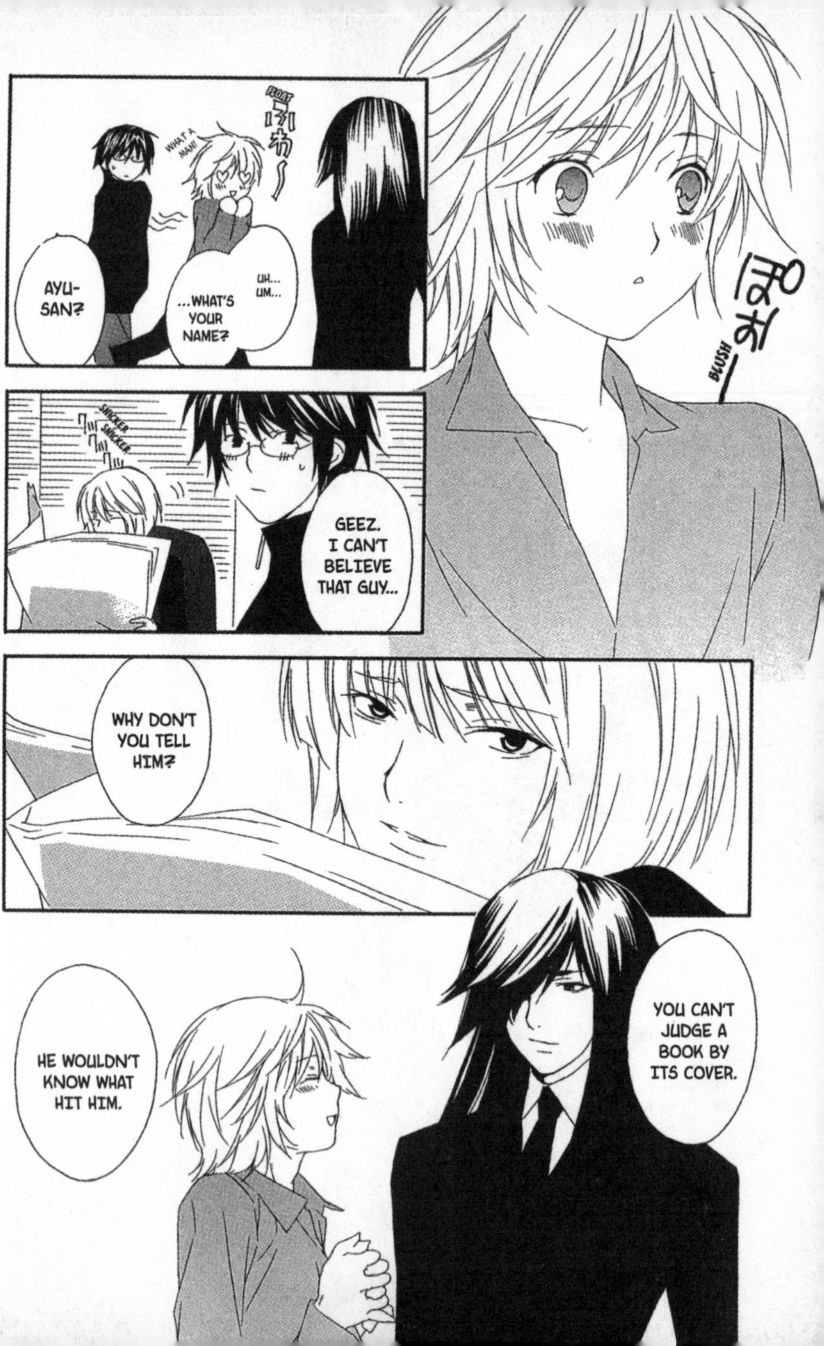
ぽぉー
BLUSH
ふわ～
FLOAT
WHAT A MAN!
UH... UM...
...WHAT'S YOUR NAME?
AYU-SAN?
SNICKER SNICKER
GEEZ. I CAN'T BELIEVE THAT GUY...
WHY DON'T YOU TELL HIM?
YOU CAN'T JUDGE A BOOK BY ITS COVER.
HE WOULDN'T KNOW WHAT HIT HIM.

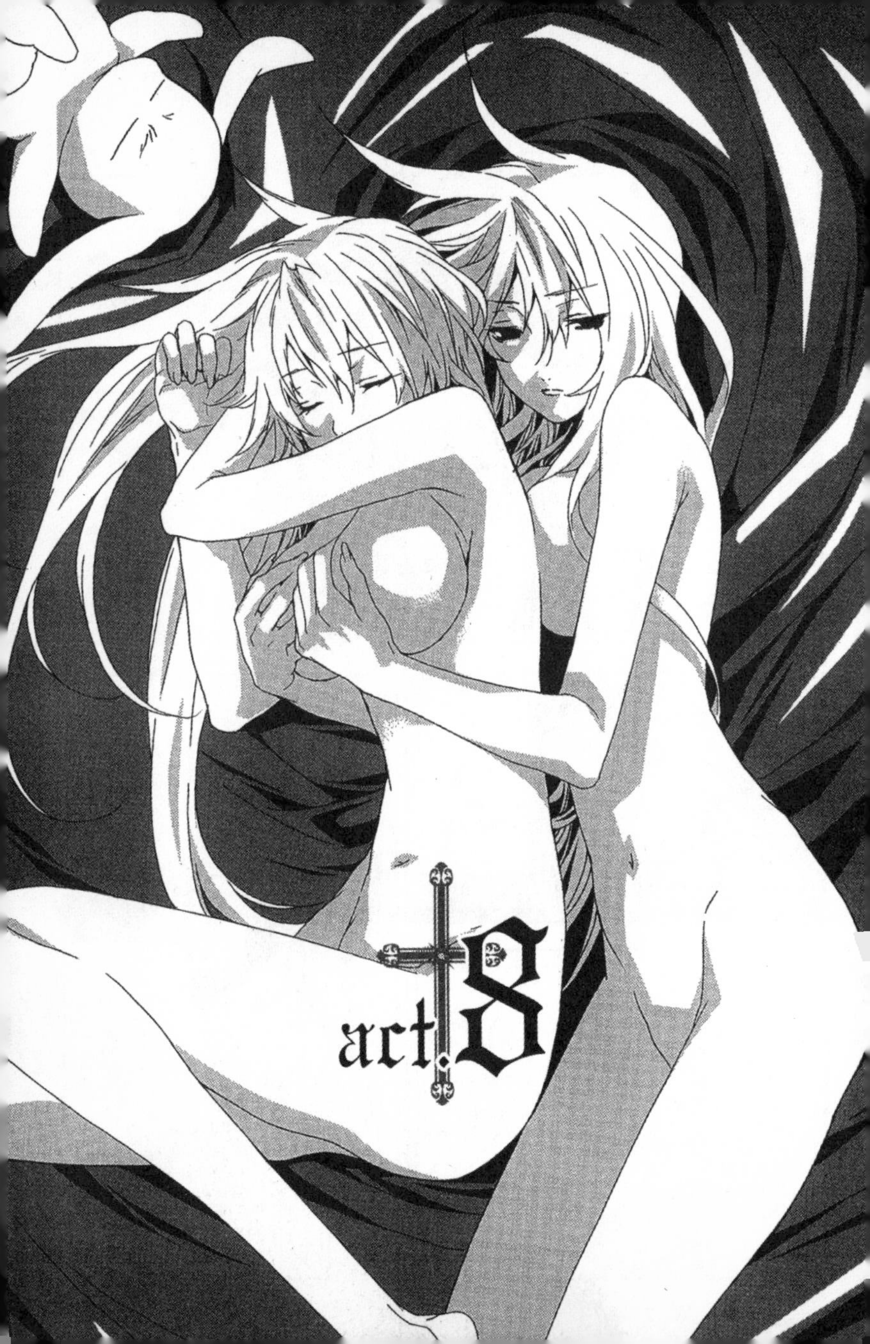
act 8

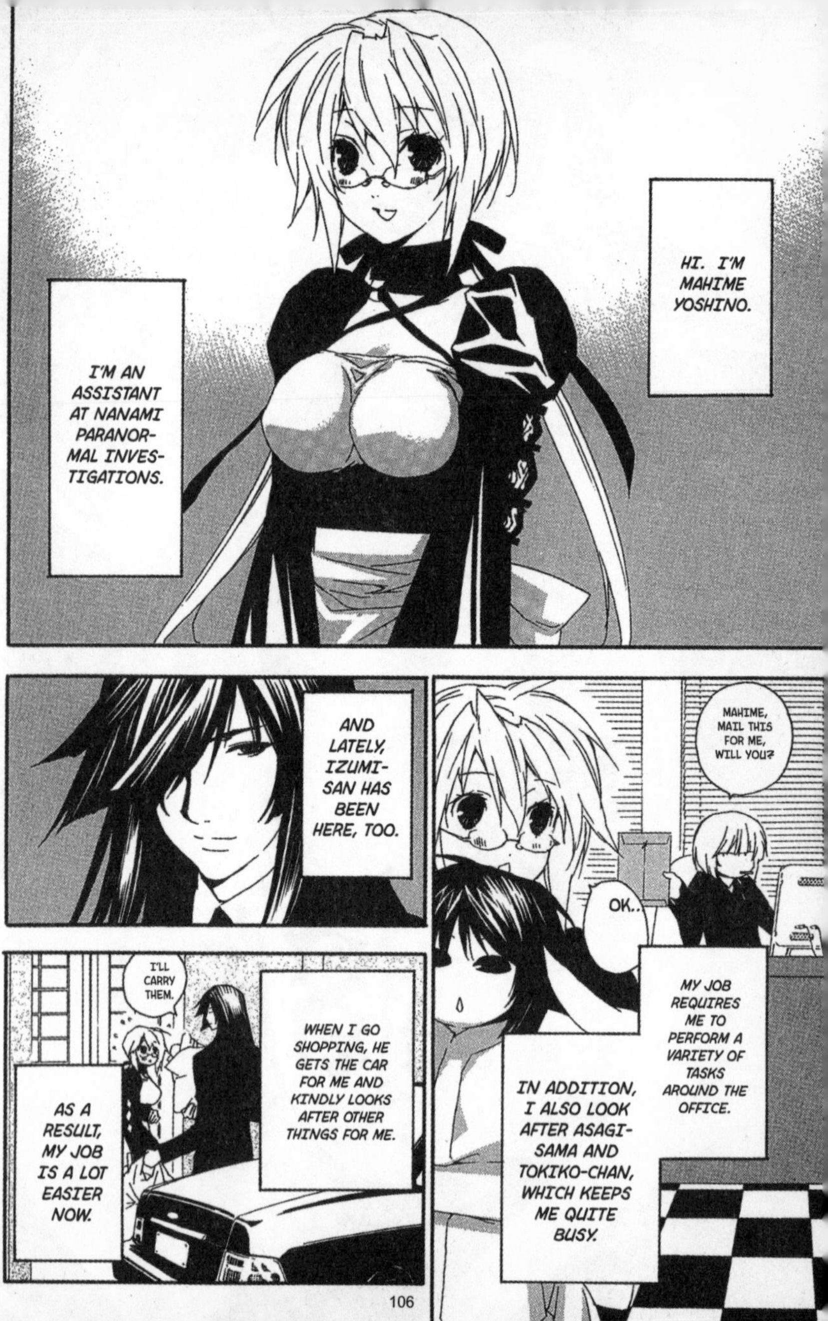
HI. I'M MAHIME YOSHINO.
I'M AN ASSISTANT AT NANAMI PARANOR-MAL INVES-TIGATIONS.
MAHIME, MAIL THIS FOR ME, WILL YOU?
OK...
MY JOB REQUIRES ME TO PERFORM A VARIETY OF TASKS AROUND THE OFFICE.
IN ADDITION, I ALSO LOOK AFTER ASAGI-SAMA AND TOKIKO-CHAN, WHICH KEEPS ME QUITE BUSY.
AND LATELY, IZUMI-SAN HAS BEEN HERE, TOO.
I'LL CARRY THEM.
WHEN I GO SHOPPING, HE GETS THE CAR FOR ME AND KINDLY LOOKS AFTER OTHER THINGS FOR ME.
AS A RESULT, MY JOB IS A LOT EASIER NOW.

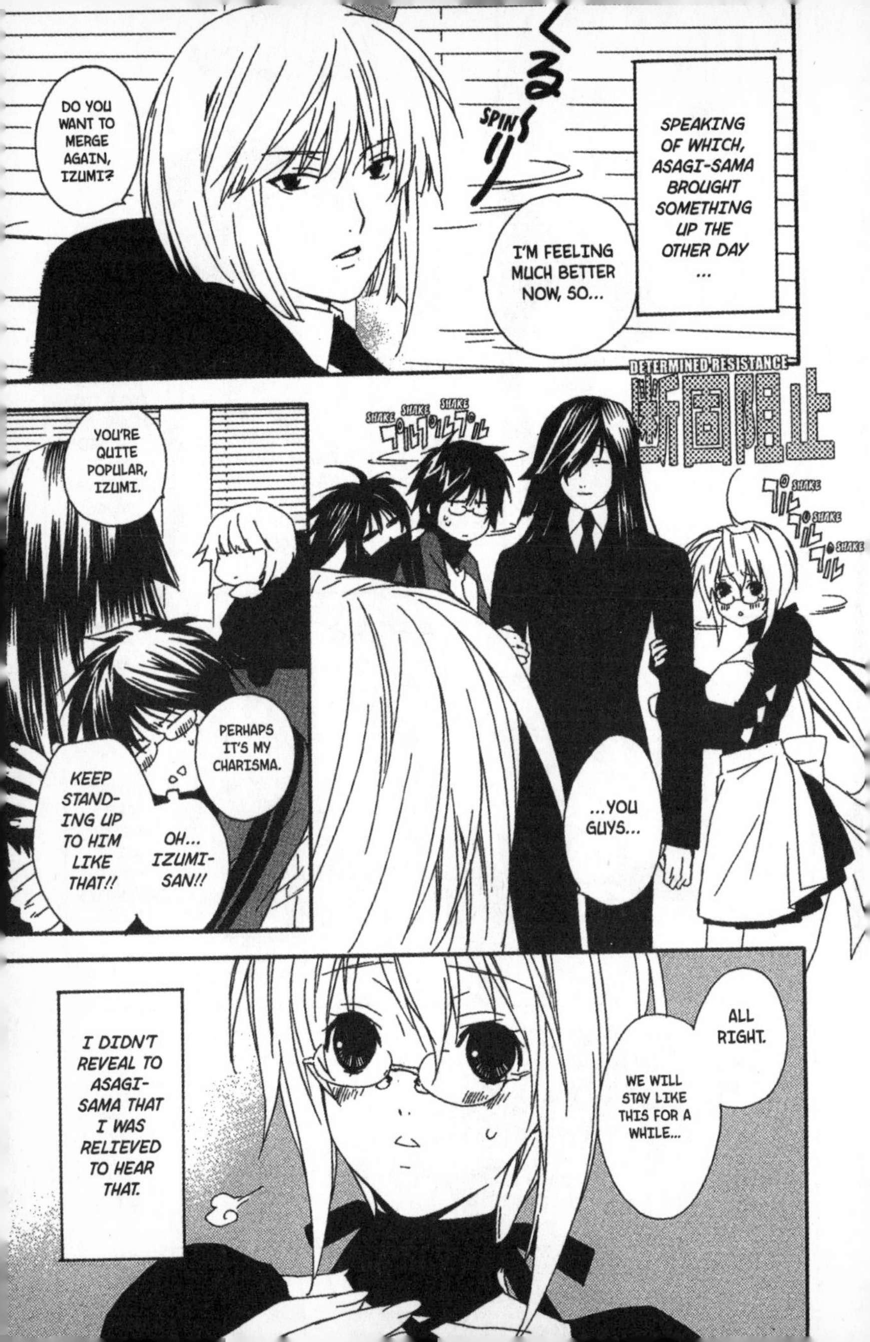
SPEAKING OF WHICH, ASAGI-SAMA BROUGHT SOMETHING UP THE OTHER DAY ...
くるり SPIN
I'M FEELING MUCH BETTER NOW, SO...
DO YOU WANT TO MERGE AGAIN, IZUMI?
DETERMINED RESISTANCE
断固阻止
プルプルプル SHAKE SHAKE SHAKE
プルプルプル SHAKE SHAKE SHAKE
...YOU GUYS...
YOU'RE QUITE POPULAR, IZUMI.
PERHAPS IT'S MY CHARISMA.
OH... IZUMI-SAN!!
KEEP STAND-ING UP TO HIM LIKE THAT!!
ALL RIGHT.
WE WILL STAY LIKE THIS FOR A WHILE...
I DIDN'T REVEAL TO ASAGI-SAMA THAT I WAS RELIEVED TO HEAR THAT.

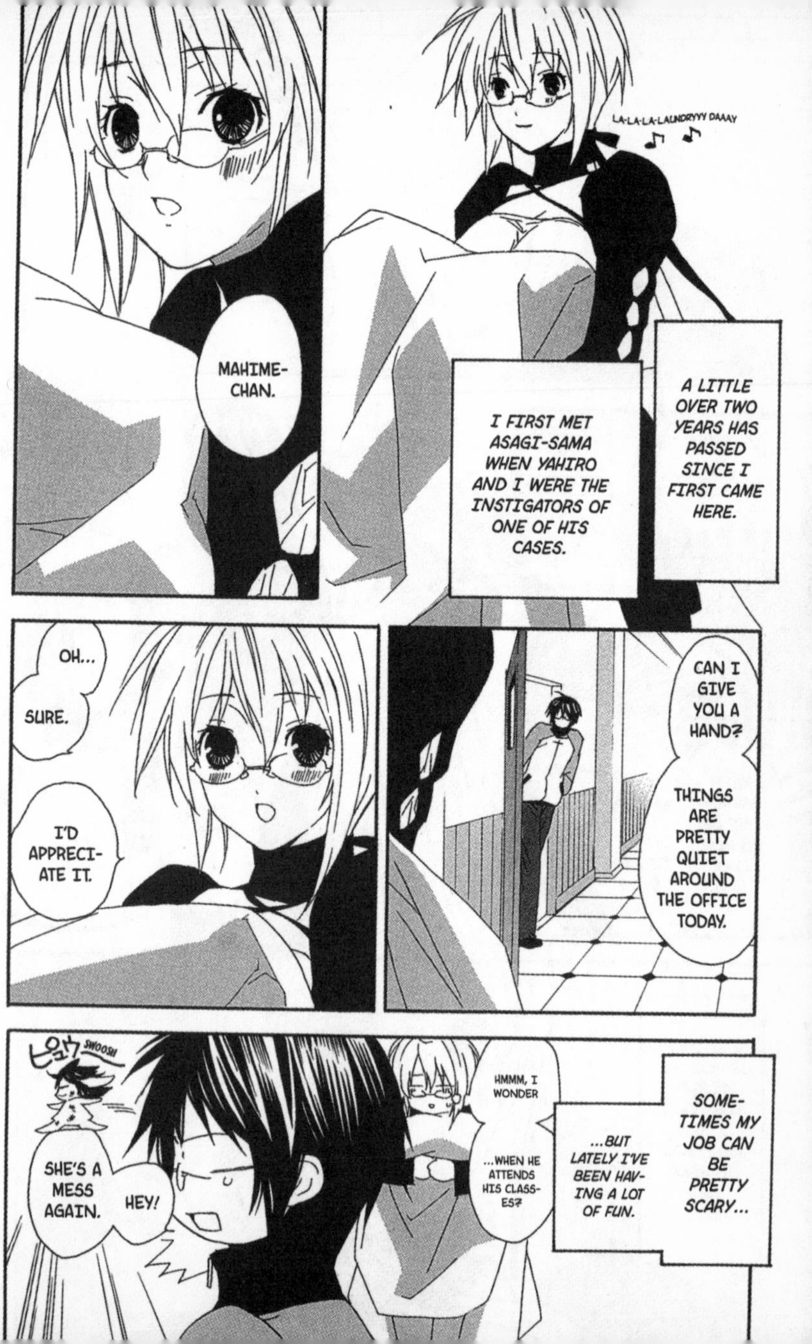
LA-LA-LA-LAUNDRYYY DAAAY
A LITTLE OVER TWO YEARS HAS PASSED SINCE I FIRST CAME HERE.
I FIRST MET ASAGI-SAMA WHEN YAHIRO AND I WERE THE INSTIGATORS OF ONE OF HIS CASES.
MAHIME-CHAN.
CAN I GIVE YOU A HAND?
THINGS ARE PRETTY QUIET AROUND THE OFFICE TODAY.
OH...
SURE.
I'D APPRECIATE IT.
SOMETIMES MY JOB CAN BE PRETTY SCARY...
...BUT LATELY I'VE BEEN HAVING A LOT OF FUN.
HMMM, I WONDER
...WHEN HE ATTENDS HIS CLASSES?
HEY!
SHE'S A MESS AGAIN.
ピュウ
SWOOSH

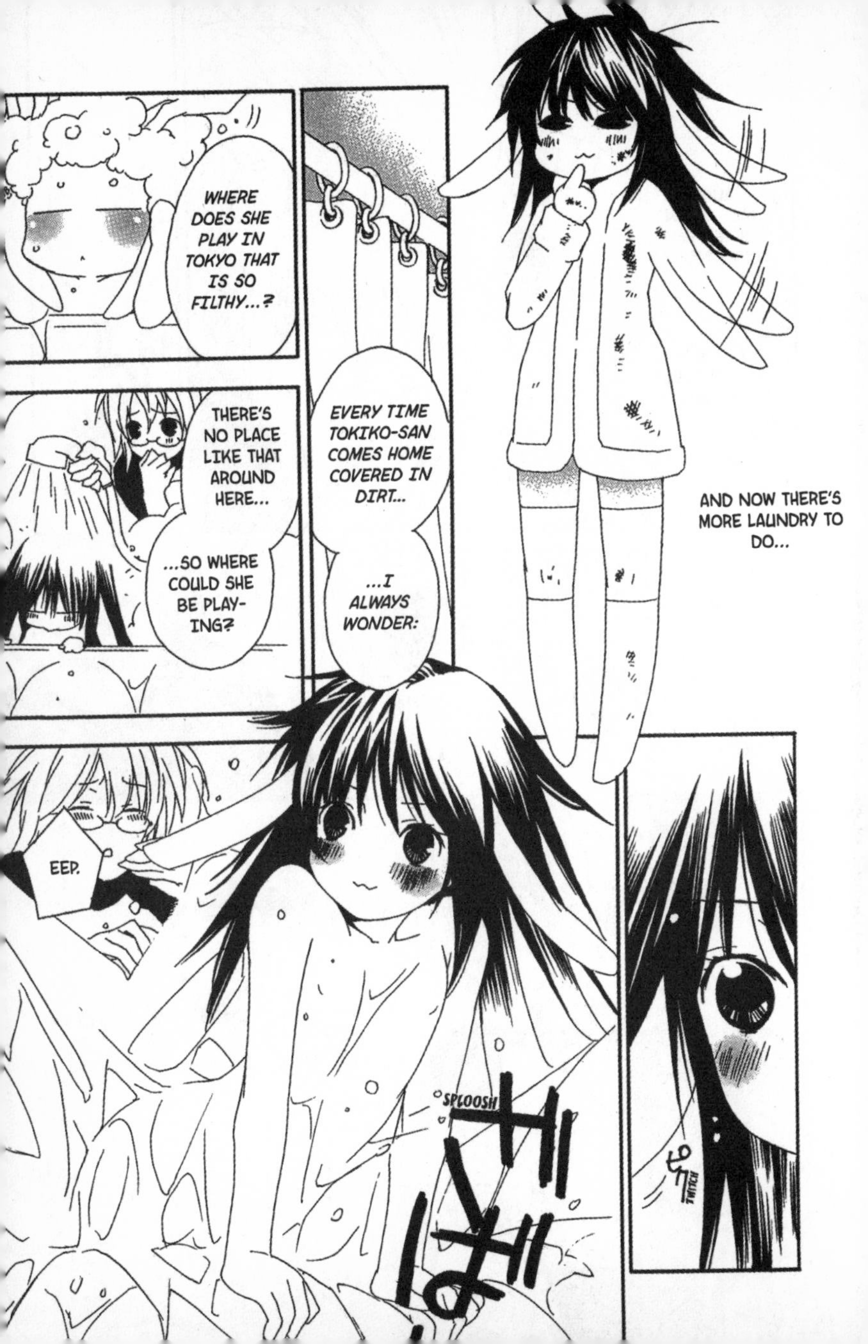
AND NOW THERE'S MORE LAUNDRY TO DO...
EVERY TIME TOKIKO-SAN COMES HOME COVERED IN DIRT...
...I ALWAYS WONDER:
WHERE DOES SHE PLAY IN TOKYO THAT IS SO FILTHY...?
THERE'S NO PLACE LIKE THAT AROUND HERE...
...SO WHERE COULD SHE BE PLAY-ING?
TWITCH
SPLOOSH
EEP.

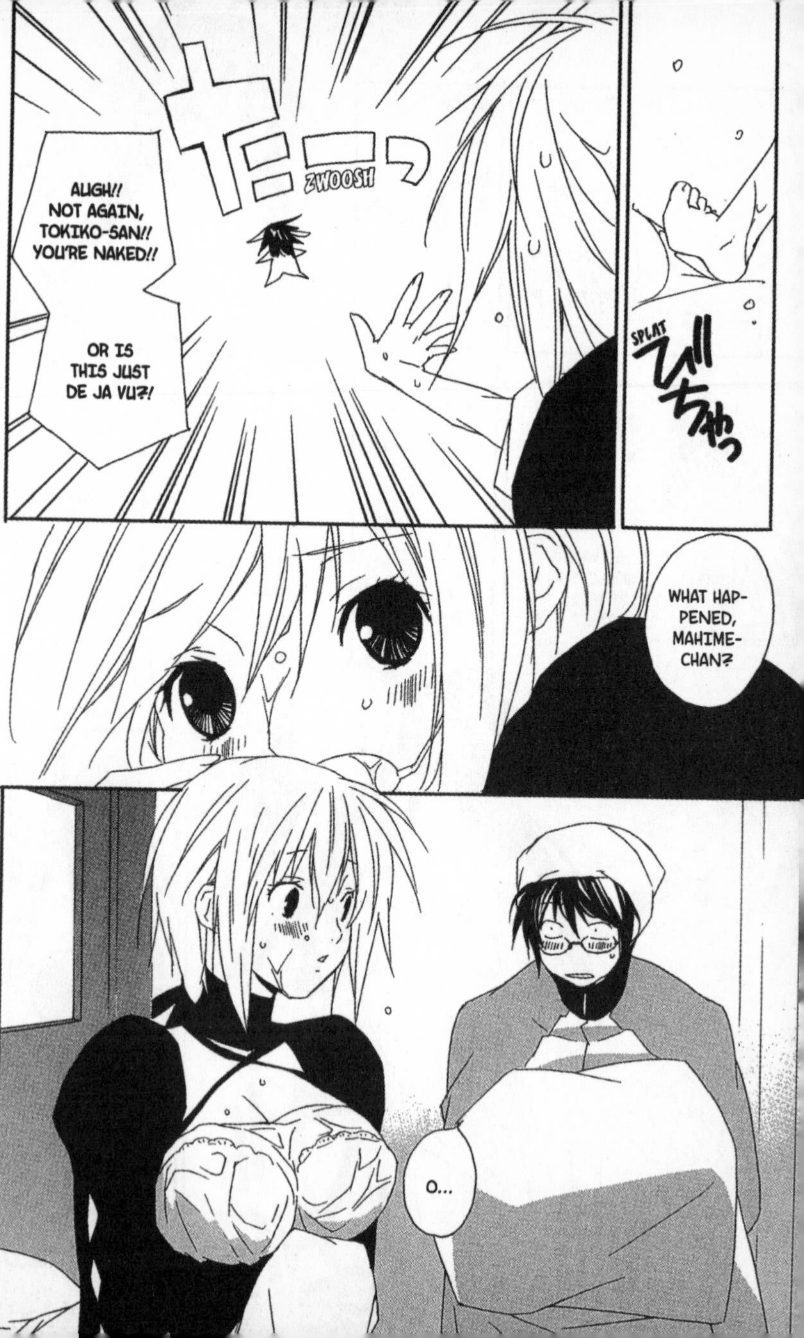
SPLAT
ZWOOSH
AUGH!! NOT AGAIN, TOKIKO-SAN!! YOU'RE NAKED!!
OR IS THIS JUST DE JA VU?!
WHAT HAP-PENED, MAHIME-CHAN?
O...

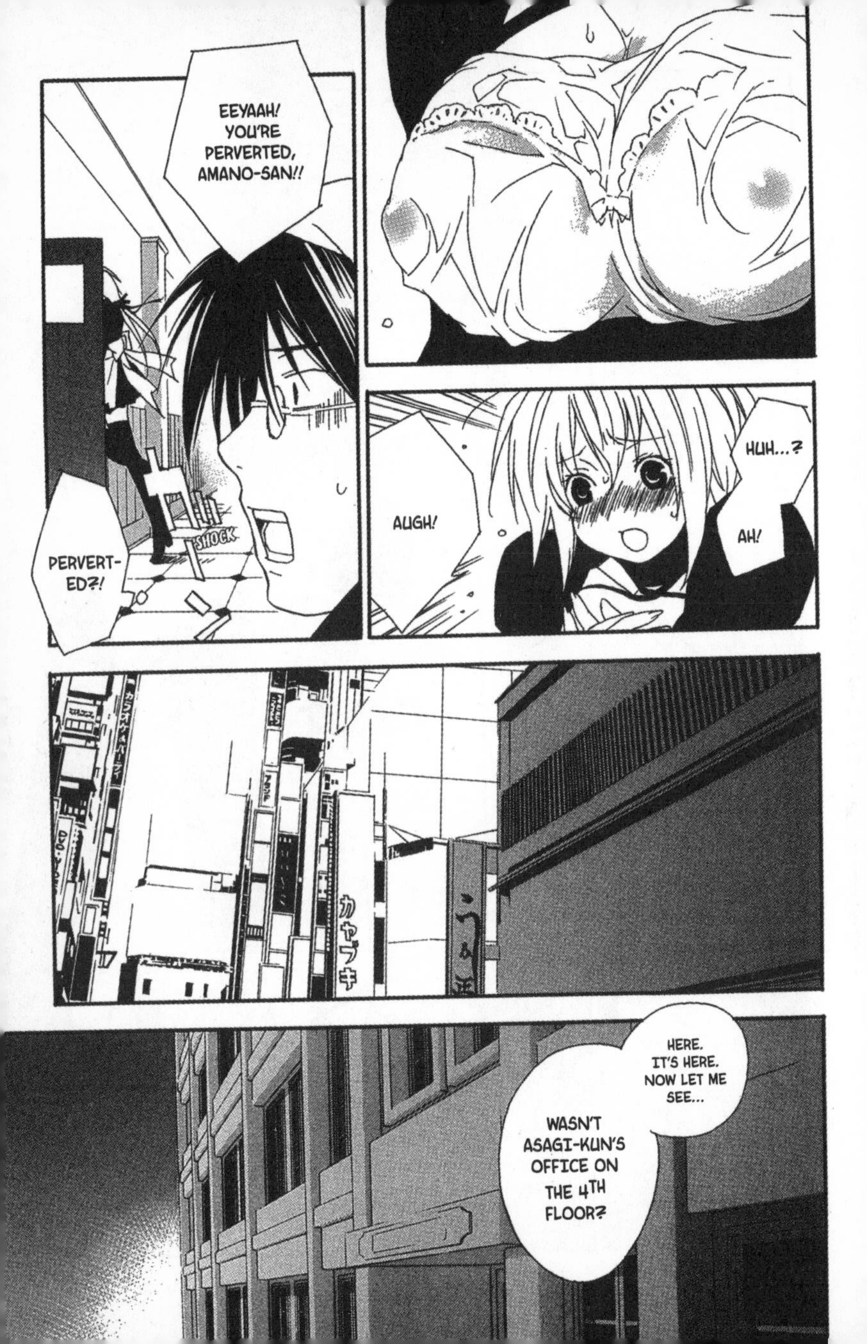
HUH...?
AH!
AUGH!
EEYAAH! YOU'RE PERVERTED, AMANO-SAN!!
SHOCK
PERVERTED?!
カヤブキ
HERE. IT'S HERE. NOW LET ME SEE...
WASN'T ASAGI-KUN'S OFFICE ON THE 4TH FLOOR?

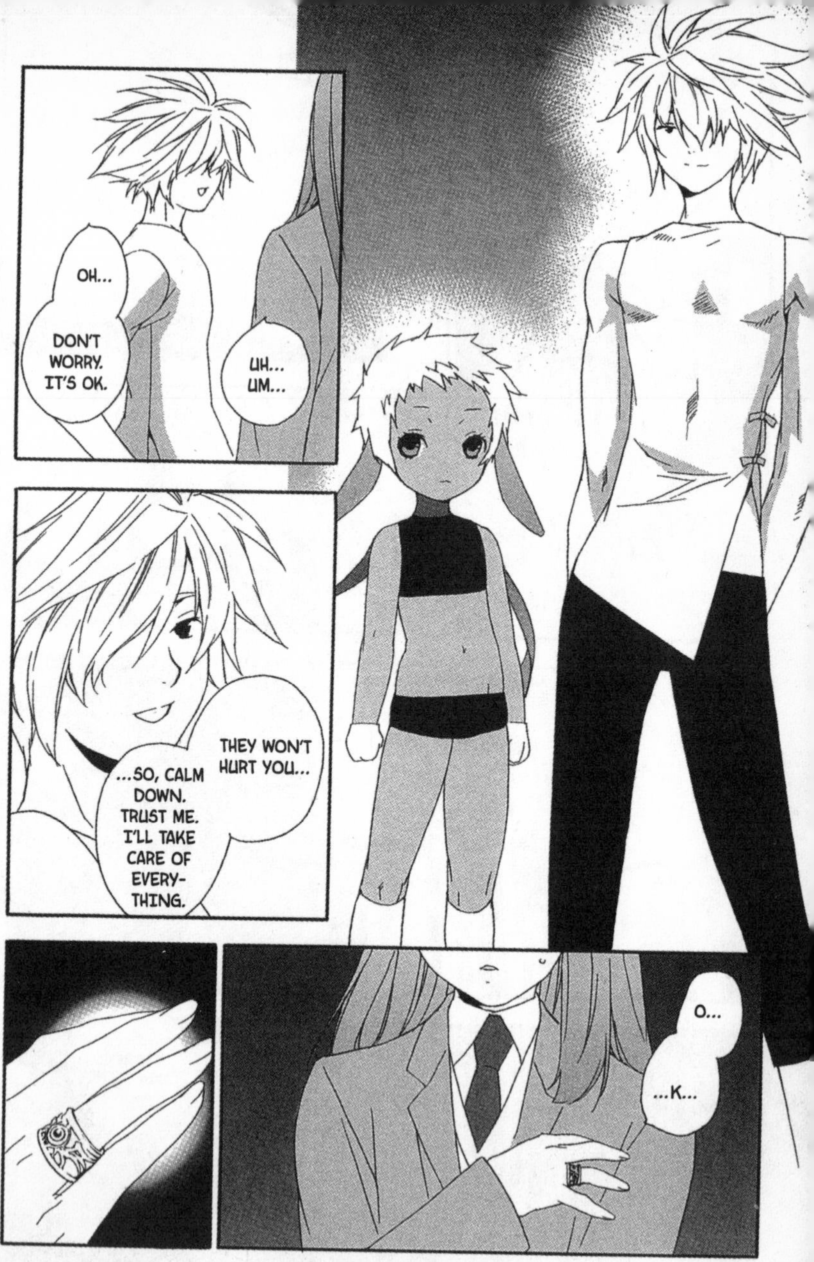
OH...
DON'T WORRY. IT'S OK.
UH... UM...
THEY WON'T HURT YOU...
...SO, CALM DOWN. TRUST ME. I'LL TAKE CARE OF EVERY-THING.
O...
...K...

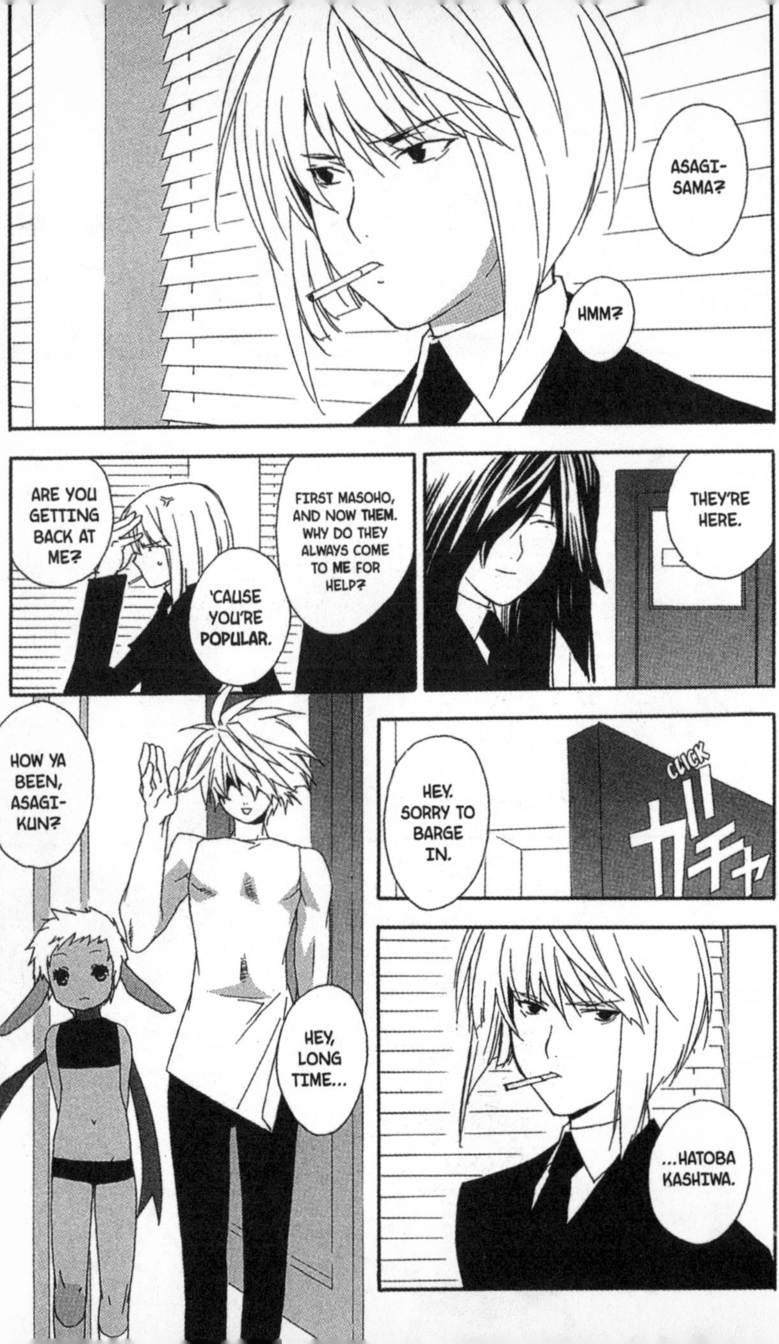
ASAGI-SAMA?
HMM?
THEY'RE HERE.
FIRST MASOHO, AND NOW THEM. WHY DO THEY ALWAYS COME TO ME FOR HELP?
'CAUSE YOU'RE POPULAR.
ARE YOU GETTING BACK AT ME?
CLICK
カチャ
HEY. SORRY TO BARGE IN.
...HATOBA KASHIWA.
HOW YA BEEN, ASAGI-KUN?
HEY, LONG TIME...

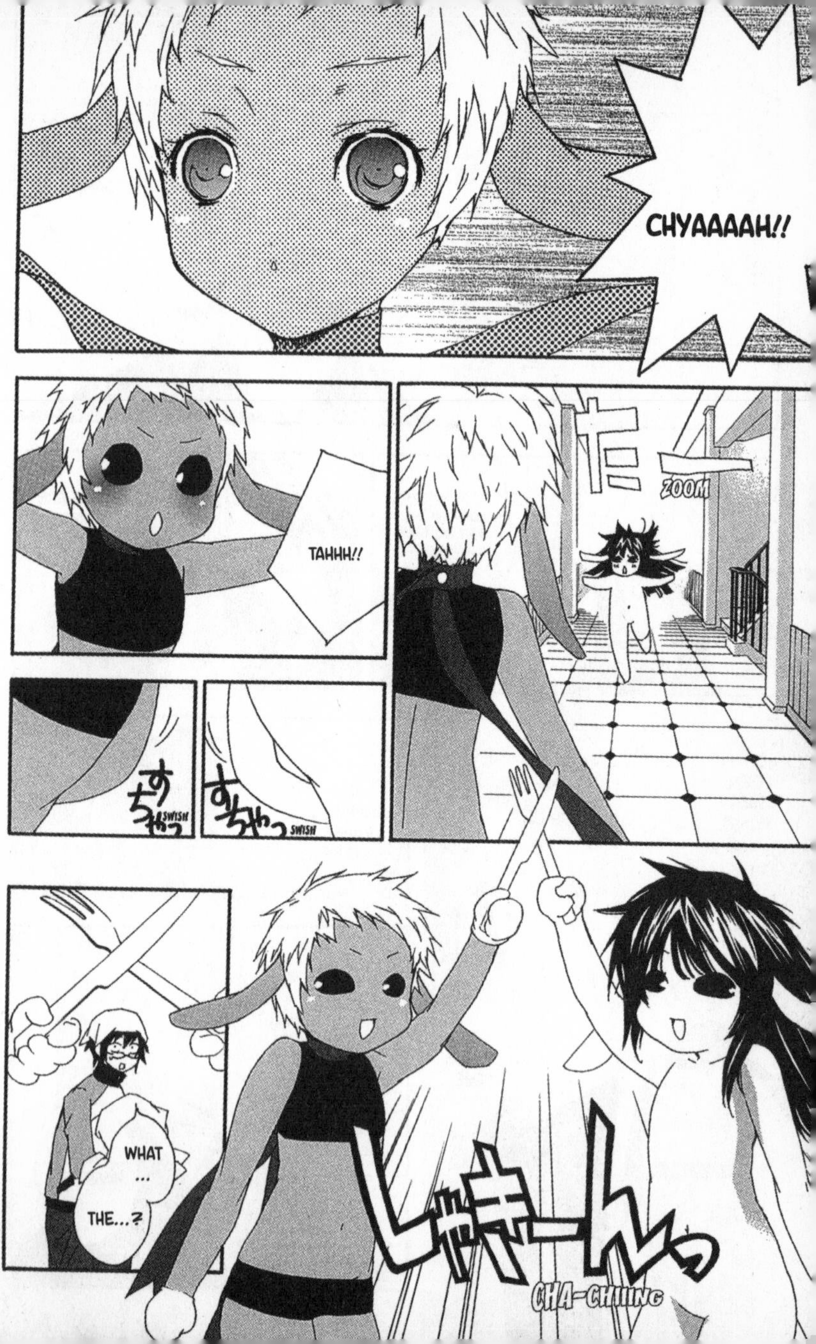
CHYAAAAH!!
たー
ZOOM
TAHHH!!
すちゃっ
SWISH
すちゃっ
SWISH
しゃきーんっ
CHA-CHIIING
WHAT ... THE...?

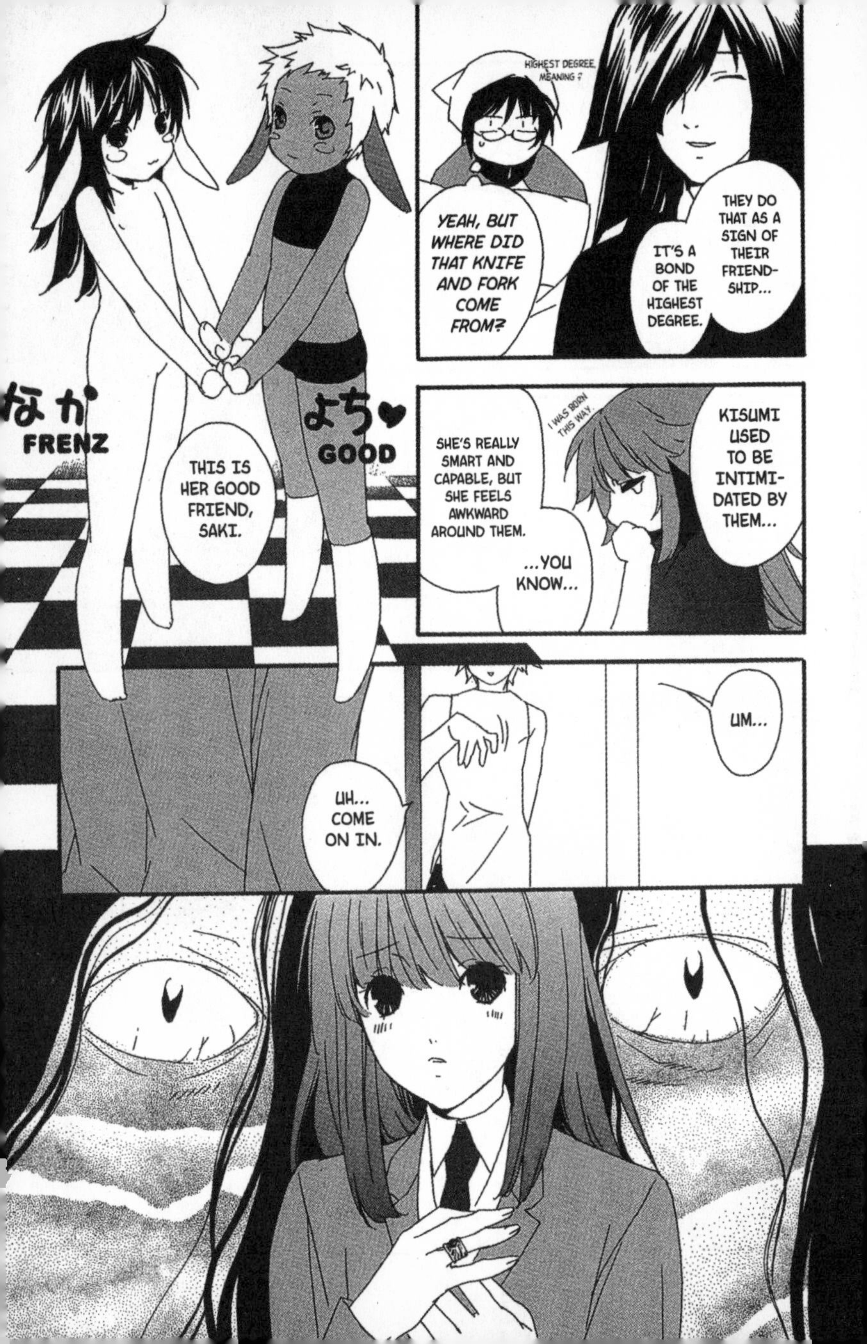
THEY DO THAT AS A SIGN OF THEIR FRIEND-SHIP...
IT'S A BOND OF THE HIGHEST DEGREE.
HIGHEST DEGREE, MEANING?
YEAH, BUT WHERE DID THAT KNIFE AND FORK COME FROM?
KISUMI USED TO BE INTIMI-DATED BY THEM...
I WAS BORN THIS WAY.
SHE'S REALLY SMART AND CAPABLE, BUT SHE FEELS AWKWARD AROUND THEM.
...YOU KNOW...
よち♥
GOOD
なが
FRENZ
THIS IS HER GOOD FRIEND, SAKI.
UM...
UH... COME ON IN.

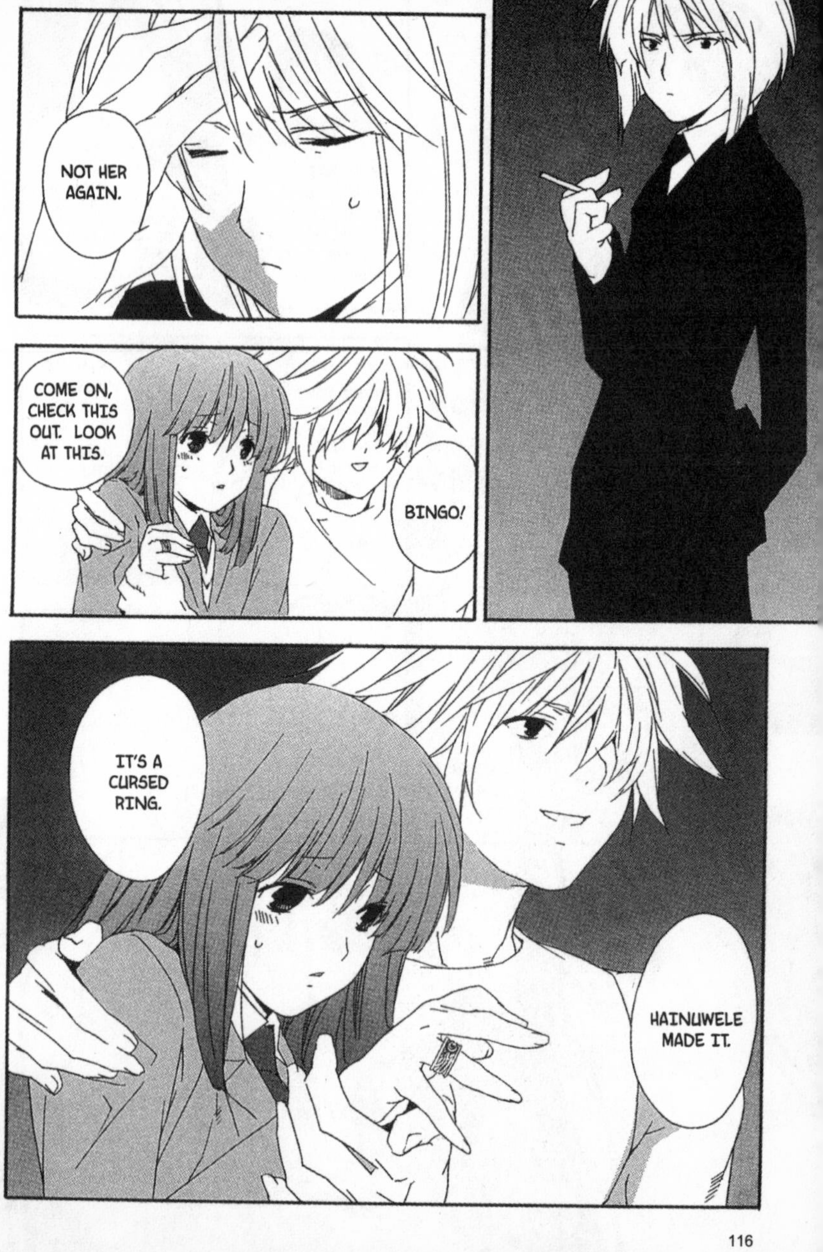
NOT HER AGAIN.
COME ON, CHECK THIS OUT. LOOK AT THIS.
BINGO!
IT'S A CURSED RING.
HAINUWELE MADE IT.

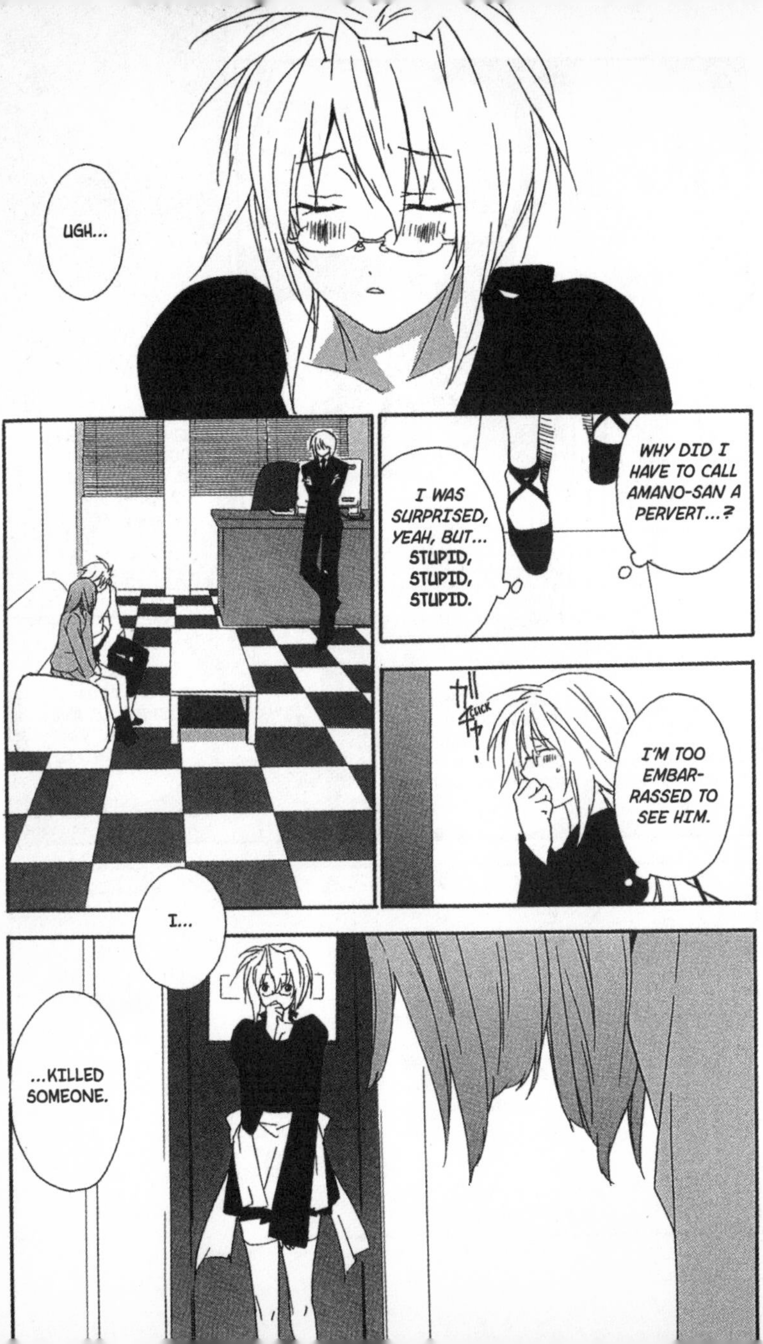
UGH...
WHY DID I HAVE TO CALL AMANO-SAN A PERVERT...?
I WAS SURPRISED, YEAH, BUT... STUPID, STUPID, STUPID.
CLICK
I'M TOO EMBAR-RASSED TO SEE HIM.
I...
...KILLED SOMEONE.

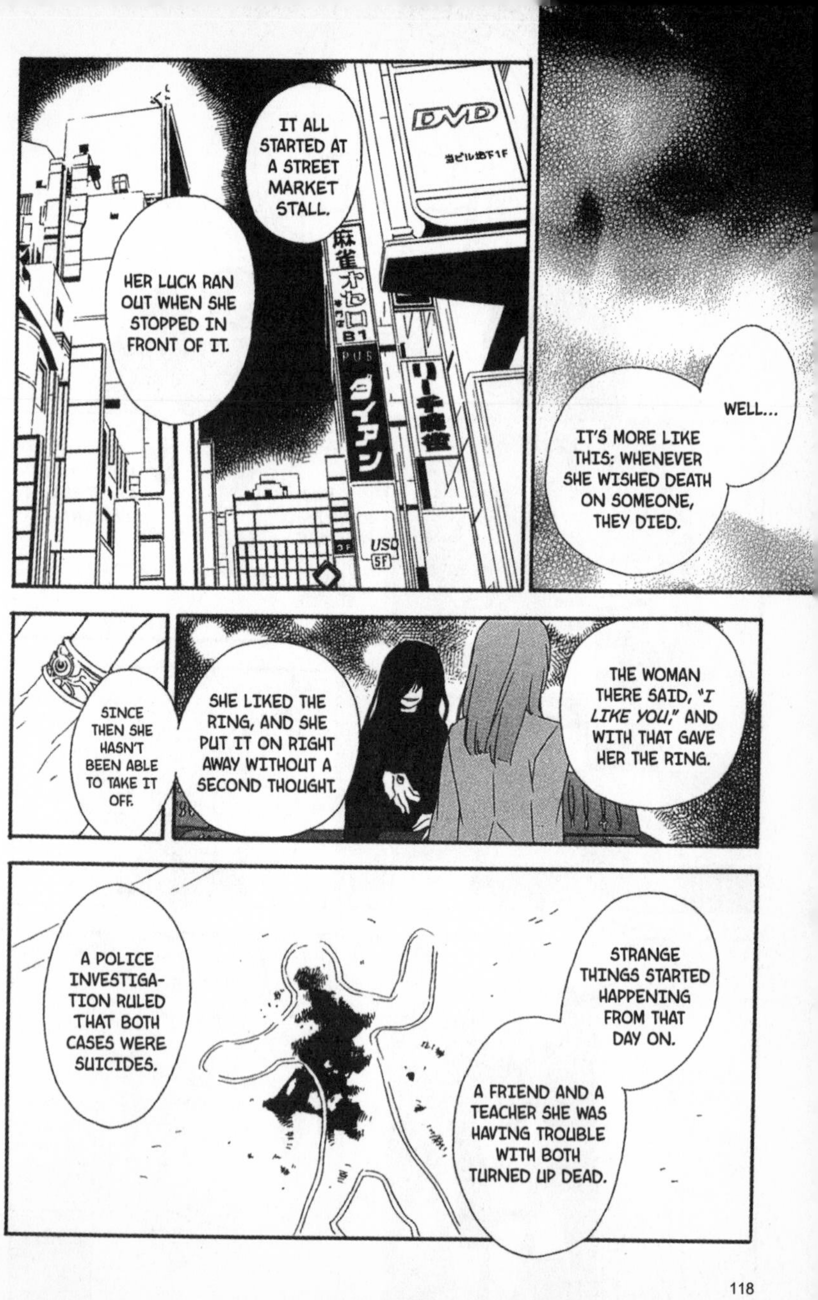
WELL...
IT'S MORE LIKE THIS: WHENEVER SHE WISHED DEATH ON SOMEONE, THEY DIED.
DVD
当ビル地下1F
IT ALL STARTED AT A STREET MARKET STALL.
HER LUCK RAN OUT WHEN SHE STOPPED IN FRONT OF IT.
麻雀
B1
ダイアン
USO
5F
THE WOMAN THERE SAID, "*I LIKE YOU,*" AND WITH THAT GAVE HER THE RING.
SHE LIKED THE RING, AND SHE PUT IT ON RIGHT AWAY WITHOUT A SECOND THOUGHT.
SINCE THEN SHE HASN'T BEEN ABLE TO TAKE IT OFF.
STRANGE THINGS STARTED HAPPENING FROM THAT DAY ON.
A FRIEND AND A TEACHER SHE WAS HAVING TROUBLE WITH BOTH TURNED UP DEAD.
A POLICE INVESTIGATION RULED THAT BOTH CASES WERE SUICIDES.

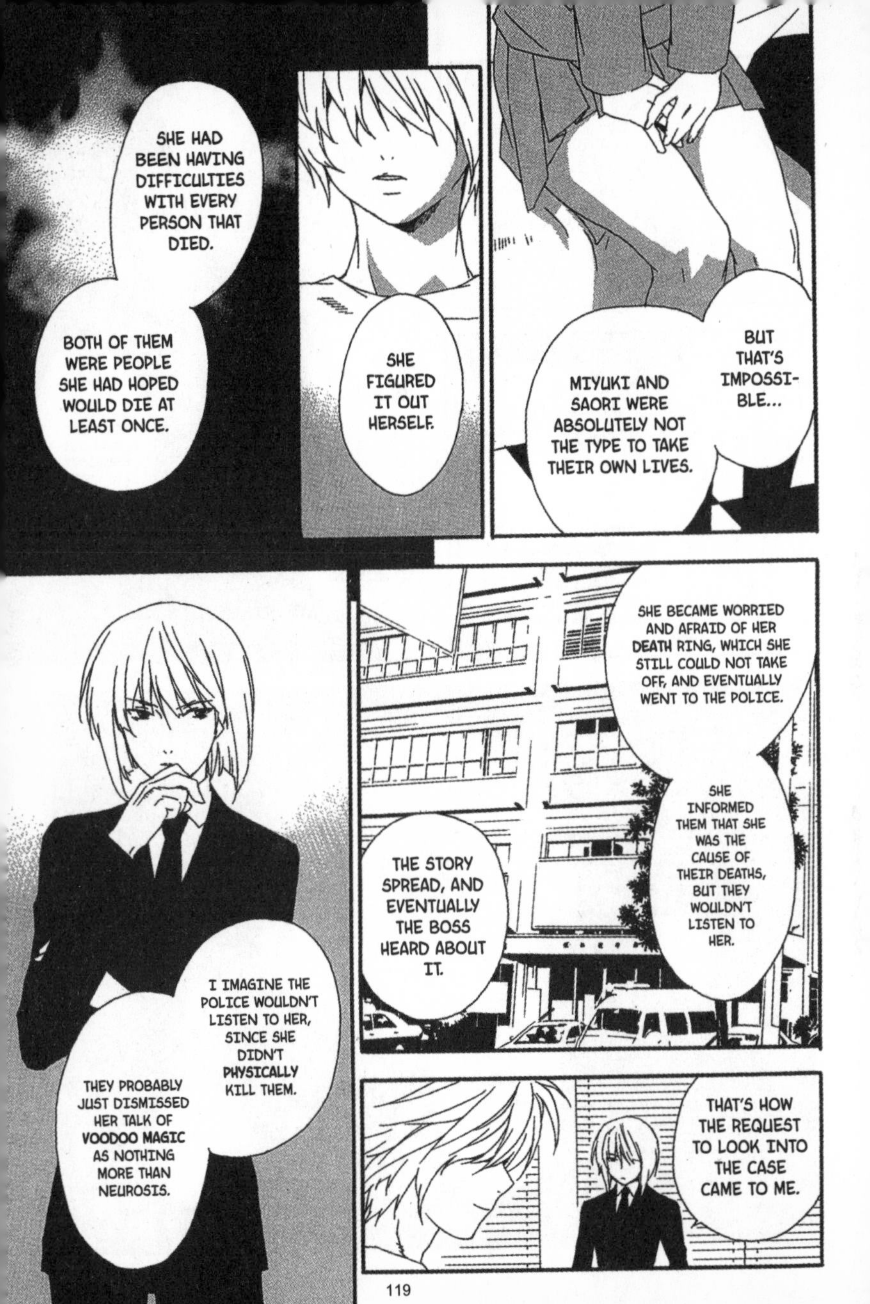
BUT THAT'S IMPOSSI-BLE...
MIYUKI AND SAORI WERE ABSOLUTELY NOT THE TYPE TO TAKE THEIR OWN LIVES.
SHE FIGURED IT OUT HERSELF.
SHE HAD BEEN HAVING DIFFICULTIES WITH EVERY PERSON THAT DIED.
BOTH OF THEM WERE PEOPLE SHE HAD HOPED WOULD DIE AT LEAST ONCE.
SHE BECAME WORRIED AND AFRAID OF HER DEATH RING, WHICH SHE STILL COULD NOT TAKE OFF, AND EVENTUALLY WENT TO THE POLICE.
SHE INFORMED THEM THAT SHE WAS THE CAUSE OF THEIR DEATHS, BUT THEY WOULDN'T LISTEN TO HER.
THE STORY SPREAD, AND EVENTUALLY THE BOSS HEARD ABOUT IT.
THAT'S HOW THE REQUEST TO LOOK INTO THE CASE CAME TO ME.
I IMAGINE THE POLICE WOULDN'T LISTEN TO HER, SINCE SHE DIDN'T PHYSICALLY KILL THEM.
THEY PROBABLY JUST DISMISSED HER TALK OF VOODOO MAGIC AS NOTHING MORE THAN NEUROSIS.

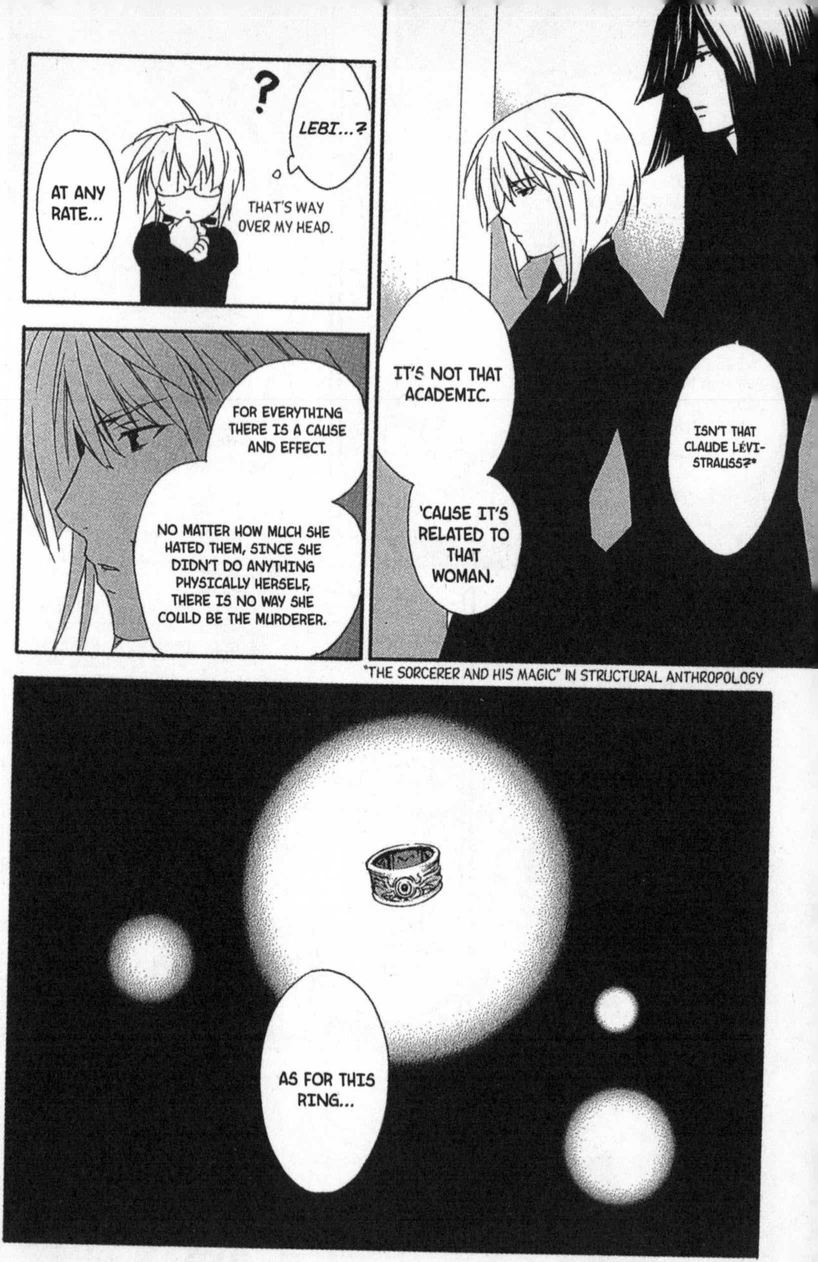
ISN'T THAT CLAUDE LÉVI-STRAUSS?*
IT'S NOT THAT ACADEMIC.
'CAUSE IT'S RELATED TO THAT WOMAN.
?
LEBI...?
THAT'S WAY OVER MY HEAD.
AT ANY RATE...
FOR EVERYTHING THERE IS A CAUSE AND EFFECT.
NO MATTER HOW MUCH SHE HATED THEM, SINCE SHE DIDN'T DO ANYTHING PHYSICALLY HERSELF, THERE IS NO WAY SHE COULD BE THE MURDERER.
AS FOR THIS RING...

*"THE SORCERER AND HIS MAGIC" IN STRUCTURAL ANTHROPOLOGY

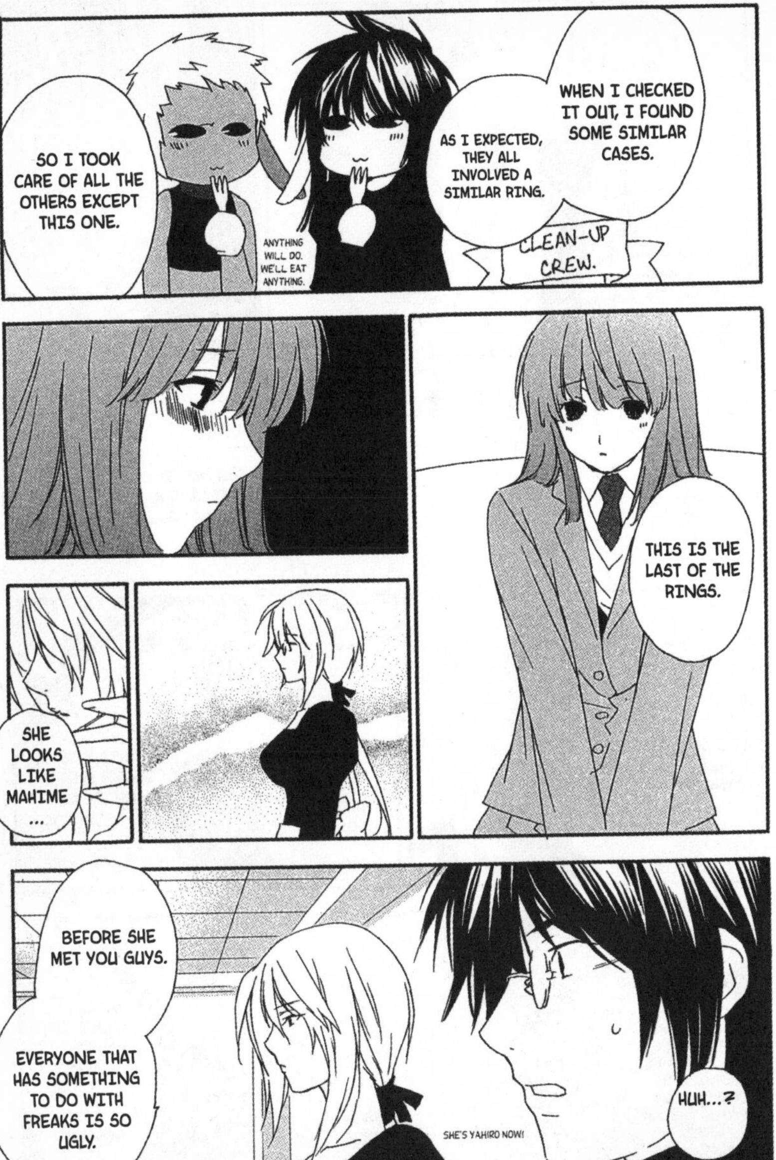
WHEN I CHECKED IT OUT, I FOUND SOME SIMILAR CASES.
AS I EXPECTED, THEY ALL INVOLVED A SIMILAR RING.
CLEAN-UP CREW.
ANYTHING WILL DO. WE'LL EAT ANYTHING.
SO I TOOK CARE OF ALL THE OTHERS EXCEPT THIS ONE.
THIS IS THE LAST OF THE RINGS.
SHE LOOKS LIKE MAHIME ...
BEFORE SHE MET YOU GUYS.
EVERYONE THAT HAS SOMETHING TO DO WITH FREAKS IS SO UGLY.
HUH...?
SHE'S YAHIRO NOW!

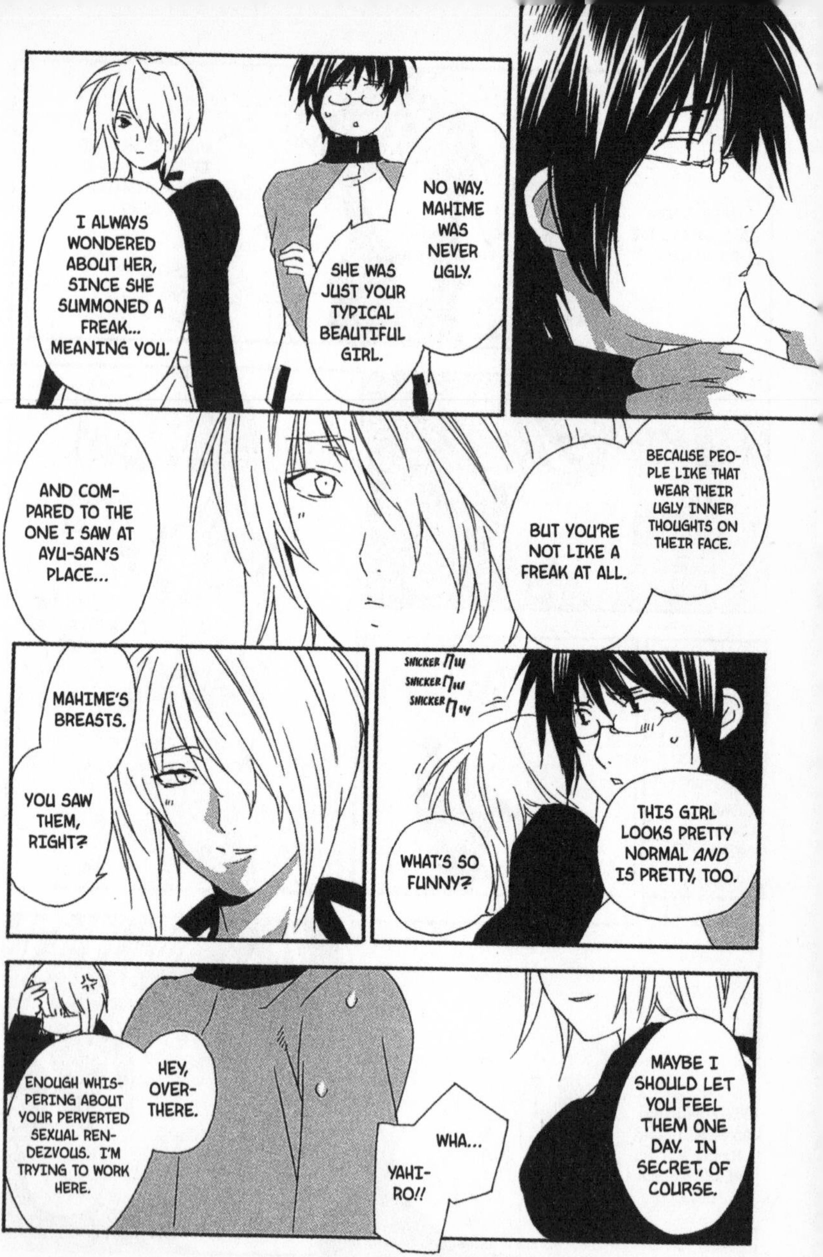
NO WAY. MAHIME WAS NEVER UGLY.
SHE WAS JUST YOUR TYPICAL BEAUTIFUL GIRL.
I ALWAYS WONDERED ABOUT HER, SINCE SHE SUMMONED A FREAK... MEANING YOU.
BECAUSE PEOPLE LIKE THAT WEAR THEIR UGLY INNER THOUGHTS ON THEIR FACE.
BUT YOU'RE NOT LIKE A FREAK AT ALL.
AND COMPARED TO THE ONE I SAW AT AYU-SAN'S PLACE...
SHICKER
SHICKER
SHICKER
THIS GIRL LOOKS PRETTY NORMAL *AND* IS PRETTY, TOO.
WHAT'S SO FUNNY?
MAHIME'S BREASTS.
YOU SAW THEM, RIGHT?
MAYBE I SHOULD LET YOU FEEL THEM ONE DAY. IN SECRET, OF COURSE.
WHA...
YAHIRO!!
HEY, OVER-THERE.
ENOUGH WHISPERING ABOUT YOUR PERVERTED SEXUAL RENDEZVOUS. I'M TRYING TO WORK HERE.

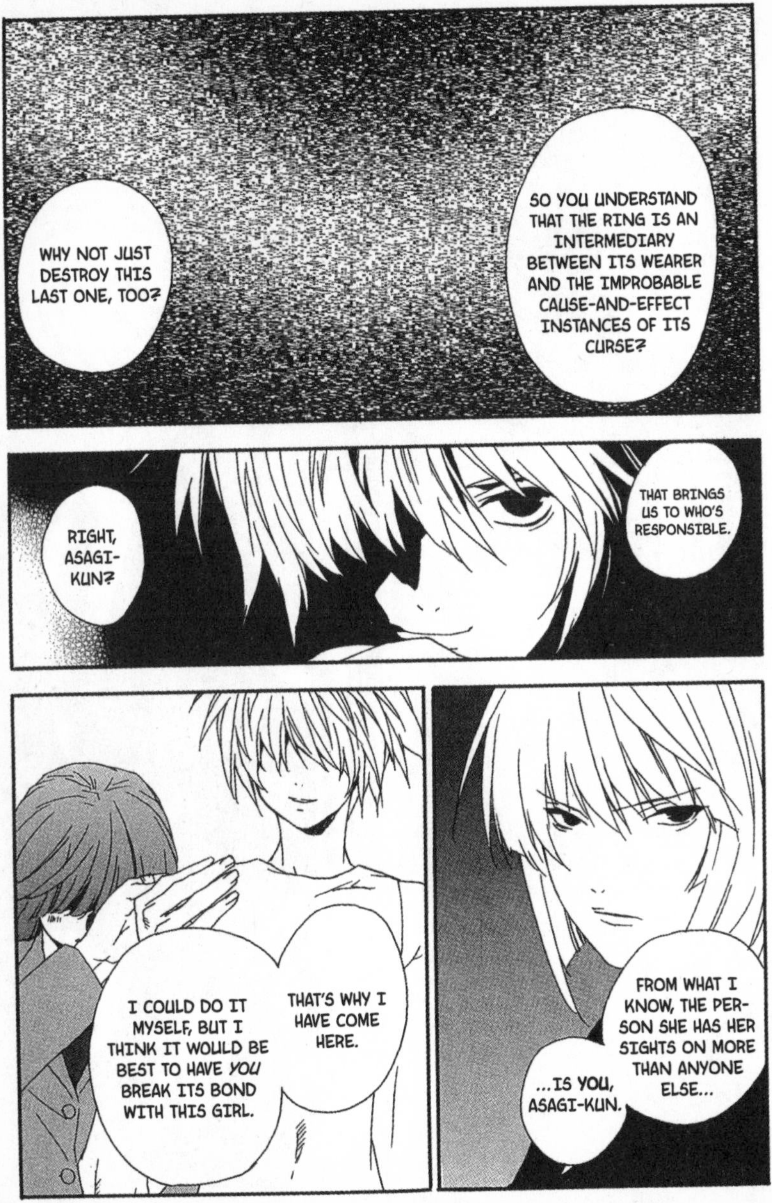
SO YOU UNDERSTAND THAT THE RING IS AN INTERMEDIARY BETWEEN ITS WEARER AND THE IMPROBABLE CAUSE-AND-EFFECT INSTANCES OF ITS CURSE?
WHY NOT JUST DESTROY THIS LAST ONE, TOO?
THAT BRINGS US TO WHO'S RESPONSIBLE.
RIGHT, ASAGI-KUN?
FROM WHAT I KNOW, THE PER-SON SHE HAS HER SIGHTS ON MORE THAN ANYONE ELSE...
...IS YOU, ASAGI-KUN.
THAT'S WHY I HAVE COME HERE.
I COULD DO IT MYSELF, BUT I THINK IT WOULD BE BEST TO HAVE *YOU* BREAK ITS BOND WITH THIS GIRL.

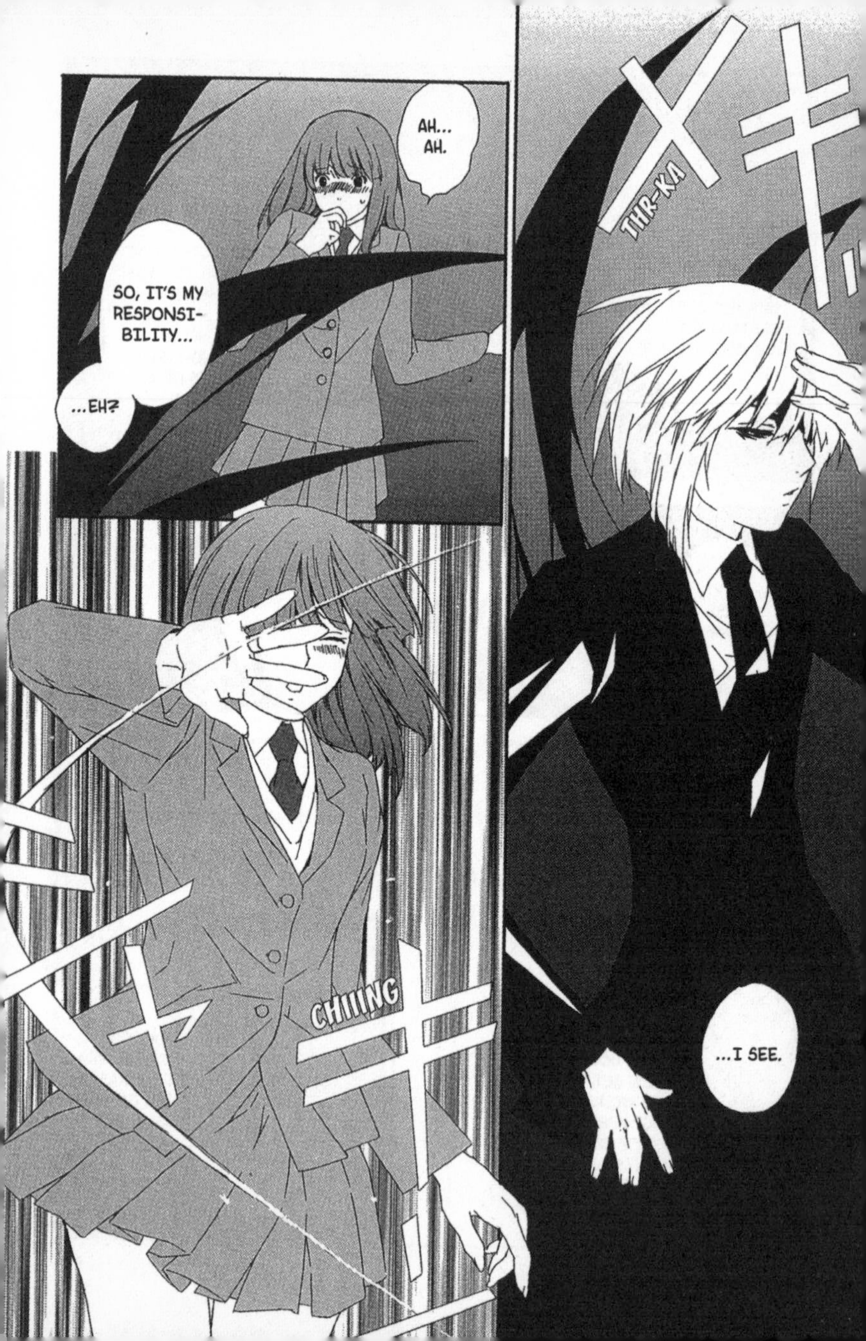
THR-KA
...I SEE.
AH... AH.
SO, IT'S MY RESPONSI-BILITY...
...EH?
CHIIING

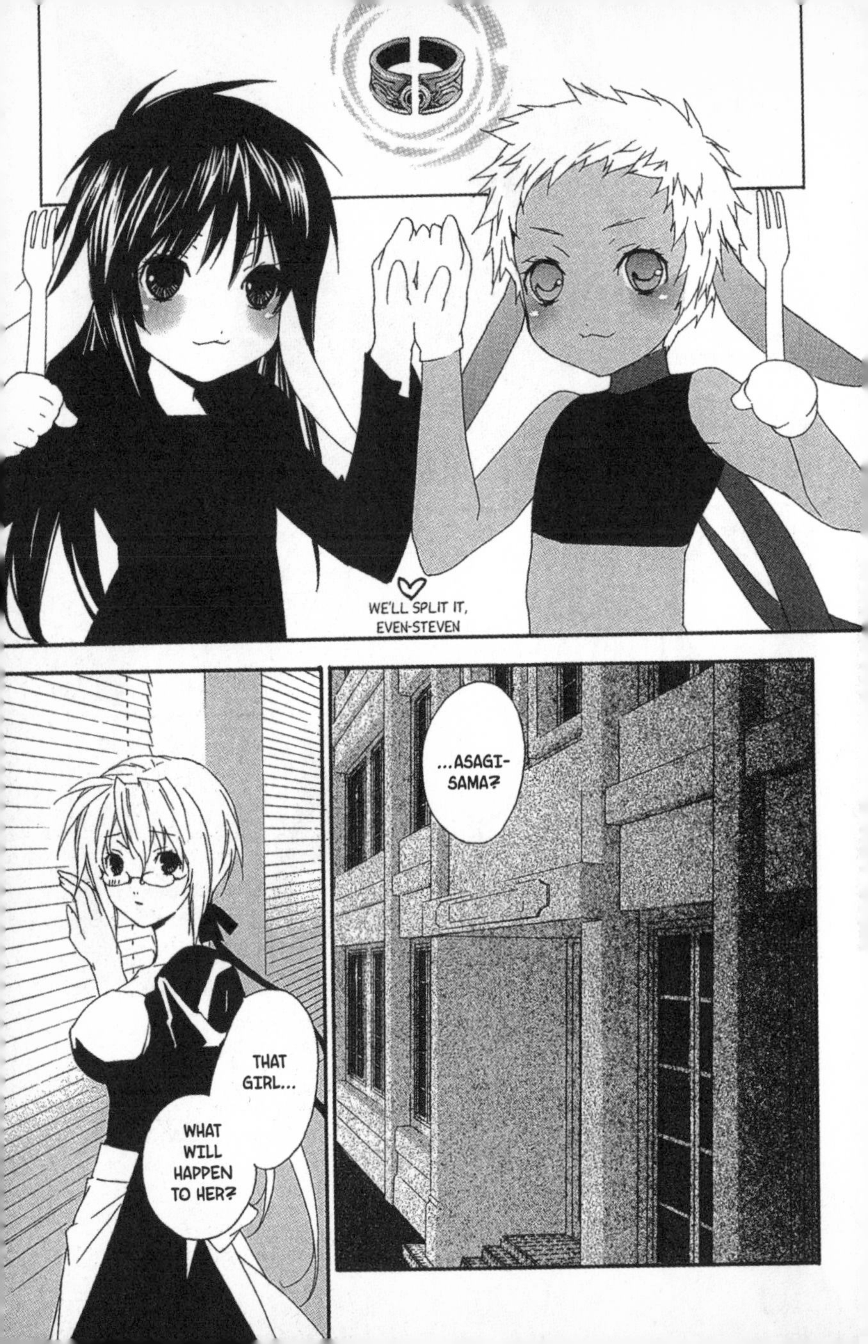
WE'LL SPLIT IT, EVEN-STEVEN
...ASAGI-SAMA?
THAT GIRL...
WHAT WILL HAPPEN TO HER?

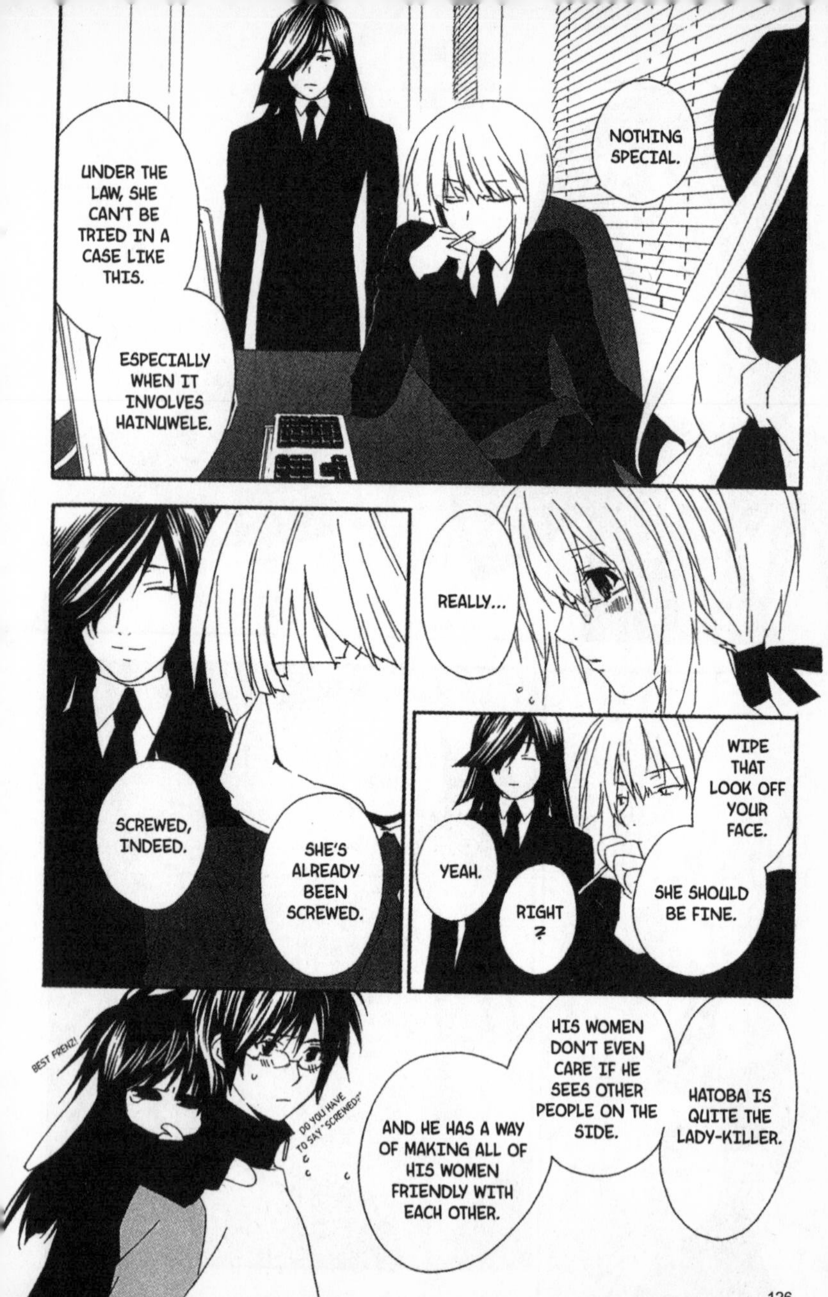
NOTHING SPECIAL.
UNDER THE LAW, SHE CAN'T BE TRIED IN A CASE LIKE THIS.
ESPECIALLY WHEN IT INVOLVES HAINUWELE.
REALLY...
WIPE THAT LOOK OFF YOUR FACE.
SHE SHOULD BE FINE.
RIGHT?
YEAH.
SHE'S ALREADY BEEN SCREWED.
SCREWED, INDEED.
HATOBA IS QUITE THE LADY-KILLER.
HIS WOMEN DON'T EVEN CARE IF HE SEES OTHER PEOPLE ON THE SIDE.
AND HE HAS A WAY OF MAKING ALL OF HIS WOMEN FRIENDLY WITH EACH OTHER.
DO YOU HAVE TO SAY "SCREWED?"
BEST FRENZ!

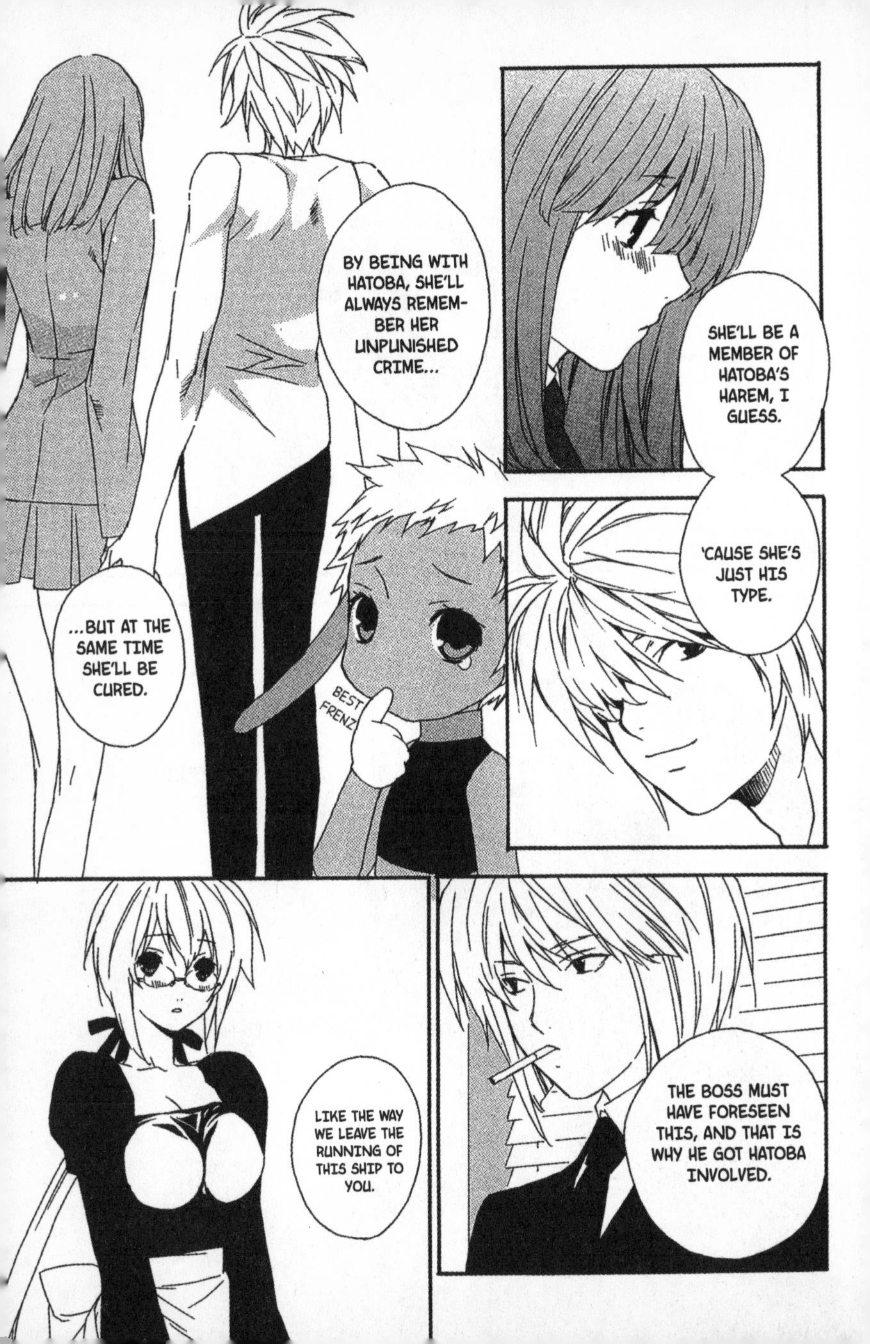
SHE'LL BE A MEMBER OF HATOBA'S HAREM, I GUESS.
'CAUSE SHE'S JUST HIS TYPE.
BY BEING WITH HATOBA, SHE'LL ALWAYS REMEM-BER HER UNPUNISHED CRIME...
...BUT AT THE SAME TIME SHE'LL BE CURED.
BEST FRENZ
THE BOSS MUST HAVE FORESEEN THIS, AND THAT IS WHY HE GOT HATOBA INVOLVED.
LIKE THE WAY WE LEAVE THE RUNNING OF THIS SHIP TO YOU.

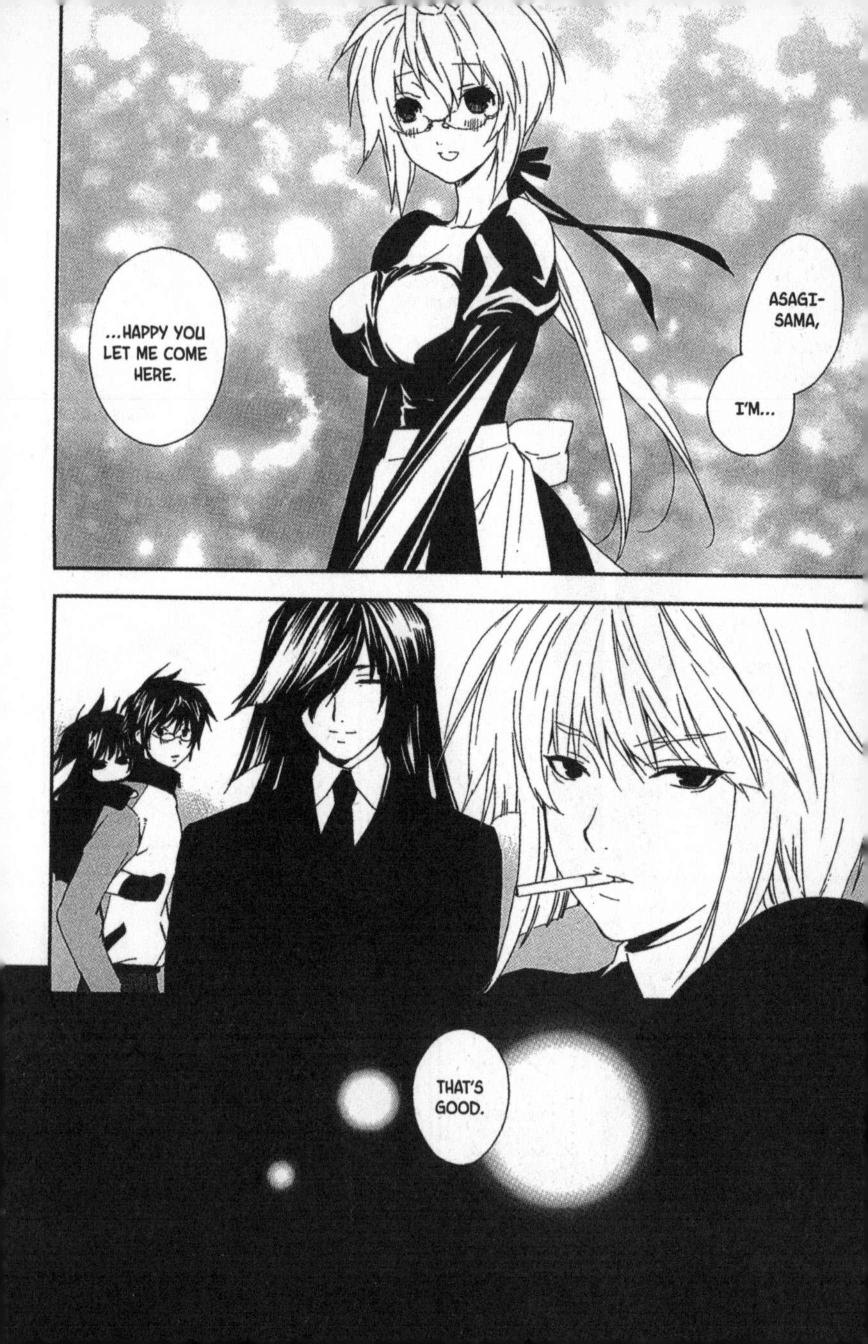
ASAGI-SAMA,
I'M...
...HAPPY YOU LET ME COME HERE.
THAT'S GOOD.

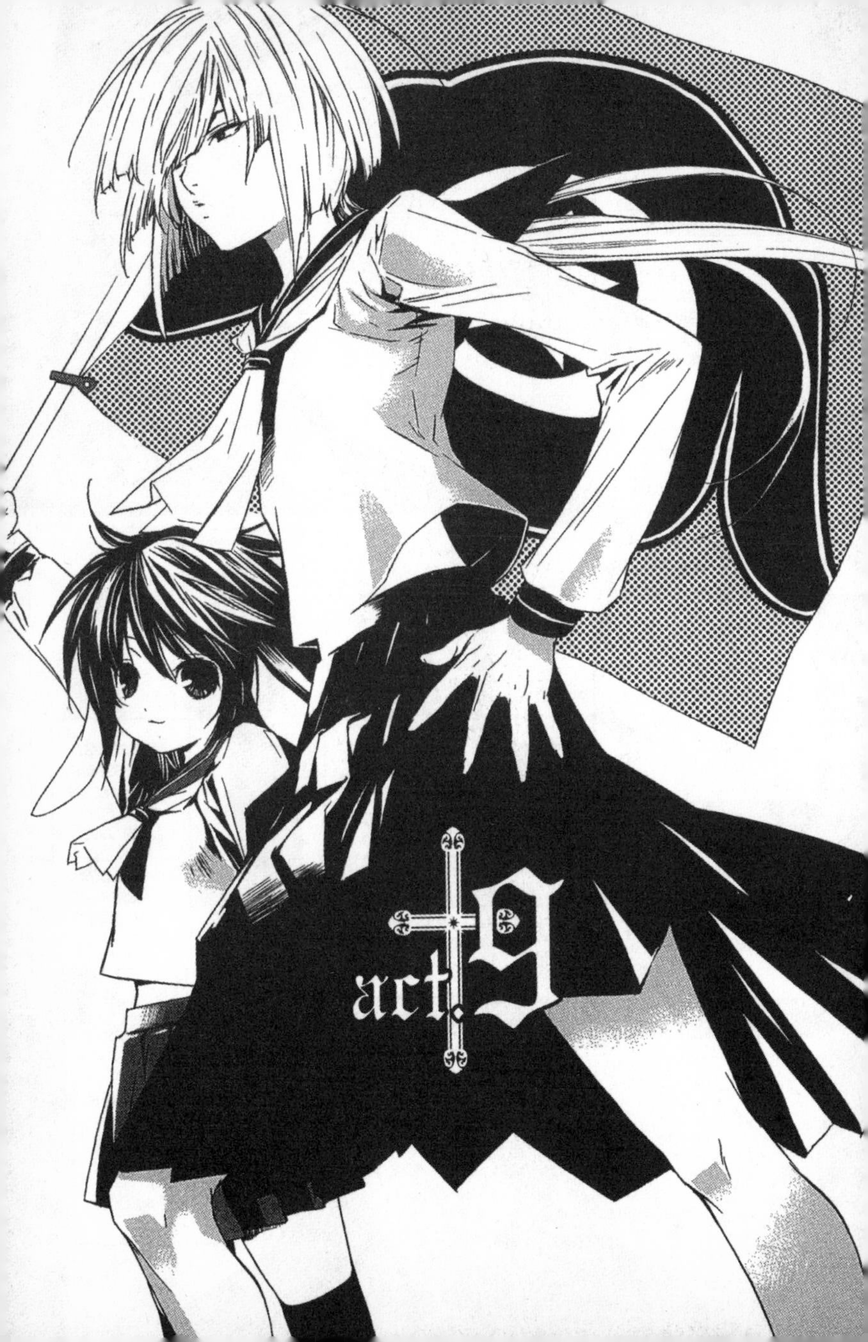
act. 9

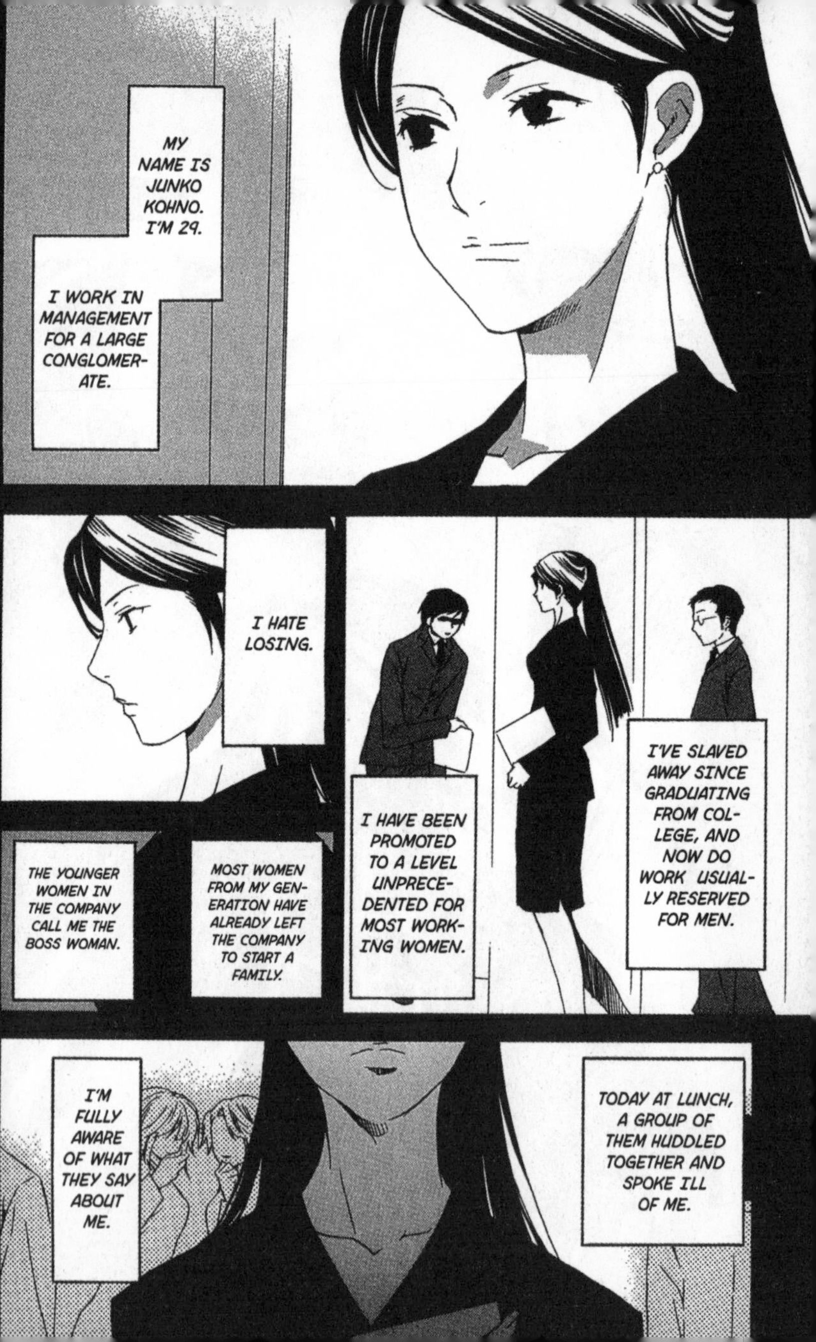
MY NAME IS JUNKO KOHNO. I'M 29.
I WORK IN MANAGEMENT FOR A LARGE CONGLOMER-ATE.
I'VE SLAVED AWAY SINCE GRADUATING FROM COL-LEGE, AND NOW DO WORK USUAL-LY RESERVED FOR MEN.
I HAVE BEEN PROMOTED TO A LEVEL UNPRECE-DENTED FOR MOST WORK-ING WOMEN.
I HATE LOSING.
MOST WOMEN FROM MY GEN-ERATION HAVE ALREADY LEFT THE COMPANY TO START A FAMILY.
THE YOUNGER WOMEN IN THE COMPANY CALL ME THE BOSS WOMAN.
TODAY AT LUNCH, A GROUP OF THEM HUDDLED TOGETHER AND SPOKE ILL OF ME.
I'M FULLY AWARE OF WHAT THEY SAY ABOUT ME.

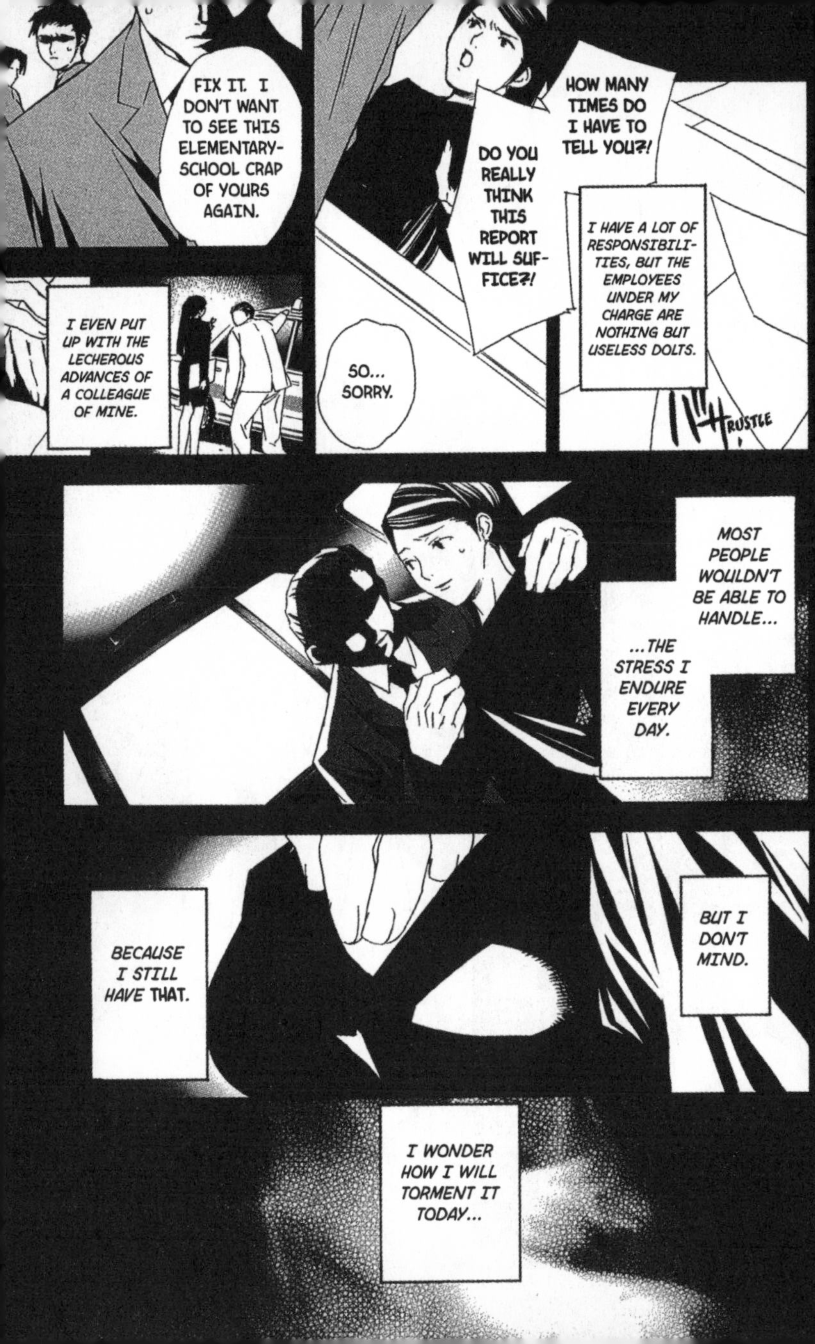
HOW MANY TIMES DO I HAVE TO TELL YOU?!
I HAVE A LOT OF RESPONSIBILI-TIES, BUT THE EMPLOYEES UNDER MY CHARGE ARE NOTHING BUT USELESS DOLTS.
RUSTLE
DO YOU REALLY THINK THIS REPORT WILL SUF-FICE?!
SO... SORRY.
FIX IT. I DON'T WANT TO SEE THIS ELEMENTARY-SCHOOL CRAP OF YOURS AGAIN.
I EVEN PUT UP WITH THE LECHEROUS ADVANCES OF A COLLEAGUE OF MINE.
MOST PEOPLE WOULDN'T BE ABLE TO HANDLE...
...THE STRESS I ENDURE EVERY DAY.
BUT I DON'T MIND.
BECAUSE I STILL HAVE THAT.
I WONDER HOW I WILL TORMENT IT TODAY...

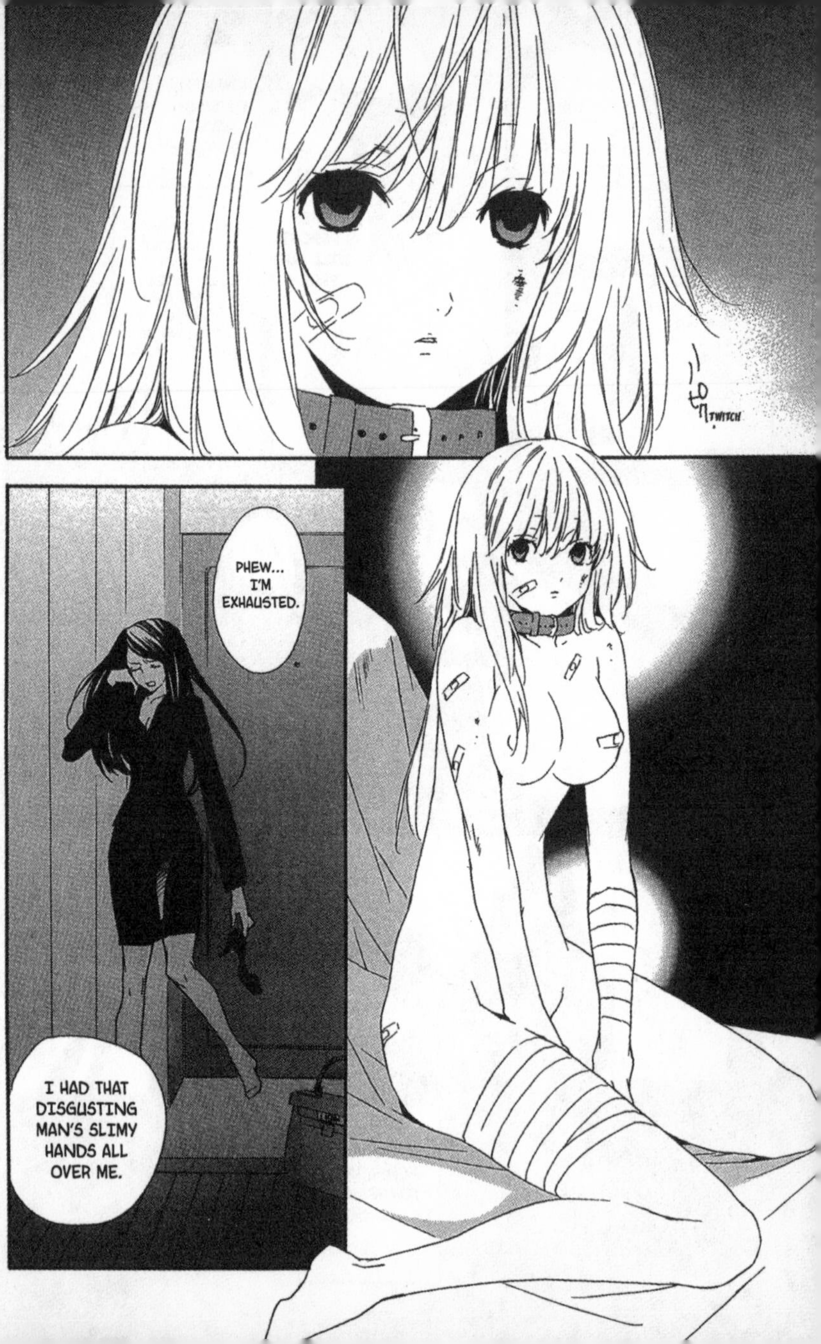
TWITCH
PHEW... I'M EXHAUSTED.
I HAD THAT DISGUSTING MAN'S SLIMY HANDS ALL OVER ME.

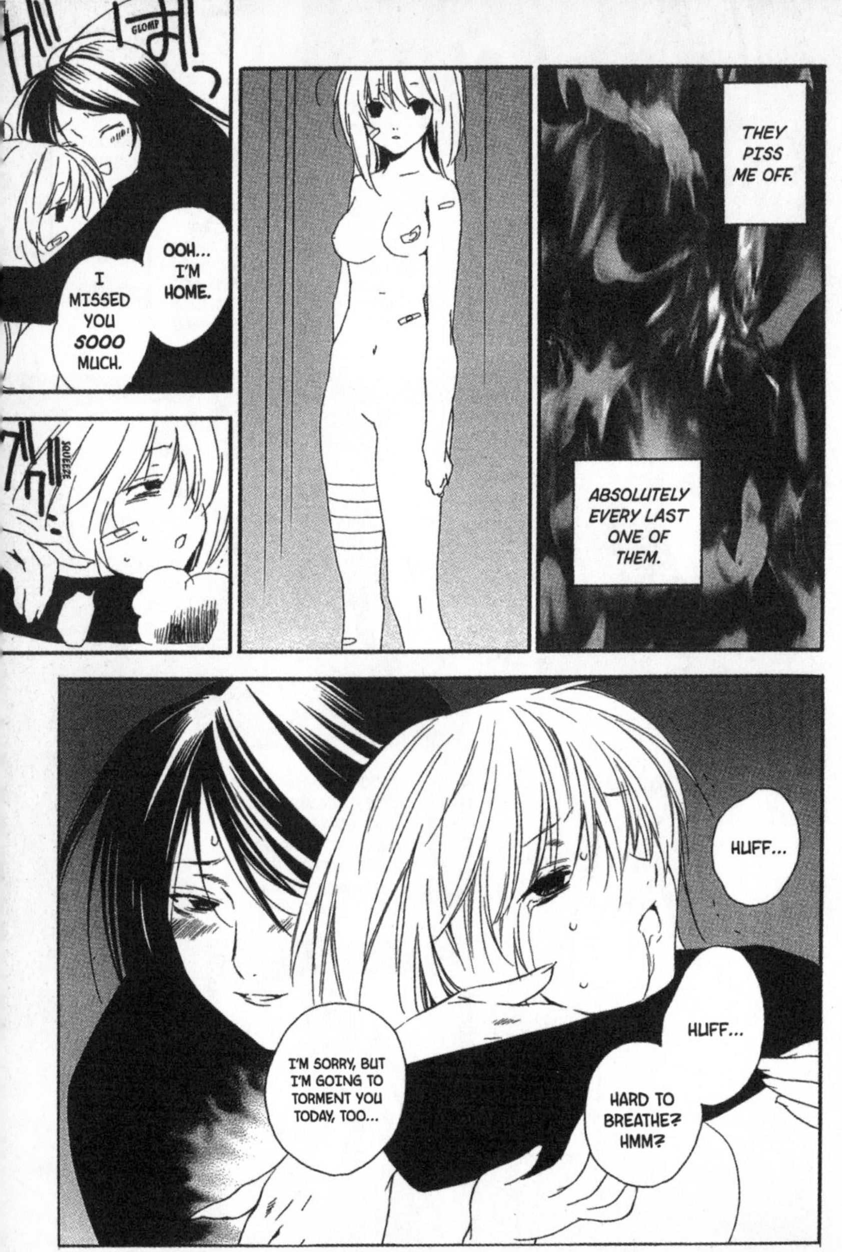
THEY PISS ME OFF.
ABSOLUTELY EVERY LAST ONE OF THEM.
GLOMP
OOH... I'M HOME.
I MISSED YOU *SOOO* MUCH.
SQUEEZE
HUFF...
HUFF...
HARD TO BREATHE? HMM?
I'M SORRY, BUT I'M GOING TO TORMENT YOU TODAY, TOO...

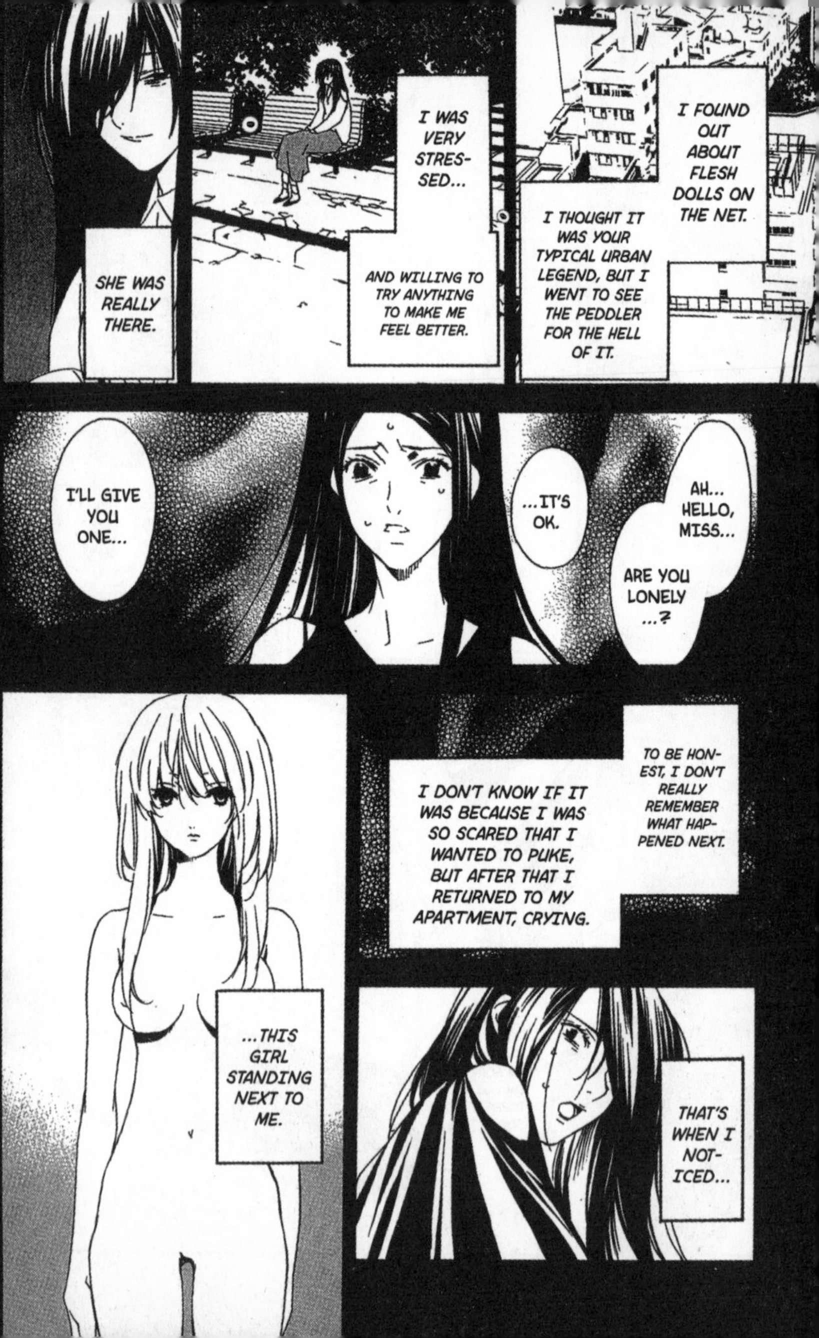
I FOUND OUT ABOUT FLESH DOLLS ON THE NET.
I THOUGHT IT WAS YOUR TYPICAL URBAN LEGEND, BUT I WENT TO SEE THE PEDDLER FOR THE HELL OF IT.
I WAS VERY STRES-SED...
AND WILLING TO TRY ANYTHING TO MAKE ME FEEL BETTER.
SHE WAS REALLY THERE.
AH... HELLO, MISS...
ARE YOU LONELY ...?
...IT'S OK.
I'LL GIVE YOU ONE...
TO BE HON-EST, I DON'T REALLY REMEMBER WHAT HAP-PENED NEXT.
I DON'T KNOW IF IT WAS BECAUSE I WAS SO SCARED THAT I WANTED TO PUKE, BUT AFTER THAT I RETURNED TO MY APARTMENT, CRYING.
THAT'S WHEN I NOT-ICED...
...THIS GIRL STANDING NEXT TO ME.

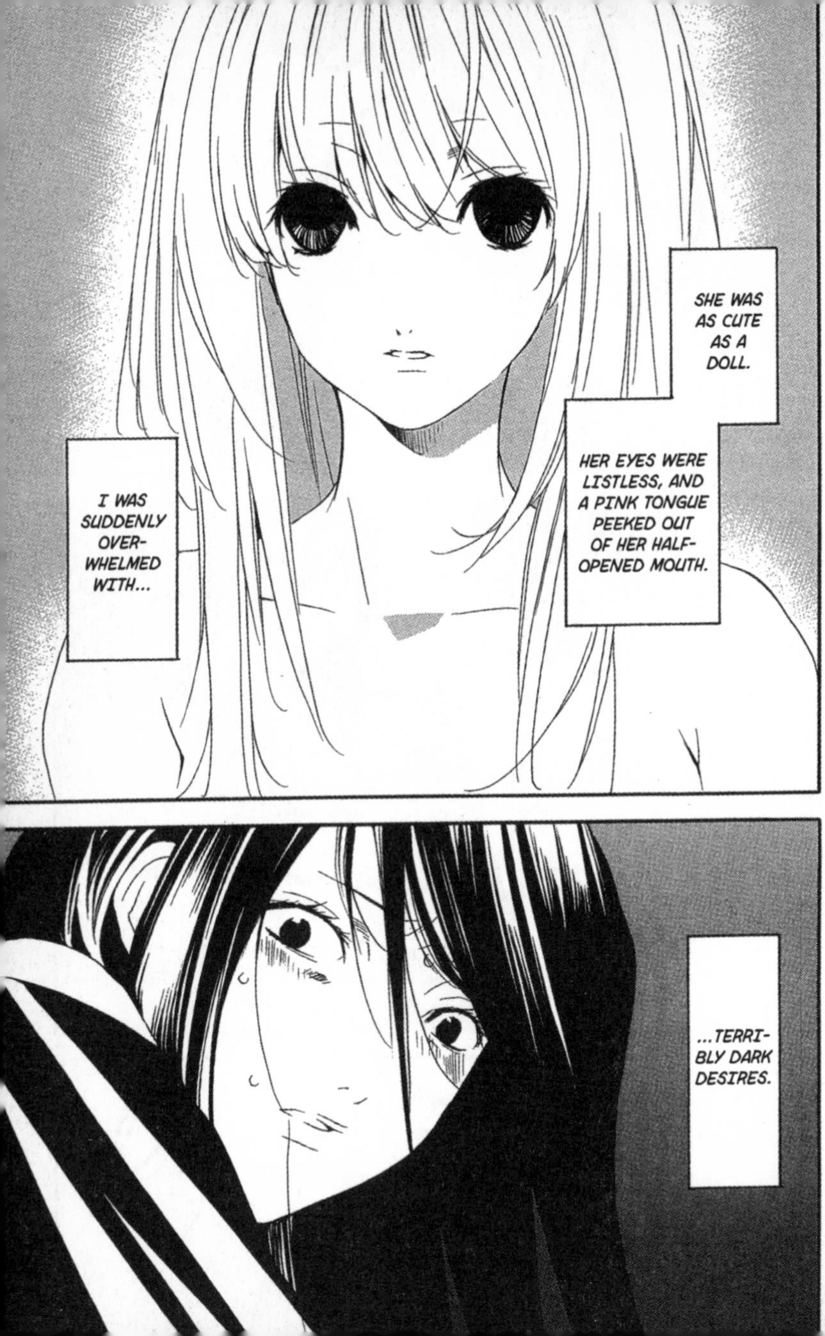
SHE WAS AS CUTE AS A DOLL.
HER EYES WERE LISTLESS, AND A PINK TONGUE PEEKED OUT OF HER HALF-OPENED MOUTH.
I WAS SUDDENLY OVER-WHELMED WITH...
...TERRI-BLY DARK DESIRES.

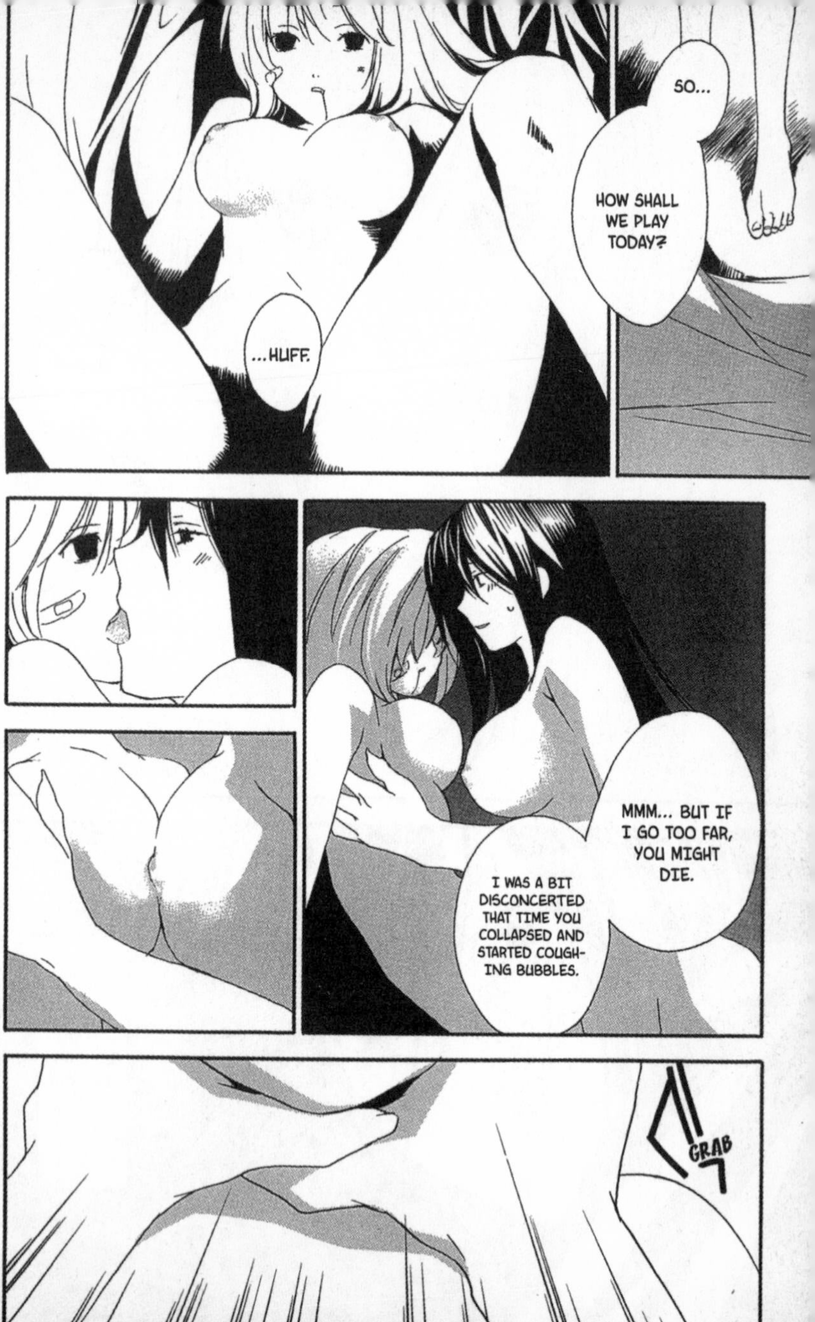
SO...
HOW SHALL WE PLAY TODAY?
...HUFF.
MMM... BUT IF I GO TOO FAR, YOU MIGHT DIE.
I WAS A BIT DISCONCERTED THAT TIME YOU COLLAPSED AND STARTED COUGHING BUBBLES.
GRAB

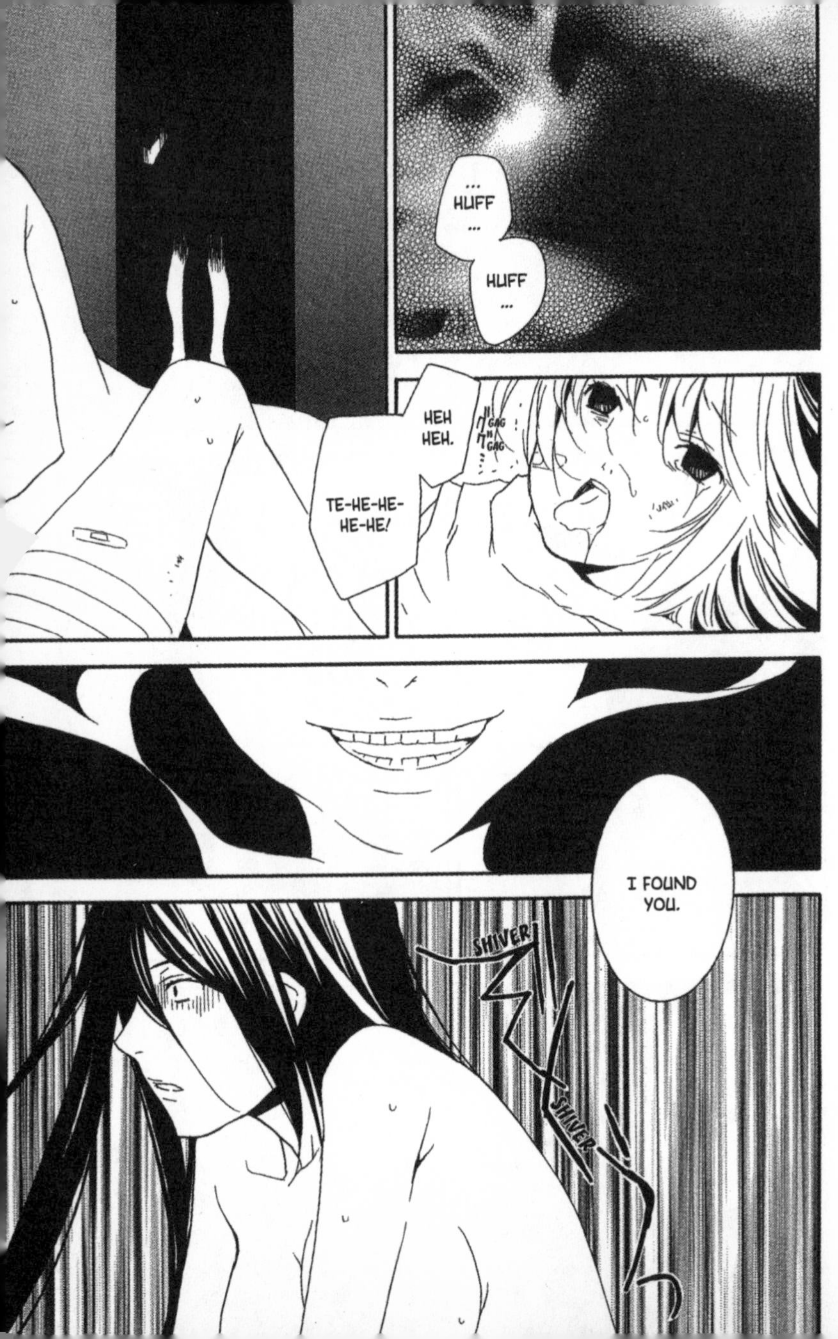
...HUFF...
HUFF...
GAG 'N GAG
HEH HEH.
TE-HE-HE-HE-HE!
I FOUND YOU.
SHIVER SHIVER

EEE...

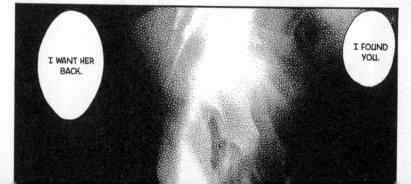

I WANT HER
BACK.

I FOUND
YOU.

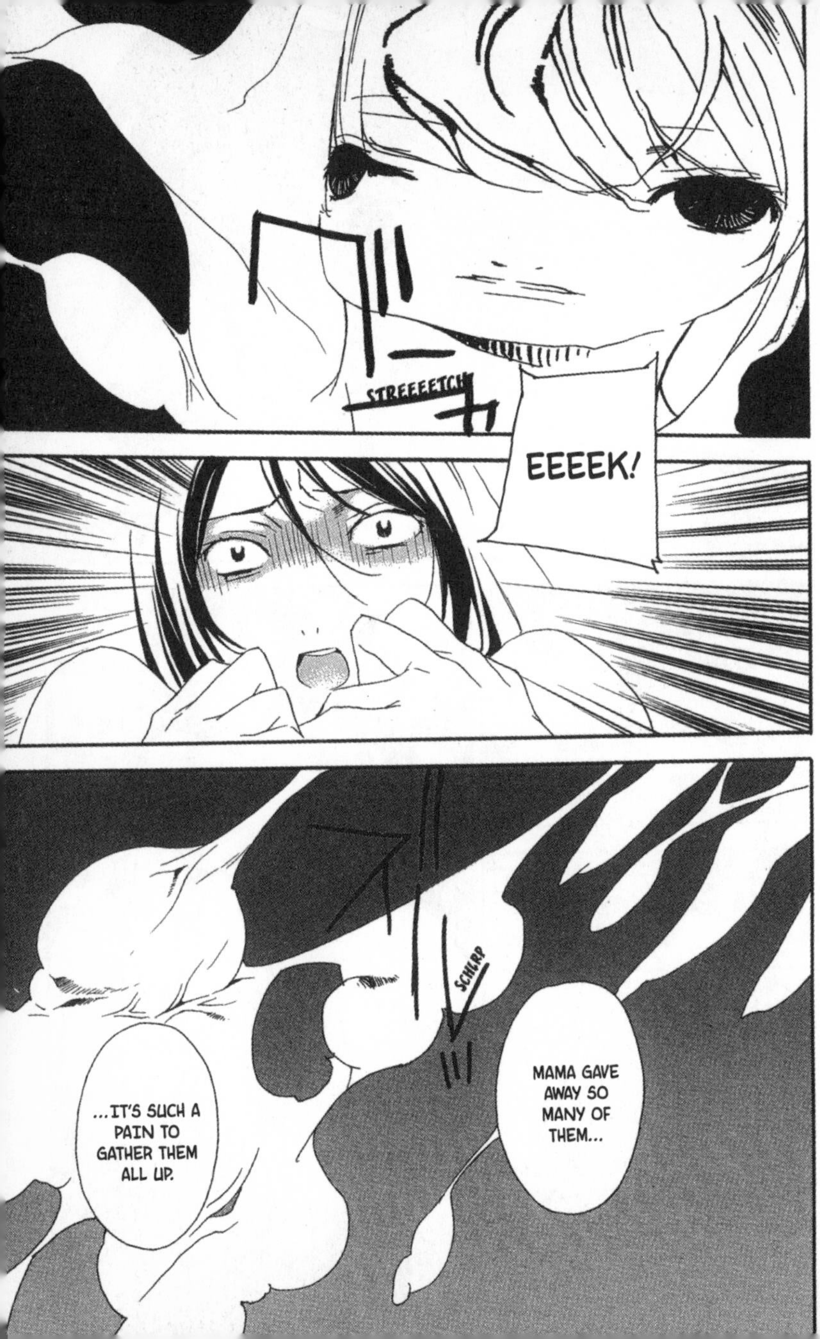
STREEEETCH
EEEEK!
SCHLRP
MAMA GAVE AWAY SO MANY OF THEM...
...IT'S SUCH A PAIN TO GATHER THEM ALL UP.

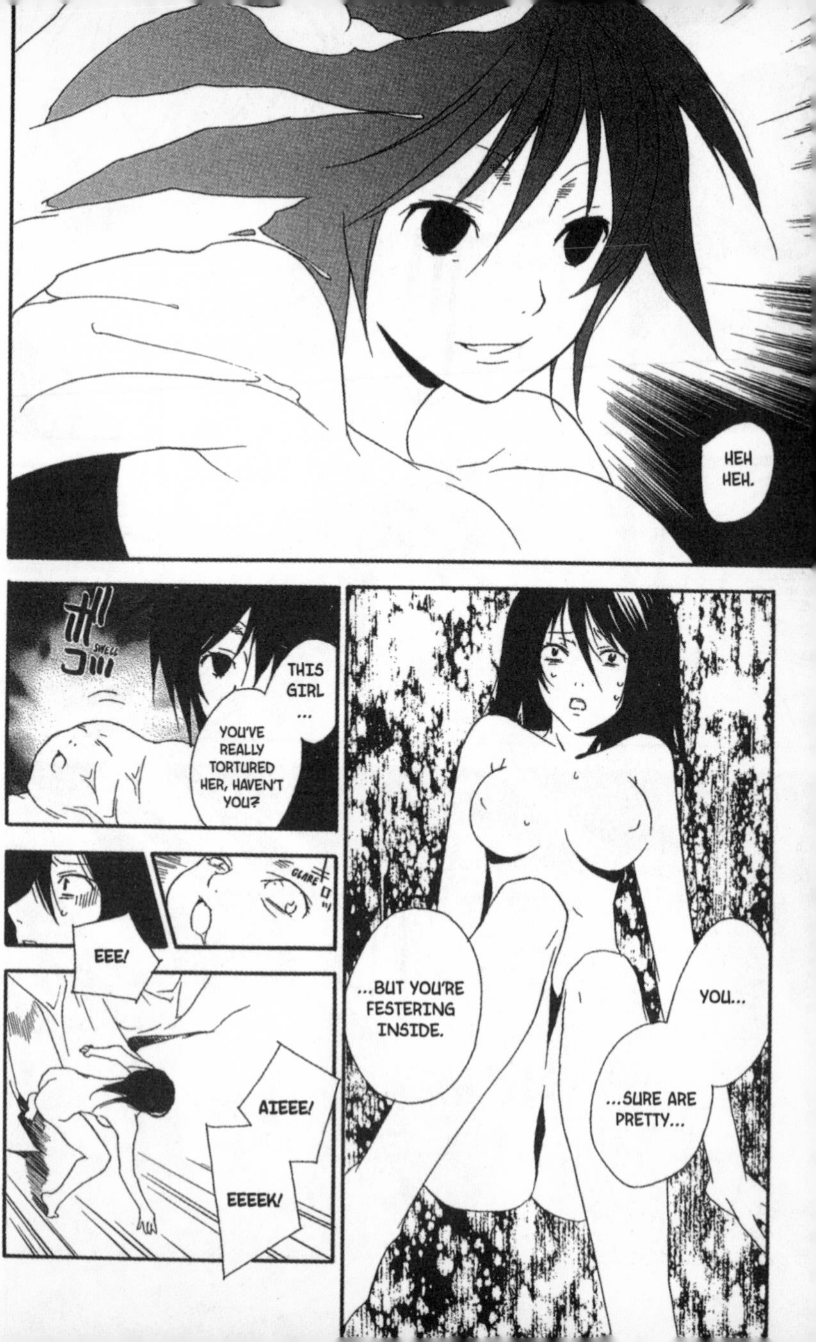
HEH HEH.
YOU...
...SURE ARE PRETTY...
...BUT YOU'RE FESTERING INSIDE.
SWELL
THIS GIRL ...
YOU'VE REALLY TORTURED HER, HAVEN'T YOU?
GLARE
EEE!
AIEEE!
EEEEK!

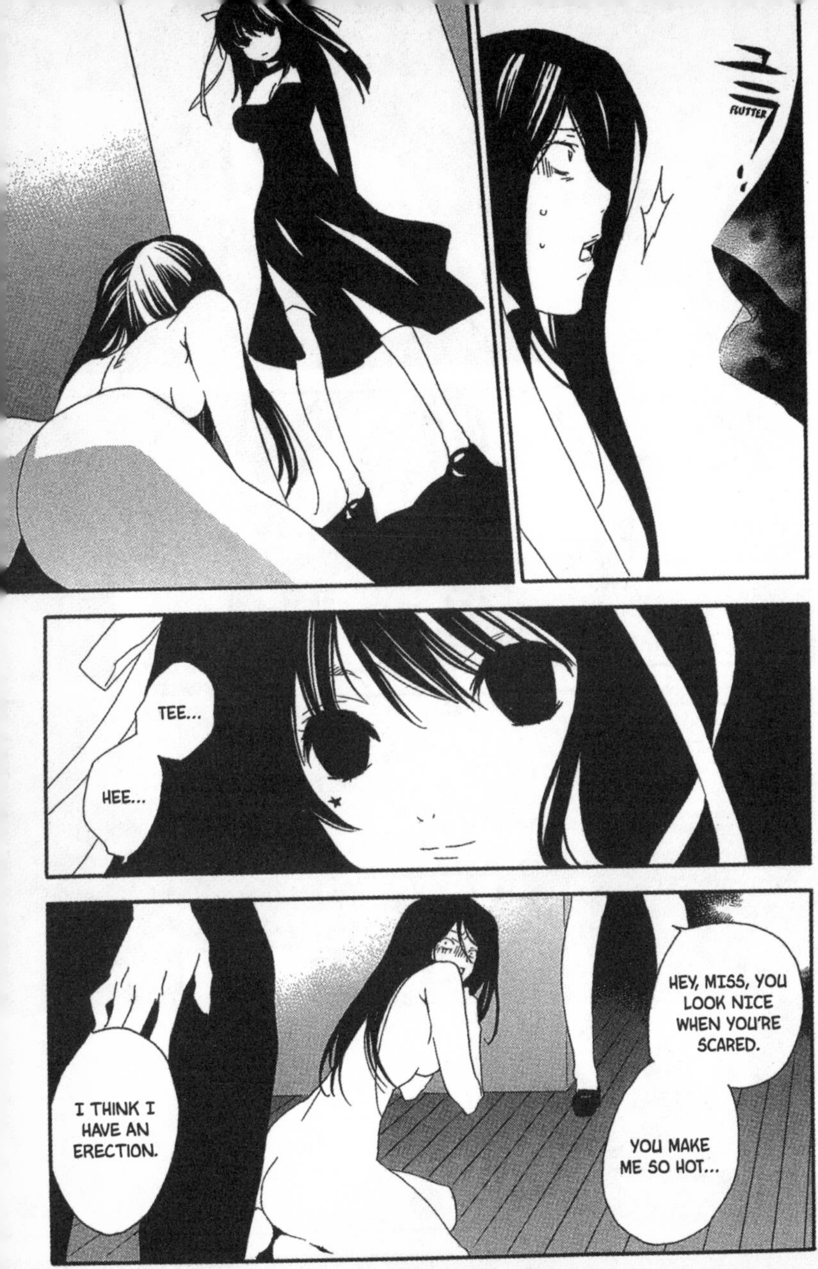
FLUTTER
TEE...
HEE...
HEY, MISS, YOU LOOK NICE WHEN YOU'RE SCARED.
YOU MAKE ME SO HOT...
I THINK I HAVE AN ERECTION.

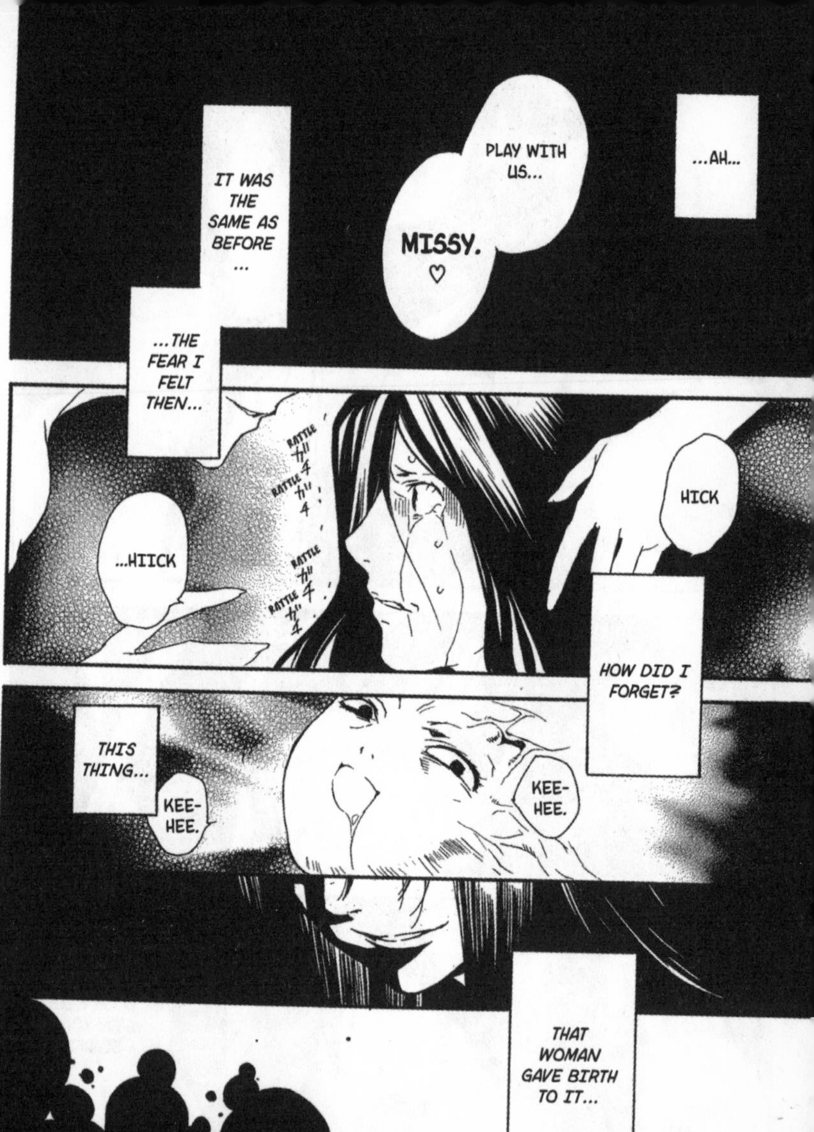
...AH...
PLAY WITH US...
MISSY. ♡
IT WAS THE SAME AS BEFORE...
...THE FEAR I FELT THEN...
HICK
RATTLE
RATTLE
RATTLE
RATTLE
...HIICK
HOW DID I FORGET?
KEE-HEE.
THIS THING...
KEE-HEE.
THAT WOMAN GAVE BIRTH TO IT...

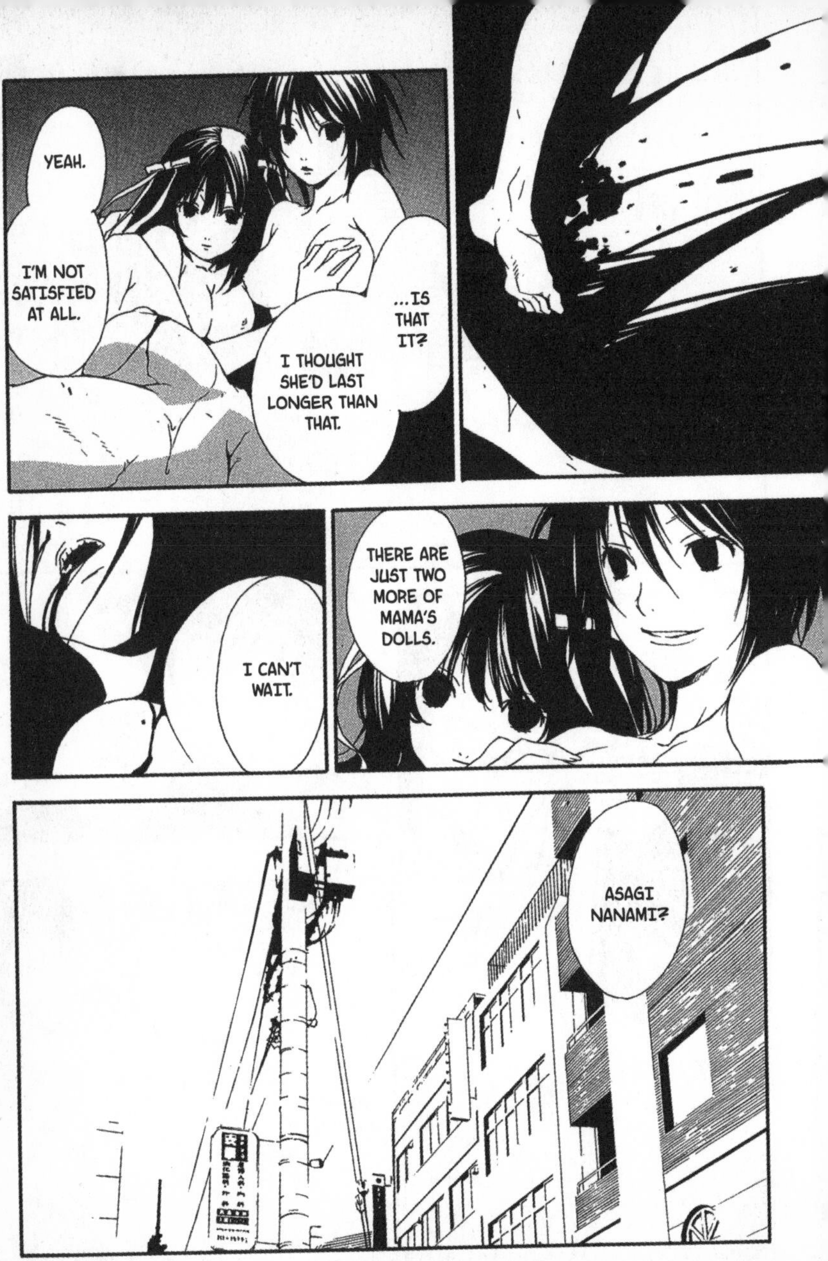
...IS THAT IT?
I THOUGHT SHE'D LAST LONGER THAN THAT.
YEAH.
I'M NOT SATISFIED AT ALL.
THERE ARE JUST TWO MORE OF MAMA'S DOLLS.
I CAN'T WAIT.
ASAGI NANAMI?

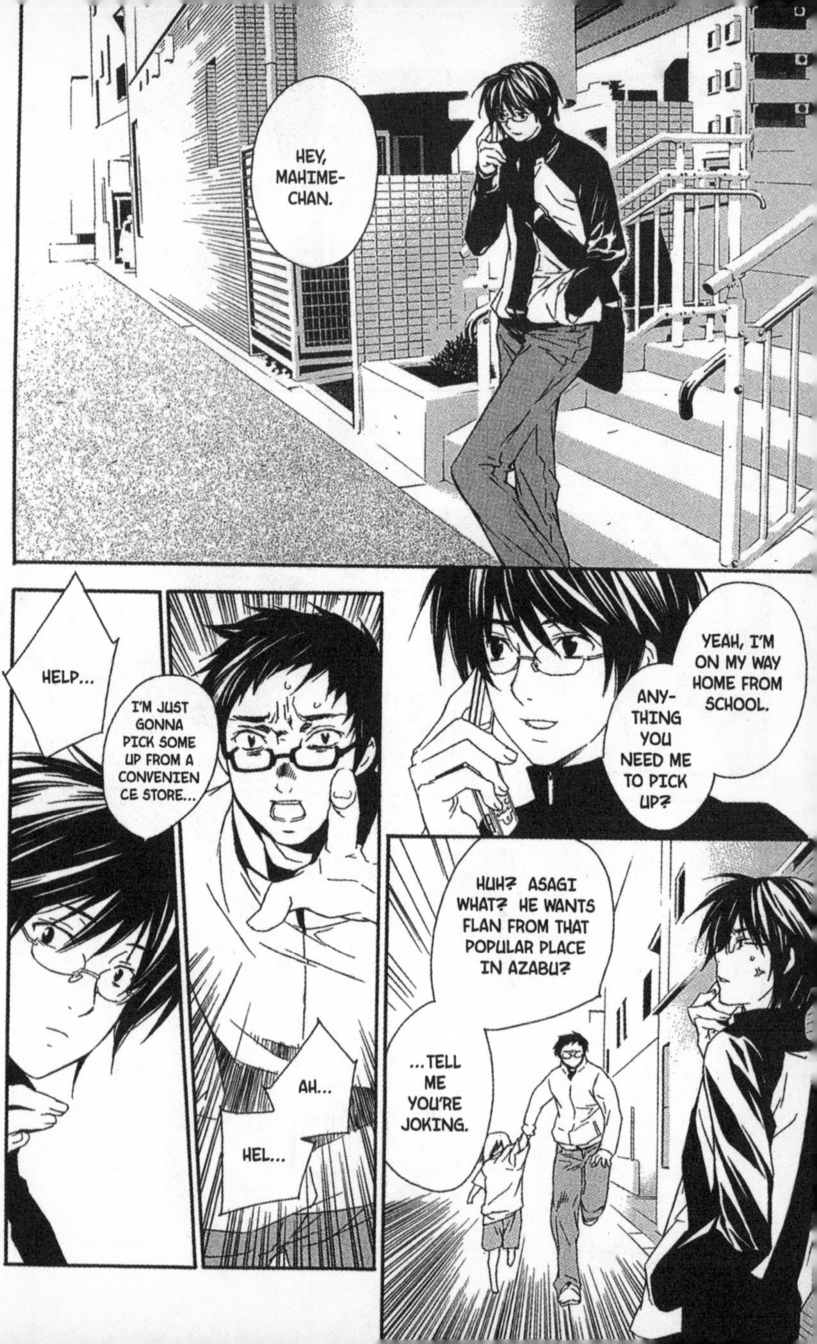
HEY, MAHIME-CHAN.
YEAH, I'M ON MY WAY HOME FROM SCHOOL.
ANY-THING YOU NEED ME TO PICK UP?
HUH? ASAGI WHAT? HE WANTS FLAN FROM THAT POPULAR PLACE IN AZABU?
...TELL ME YOU'RE JOKING.
I'M JUST GONNA PICK SOME UP FROM A CONVENIEN CE STORE...
AH...
HEL...
HELP...

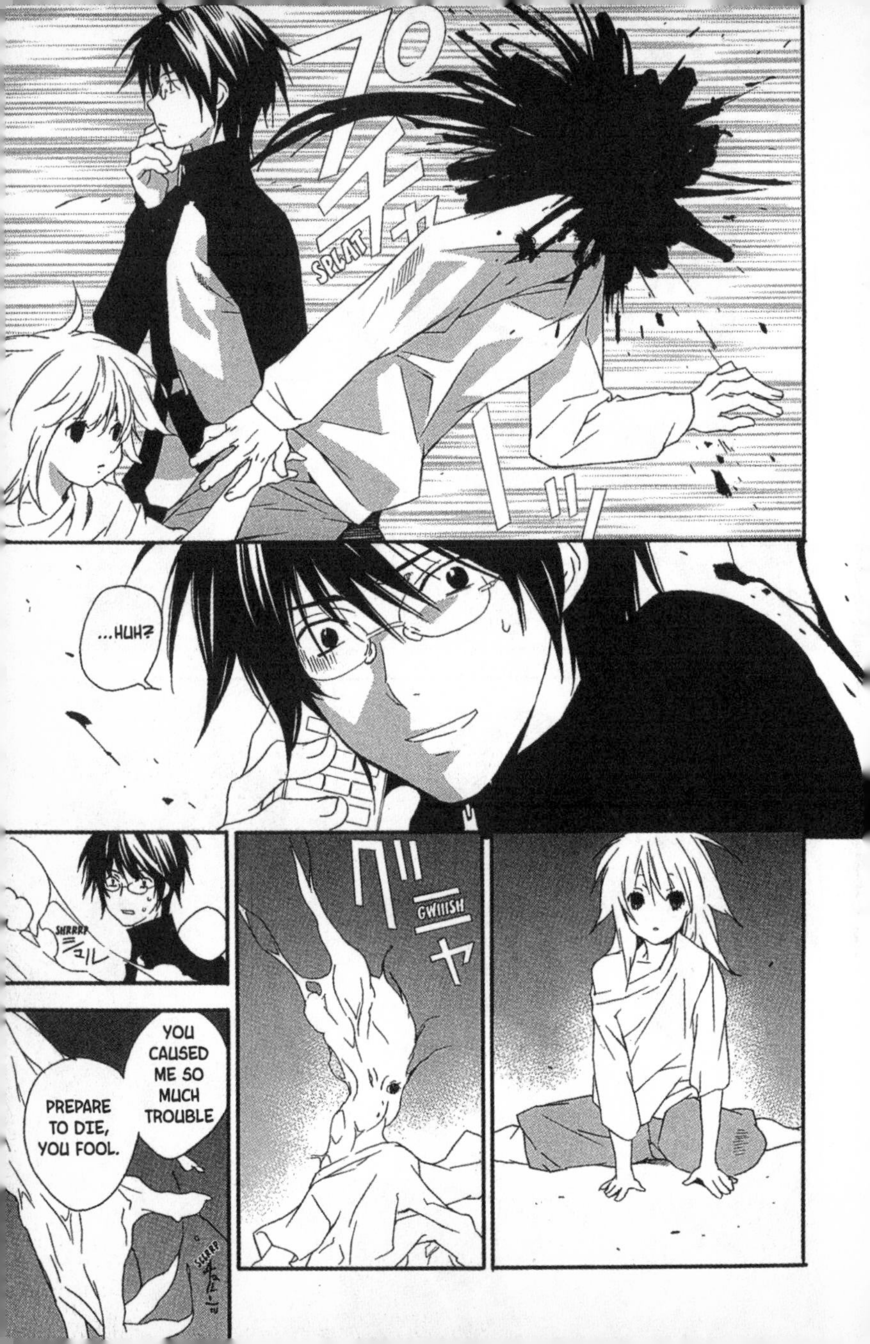
SPLAT
...HUH?
GWIIISH
SHRRRP
YOU CAUSED ME SO MUCH TROUBLE
PREPARE TO DIE, YOU FOOL.
SCLRRP

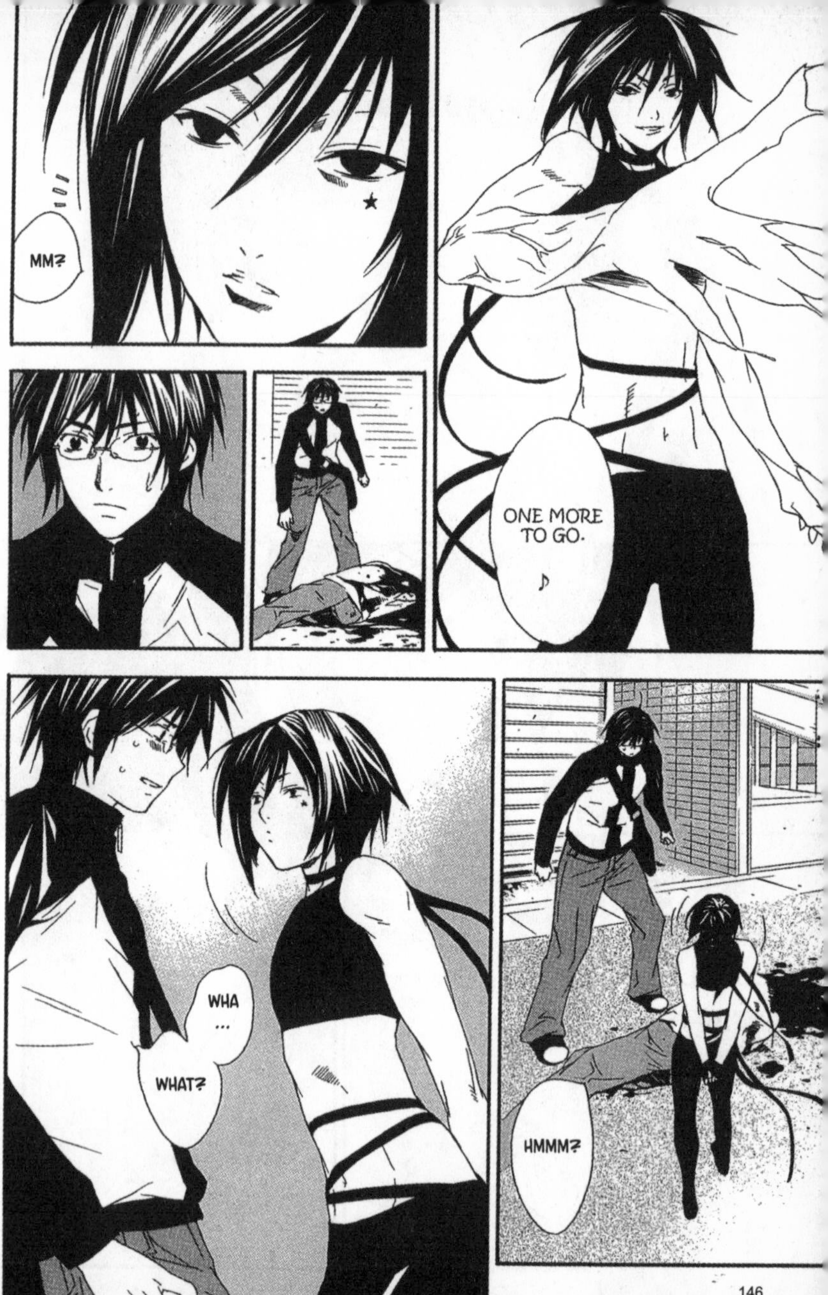
ONE MORE TO GO. ♪
MM?
HMMM?
WHA ...
WHAT?

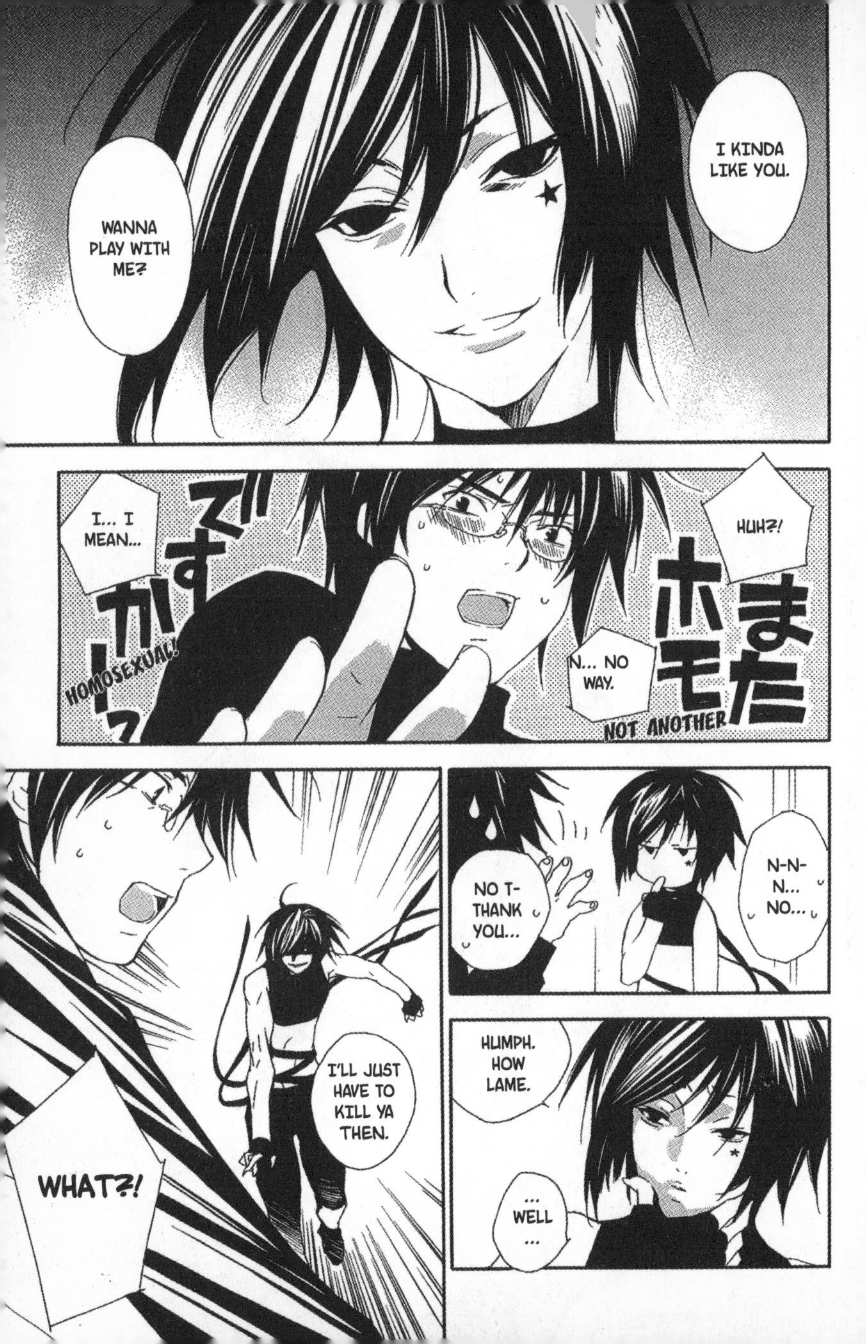
I KINDA LIKE YOU.
WANNA PLAY WITH ME?
HUH?!
またホモ
NOT ANOTHER
N... NO WAY.
I... I MEAN...
ですかーっ
HOMOSEXUAL!
N-N-N... NO...
NO T-THANK YOU...
HUMPH. HOW LAME.
... WELL ...
I'LL JUST HAVE TO KILL YA THEN.
WHAT?!

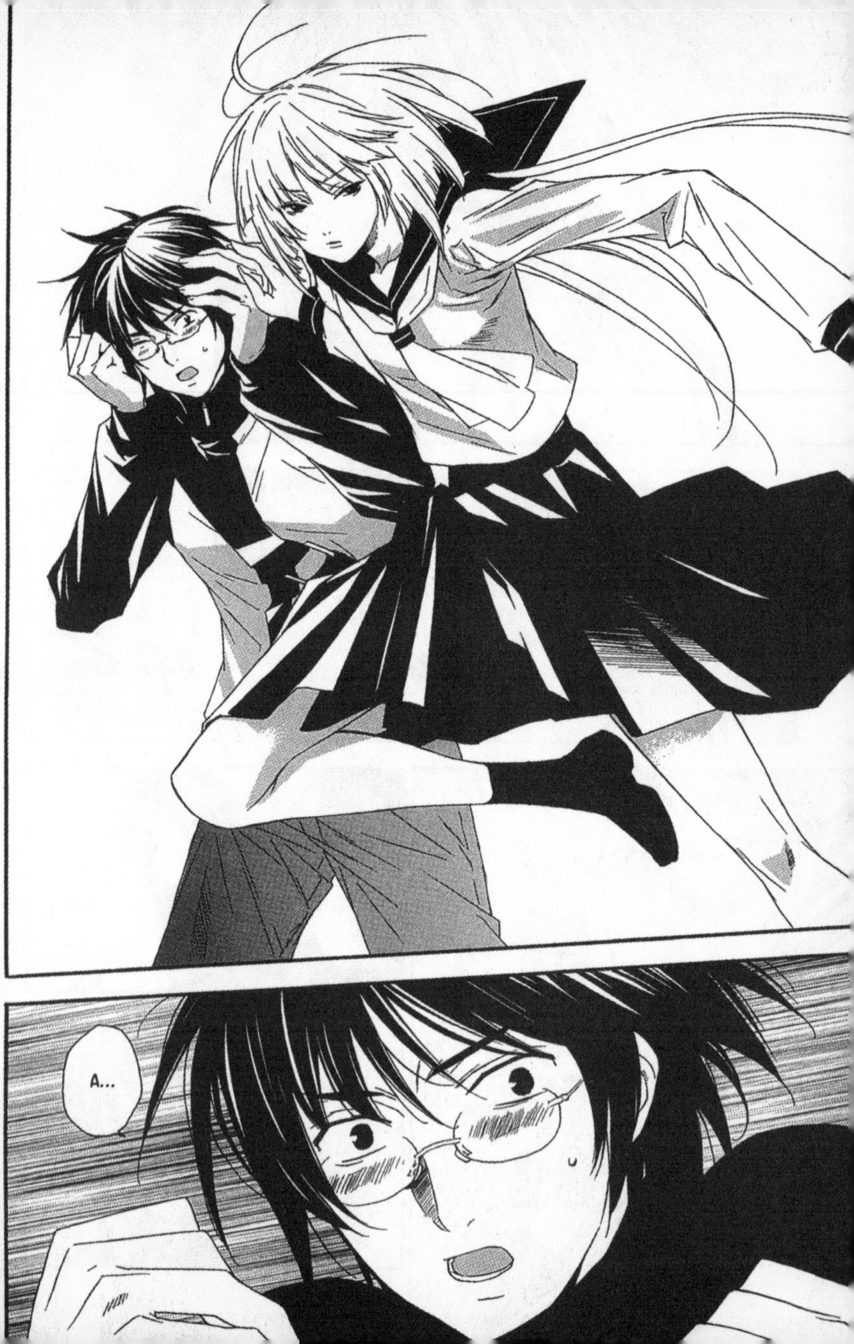
A...

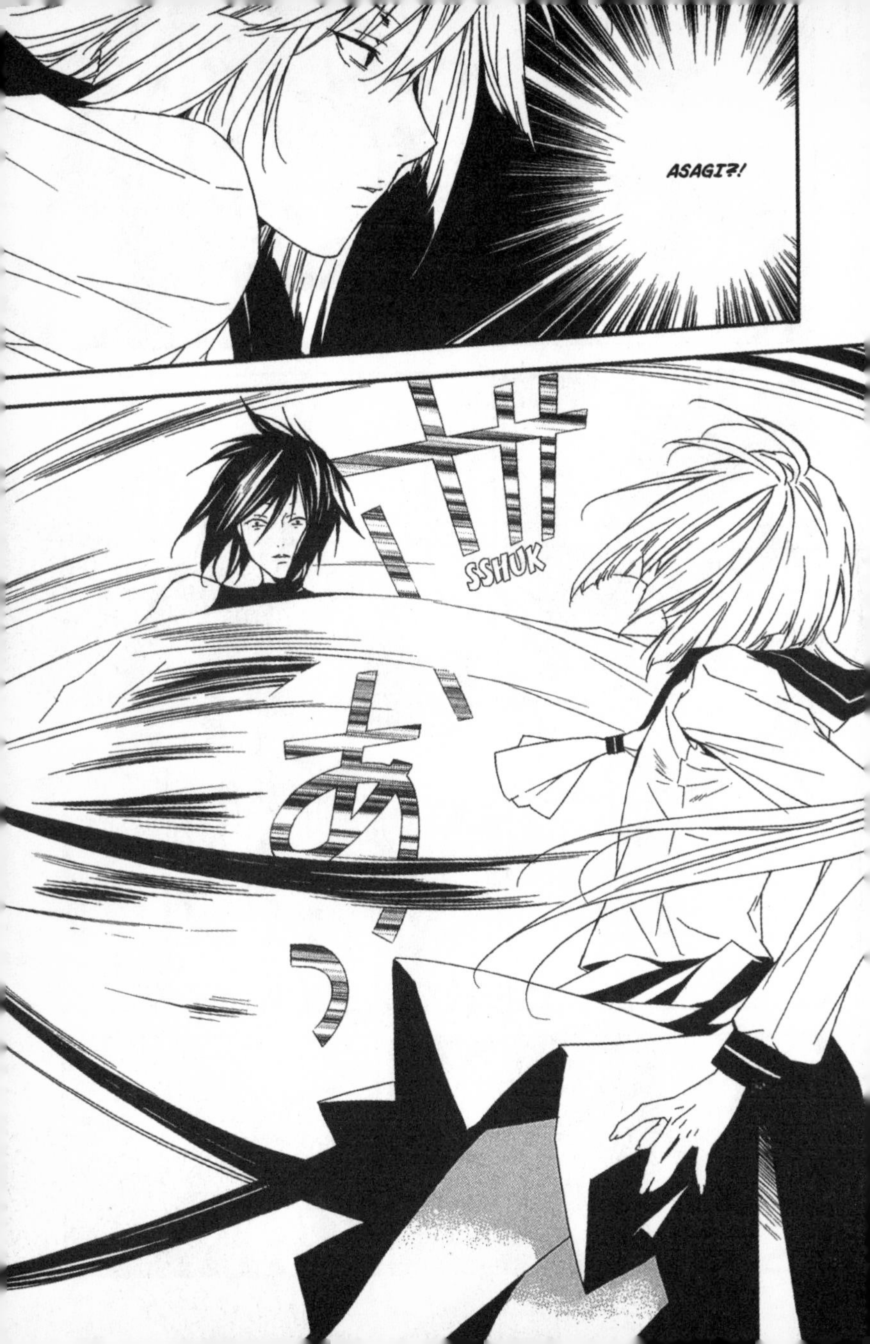
ASAGI?!
SSHUK

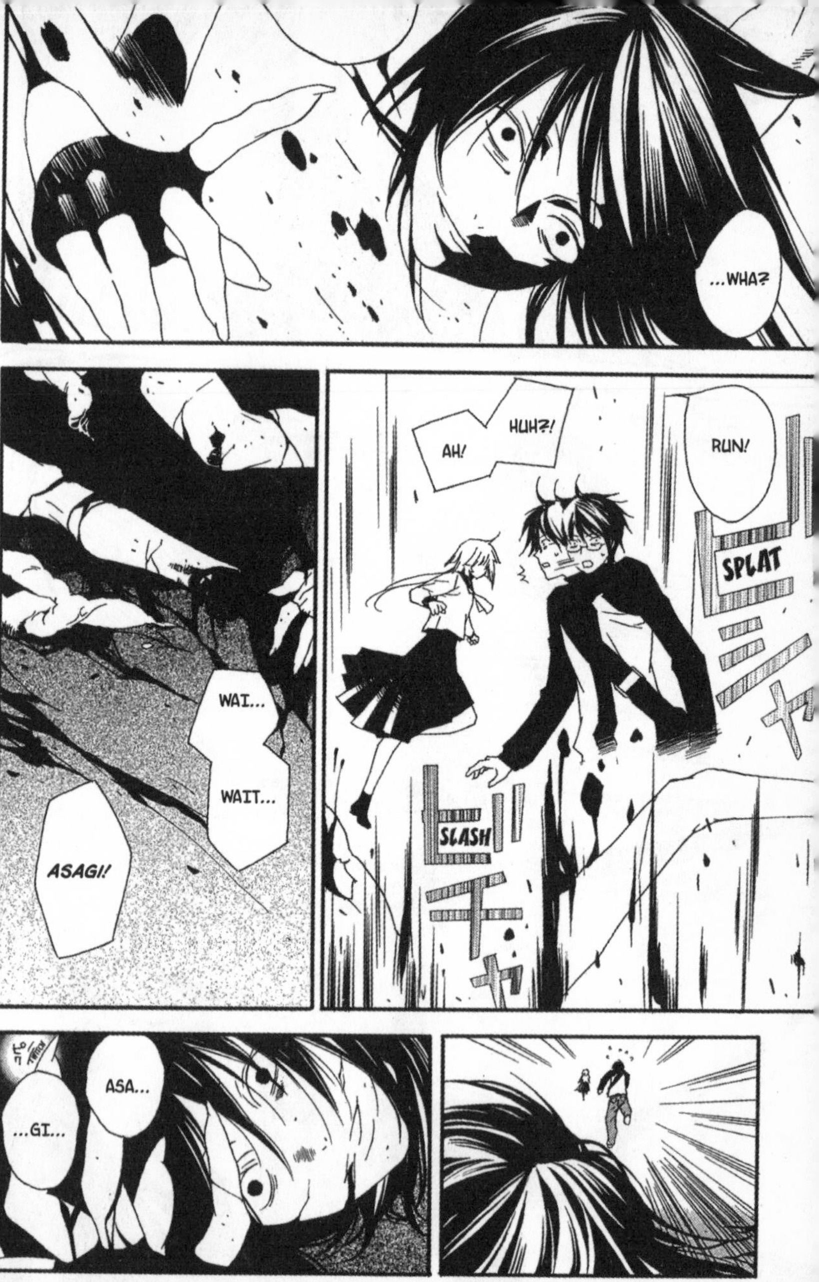
...WHA?
RUN!
HUH?!
AH!
SPLAT
SLASH
WAI...
WAIT...
ASAGI!
TWITCH
ASA...
...GI...

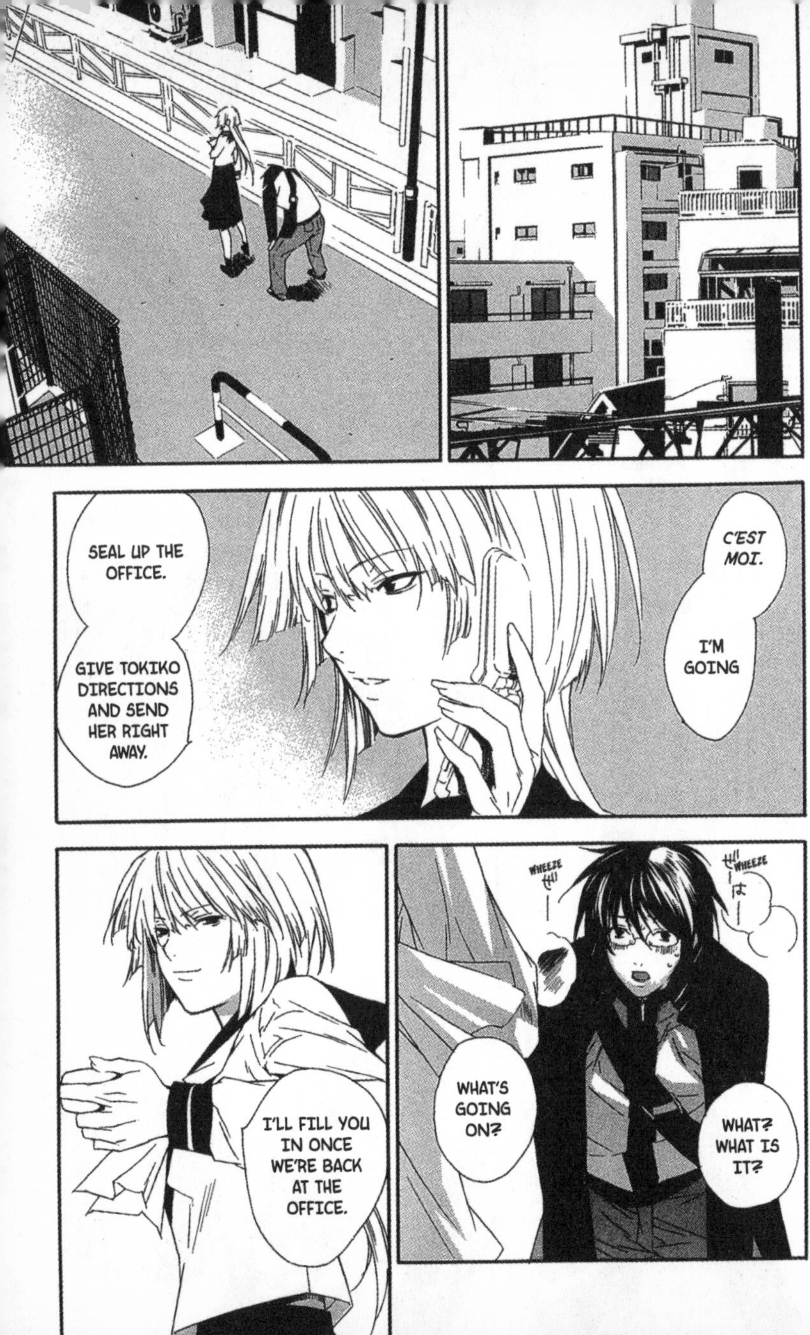
C'EST MOI.
I'M GOING
SEAL UP THE OFFICE.
GIVE TOKIKO DIRECTIONS AND SEND HER RIGHT AWAY.
WHEEZE
WHEEZE
WHAT? WHAT IS IT?
WHAT'S GOING ON?
I'LL FILL YOU IN ONCE WE'RE BACK AT THE OFFICE.

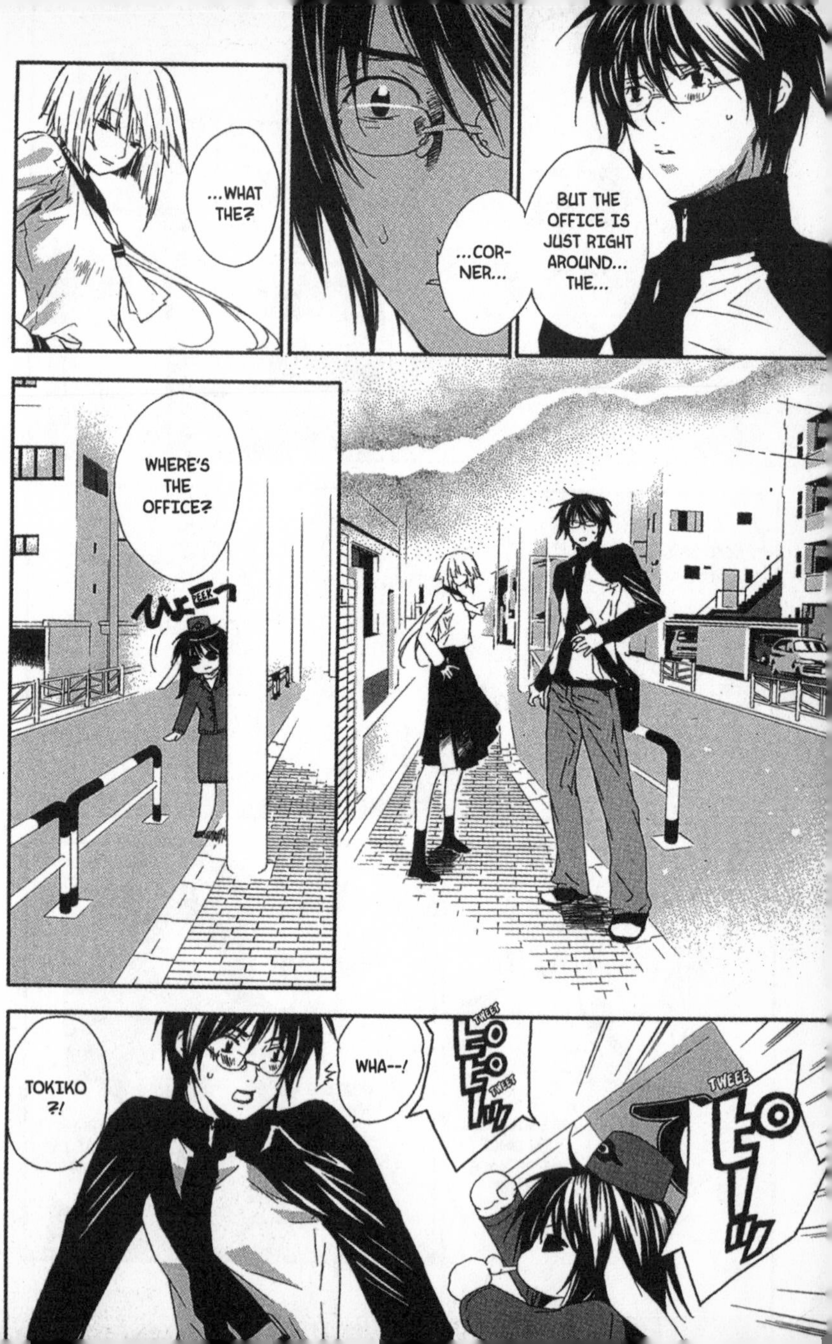
BUT THE OFFICE IS JUST RIGHT AROUND... THE...
...COR-NER...
...WHAT THE?
WHERE'S THE OFFICE?
PEEK
TWEEE
TWEET
TWEET
TWEET
WHA--!
TOKIKO?!

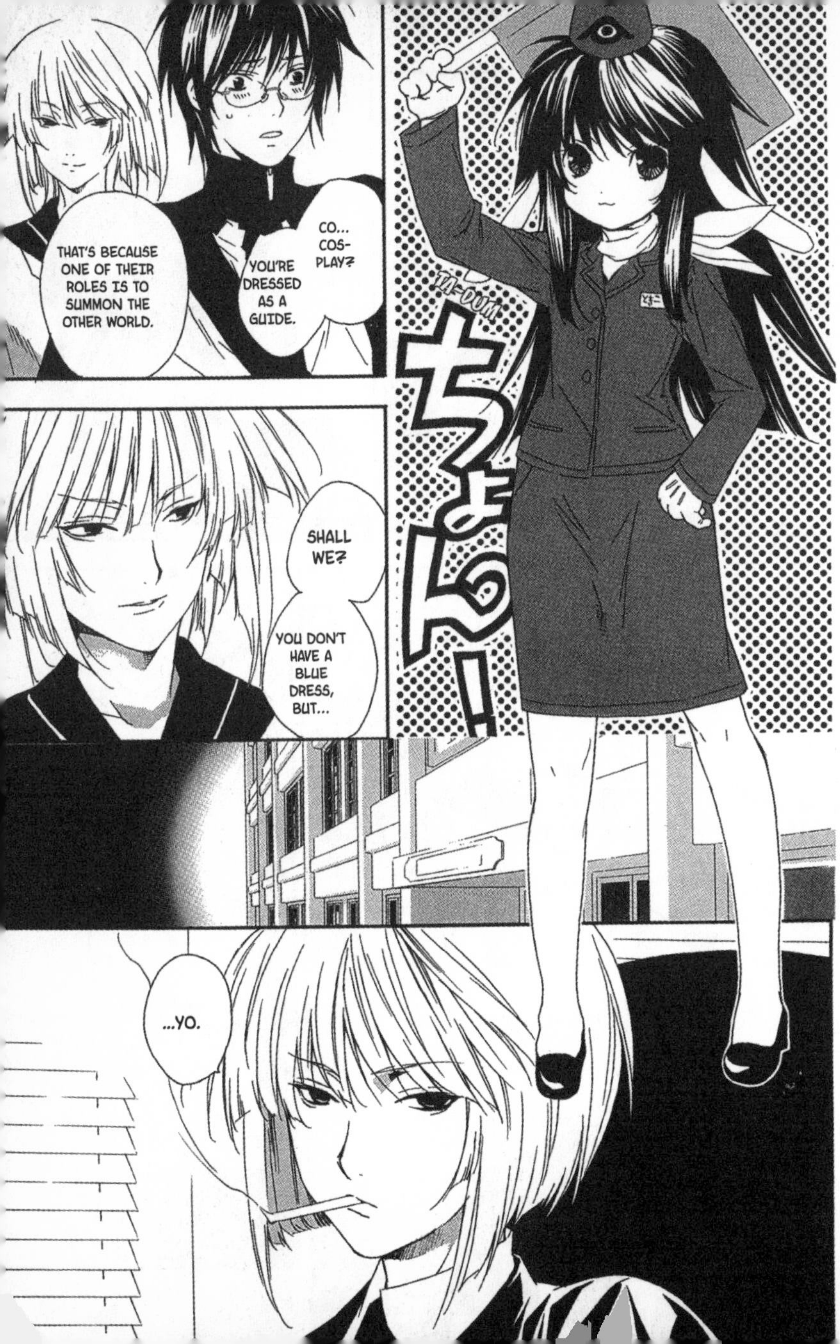
TA-DUM
ちょん!
CO... COS-PLAY?
YOU'RE DRESSED AS A GUIDE.
THAT'S BECAUSE ONE OF THEIR ROLES IS TO SUMMON THE OTHER WORLD.
SHALL WE?
YOU DON'T HAVE A BLUE DRESS, BUT...
...YO.

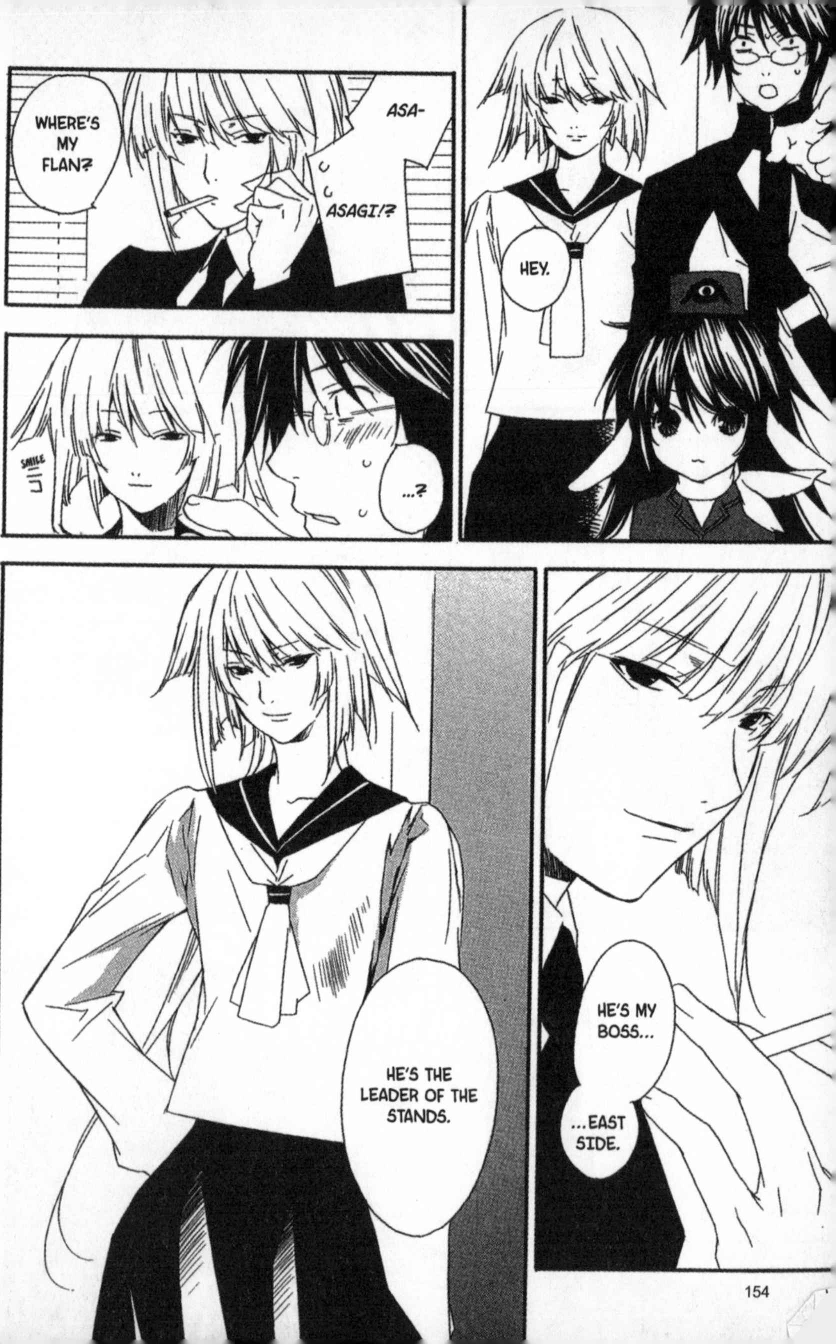
HEY.
ASA-
ASAGI!?
WHERE'S MY FLAN?
...?
SMILE
HE'S MY BOSS...
...EAST SIDE.
HE'S THE LEADER OF THE STANDS.

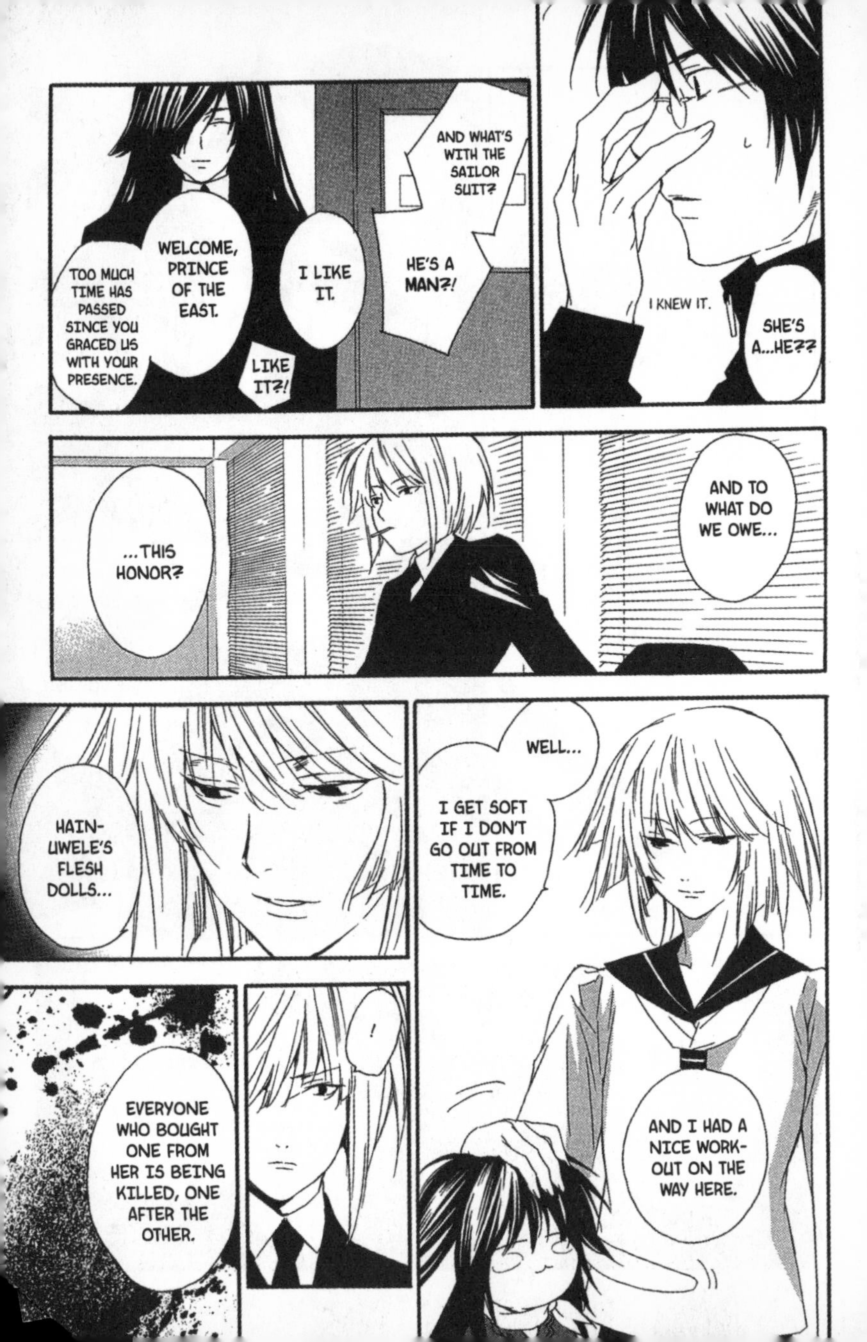
SHE'S A...HE??
I KNEW IT.
AND WHAT'S WITH THE SAILOR SUIT?
HE'S A MAN?!
I LIKE IT.
LIKE IT?!
WELCOME, PRINCE OF THE EAST.
TOO MUCH TIME HAS PASSED SINCE YOU GRACED US WITH YOUR PRESENCE.
AND TO WHAT DO WE OWE...
...THIS HONOR?
WELL...
I GET SOFT IF I DON'T GO OUT FROM TIME TO TIME.
AND I HAD A NICE WORK-OUT ON THE WAY HERE.
HAIN-UWELE'S FLESH DOLLS...
!
EVERYONE WHO BOUGHT ONE FROM HER IS BEING KILLED, ONE AFTER THE OTHER.

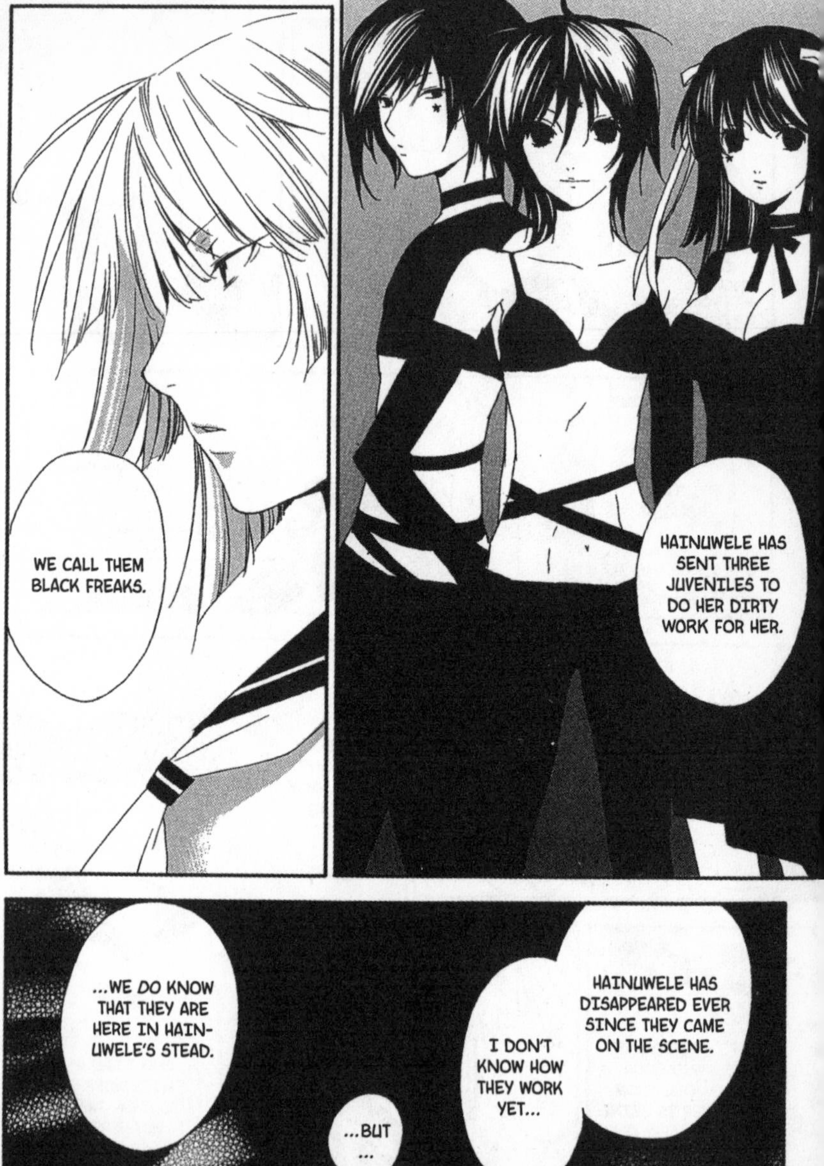
HAINUWELE HAS SENT THREE JUVENILES TO DO HER DIRTY WORK FOR HER.
WE CALL THEM BLACK FREAKS.
HAINUWELE HAS DISAPPEARED EVER SINCE THEY CAME ON THE SCENE.
I DON'T KNOW HOW THEY WORK YET...
...BUT ...
...WE *DO* KNOW THAT THEY ARE HERE IN HAIN-UWELE'S STEAD.

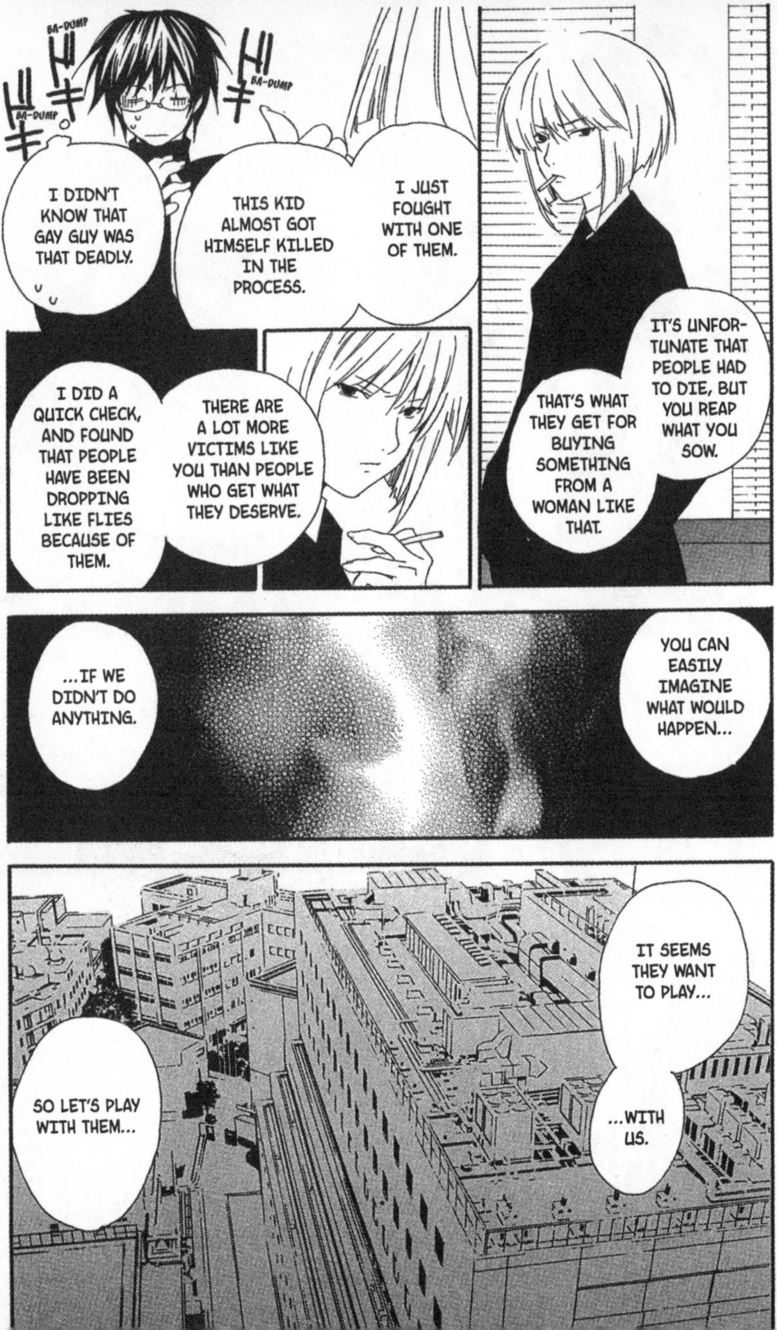
IT'S UNFOR-TUNATE THAT PEOPLE HAD TO DIE, BUT YOU REAP WHAT YOU SOW.
THAT'S WHAT THEY GET FOR BUYING SOMETHING FROM A WOMAN LIKE THAT.
BA-DUMP
BA-DUMP
BA-DUMP
I JUST FOUGHT WITH ONE OF THEM.
THIS KID ALMOST GOT HIMSELF KILLED IN THE PROCESS.
I DIDN'T KNOW THAT GAY GUY WAS THAT DEADLY.
THERE ARE A LOT MORE VICTIMS LIKE YOU THAN PEOPLE WHO GET WHAT THEY DESERVE.
I DID A QUICK CHECK, AND FOUND THAT PEOPLE HAVE BEEN DROPPING LIKE FLIES BECAUSE OF THEM.
YOU CAN EASILY IMAGINE WHAT WOULD HAPPEN...
...IF WE DIDN'T DO ANYTHING.
IT SEEMS THEY WANT TO PLAY...
...WITH US.
SO LET'S PLAY WITH THEM...

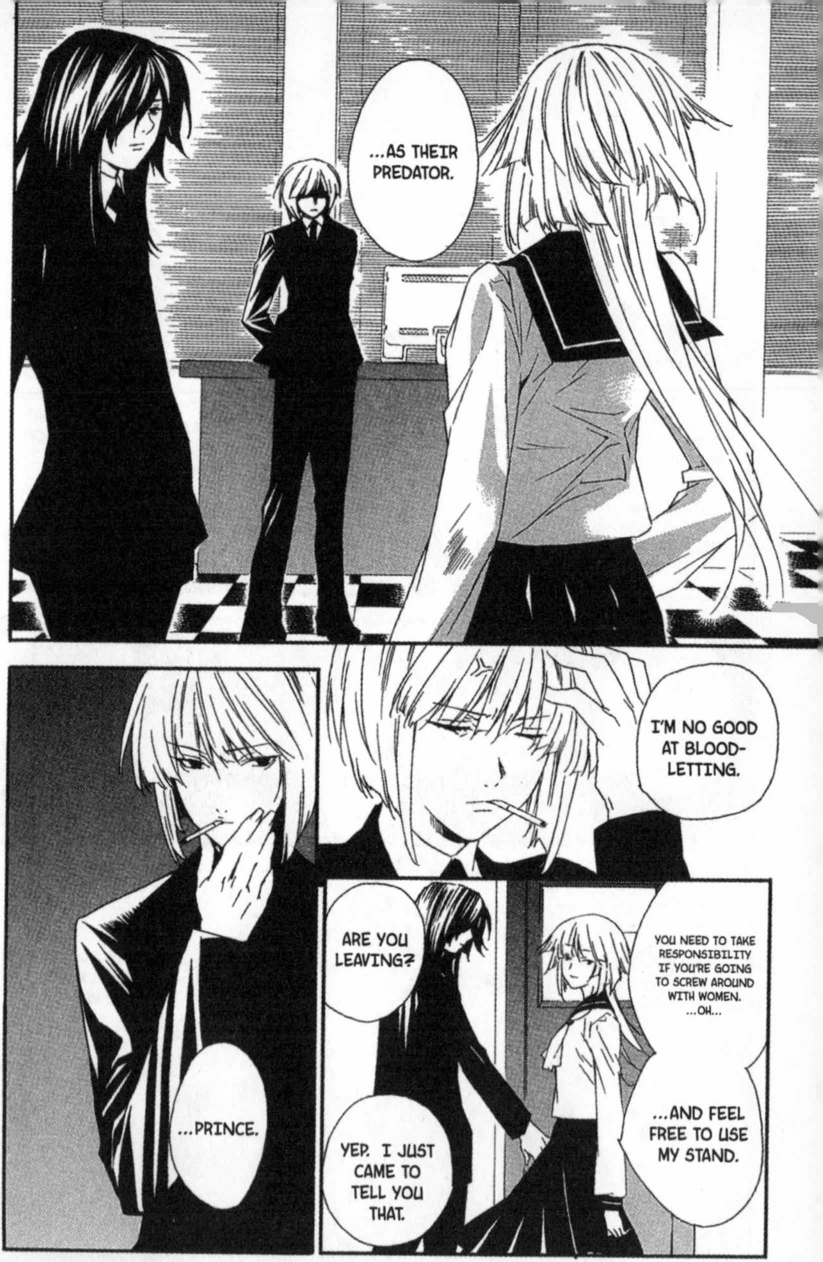
...AS THEIR PREDATOR.
I'M NO GOOD AT BLOOD-LETTING.
YOU NEED TO TAKE RESPONSIBILITY IF YOU'RE GOING TO SCREW AROUND WITH WOMEN. ...OH...
...AND FEEL FREE TO USE MY STAND.
ARE YOU LEAVING?
YEP. I JUST CAME TO TELL YOU THAT.
...PRINCE.

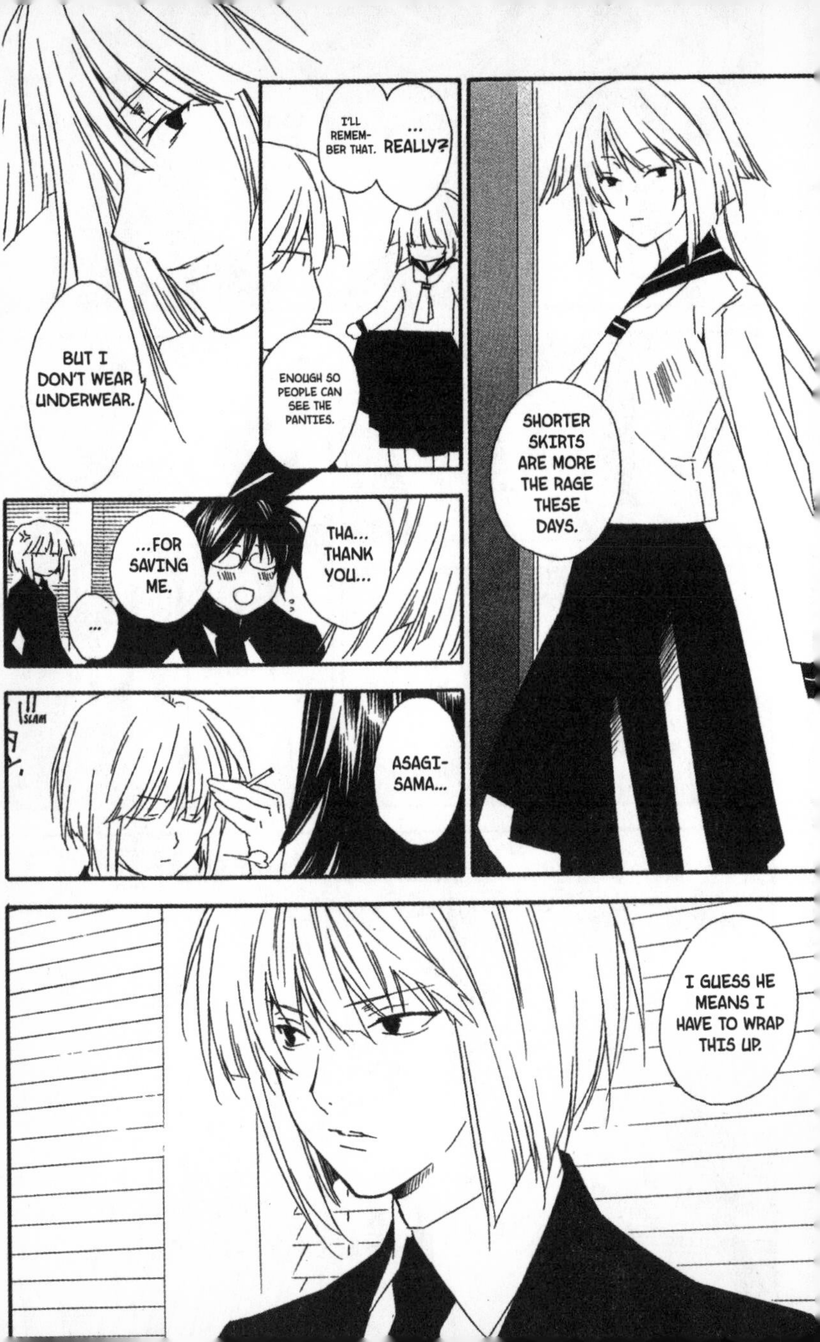
SHORTER SKIRTS ARE MORE THE RAGE THESE DAYS.
... REALLY?
I'LL REMEMBER THAT.
ENOUGH SO PEOPLE CAN SEE THE PANTIES.
BUT I DON'T WEAR UNDERWEAR.
THA... THANK YOU...
...FOR SAVING ME.
...
ASAGI-SAMA...
SLAM
I GUESS HE MEANS I HAVE TO WRAP THIS UP.

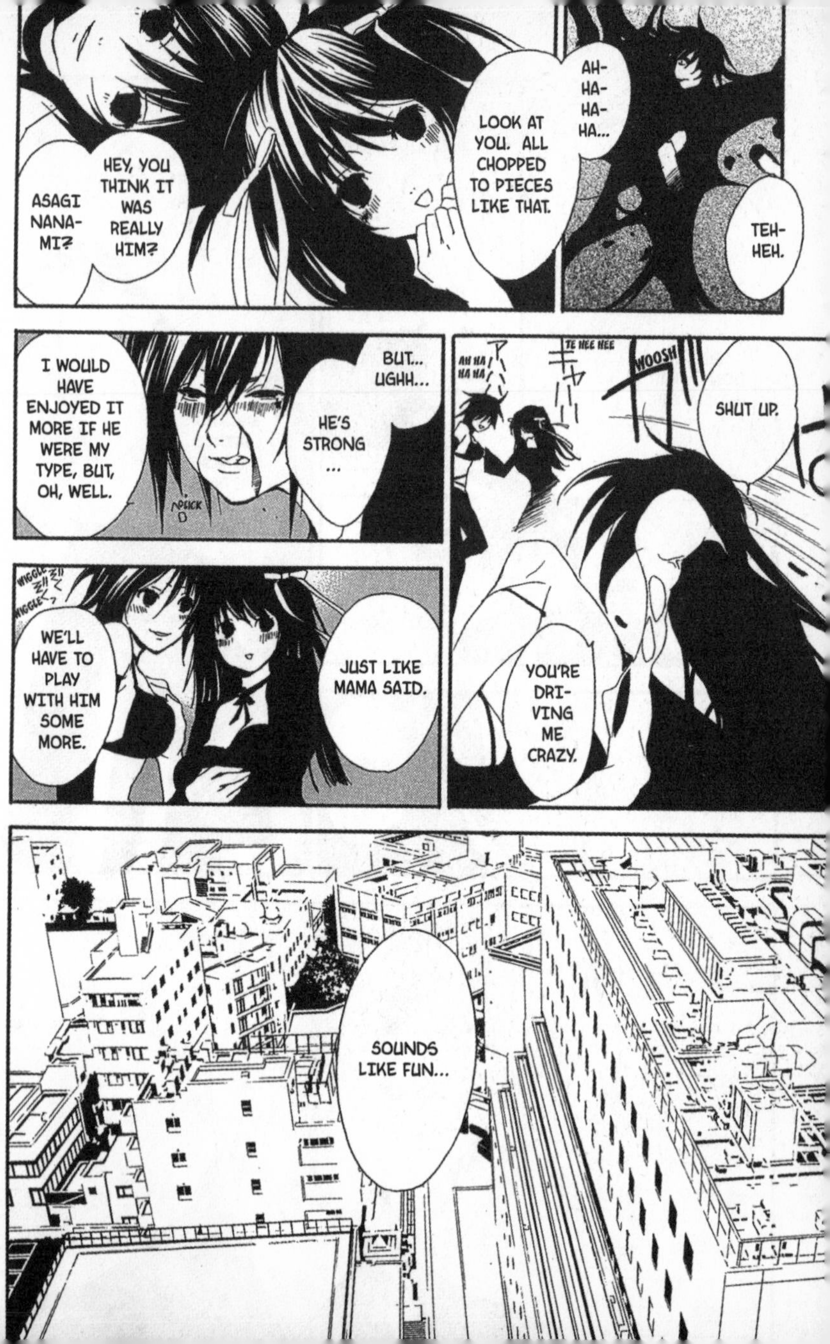
AH-HA-HA-HA...
TEH-HEH.
LOOK AT YOU. ALL CHOPPED TO PIECES LIKE THAT.
HEY, YOU THINK IT WAS REALLY HIM?
ASAGI NANAMI?
AH HA HA HA
TE HEE HEE
WOOSH
SHUT UP.
YOU'RE DRI-VING ME CRAZY.
BUT... UGHH...
HE'S STRONG ...
I WOULD HAVE ENJOYED IT MORE IF HE WERE MY TYPE, BUT, OH, WELL.
JUST LIKE MAMA SAID.
WE'LL HAVE TO PLAY WITH HIM SOME MORE.
WIGGLE WIGGLE
SOUNDS LIKE FUN...

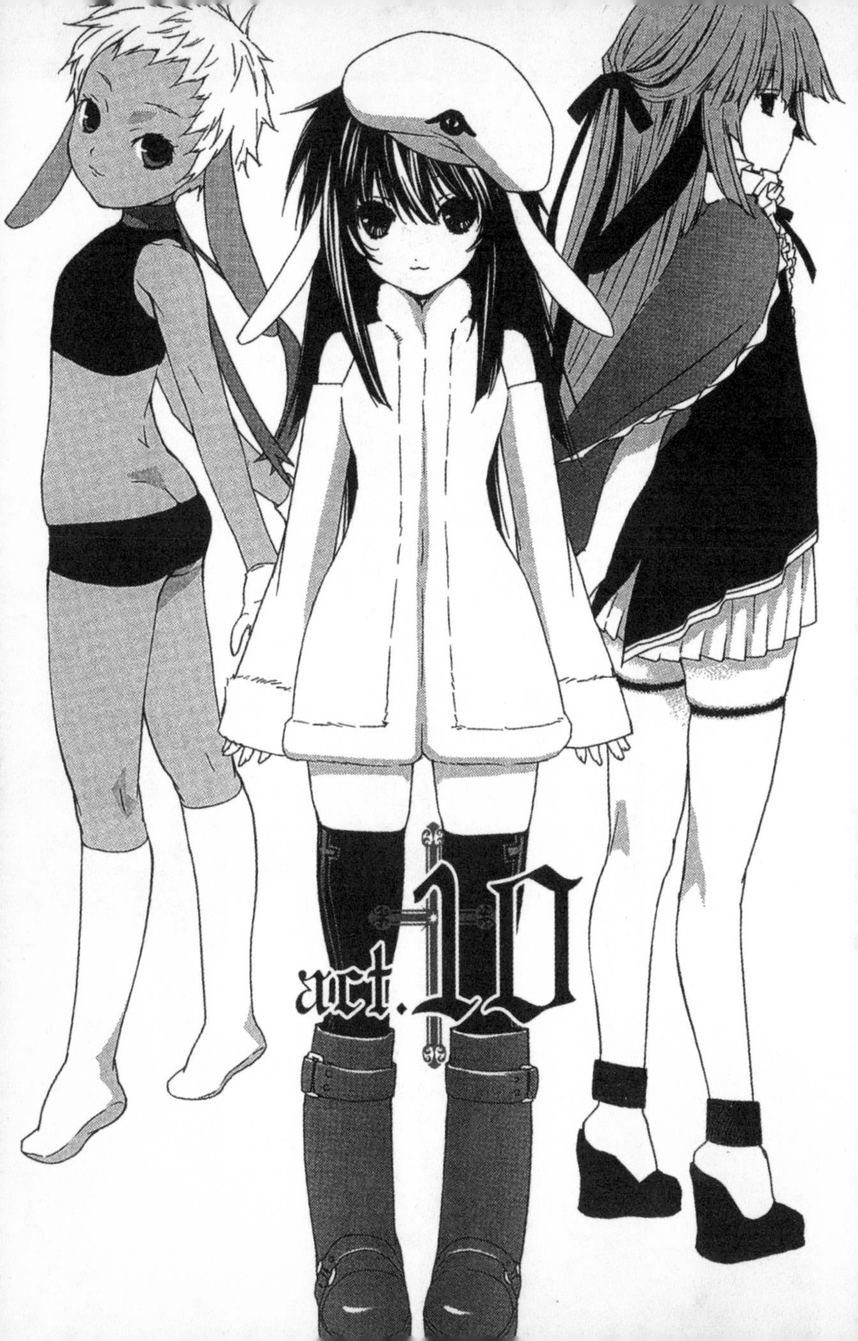
act.10

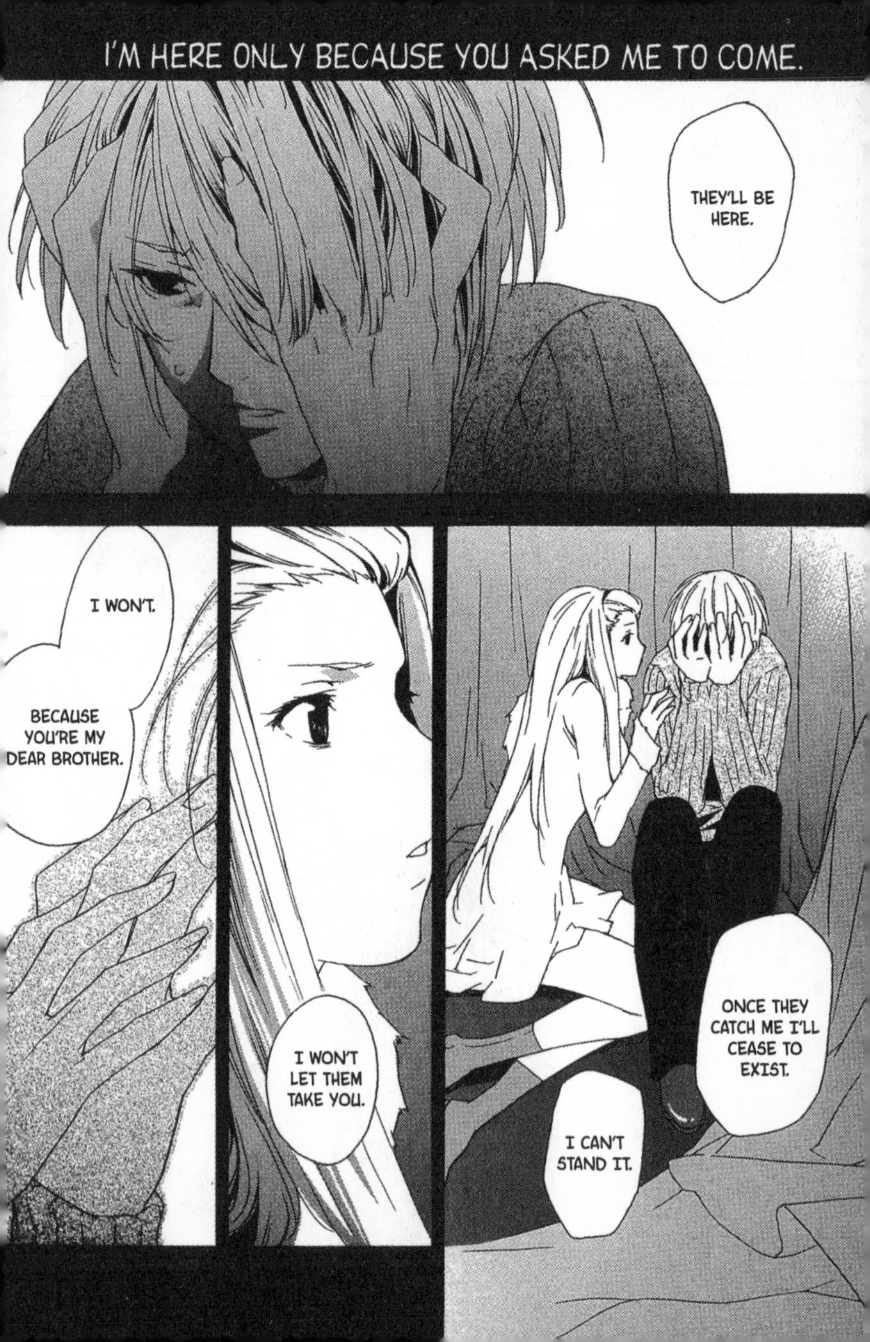
I'M HERE ONLY BECAUSE YOU ASKED ME TO COME.
THEY'LL BE HERE.
ONCE THEY CATCH ME I'LL CEASE TO EXIST.
I CAN'T STAND IT.
I WON'T LET THEM TAKE YOU.
I WON'T.
BECAUSE YOU'RE MY DEAR BROTHER.

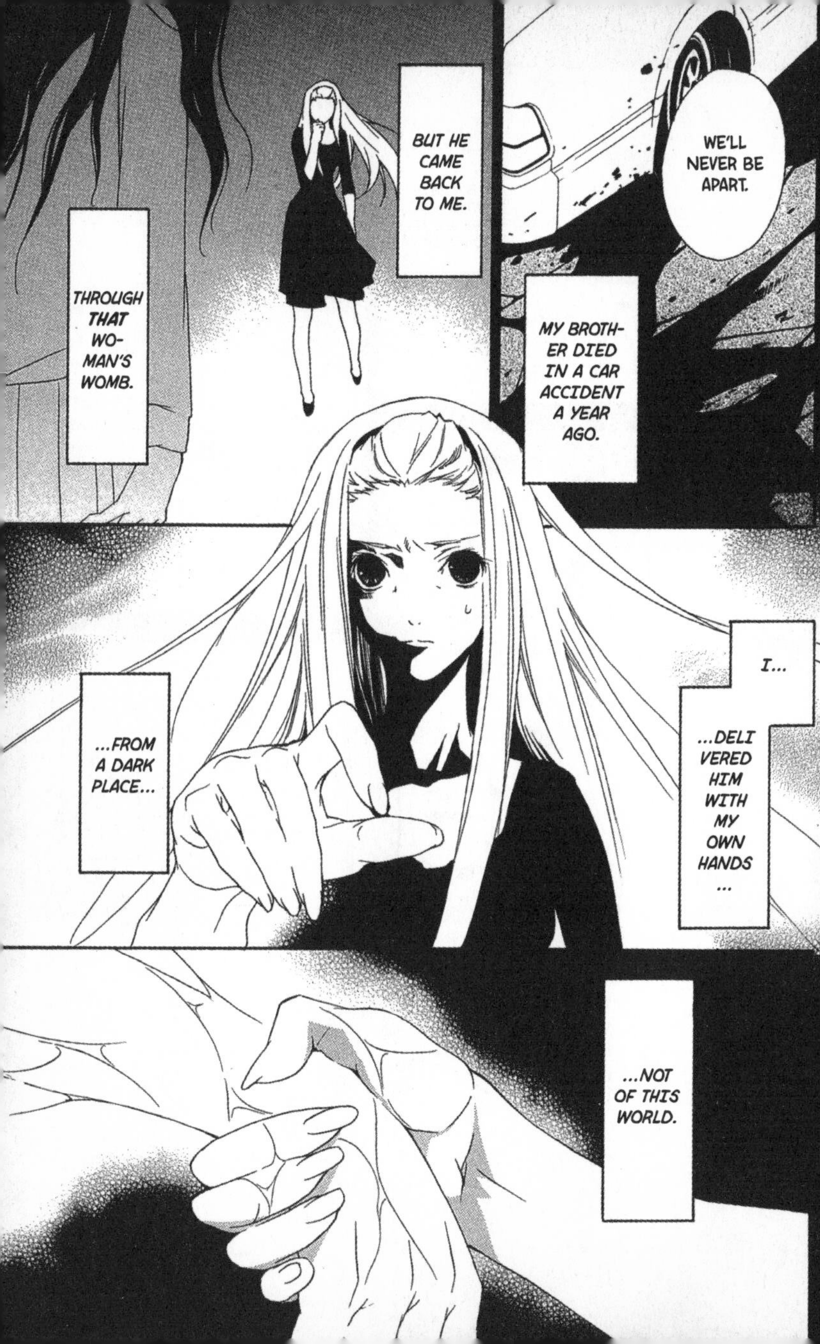
WE'LL NEVER BE APART.
MY BROTHER DIED IN A CAR ACCIDENT A YEAR AGO.
BUT HE CAME BACK TO ME.
THROUGH THAT WOMAN'S WOMB.
I...
...DELIVERED HIM WITH MY OWN HANDS...
...FROM A DARK PLACE...
...NOT OF THIS WORLD.

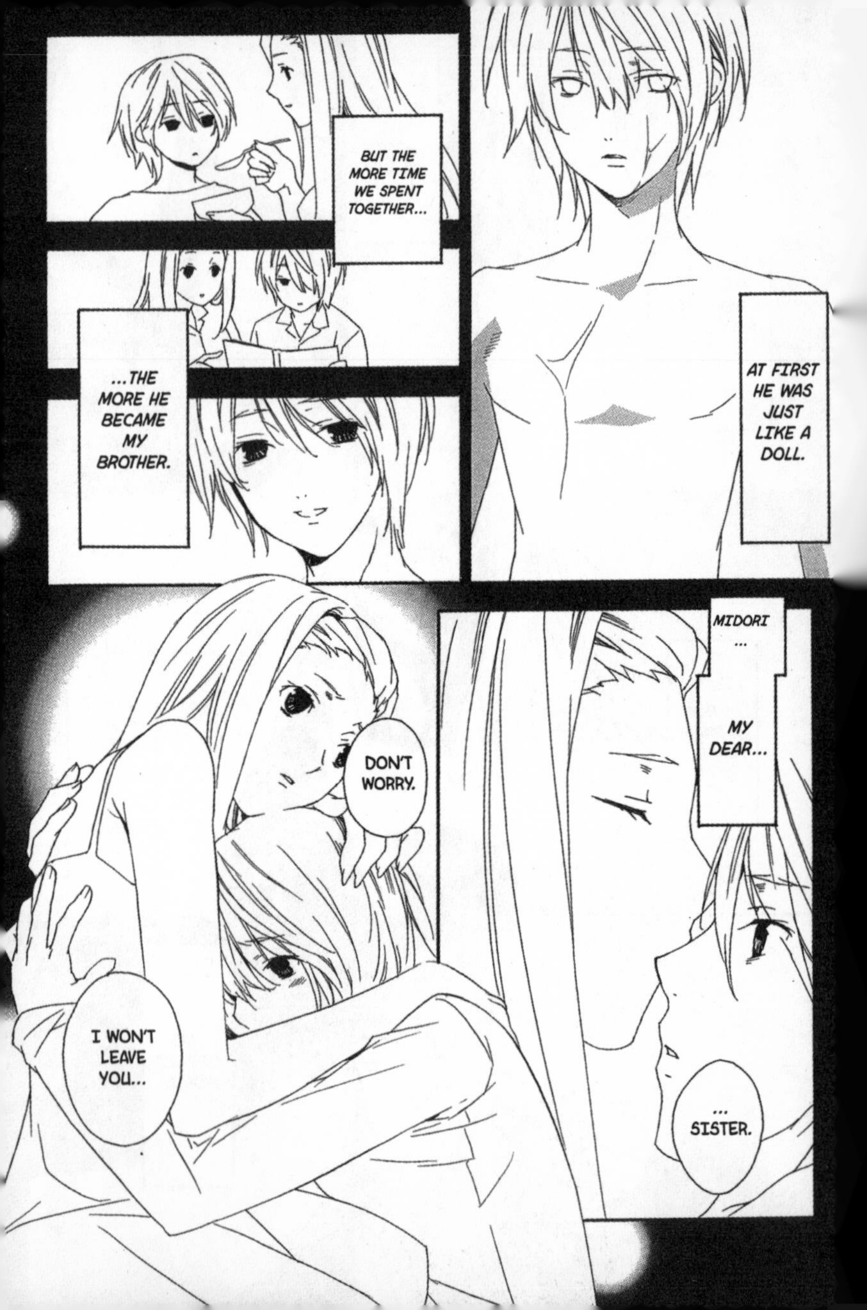
AT FIRST HE WAS JUST LIKE A DOLL.
BUT THE MORE TIME WE SPENT TOGETHER...
...THE MORE HE BECAME MY BROTHER.
MIDORI...
MY DEAR...
...SISTER.
DON'T WORRY.
I WON'T LEAVE YOU...

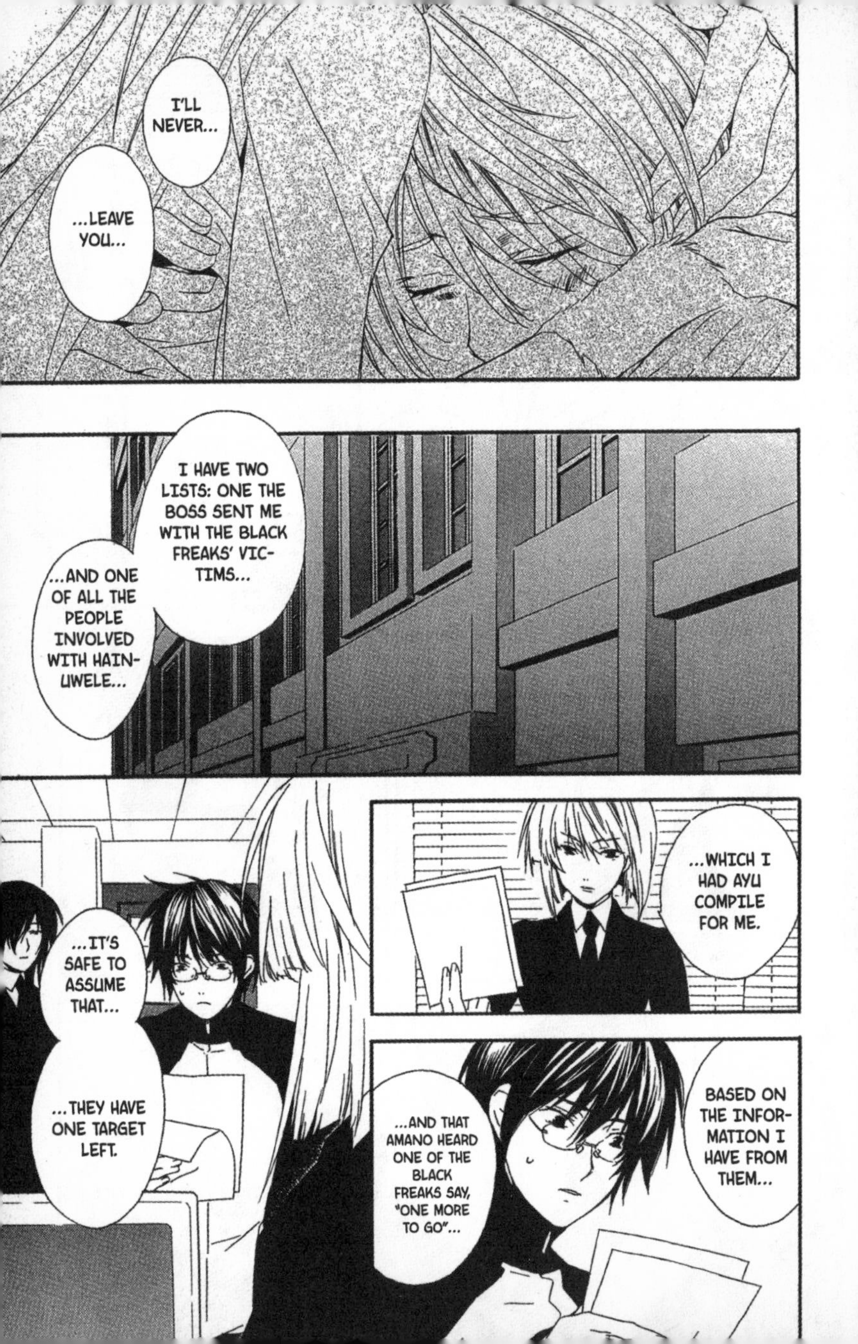
I'LL NEVER...
...LEAVE YOU...
I HAVE TWO LISTS: ONE THE BOSS SENT ME WITH THE BLACK FREAKS' VIC-TIMS...
...AND ONE OF ALL THE PEOPLE INVOLVED WITH HAIN-UWELE...
...WHICH I HAD AYU COMPILE FOR ME.
BASED ON THE INFOR-MATION I HAVE FROM THEM...
...AND THAT AMANO HEARD ONE OF THE BLACK FREAKS SAY, "ONE MORE TO GO"...
...IT'S SAFE TO ASSUME THAT...
...THEY HAVE ONE TARGET LEFT.

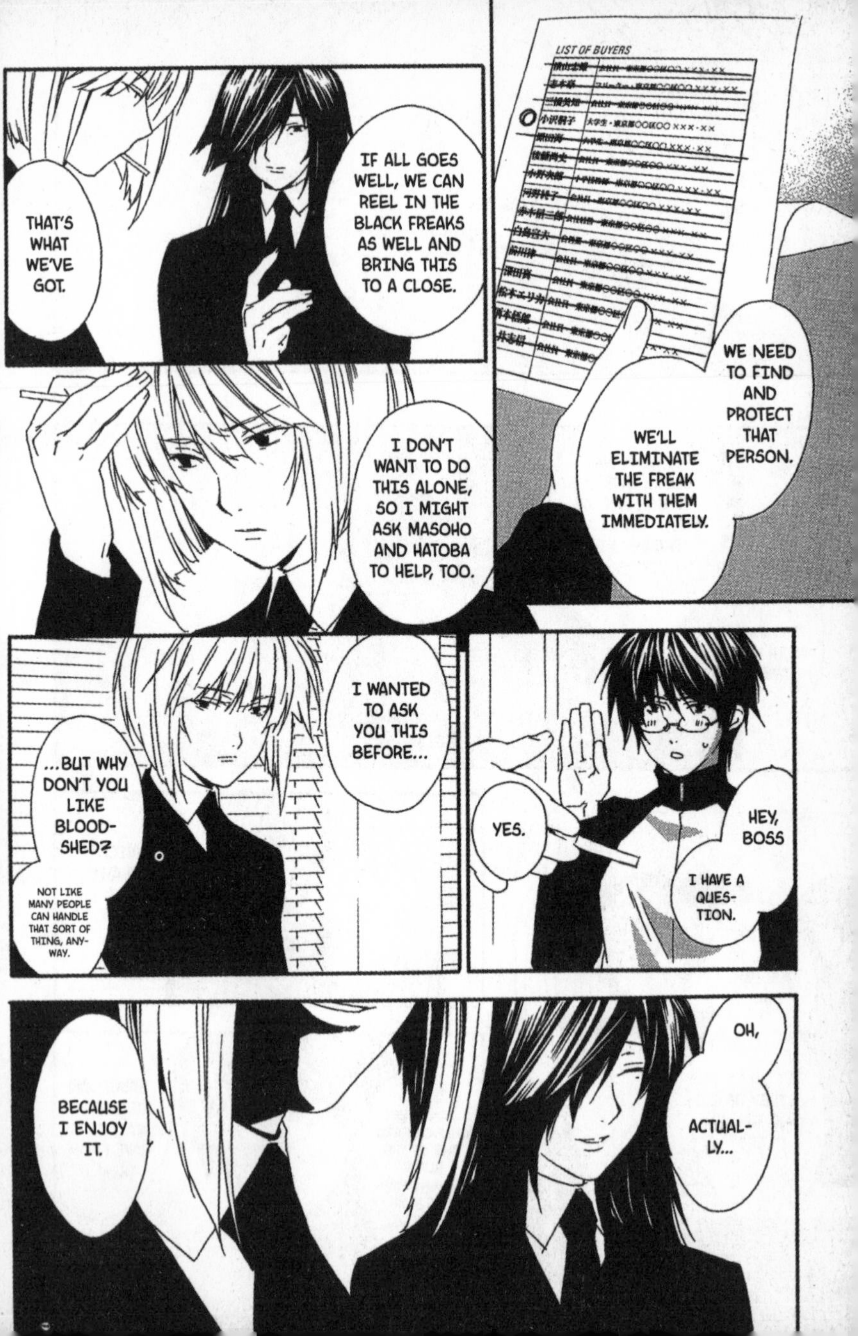
LIST OF BUYERS
WE NEED TO FIND AND PROTECT THAT PERSON.
WE'LL ELIMINATE THE FREAK WITH THEM IMMEDIATELY.
IF ALL GOES WELL, WE CAN REEL IN THE BLACK FREAKS AS WELL AND BRING THIS TO A CLOSE.
THAT'S WHAT WE'VE GOT.
I DON'T WANT TO DO THIS ALONE, SO I MIGHT ASK MASOHO AND HATOBA TO HELP, TOO.
HEY, BOSS
I HAVE A QUES-TION.
YES.
I WANTED TO ASK YOU THIS BEFORE...
...BUT WHY DON'T YOU LIKE BLOOD-SHED?
NOT LIKE MANY PEOPLE CAN HANDLE THAT SORT OF THING, ANY-WAY.
OH,
ACTUAL-LY...
BECAUSE I ENJOY IT.

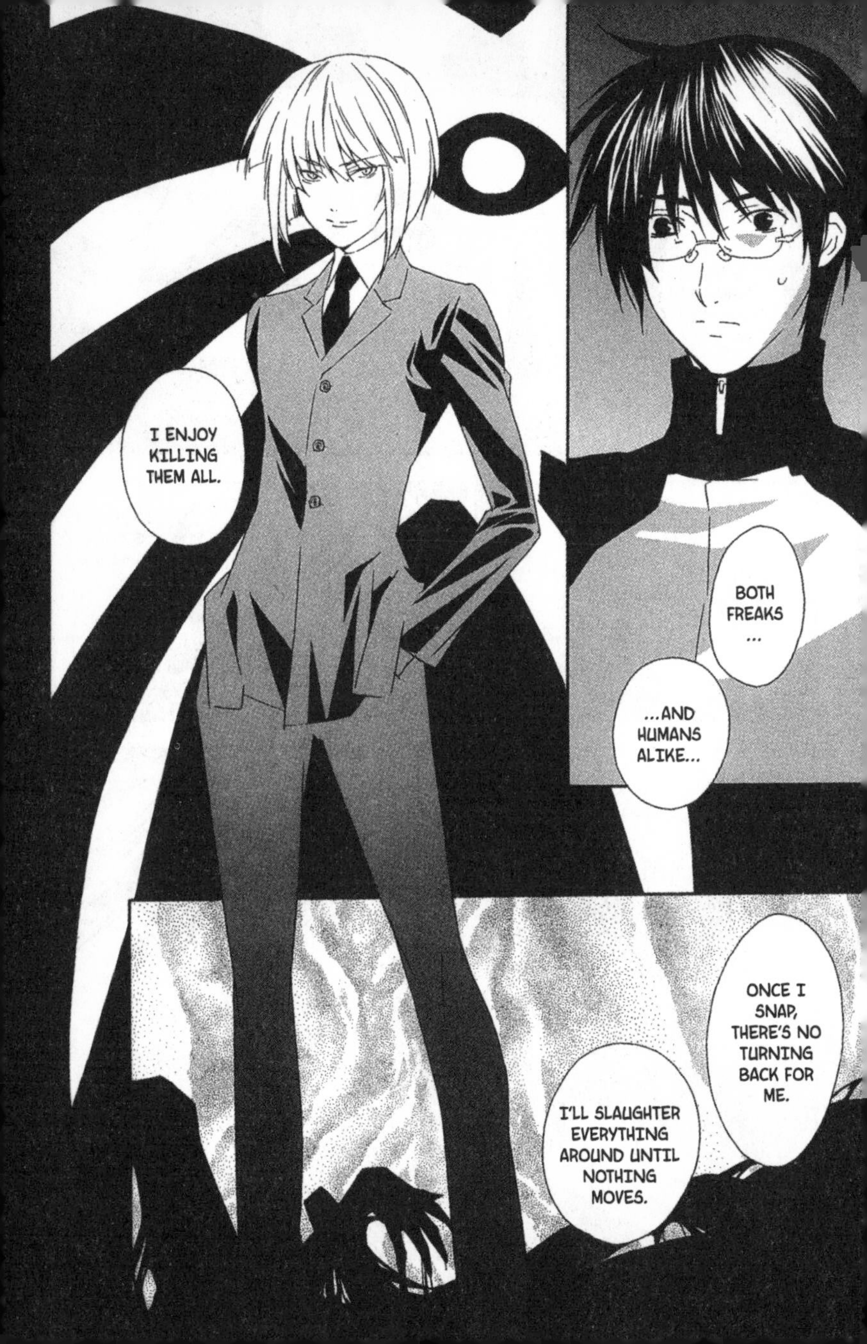
BOTH FREAKS ...
...AND HUMANS ALIKE...
I ENJOY KILLING THEM ALL.
ONCE I SNAP, THERE'S NO TURNING BACK FOR ME.
I'LL SLAUGHTER EVERYTHING AROUND UNTIL NOTHING MOVES.

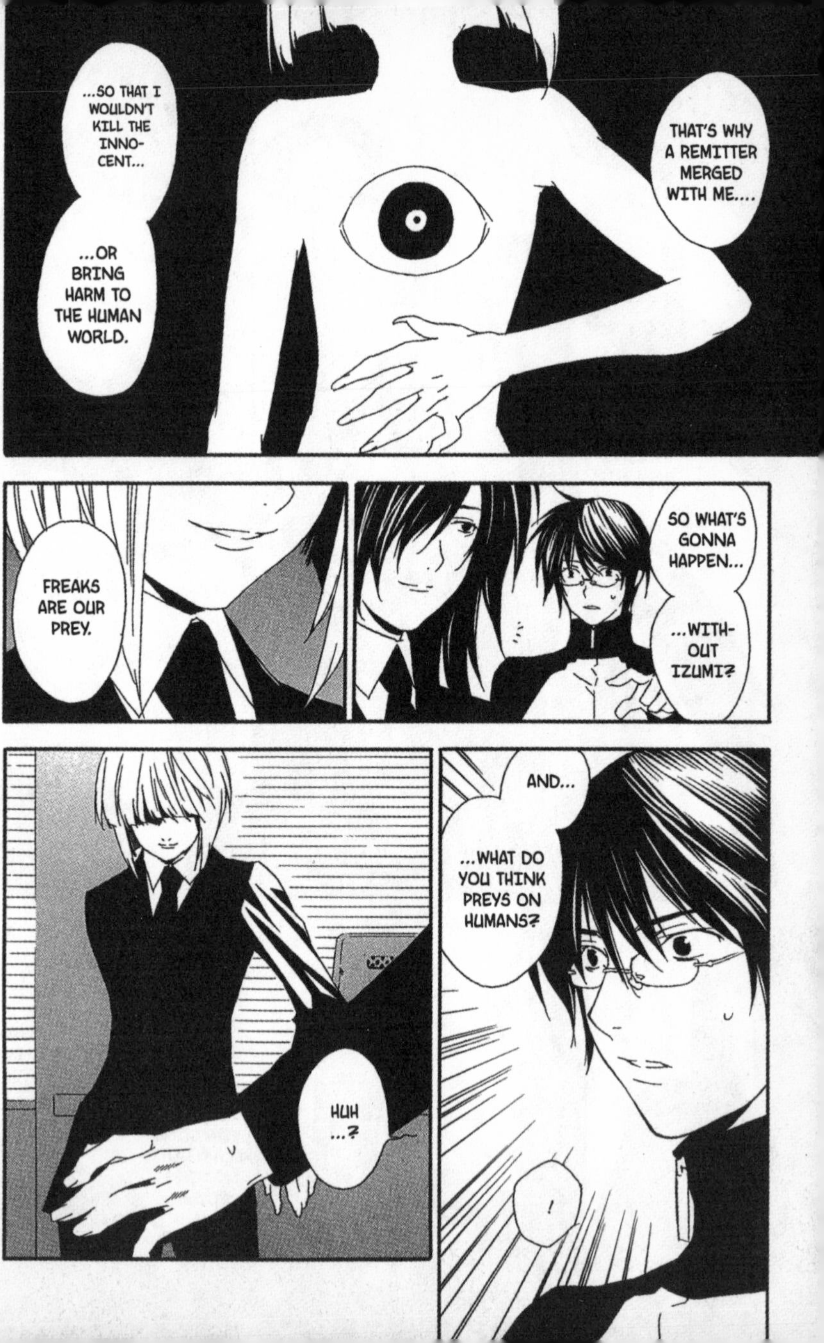
THAT'S WHY A REMITTER MERGED WITH ME....
...SO THAT I WOULDN'T KILL THE INNO-CENT...
...OR BRING HARM TO THE HUMAN WORLD.
SO WHAT'S GONNA HAPPEN...
...WITH-OUT IZUMI?
FREAKS ARE OUR PREY.
AND...
...WHAT DO YOU THINK PREYS ON HUMANS?
!
HUH ...?

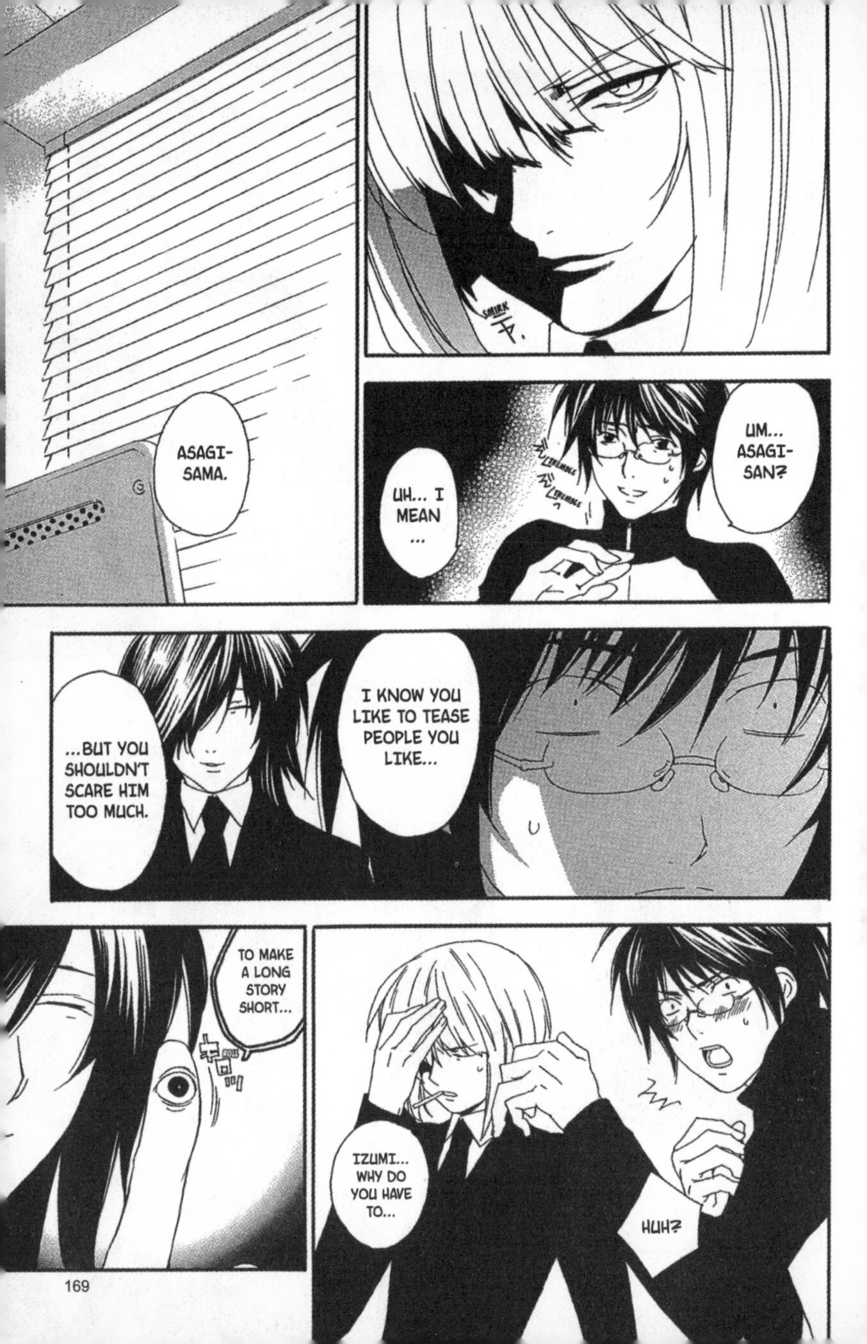
SMIRK
UM... ASAGI-SAN?
TREMBLE
TREMBLE
UH... I MEAN ...
ASAGI-SAMA.
I KNOW YOU LIKE TO TEASE PEOPLE YOU LIKE...
...BUT YOU SHOULDN'T SCARE HIM TOO MUCH.
HUH?
IZUMI... WHY DO YOU HAVE TO...
TO MAKE A LONG STORY SHORT...
ROLL

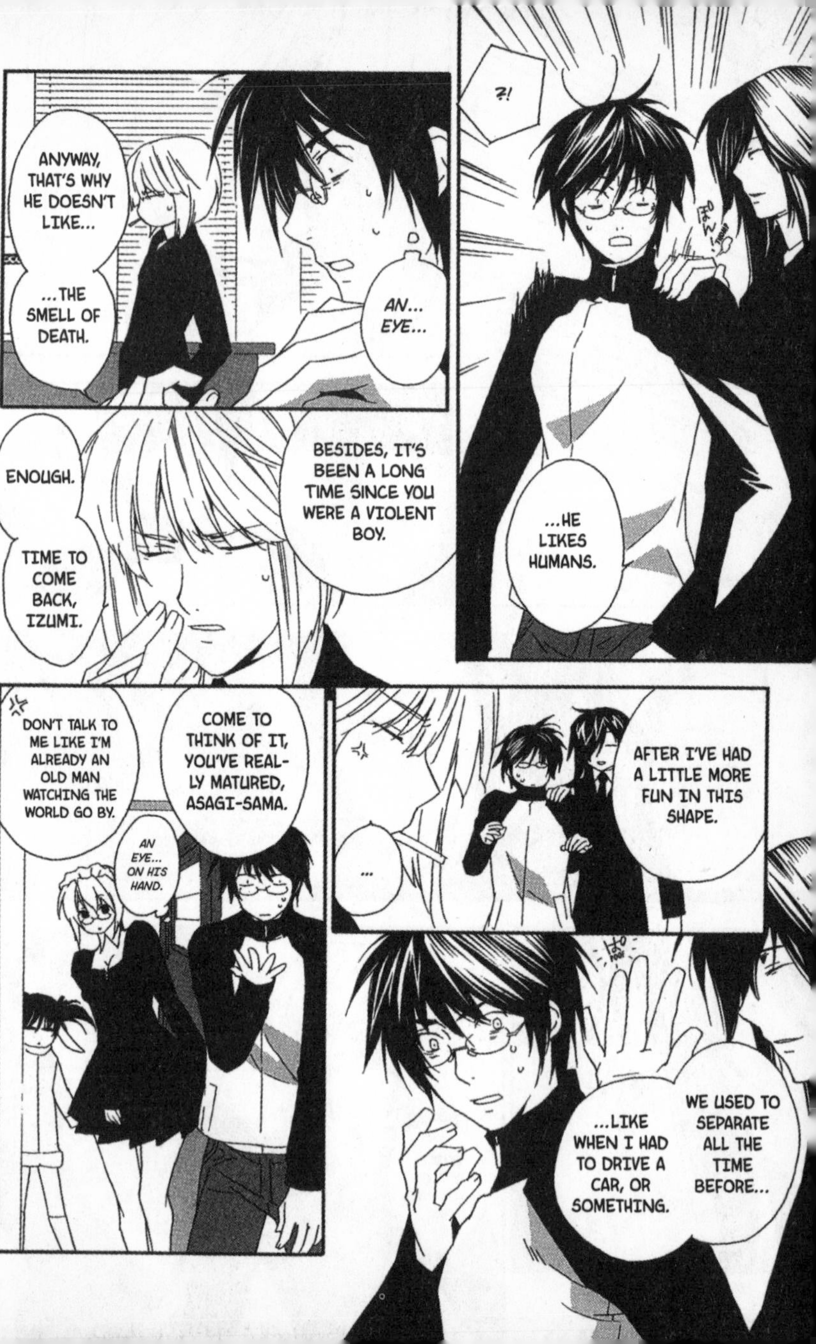
?!
...HE LIKES HUMANS.
ANYWAY, THAT'S WHY HE DOESN'T LIKE...
...THE SMELL OF DEATH.
AN... EYE...
BESIDES, IT'S BEEN A LONG TIME SINCE YOU WERE A VIOLENT BOY.
ENOUGH.
TIME TO COME BACK, IZUMI.
AFTER I'VE HAD A LITTLE MORE FUN IN THIS SHAPE.
...
WE USED TO SEPARATE ALL THE TIME BEFORE...
...LIKE WHEN I HAD TO DRIVE A CAR, OR SOMETHING.
COME TO THINK OF IT, YOU'VE REAL-LY MATURED, ASAGI-SAMA.
DON'T TALK TO ME LIKE I'M ALREADY AN OLD MAN WATCHING THE WORLD GO BY.
AN EYE... ON HIS HAND.

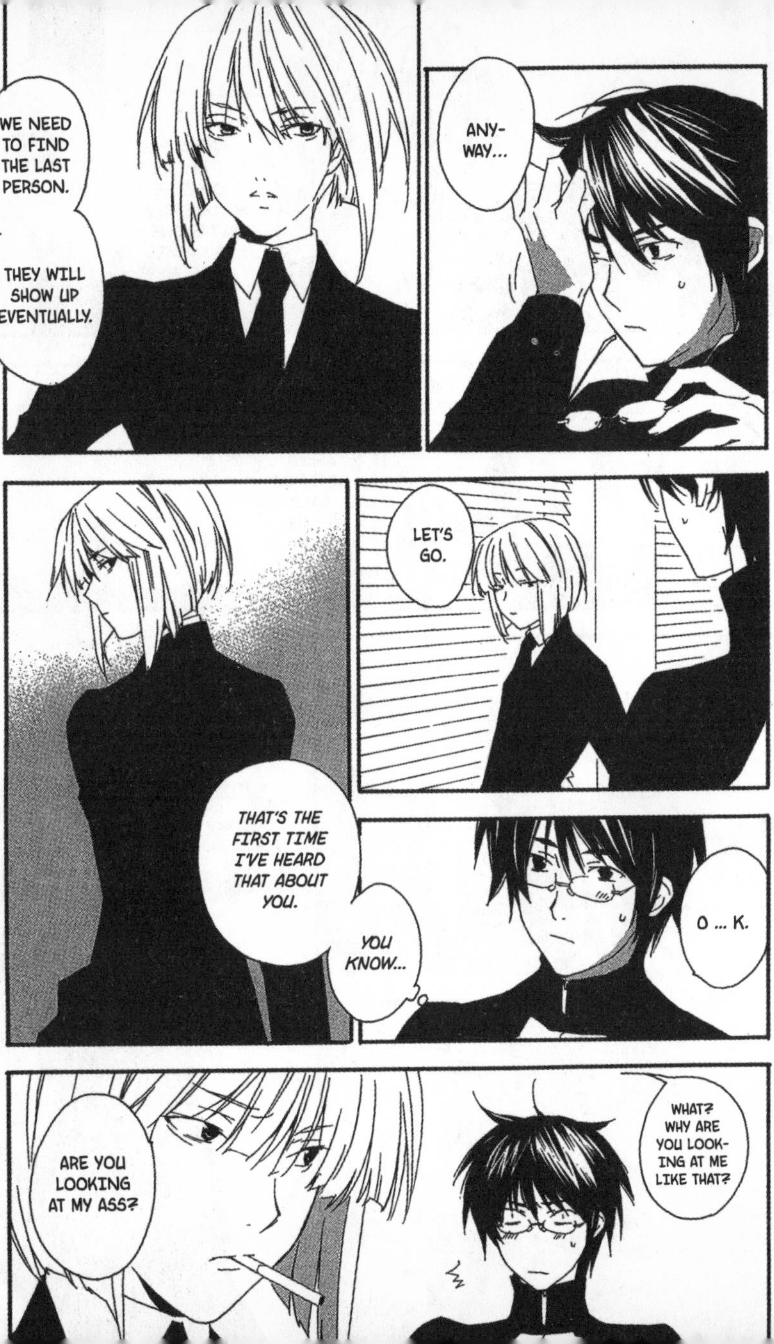
ANY-WAY...
WE NEED TO FIND THE LAST PERSON.
THEY WILL SHOW UP EVENTUALLY.
LET'S GO.
O ... K.
YOU KNOW...
THAT'S THE FIRST TIME I'VE HEARD THAT ABOUT YOU.
WHAT? WHY ARE YOU LOOKING AT ME LIKE THAT?
ARE YOU LOOKING AT MY ASS?

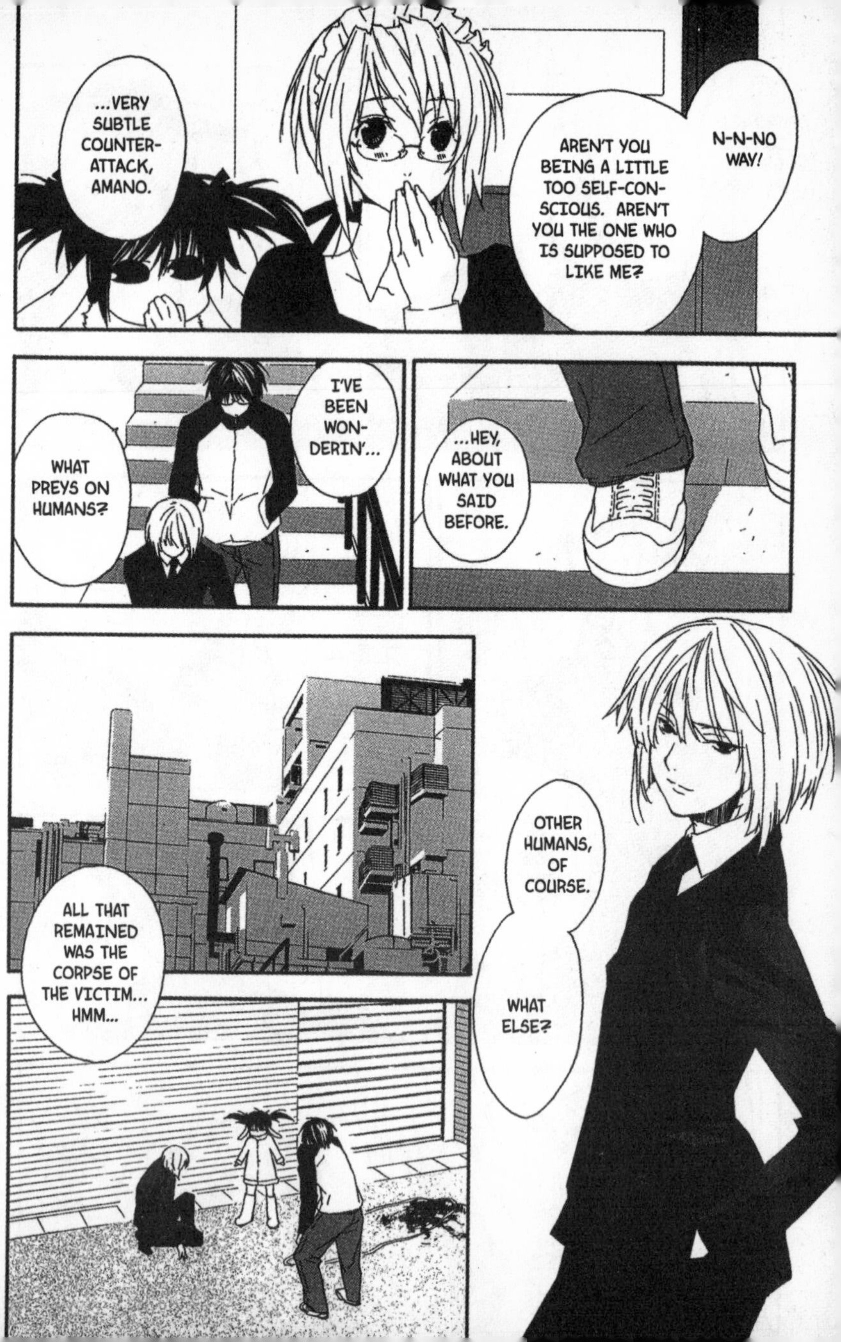
N-N-NO WAY!
AREN'T YOU BEING A LITTLE TOO SELF-CON-SCIOUS. AREN'T YOU THE ONE WHO IS SUPPOSED TO LIKE ME?
...VERY SUBTLE COUNTER-ATTACK, AMANO.
...HEY, ABOUT WHAT YOU SAID BEFORE.
I'VE BEEN WON-DERIN'...
WHAT PREYS ON HUMANS?
OTHER HUMANS, OF COURSE.
WHAT ELSE?
ALL THAT REMAINED WAS THE CORPSE OF THE VICTIM... HMM...

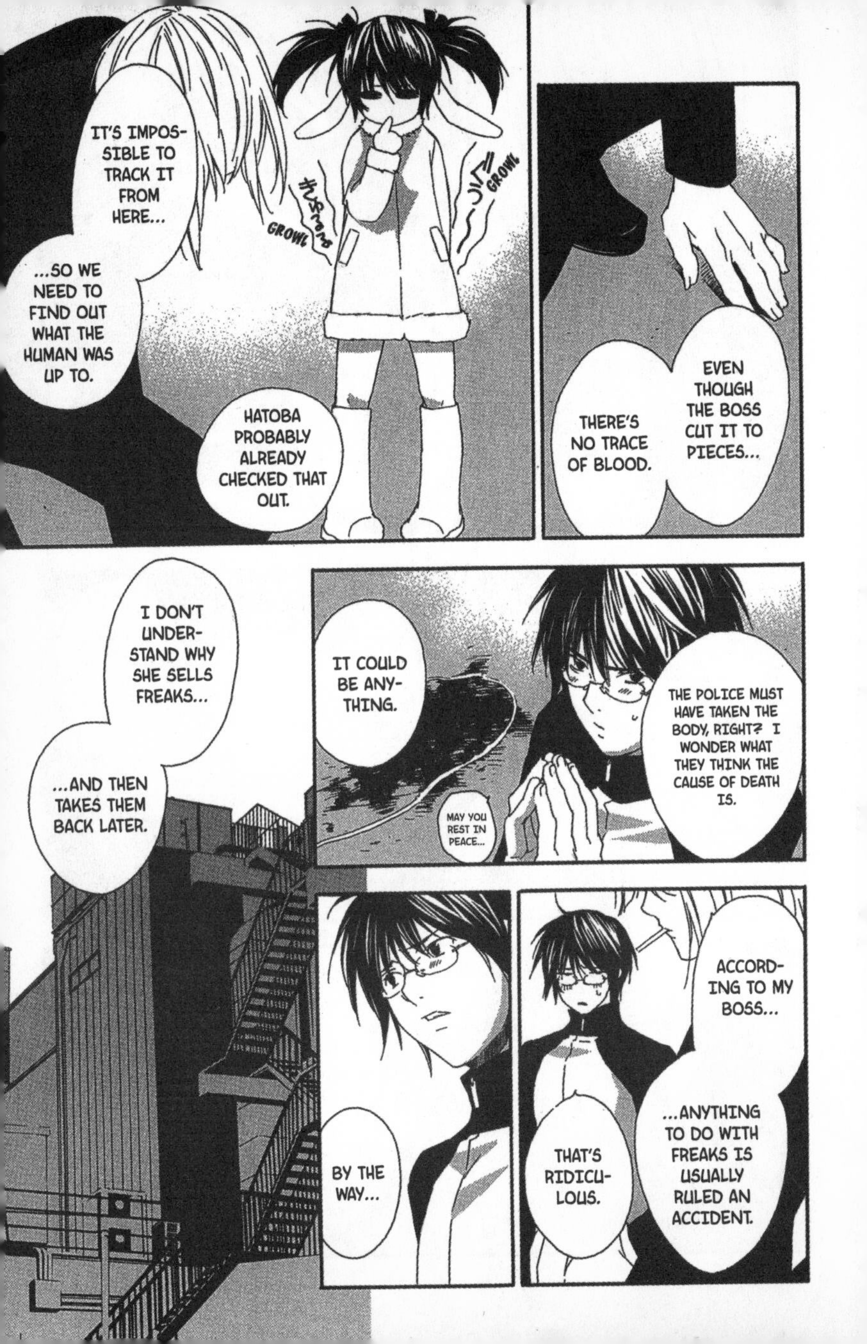
EVEN THOUGH THE BOSS CUT IT TO PIECES...
THERE'S NO TRACE OF BLOOD.
GROWL
IT'S IMPOSSIBLE TO TRACK IT FROM HERE...
GROWL
...SO WE NEED TO FIND OUT WHAT THE HUMAN WAS UP TO.
HATOBA PROBABLY ALREADY CHECKED THAT OUT.
THE POLICE MUST HAVE TAKEN THE BODY, RIGHT? I WONDER WHAT THEY THINK THE CAUSE OF DEATH IS.
IT COULD BE ANYTHING.
MAY YOU REST IN PEACE...
ACCORDING TO MY BOSS...
...ANYTHING TO DO WITH FREAKS IS USUALLY RULED AN ACCIDENT.
THAT'S RIDICULOUS.
BY THE WAY...
I DON'T UNDERSTAND WHY SHE SELLS FREAKS...
...AND THEN TAKES THEM BACK LATER.

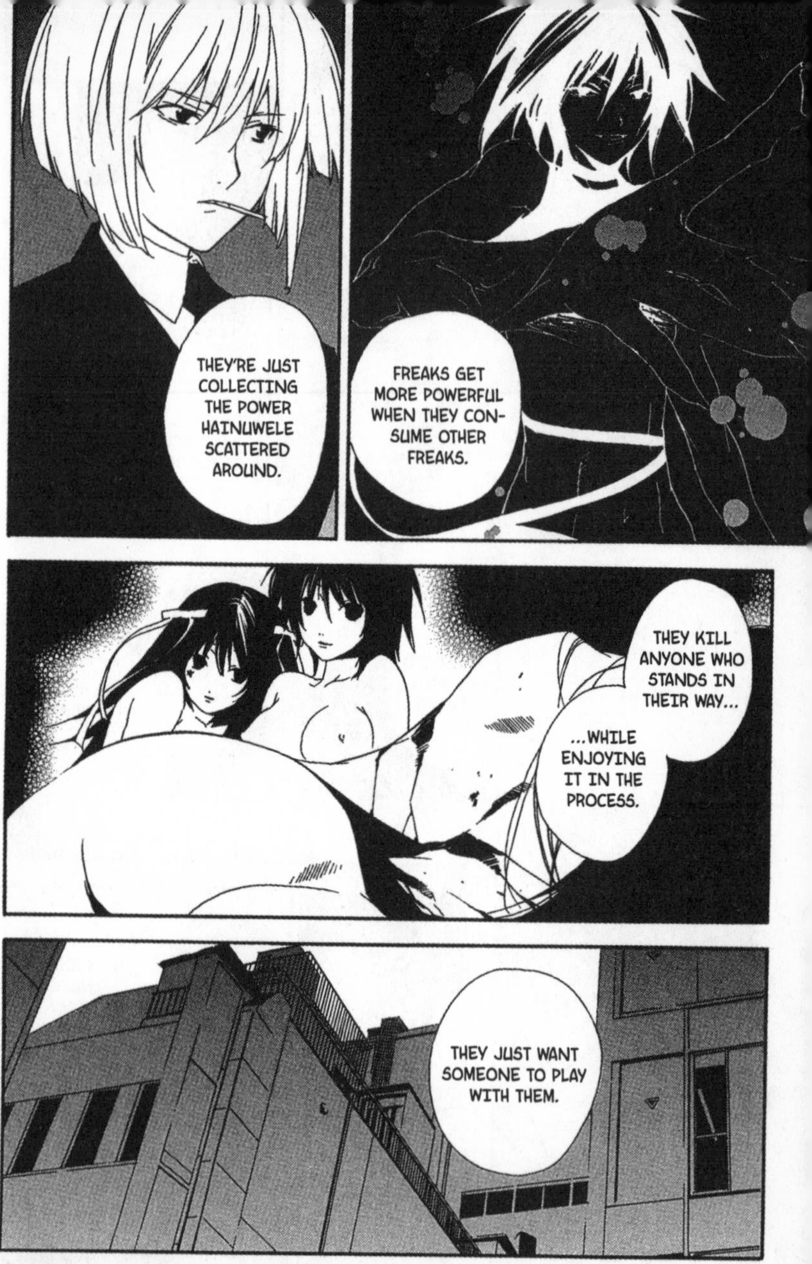
FREAKS GET MORE POWERFUL WHEN THEY CON- SUME OTHER FREAKS.
THEY'RE JUST COLLECTING THE POWER HAINUWELE SCATTERED AROUND.
THEY KILL ANYONE WHO STANDS IN THEIR WAY...
...WHILE ENJOYING IT IN THE PROCESS.
THEY JUST WANT SOMEONE TO PLAY WITH THEM.

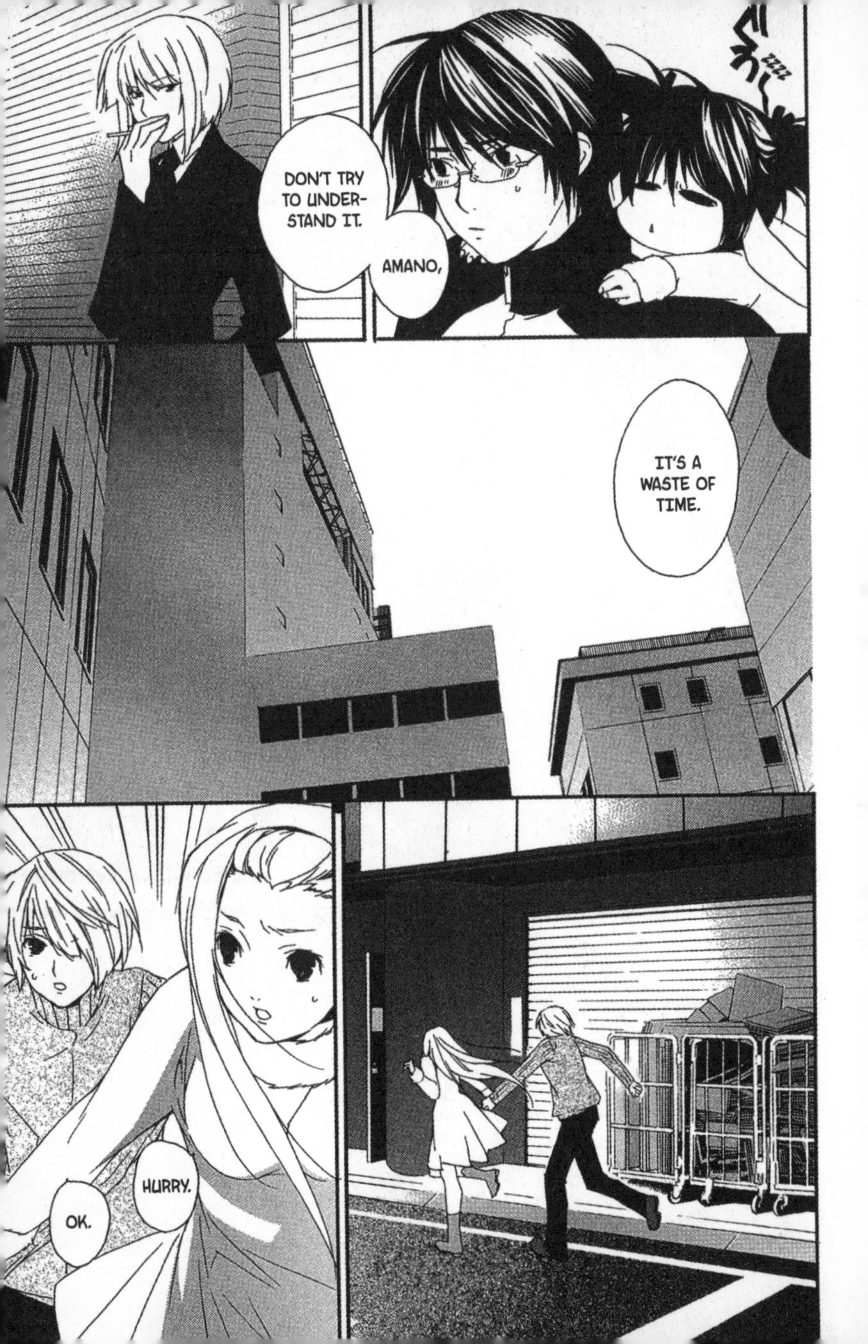
AMANO,
DON'T TRY TO UNDER-STAND IT.
IT'S A WASTE OF TIME.
HURRY.
OK.

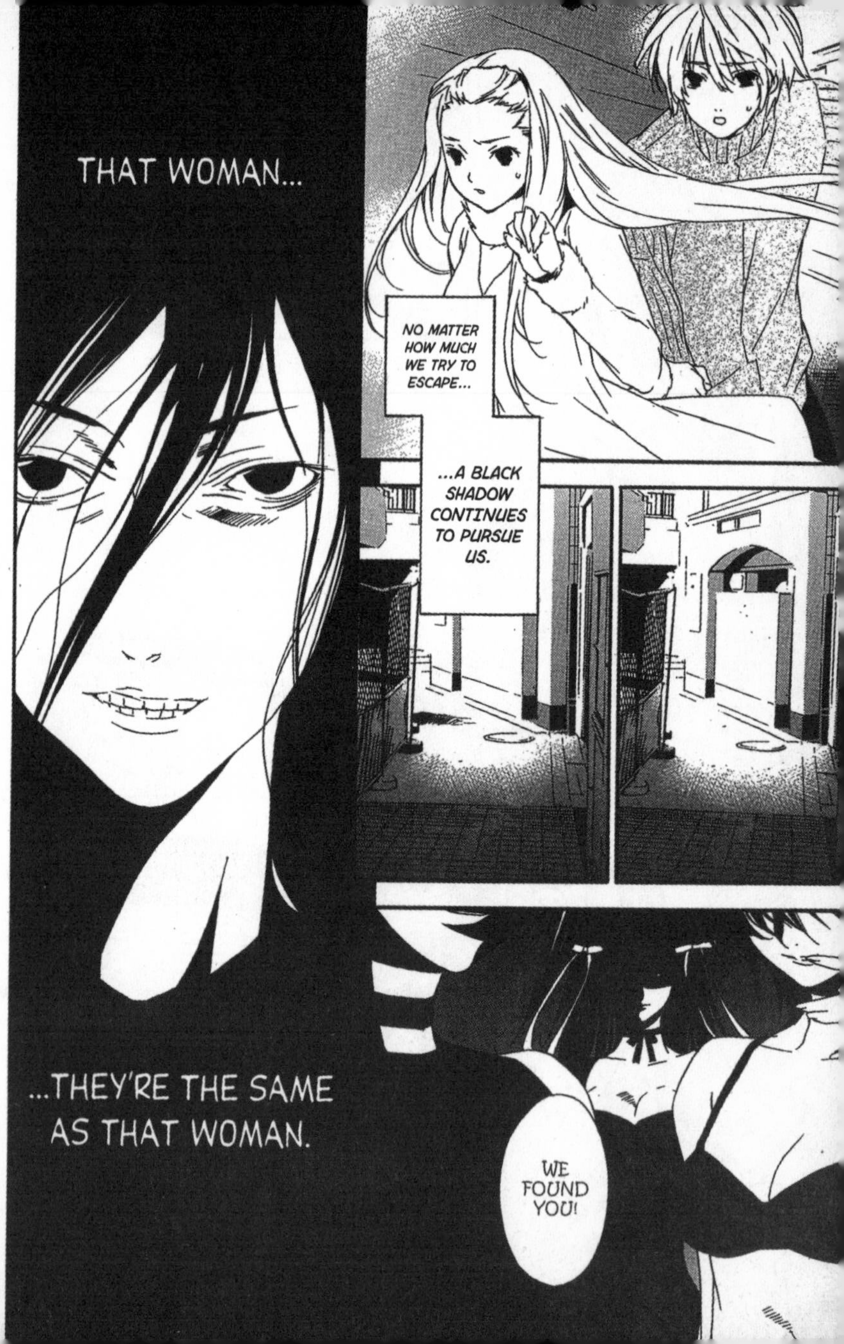
NO MATTER HOW MUCH WE TRY TO ESCAPE...
...A BLACK SHADOW CONTINUES TO PURSUE US.
WE FOUND YOU!
THAT WOMAN...
...THEY'RE THE SAME AS THAT WOMAN.

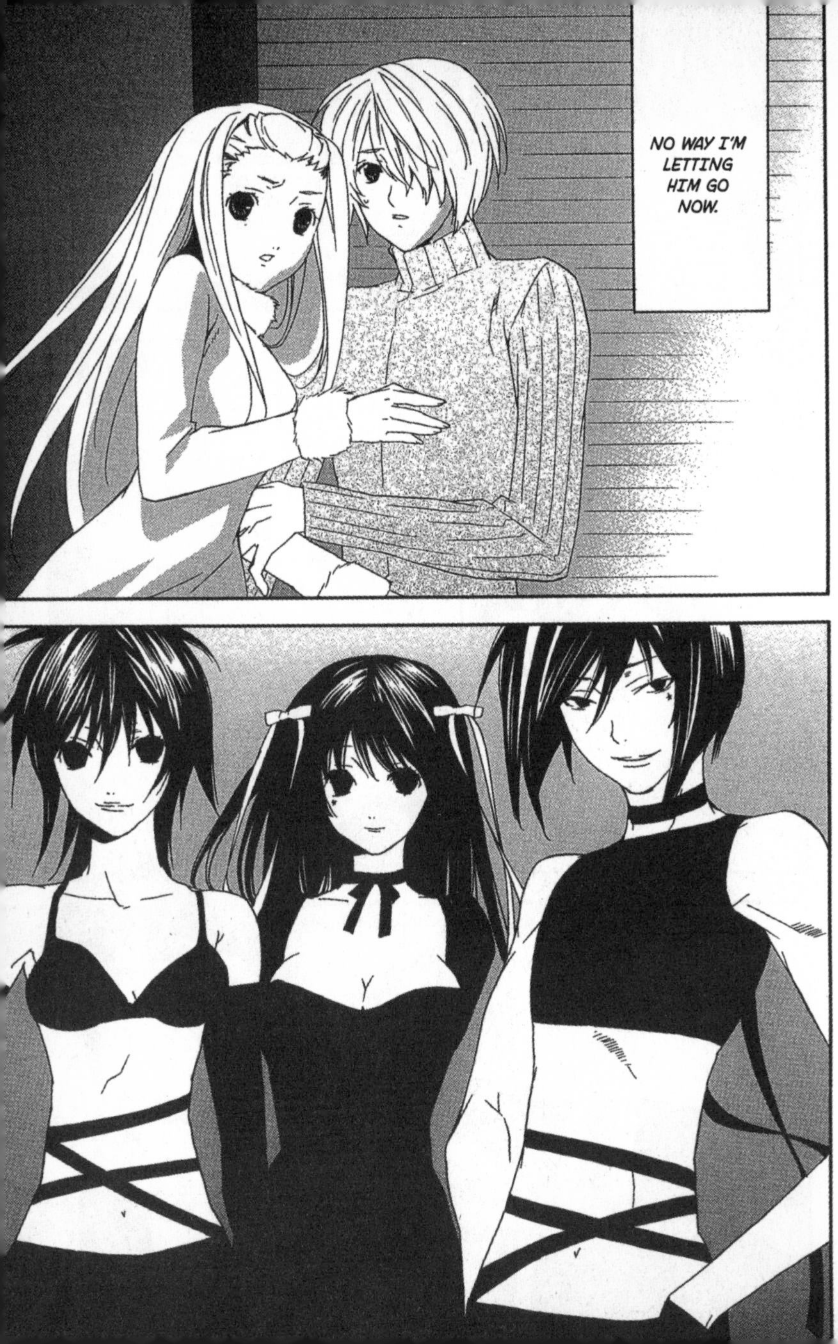
NO WAY I'M LETTING HIM GO NOW.

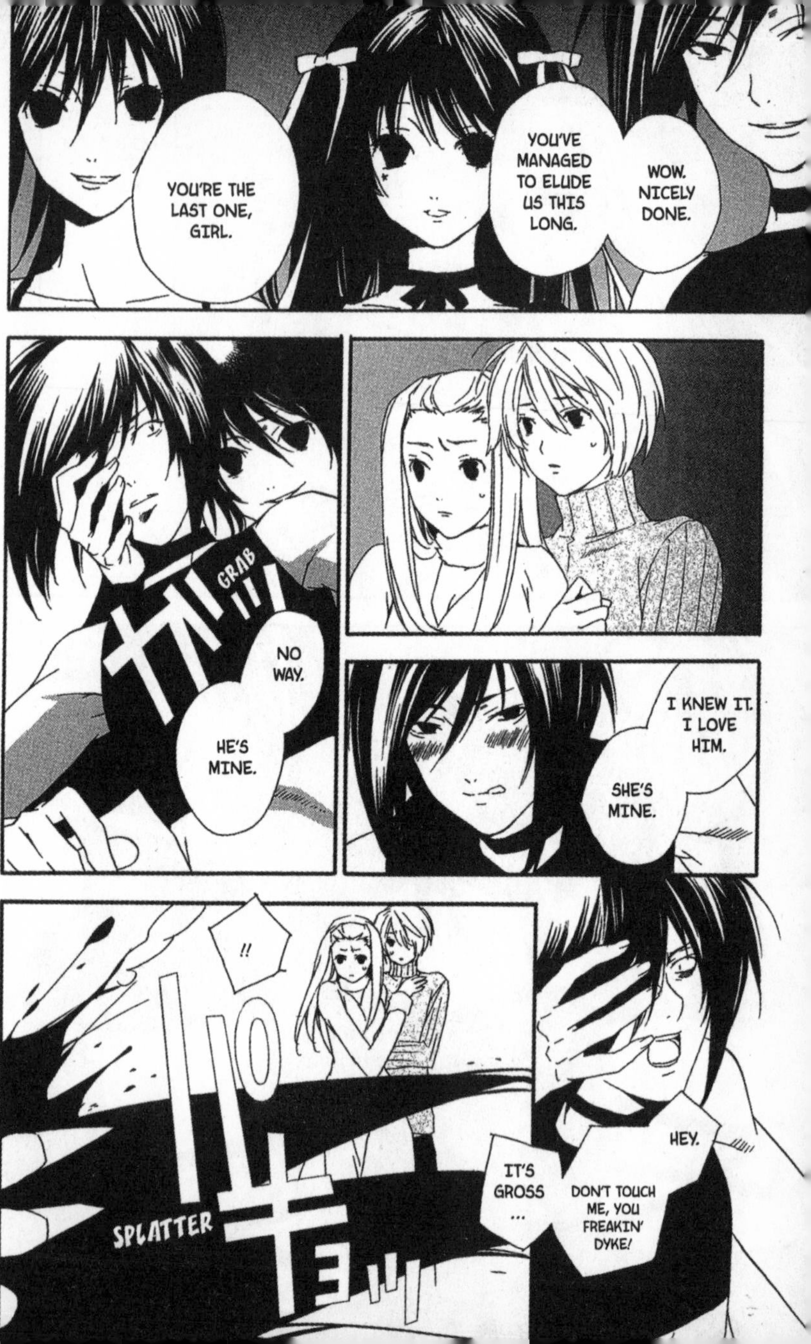
WOW. NICELY DONE.
YOU'VE MANAGED TO ELUDE US THIS LONG.
YOU'RE THE LAST ONE, GIRL.
I KNEW IT. I LOVE HIM.
SHE'S MINE.
GRAB
NO WAY.
HE'S MINE.
HEY.
DON'T TOUCH ME, YOU FREAKIN' DYKE!
IT'S GROSS ...
!!
SPLATTER

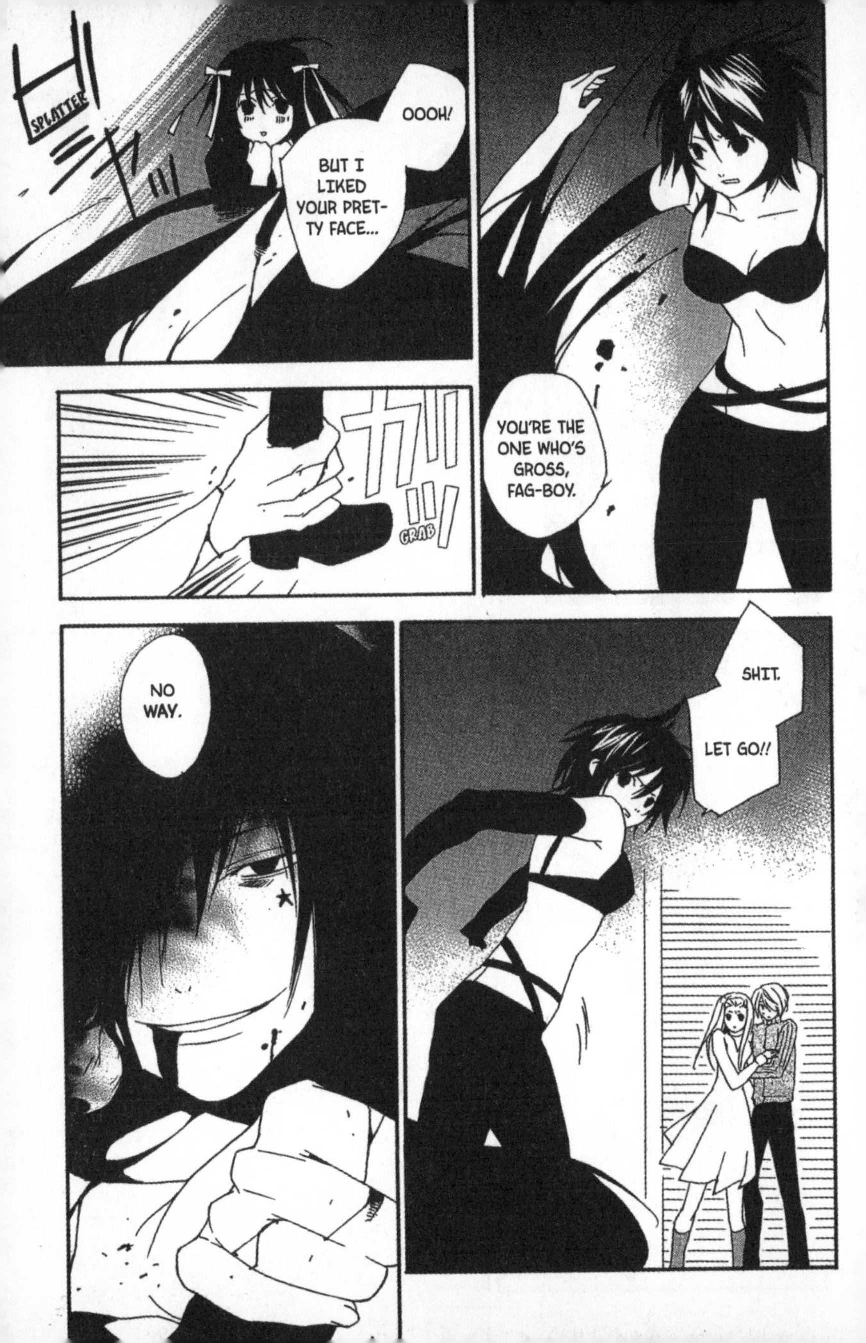
YOU'RE THE ONE WHO'S GROSS, FAG-BOY.
SPLATTER
OOOH!
BUT I LIKED YOUR PRET-TY FACE...
GRAB
SHIT.
LET GO!!
NO WAY.

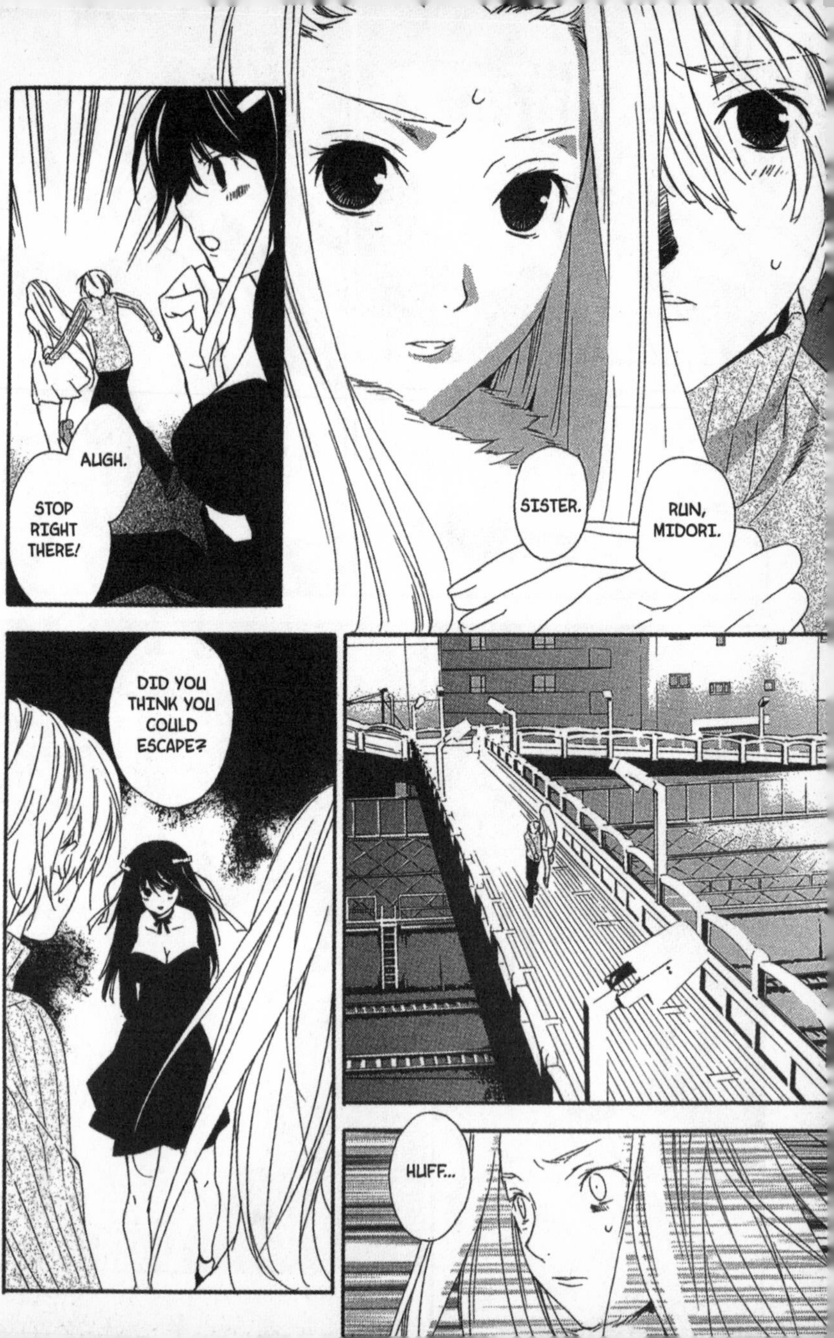
RUN, MIDORI.
SISTER.
AUGH.
STOP RIGHT THERE!
HUFF...
DID YOU THINK YOU COULD ESCAPE?

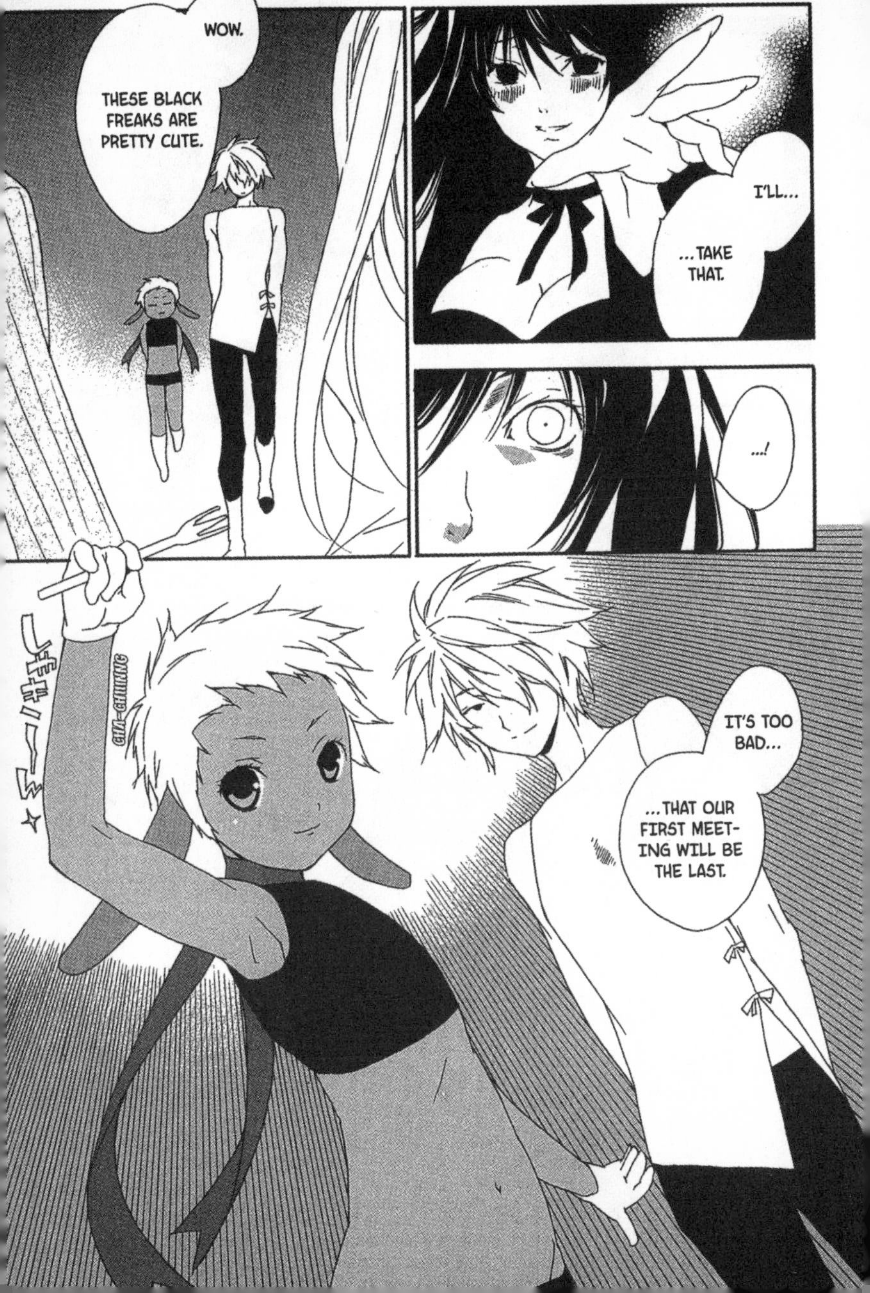
I'LL...
...TAKE THAT.
...!
WOW.
THESE BLACK FREAKS ARE PRETTY CUTE.
IT'S TOO BAD...
...THAT OUR FIRST MEETING WILL BE THE LAST.
CHA-CHIIIING

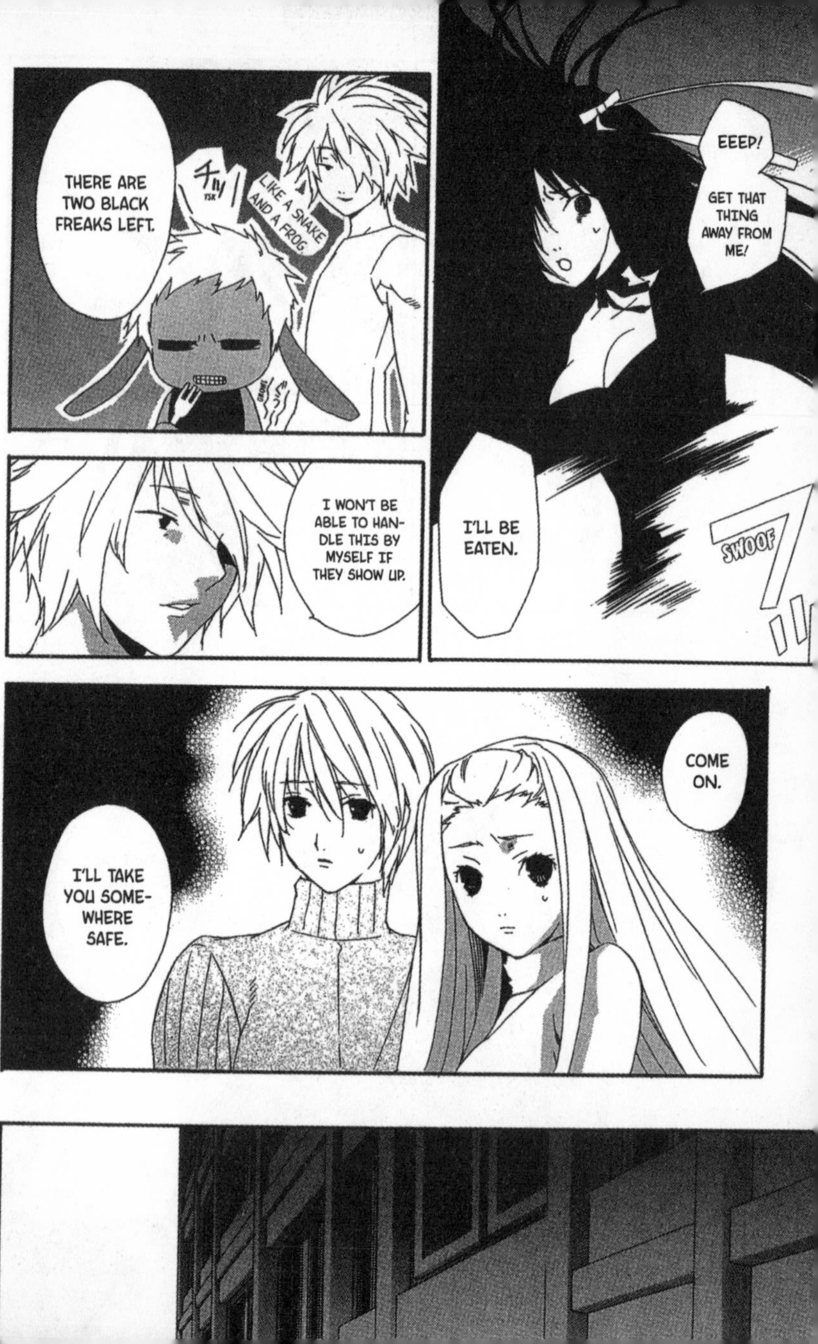
EEEP!
GET THAT THING AWAY FROM ME!
I'LL BE EATEN.
SWOOF
LIKE A SNAKE AND A FROG.
TSK
THERE ARE TWO BLACK FREAKS LEFT.
GROWL
I WON'T BE ABLE TO HANDLE THIS BY MYSELF IF THEY SHOW UP.
COME ON.
I'LL TAKE YOU SOMEWHERE SAFE.

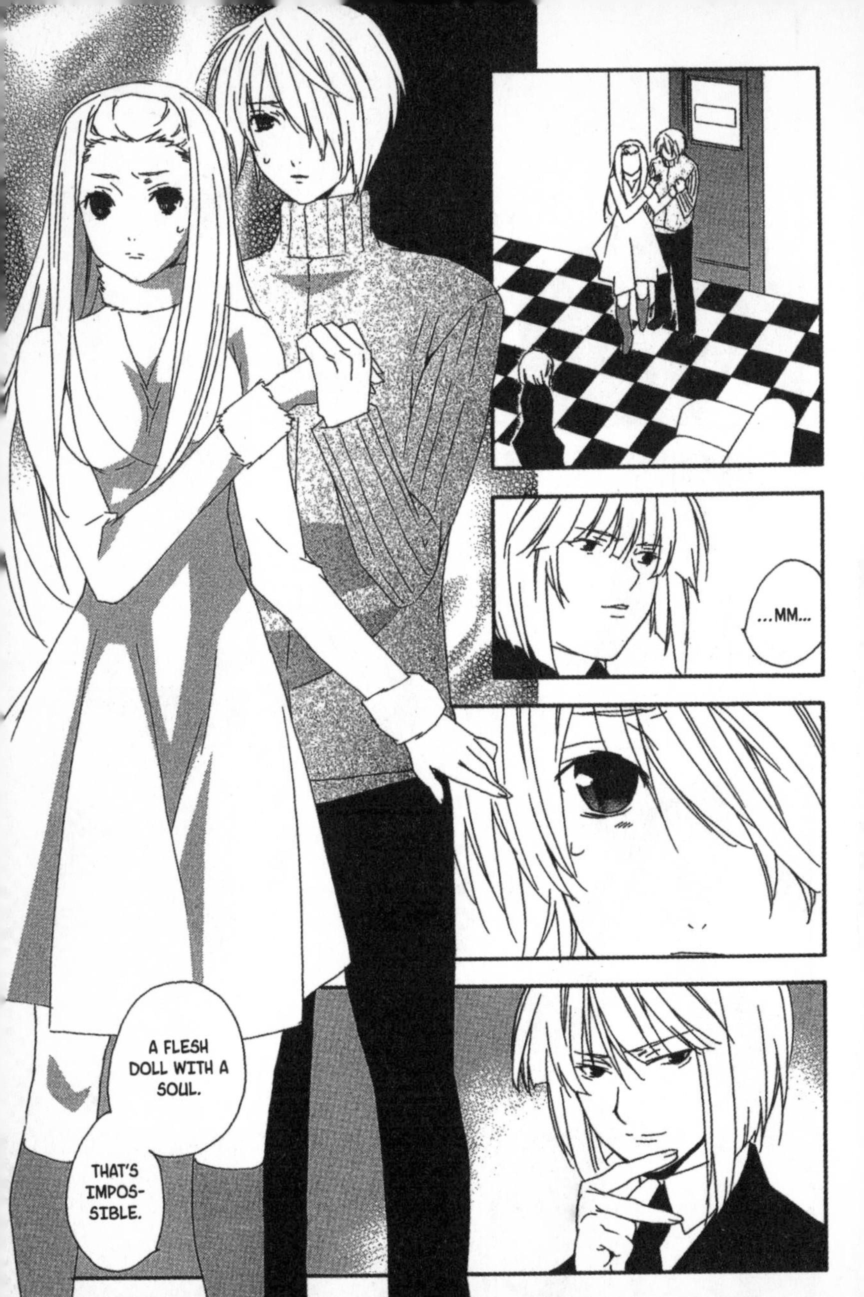
...MM...
A FLESH DOLL WITH A SOUL.
THAT'S IMPOSSIBLE.

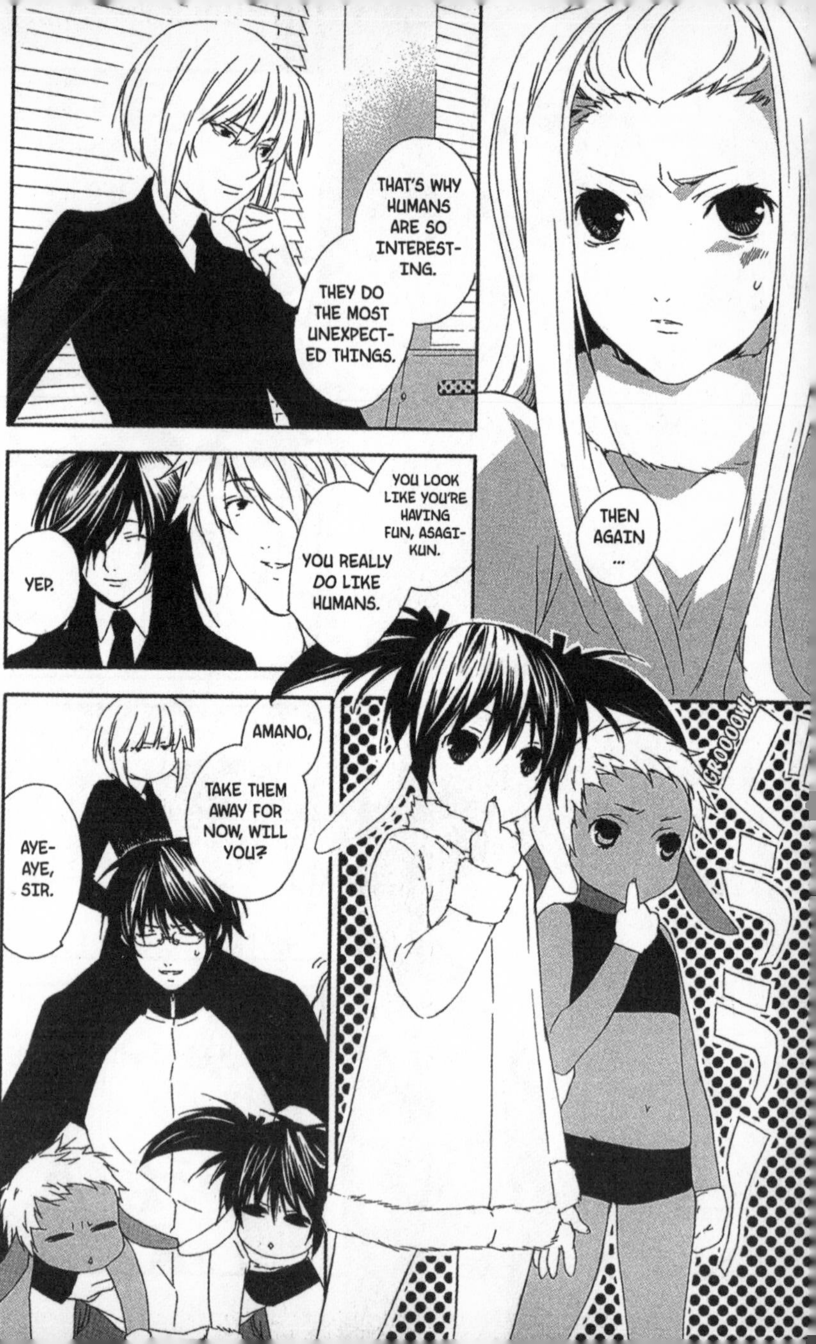
THEN AGAIN ...
THAT'S WHY HUMANS ARE SO INTEREST-ING.
THEY DO THE MOST UNEXPECT-ED THINGS.
YOU LOOK LIKE YOU'RE HAVING FUN, ASAGI-KUN.
YOU REALLY DO LIKE HUMANS.
YEP.
GROOOOWL
AMANO,
TAKE THEM AWAY FOR NOW, WILL YOU?
AYE-AYE, SIR.

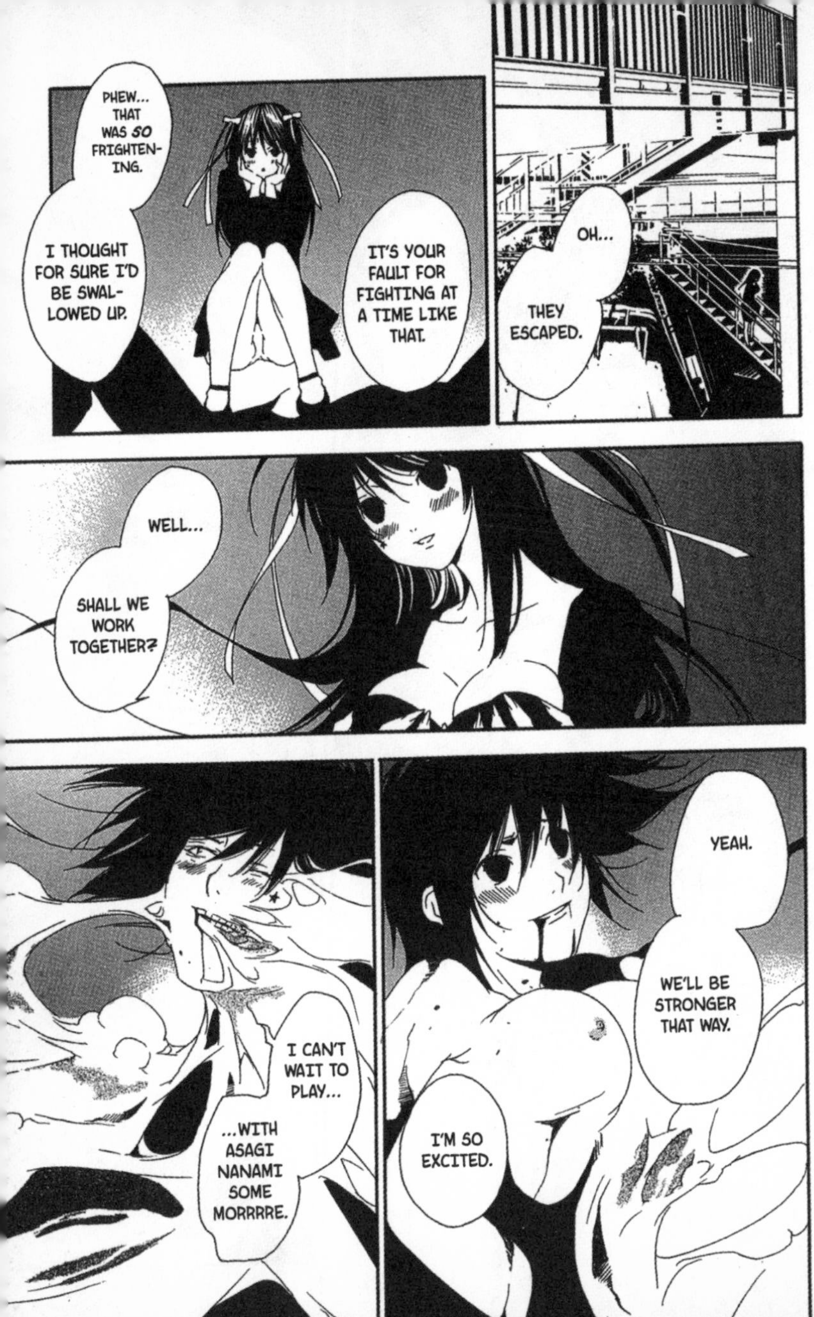
OH...
THEY ESCAPED.
PHEW... THAT WAS *SO* FRIGHTENING.
I THOUGHT FOR SURE I'D BE SWALLOWED UP.
IT'S YOUR FAULT FOR FIGHTING AT A TIME LIKE THAT.
WELL...
SHALL WE WORK TOGETHER?
YEAH.
WE'LL BE STRONGER THAT WAY.
I'M SO EXCITED.
I CAN'T WAIT TO PLAY...
...WITH ASAGI NANAMI SOME MORRRRE.

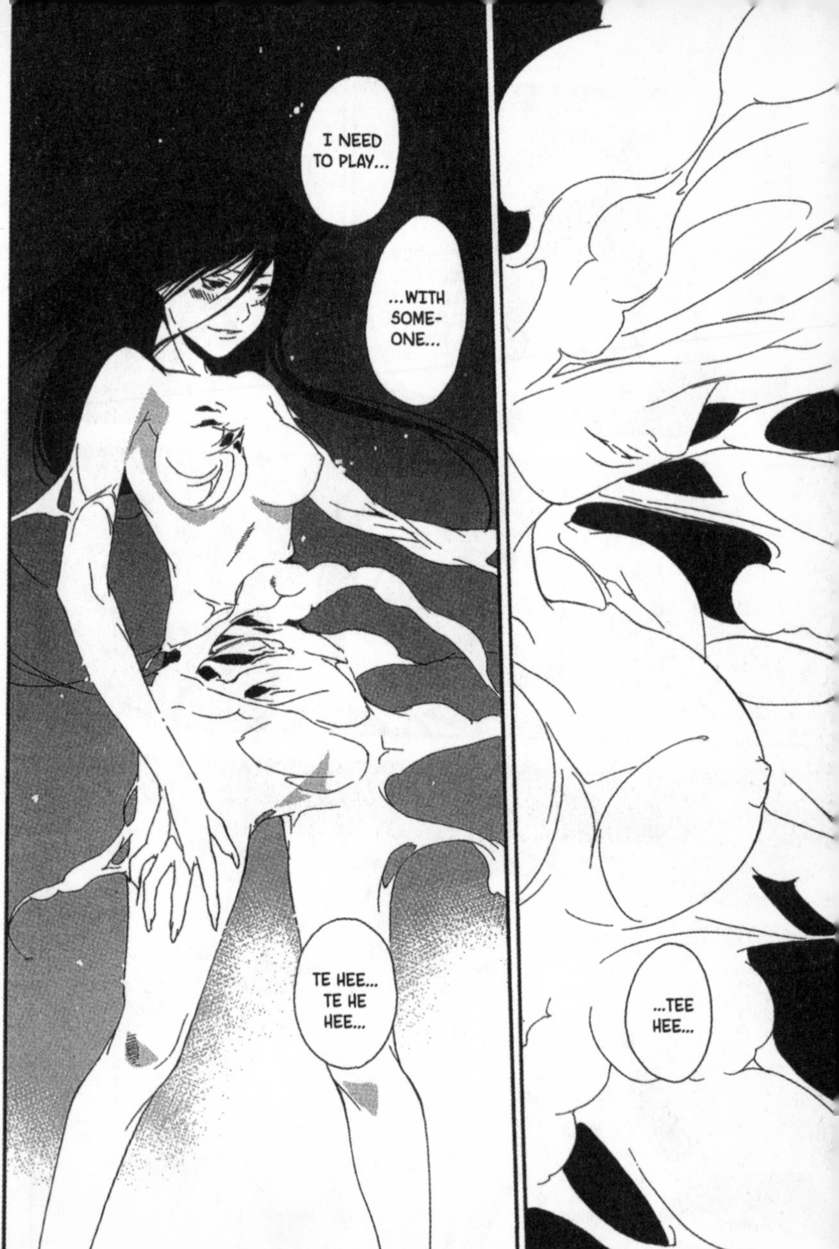
...TEE HEE...
I NEED TO PLAY...
...WITH SOME-ONE...
TE HEE... TE HE HEE...

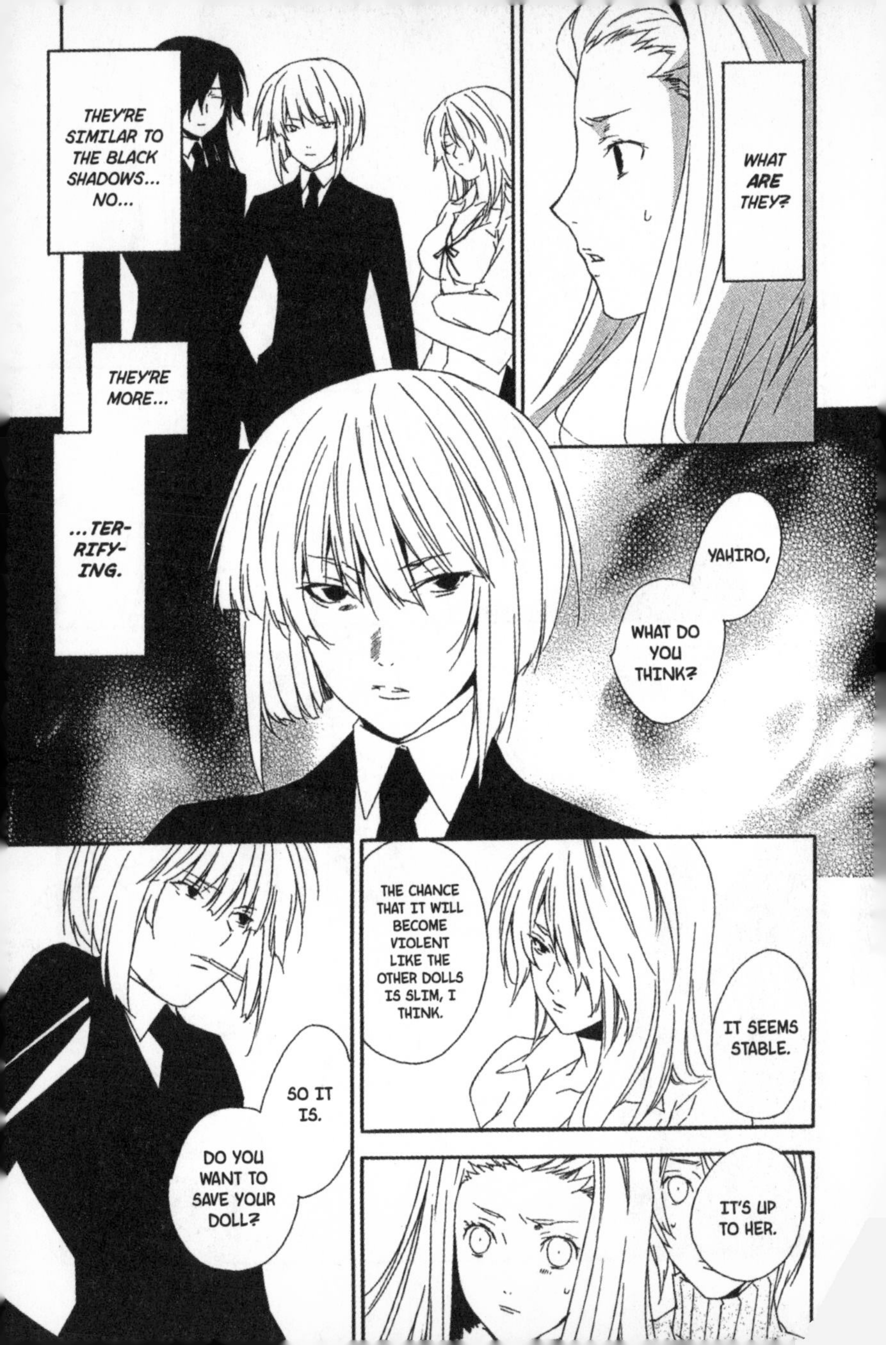
WHAT ARE THEY?
THEY'RE SIMILAR TO THE BLACK SHADOWS... NO...
THEY'RE MORE...
...TER-RIFY-ING.
YAHIRO,
WHAT DO YOU THINK?
IT SEEMS STABLE.
THE CHANCE THAT IT WILL BECOME VIOLENT LIKE THE OTHER DOLLS IS SLIM, I THINK.
IT'S UP TO HER.
SO IT IS.
DO YOU WANT TO SAVE YOUR DOLL?

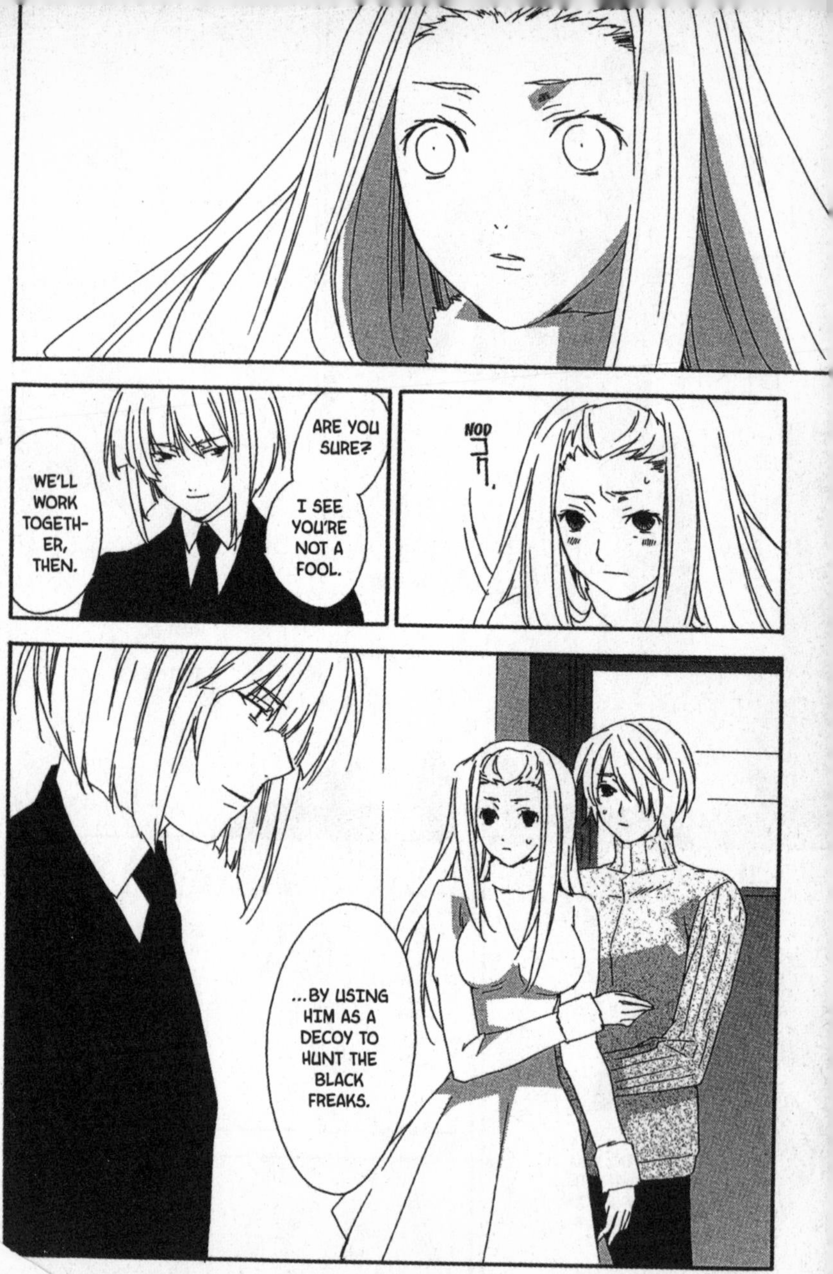
NOD
コク
ARE YOU SURE?
I SEE YOU'RE NOT A FOOL.
WE'LL WORK TOGETH-ER, THEN.
...BY USING HIM AS A DECOY TO HUNT THE BLACK FREAKS.

Category: Freaks

to be Continued

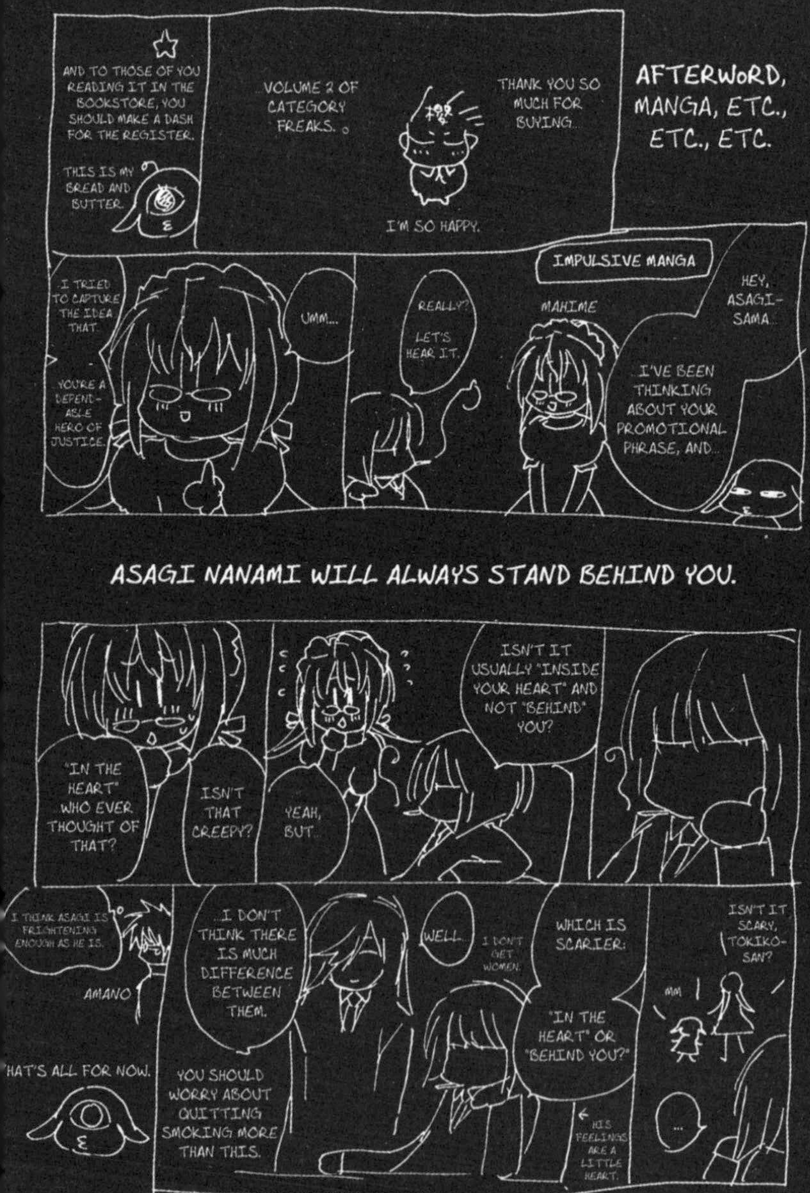
AFTERWORD, MANGA, ETC., ETC., ETC.
THANK YOU SO MUCH FOR BUYING...
...VOLUME 2 OF CATEGORY FREAKS.
I'M SO HAPPY.
AND TO THOSE OF YOU READING IT IN THE BOOKSTORE, YOU SHOULD MAKE A DASH FOR THE REGISTER.
THIS IS MY BREAD AND BUTTER.
IMPULSIVE MANGA
HEY, ASAGI-SAMA...
MAHIME
...I'VE BEEN THINKING ABOUT YOUR PROMOTIONAL PHRASE, AND...
REALLY?
LET'S HEAR IT.
UMM...
I TRIED TO CAPTURE THE IDEA THAT...
YOU'RE A DEPENDABLE HERO OF JUSTICE.
ASAGI NANAMI WILL ALWAYS STAND BEHIND YOU.
ISN'T IT USUALLY "INSIDE YOUR HEART" AND NOT "BEHIND" YOU?
YEAH, BUT...
"IN THE HEART" ...WHO EVER THOUGHT OF THAT?
ISN'T THAT CREEPY?
ISN'T IT SCARY, TOKIKO-SAN?
MM
...
WHICH IS SCARIER:
"IN THE HEART" OR "BEHIND YOU?"
I DON'T GET WOMEN.
HIS FEELINGS ARE A LITTLE HEART.
WELL.
...I DON'T THINK THERE IS MUCH DIFFERENCE BETWEEN THEM.
YOU SHOULD WORRY ABOUT QUITTING SMOKING MORE THAN THIS.
I THINK ASAGI IS FRIGHTENING ENOUGH AS HE IS.
AMANO
HAT'S ALL FOR NOW.

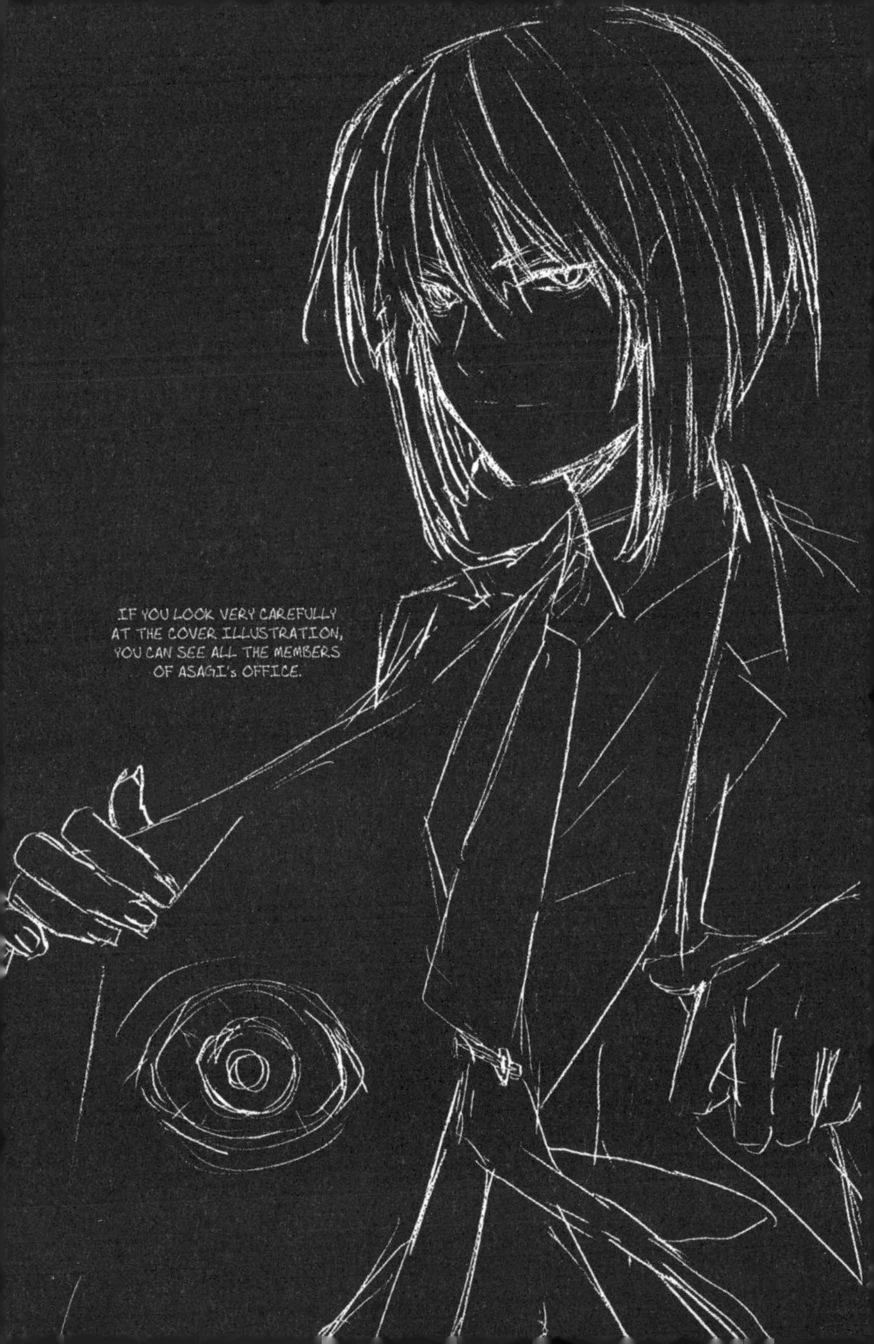
IF YOU LOOK VERY CAREFULLY
AT THE COVER ILLUSTRATION,
YOU CAN SEE ALL THE MEMBERS
OF ASAGI's OFFICE.

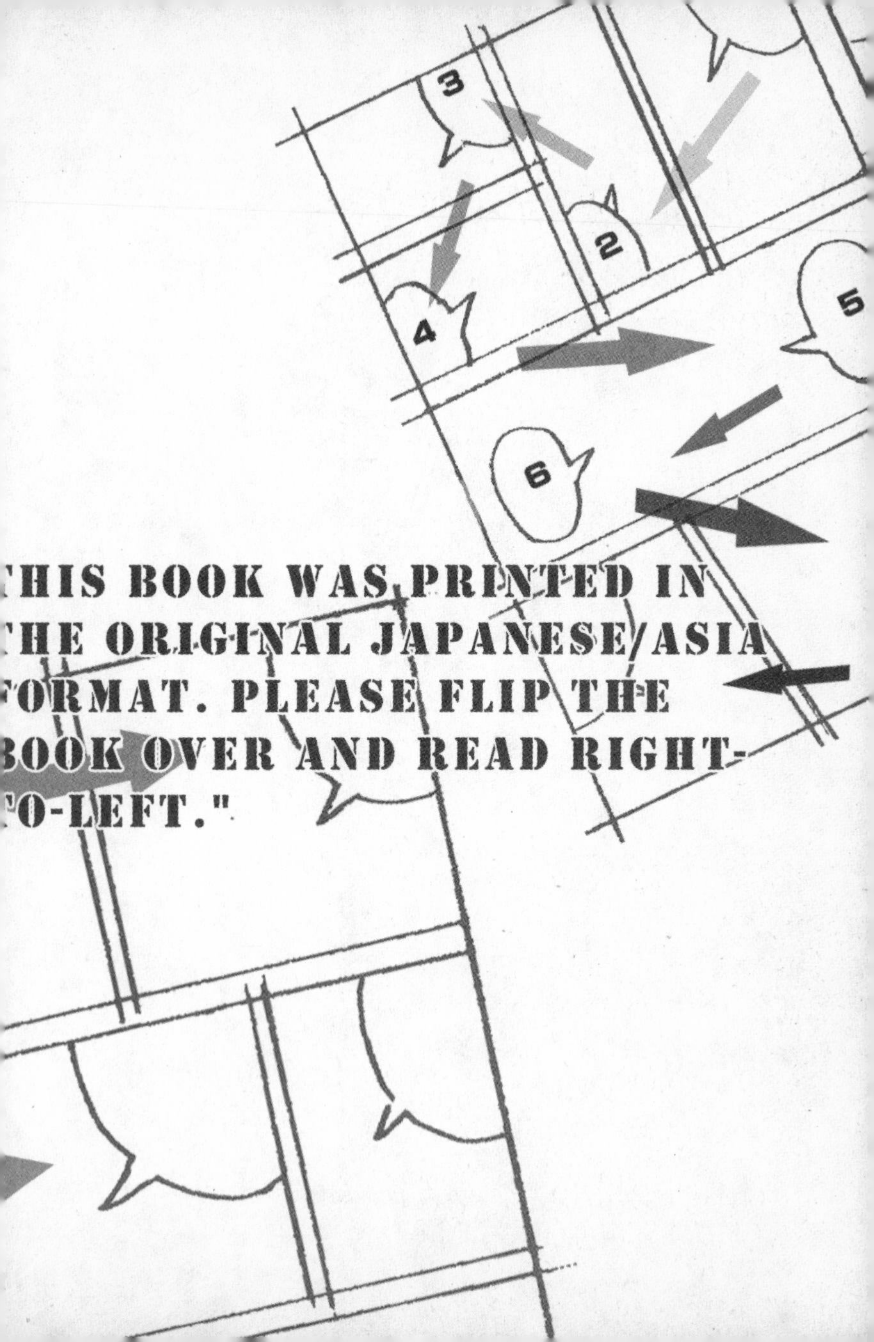
3
2
4
5
6

"THIS BOOK WAS PRINTED IN THE ORIGINAL JAPANESE/ASIA FORMAT. PLEASE FLIP THE BOOK OVER AND READ RIGHT-TO-LEFT."